E. Michael Gerli
1515 Still Meadow Cove
Charlottesville, VA 22901

Baroque Sovereignty

Baroque Sovereignty

CARLOS DE SIGÜENZA Y GÓNGORA
AND THE CREOLE ARCHIVE
OF COLONIAL MEXICO

Anna More

PENN

UNIVERSITY OF PENNSYLVANIA PRESS   *Philadelphia*

THIS BOOK IS MADE POSSIBLE BY A COLLABORATIVE GRANT
FROM THE ANDREW W. MELLON FOUNDATION.

© 2013 University of Pennsylvania Press

All rights reserved. Except for brief quotations used for purposes of review or scholarly citation, none of this book may be reproduced in any form by any means without written permission from the publisher.

Published by
University of Pennsylvania Press
Philadelphia, Pennsylvania 19104-4112
www.upenn.edu/pennpress

Printed in the United States of America
on acid-free paper

10 9 8 7 6 5 4 3 2 1

Library of Congress Cataloging-in-Publication Data

More, Anna Herron.
  Baroque sovereignty : Carlos de Sigüenza y Góngora and the Creole archive of colonial Mexico / Anna More. — 1st ed.
    p. cm.
  Includes bibliographical references and index.
  ISBN 978-0-8122-4469-4 (hardcover : alk. paper)
  1. Sigüenza y Góngora, Carlos de, 1645–1700—Political and social views. 2. Sigüenza y Góngora, Carlos de, 1645–1700—Library. 3. Archives—Political aspects—Mexico—History—17th century. 4. Creoles—Mexico—Intellectual life—17th century. 5. Civilization, Baroque—Mexico. 6. Mexico—History—Spanish colony, 1540–1810—Sources. 7. Mexico—Intellectual life—17th century. I. Title.
PQ7296.S5Z77 2013
972'.02092—dc23

2012024668

For Bene, Clarice, and Olivia

"The Renaissance explores the universe;
the Baroque explores libraries..."
—Walter Benjamin,
The Origin of German Tragic Drama

CONTENTS

Introduction: Sigüenza y Góngora and the Creole Archive ... 1
1. Allegory, Archives, and Creole Sovereignty ... 29
2. "*Nostra Academia in Barbara . . .* ": Building an Archive on the Imperial Frontier ... 57
3. Mexican Hieroglyphics: Creole Antiquarianism and the Politics of Empire ... 110
4. Counterhistory and Creole Governance in the Riot of 1692 ... 158
5. Creole Citizenship, Race, and the Modern World System ... 202
Conclusion: The Afterlife of a Baroque Archive ... 250

Notes ... 263
Bibliography ... 317
Index ... 337
Acknowledgments ... 347

Introduction

Sigüenza y Góngora and the Creole Archive

BIOMBO: THE FISSURES OF HISTORY

The Museo Franz Mayer in Mexico City houses a decorative standing screen (*biombo*) whose magnificent double-sided painting strikingly evokes the tension between the imaginary order of seventeenth-century New Spain and the region's violent origins (Figure 1). On one side, the Spanish conquest of Tenochtitlan unfolds as a series of battles erupting simultaneously throughout the pre-Columbian city. Although a legend in the lower left-hand corner labels key moments of the conquest depicted in the painting, the composition itself is geographical and spatial rather than chronological. A strong chiaroscuro marks the events represented: while light bathes the depiction of the Spanish approach to the mainland and Moctezuma's reception of Hernán Cortés in the upper left edges, the darkened lower corners reveal indigenous families fleeing into the surrounding forests as well as the infamous "sad night" (noche triste), when the Spanish were temporarily forced to retreat from the city. Rather than a chronological narrative, the painting presents the conquest as a palimpsest in which Moctezuma's initial reception of the Spanish gives way to bloody battles that force residents to flee into the wilderness. The depiction thus actively undermines sixteenth-century accounts such as Francisco López de Gómara's official history, which narrated the Mexican conquest as an act of providence.[1] Although the biombo includes stock events from this providentialist historiography, such as the appearance of Santiago to the Spanish conquerors and Moctezuma's death at the hands of his own vassals, these scenes are not given priority over what one critic

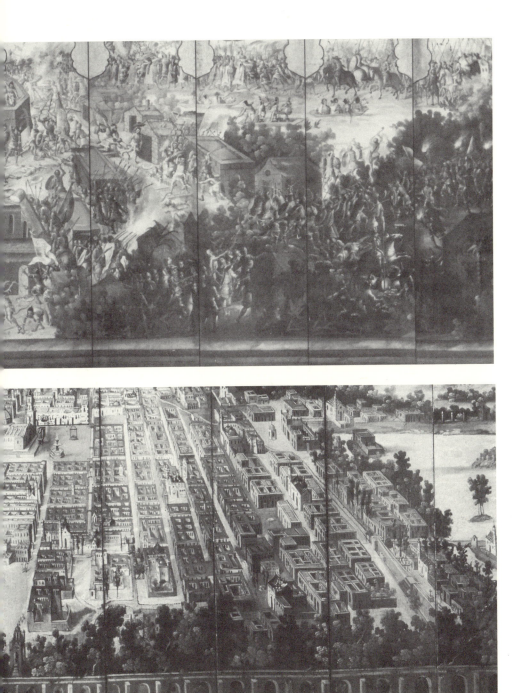

has called the "motley banquet of violence" (abigarrada festín de violencia).[2] Indeed, the overall impression is one of violent disorder in which bodies, spears, and horses point outward from empty buildings. Perhaps the most spectacular of these constructions, labeled the "temple that was in the central plaza of Mexico where the palace stands today" (cue que estaba en la plaza de México donde oi esta el Palacio), is fantastically represented as a hollowed-out octagon rather than the towering pyramid depicted in other colonial sources. The biombo, in short, portrays the conquest as a disordering event rather than the conclusive *translatio imperii* found in official historical representations.[3]

The contrast between this representation and that of the second side of the biombo could not be greater. On this, a serene map of seventeenth-century Mexico City spreads out as if before the eyes of a traveler who has paused on his journey through the hills outside the city. As opposed to the violent chiaroscuro of the previous side, the viceregal buildings are homogenous in color and shape, differing occasionally in size and form and distributed symmetrically around the central plaza. This time, the legend identifies an ordered urban geography, naming all the buildings whose repetitive geometry and red roofs would be indistinguishable from one another otherwise. The soft and graceful wooded landscape that rings the city sets a bucolic tone and complements the gardens inside. The geometrical symmetry, which extends even to the watery canals that cut through the city, is broken only by the sweeping curve of the aqueduct that points a path to the heart of the city: the central plaza (zócalo) and the cathedral. But what is perhaps most remarkable, after the chaos of the previous side, is the complete absence of human figures from the urban scene, as if the order of the city depended on their exile. What embodiment may be found is funneled through the perspective of the viewer atop Chapultepec, one of the symbolic centers of the colonial government, whose hill provides the best vantage point from which to survey the city. In fact, the painting follows a generic chorographic perspective often used in seventeenth-century cartographic representations, in this case lifted directly from a popular Dutch atlas of the seventeenth century. The original drawing was completed in 1628 by Juan Gómez de Trasmonte, the architect of Mexico City's cathedral. This he made at the request of Adrian Boot, a Dutch engineer who was helping with the

Figure 1 (previous page). *The Very Noble and Loyal City of Mexico* (*La mui noble y leal ciudad de Mexico*). Folding screen, late seventeenth century. Courtesy of the Museo Franz Mayer, Mexico City.

Introduction   5

desagüe project, the perennial attempt to solve the city's flooding problems. The map sought to represent the city as it should appear after further draining of the lake.[4] As the late seventeenth-century biombo was likely a gift to the new viceroy, the Conde de Galve, the incorporation of the map's chorographic perspective surely sought to symbolize the relationship between colonial governance and an orderly city, cleansed of any visual impediments to the sweeping gaze.[5]

Although it would be easy to read the biombo's antipodal sides as depicting the civilizing triumph of Spanish urbanity, the lack of providentialism in the representation of the conquest and the absence of bodies in the viceregal city force us to question such a clear moral conclusion. In fact, the pairing of urban order with violent conquest produces not so much a teleology as the uncomfortable meeting of two planes of history around sites in the city.[6] The biombo's physical structure further suggests the fragility of a viceregal order built on conquest. Although modern reproductions customarily represent the screen in its full extension, the material object in the Museo Franz Mayer is not one solid plane but rather a series of panels, fissured to allow it to stand freely in space. In this way, the voids that interrupt the screen negatively register the presence of the opposite side. In fact, if we imagine walking around the freestanding object, its very structure denies a clear chronological order. Instead, past and present are locked in a dialectical embrace suggesting as much the desire as the impossibility of overcoming the Spanish conquest at the end of the seventeenth century. Although the legend on the first side orients the viewer by noting the viceregal transformation of several pre-Columbian buildings, the absence of bodies in the viceregal city abstracts its order from any human chronology, as if the human form would be the most palpable point of connection to the violence displayed on the other side. Rather than a document of historical transformation, then, the biombo appears to retreat from history into an idealized urban plane. If nothing else, the biombo presents the problem of relating an imagined seventeenth-century viceregal order to its historical foundations in violence nearly a century and a half before.

As a material object, the biombo is a salutary reminder of the specificity of historical artifacts, even those whose representational power transcends their immediate history of production and reception. A decorative art form initially imported from Asia, the colonial biombo is an excellent example of the hybridity of cultural production in seventeenth-century New Spain. In fact, it is possible that biombos became popular in the houses of the colonial elite precisely because their form condensed a history of cultural incorporation that was itself an essential characteristic of New Spain. The Franz Mayer biombo suggests this history by framing the battle scenes of the first side with a golden arabesque arch, a Moorish motif that gloriously remembers the Reconquest of Spain.[7] On the reverse side, however, this frame has been replaced by a border of flowers, a common trope for America as an earthly paradise that avoids all reference to the violence of conquest. While framing the transformation of urban space after the conquest in moral terms, these juxtaposed motifs do little to provide a historical account of that transformation.[8] If the Franz Mayer biombo thus suggests the problem of representing the history of New Spain after the conquest, it is important to remember that it was very likely given by a member of the local elite to the highest Spanish official in New Spain.[9] Rather than expressing a universally held problem, the biombo suggests that at least part of the Mexican elite believed that at the end of the seventeenth century the viceregal order was still fragile, subject to reversals and an unresolved violent foundation. Thus, while the biombo's representation of urban order was perhaps at some level satisfying to the viceregal official to whom it was presented, its mixed cultural references and memory of violence also implied that a conclusive viceregal order in New Spain was a task still to be accomplished, despite a century and a half of Spanish rule.

This book will argue that in the second half of the seventeenth century, precisely at the moment when Spanish Habsburg rule entered into its definitive period of decline, it was this task that most concerned the Novohispanic elite, or Creoles.[10] It will also argue that Creole solutions to the problem of local governance entailed far more complex archival politics than that which the biombo's idealized planes suggest. On the one hand, Creoles imagined themselves as heirs to a continuous genealogy of conquerors and indigenous nobility leading back to the conquest. On the other, they were also acutely aware of the social fragmentation that had occurred in the intervening century as these same lineages entered into decay and a new racially mixed society developed in urban centers of the viceroyalty. Despite the façade of unity that the Novohispanic elite and viceregal administrators presented at official events, moreover, many in the viceroyalty were conscious of the problems facing the Spanish Empire at the end of the seventeenth century. The numerous reports of political disarray in Spain and pirate attacks in the Caribbean exposed a weakened Spanish Crown and augmented a general sense of crisis. For many Creoles, historical continuity became the key to restoring order to late seventeenth-century Novohispanic society. The history they imagined, however, was not a providential teleology confirming the justice of the Spanish conquest. Rather, Creoles conceived of history on a much more parochial and regional level, as an archive of deep history that predated the Spanish. In expanding their archive beyond the conquest, they tapped into a project that had begun virtually simultaneously with the conquest itself: the registering, decoding, and preserving of the pre-Columbian past. But while seventeenth-century Creoles inherited the projects, and at times the archives, of early mendicant and indigenous historians, they did so under distinct auspices. Friars, from Bartolomé de las Casas to Juan de Torquemada, had been principally interested in studying the indigenous past in order to eradicate its persistence in the present.[11] While they often worked closely with these mendicant projects, indigenous and native-identified mestizo historians, such as Juan Bautista Pomar or Fernando de Alva Ixtlilxochitl, had the additional objective of preserving a genealogical record of ethnic kingship.[12]

The seventeenth-century Creole archive, by contrast, was at once more secular and less genealogical than these earlier projects. Rather than being a reflection of the discrete interests of one particular lineage, history became tied to problems of governance, a sense of political crisis, and the racial insecurities of the local elite. Despite drawing on previous archives, therefore, the Creole archive required a hermeneutics distinct from those that had preceded it. This meant not only gathering objects and documents that had not previously figured in Spanish writings but also reinterpreting those already found in earlier works. Forming a regional history, furthermore, entailed plotting the territorial and social boundaries of a local citizenry that would receive the truth it documented. Through a language of republican patriotism Creoles introduced the notion of citizenship even as they limited this to a small minority of Spanish descent. Indeed, appealing to their own virtue, purity of blood, and local knowledge, Creoles placed themselves on the top of the racial hierarchy that was beginning to define viceregal society during this period. To the authority of the humanist historical practices they inherited, therefore, Creoles added their unique access to local knowledge. This knowledge, moreover, was closely related to the Neoplatonic rhetorical form in which it was often expressed. From the Creole vantage point, the cultural landscape of seventeenth-century New Spain became a cipher for a hidden and secret past. The hope for New Spain's future lay in these arcane local truths, inaccessible to Spanish peninsular administration. Without overtly breaking with Spanish administration, then, by the end of the seventeenth century Novohispanic Creoles had begun to invent a deep history extending beyond the Spanish conquest. Through this body of knowledge stored in writings, collections, and visual artifacts, they began to set the foundations of a local patrimonial order that could stand in for a distant monarch who appeared increasingly unable to secure his faltering empire.

THE INVENTION OF CREOLE TRADITION

The subject of this book, the concept of a local community in New Spain as it developed in Creole writings over the course of the seventeenth century, has most often been addressed as the emergence of a "consciousness" or "identity."[13] One of the strongest sources of evidence that members of the seventeenth-century Spanish American elite increasingly thought of themselves in collective terms was their appropriation of the term *criollo* (Creole). Employed as early as 1563 to describe persons of Spanish descent born in the Americas, the term *criollo* originally carried the connotation of degeneration among American-born subjects.[14] By the mid-seventeenth century, however, in a clear attempt to reverse the association of the American climate with degeneration, the American-born colonial elite began to employ the term as a more positive form of self-identification. Etymologically related to the term *criar*, and thus connoting local cultivation, in Spanish the adjective *criollo* was used to designate any person born in the Americas of nonindigenous heritage. Although its use for subjects of African descent remained an oppositional qualifier—for instance a *negro criollo* was distinguished from a *negro bozal* born in Africa—in the case of persons of Spanish descent the term "Creole" came to stand alone.[15] Through its association with persons of Spanish descent, "Creole" thus became defined by the combination of racial purity and an attachment to local origins.[16] During this period, Creoles also began to employ the term *patria* to designate a homeland or polity that encompassed a geographical area beyond that of an individual birthplace and the term *nación* to refer to a collective Creole citizenry.[17] Together with these linguistic changes, seventeenth-century Spanish American writings wove a range of themes and topics into regional patriotic imaginaries. These themes included the representation of the American landscape as a new paradise, an antiquarian interest in the pre-Columbian past, and the promotion of local apparitions and saints such as the Virgin of Guadalupe and Saint Rose of Lima.[18]

Because seventeenth-century Creole patriotism harbored no desire for political autonomy from the Spanish Crown, scholarship has tended to see it as a defensive reaction to Creoles' exclusion from viceregal administrative privileges and rights of citizenship.[19] Whether historical or literary, studies have thus tended to present seventeenth-century Creoles as conflicted subjects, torn between loyalty to Spain and resentment at their unequal treatment by the Crown. According to this line of reasoning, Creoles expressed this contradictory subjectivity in racial and ethnic terms by insisting on their Spanish descent even while they claimed to be "patrimonial sons of the land" (hijos patrimoniales de la tierra).[20] Creoles also tended to denigrate present indigenous culture even as they projected and appropriated a glorious indigenous past. Most studies conclude that after several generations of Spanish immigration to the Americas, Creoles were unable to identify fully with the two major social groups of early colonization: Spaniards or Amerindians. Meanwhile, their desire for inclusion in the Spanish monarchy as a "kingdom" (reino) with full standing was matched only by their equally strong desire to differentiate themselves from Spain through patriotic pride in regional homelands.[21] Finally, while they presented themselves as heirs to the first generation of conquistadors, whose right to self-rule had been sharply curtailed by the rationalization and centralization of Spanish imperial administration, seventeenth-century Creoles couched their politics in the language of recognition rather than political autonomy, as had their sixteenth-century forebears.[22] It has been difficult to assign a priority to or at times even to find a relationship among these competing demands upon Creoles. As a result, Creole identity has been called "ambiguous," "hybrid," and "oscillating" and Creole politics "confused," at best the sign of a strategic ploy to work within a system stacked against American-born subjects and at worst a sign of indecision and political immaturity.[23]

Both literary and intellectual historians have further related this divided Creole subjectivity to Baroque aesthetics, the dominant style of Spanish American writing at the time. Although the literary Baroque took several forms, it was the rhetoric and poetics of Gongorism that was most prominently institutionalized in seventeenth-century Spain and Spanish America through university training and court culture.[24] Indeed, historical and literary studies have tended to equate Baroque aesthetics with this common stylistic form, whose hallmark was excessive ornamentation, classical references, Latinisms, and obscure metaphors. Their assessments of its value have differed, however. While historians have often associated Baroque aesthetics with Neoplatonism, scholasticism, and Jesuit universalism, and have questioned its intellectual merit, literary studies are more prone to defend the Creole Baroque as an appropriate medium for the expression of Creole identity. In his study of the Novohispanic nun and poet Sor Juana Inés de la Cruz, for instance, Octavio Paz asserts:

> the aesthetic singularity of the Mexican Baroque corresponded to the historical and existential singularity of the Creoles. Their relationship to Baroque art was not one of cause and effect, but of affinity and coincidence. Creoles breathed naturally in a world of strangeness because they themselves were, and knew themselves to be, strange beings.
>
> (la singularidad estética del barroco mexicano correspondía a la singularidad histórica y existencial de los criollos. Entre ellos y el arte barroco había una relación inequívoca, no de causa y efecto, sino de afinidad y coincidencia. Respiraban con naturalidad en el mundo de la extrañeza porque ellos mismos eran y se sabían seres extraños.)[25]

Even while they assign a more positive value to Baroque form, therefore, literary studies have implicitly accepted the depiction of seventeenth-century Creoles as partially elaborated subjects in a corresponding teleology leading to nineteenth-century Creole independence from Spain.

By contrast, this book begins with the idea that identity and subjectivity, insofar as they suggest psychological conditions or consciousness, are insufficient analytical categories through which to interpret seventeenth-century Creole writings. Not only does the language of paradox and ambivalence foreclose the possibility that Creoles' political perspectives on Spanish rule were directly related to historical circumstances, but it does little to relate the racial or patriarchal overtones of Creole patriotism to the juridical and political structures of Spanish imperialism.[26] In fact, the ideals of Spanish imperialism were an important factor in defining seventeenth-century Creole political discourse. Any account of Creole political ideas must therefore be placed within a history of colonial social categories and the daily and institutional practices related to them. These, in turn, were closely tied to the issue of Spanish sovereignty in the Americas, the full contradictions of which became most pronounced with the crisis of Habsburg rule in the second half of the seventeenth century. Although active debates on Spanish imperial sovereignty were for the most part concluded by the end of the sixteenth century, the issue continued to vex the Crown throughout the seventeenth century. One only has to note that in 1681 the Spanish

Crown finally printed the *Recopilación de leyes de los re[ynos de las] Indias* (Recopilation of the Laws of the Kingdoms of the In[dies]), [real]ize that the Crown sought to preserve the juridical langu[age of] colonization even as it entered its late seventeenth-century crisis.

What was the relationship between this attempt to conserve the sixteenth-century basis of Spanish sovereignty in the Americas and the emergence of a Creole political discourse during the seventeenth century? How did Creoles react to the perceptible weakness of the Habsburg monarchy in Spain, especially after the death of Felipe IV in 1665? In short, what was the structural relationship between the emergence of a Creole political discourse and the social and political crisis of seventeenth-century Spanish imperialism?

It might appear that approaching seventeenth-century Creole political discourse in terms of patriotism, rather than identity, would be one means to address these questions. After all, Creoles often invoked the language of republican patriotism, particularly Ciceronian, in their writings. But as in approaches to Creole identity, there has been a tendency to interpret these statements as clear reflections of a natural bond to a homeland rather than as projections of an ideal or a desire.[28] As Maurizio Viroli has written, the classical notions of patria that were appropriated by early modern humanism implied ideas of polity and citizenship that, at the very least, had to be reinterpreted in the context of European political modernity.[29] Interestingly, Viroli himself argues that the humanist discourse of patria was on the wane in seventeenth-century absolutist states, except in pointed cases of rebellion or open dissent.[30] The fact that this is not borne out by studies of Spanish America points to a possible distinction between the Spanish American use of the term patria and its appropriation as an emblem of "liberty" in European contexts. The Creole notion of patria, it is clear, was not a bid for political separation from the Spanish monarchy, nor even an act of political dissent. Rather, when they invoked the classical notion of *amor patriae*, Creoles were attempting to naturalize what in fact was a political condition fraught with problems.[31] Chief among these problems were issues of who exactly the citizens of a local patria were and what their relationship was to a land that had been colonized only a century beforehand. These questions often appear in Creole writings through two repeated themes: on the one hand the relationship between Creoles and other colonial subjects of the greater Spanish Empire and, on the other, the espousal of a regional history that would soften or even avoid a providentialist reading of the Spanish conquest.

In fact, one of the most cogent assessments in scholarship on seventeenth-century Creoles is that they understood themselves to be the "natural lords" of their lands, thus inheriting the mantel of an indigenous nobility in decline.[32] Yet while it is true that the Creole discourse of indigenous nobility extended the privileges that Spanish imperialism had awarded native lords, it is important to note that Creoles did not understand themselves to be direct *genealogical* descendents of pre-Columbian peoples, even when this was actually the case.[33] Rather, seventeenth-century Creoles appropriated an indigenous past in what might be called, following Eric Hobsbawm, an "invention of tradition." Hobsbawm's phrase, which he employs to argue that state rituals in late nineteenth-century Europe actually had quite shallow roots, has slightly distinct implications for colonial Spanish America.[34] In seventeenth-century documents, for instance, the word "tradition" (*tradición*) was used to describe nonwritten beliefs, particularly those associated with indigenous culture.[35] Such usage suggested the authority of an untraceable origin even while it admitted the problems associated with oral transmission. The eighteenth-century *Diccionario de autoridades* (Dictionary of the Authorities), for instance, defines "tradition" as the "notice of some ancient thing, which is transmitted from parents to children through successive retellings" (Noticia de alguna cosa antigua, que se difunde de padres a hijos y se comunica por relacion sucesiva de unos en otros) and then provides the following illustration: "I do not rely on traditions, which run the grave risk of being apocryphal, but rather on ancient documents" (pues me fundo no en tradiciones, que tienen gran peligro de dar en apócryphas, sino en papeles antiquissimos).[36] If "tradition" was thus closely related to contemporary notions of the term, the seventeenth-century term "invention" had a much more complex meaning than current usage would allow. Even in late seventeenth-century Spanish America *invención* often still followed the classical definition of *inventio* as "discovery" rather than creation.[37] But it was also heir to a shift in the rhetorical and poetic priority given to received topics. While in classical rhetoric, "invention" often designated the choice of subject matter, to be distinguished from delivery itself, in Renaissance poetics it began to take on a stronger imaginative quality.[38] By the seventeenth century the treatises of Balthasar Gracián and Emanuele Tesauro related "invention" to wit or *ingenium*, thus designating the power of metaphor and conceit to signify and even create what nature could not.[39]

In contrast to Hobsbawm's use of the term, then, the seventeenth-century Creole "invention of tradition" was a rhetorical exercise, in which rhetoric itself reached well beyond expression to incorporate a logic and epistemology bordering on European hermeticism. Unlike European hermeticism, however, Creoles were privy to a storehouse not just of European topics and artifacts, including the Egyptian hieroglyphs that had influenced Renaissance Neoplatonism, but also indigenous ones. Their challenge was to find a connection among these sources of ancient wisdom and thus recover hidden points of unity. In Creole texts this could be thought of as an *ars inveniendi* best described by Gracián's definition of *ingenio*: "this conceitful artifice consists, then, of a perfect correspondence, a harmonious correlation between two or three knowable extremes, expressed by an act of understanding" (consiste, pues, este artificio conceptuoso, en una primorosa concordancia, en una armónica correlación entre dos o tres conoscibles extremos, expresada por un acto del entendimiento).[40] As Gracian's definition suggests, seventeenth-century recombinations went beyond paradox and hybridity, often interpreted as a transgressive or even liberational element of the Latin American Baroque,[41] to include the creation of meaning. The ability to access a hidden truth through the creative recombination of objects was especially powerful in areas in which indigenous traditions themselves had become dislodged from endogamous transmission, either through active or passive imperial policy. In this context, Creoles could derive a specific form of authority from the interpretation of non-European objects. What has often been interpreted as a paradoxical Creole appropriation of pre-Columbian indigenous artifacts and history even as they emphasized their own European roots, therefore, was in fact a bid to establish an authority based on knowledge available only to those who understood both traditions.[42]

While not often applied to Spanish America, Walter Benjamin's concept of Baroque allegory provides a theoretical approach to understanding seventeenth-century Creole hermeticism. In his well-known 1929 study of German Baroque drama, Walter Benjamin related Baroque aesthetics to the politico-theological crisis of seventeenth-century Europe. As in his later theory of dialectical images, Benjamin argued that Baroque allegory "froze" or spatialized objects by drawing them out of a temporal continuum. Yet whereas Benjamin argued that dialectical images counteracted historical alienation, he understood Baroque allegory as an attempt to offset guilt and profanity at a moment when theological transcendence had begun to experience a crisis.⁴³ Benjamin's theory of Baroque allegory allows us to relate Spanish American hybridity, as expressed in seventeenth-century Creole texts, to the evangelical projects that were the centerpiece of Spanish sovereignty in the Americas. Unlike in Europe, where salvation was ultimately an individual condition, in Spanish America redemption was the cornerstone of Spain's justification of its presence in the Americas. After the collapse of sixteenth-century utopian projects, particularly those of the Franciscans and Dominicans, seventeenth-century clerics were more sober about the feasibility, and indeed desirability, of the full redemption of indigenous subjects.⁴⁴ The decline of the utopian rhetoric of sixteenth-century evangelization led to a greater emphasis on the management of indigenous communities and the elimination of obstacles to Christianity over the long term.⁴⁵ Although seventeenth-century missionary projects continued to work toward the goal of the redemption of "barbarous" subjects on the frontiers of Spanish America, a specifically Creole version of seventeenth-century pragmatism treated indigenous culture of central viceregal areas as an object of antiquarian interest. Not coincidentally, these were precisely the geographical areas already substantially transformed by Spanish rule. As indigenous cultural objects, from codices to ruins, became disassociated from indigenous practices, allegory allowed Creoles to pull them into European systems of hermetic meaning.

Unlike the sundry profane objects that, according to Benjamin, made up Baroque allegory in Europe, therefore, Creole texts combined traditions that had been interrupted by colonization. In the hands of seventeenth-century Creoles, therefore, what Benjamin calls Baroque allegory lent itself to the recuperation of a local archive as an approach to combating indigenous systems of meaning. In recent literary and cultural studies, the concept of the archive has been an important trope for understanding the way in which Spanish American writings rework received traditions.⁴⁶ What has not been sufficiently recognized by these studies is the fact that the archive is also a source of authority. As Jacques Derrida has argued, the archive produces a nomological authority by projecting the origin of the law onto an archaic past. This form of authority depends on an interruption and recomposition, a "consignment" in Derrida's terms, of documents within the confines of a place.⁴⁷ Thus, like Benjamin's allegory, the archive resignifies objects that have been temporally dislocated. Indeed, it is only too clear that simply by collecting objects, particularly indigenous ones, seventeenth-century Creoles already assigned them a meaning distinct from that which they had previously held. But unlike in Benjamin's notion of allegory, the Creole archive did not wish to redeem these profane objects within an eschatological time frame. Rather, the project to establish a local archive in seventeenth-century New Spain was an attempt to salvage historical time from narratives of religious eschatology by projecting indigenous paganism onto a distant past. This is not to say that seventeenth-century Creoles absolved contemporary indigenous subjects from any association with paganism. Indeed, throughout the seventeenth century, indigenous subjects were periodically accused of continuing to practice and propagate "idolatry." But these accusations were part of the larger context of Creole antiquarianism that was, above all, a discourse of nobility that denigrated commoners as ignorant of their own glorious past.[48]

This Creole turn to history, as an archive rather than a chronological narrative, became an answer to the impasse of seventeenth-century Spanish imperialism. In contrast to the first wave of Spanish colonization, seventeenth-century Creoles in Spanish America did not look to conversion as an eschatological resolution of indigenous paganism. Rather, they took the opposite tack by searching for a lost totality in an archaic past. For this reason, Creole hermeneutics held affinities to Neoplatonic hermeticism through which pagan difference was resignified as a hidden truth.[49] Yet, as in the widespread Creole narrative of St. Thomas's apostolic evangelization of the Americas well before the arrival of the Spanish, the truth Creoles derived from a local archive established authority rather than esoteric dissent. At the same time, the recombination of traditions, particularly indigenous and Western, highlighted the need for an allegorical hermeneutics that could establish a common archive after the confrontational division of the conquest. If Creoles combined European and non-European artifacts in novel and hybrid forms, then, it was not only out of desire to differentiate themselves from Europe but equally to find meaning in local objects that had become separated from their original traditions. Not only did Creoles desire to maintain the authority of the Spanish monarch but equally, and perhaps more insistently, they wished to establish a local authority and tradition following the fragmentation of indigenous communities and the demise of evangelical utopianism. The problem, in all cases, was one of preserving authority even while shifting it to Creole hands. As substitutes for more institutional forms of authority Creoles founded hybrid traditions but locked these up in a hermetic archive.

For this reason, late seventeenth-century Creole texts went well beyond anxieties of identity and subjectivity to touch upon the social organization and governance of seventeenth-century Spanish America. Against what was seen as the vertiginous loss of order, Creole hermeneutics preserved authority and social hierarchy based on epistemological privilege. But by inventing a tradition that was confined to written, archivable documents Creoles also broke with the symbolic aura of local authority and custom that underwrote both indigenous and European political leadership. By the end of the seventeenth century, Creoles had thus begun to reformulate sovereignty from the grandiose project of Spanish imperialism—the *monarchia universalis*—to a provincial polity defined by a racially limited citizenry. Faced with the decline of the power and privilege of the local indigenous nobility and the rise of a Hispanicized and Christianized indigenous and mixed-race population, Creoles sought to promote themselves as natural lords of their regions through the artifice of epistemology rather than through the genealogical arguments of indigenous *caciques* or the entitlement to the spoils of conquest of sixteenth-century Spanish *conquistadores*. Key to Creole authority was an allegorical hermeneutics that dedicated objects to a local archive of which Creoles claimed to be the magistrates.

SIGÜENZA Y GÓNGORA AND REGIONALISM IN NEW SPAIN

While the goal of this study is to elucidate the consequences of Spanish imperial decline for late seventeenth-century Spanish American political ideas, it is organized around close readings of the works of one prominent Creole author of the period. Carlos de Sigüenza y Góngora (1645–1700) has long been understood to be a key figure in the transition between the late sixteenth-century discourse of resentful *encomenderos* and the more mature eighteenth-century Creole political imaginary.[50] His varied works are the clearest expression of how issues of governance, history, and citizenship combined to form a discourse of Creole patriotism in late seventeenth-century New Spain. Because of its focus, this study cannot generalize about all Creole politics in seventeenth-century Spanish America. In fact, it begins with the assumption that regional and even authorial conditions greatly shaped the form of early Spanish American political discourse. The regional nature of seventeenth-century Creole politics stemmed partly from the geographical distances that separated the major viceregal centers, Mexico and Lima, but was also the consequence of a conscious policy on the part of the Spanish Crown to prevent direct commercial and administrative contacts between the viceroyalties.[51] Although Creole elites across Spanish America, especially those in viceregal centers, could and did imagine themselves to be in analogous situations, they also competed for prestige and recognition and their ideas of homeland were highly inflected by local political and social conditions. The decline of the Habsburg monarchy had a paradoxical effect on this situation. While the second half of the seventeenth century witnessed political fragmentation in Spain, it was also an intensely global moment, when imperial competition among European states created new requirements for the Spanish American viceroyalties, who were forced to compensate for a depleted royal treasury by contributing more resources to their own defense. The sum of these conditions meant that Creole politics emerged together with what can best be described as regional geopolitical perspectives.[52]

The development of a Creole patriotism in New Spain, the larger of the Spanish American viceroyalties and its central administrative center, entailed several idiosyncrasies. Beginning with Miguel Sanchez's 1648 treatise, seventeenth-century Novohispanic Creoles increasingly promoted the Virgin of Guadalupe as a regional cult that linked points in the viceroyalty's vast territory.[53] Through this and other local historical interests Creoles also took advantage of the indigenous written record in the region. Despite the destruction of most of the preconquest codices in the sixteenth century, the tradition of graphic memory systems in Mesoamerica meant that by the end of the sixteenth century there existed a rich indigenous record preserved in both alphabetic and pictorial forms. The interest of late sixteenth-century friars in these documents, as well as the attempts among the indigenous elite to preserve familial and dynastic records, provided seventeenth-century Creoles with diverse sources for the human and natural history of the region.[54] Early in the sixteenth century, New Spain had also become home to both a university and printing press, conditions that soon led to the development of a locally educated elite. By the seventeenth century, this intellectual culture was further strengthened by Jesuit institutions, which came to hold a virtual monopoly over higher education in the viceroyalty.[55] The reservedly critical attitude of the Jesuits, together with frankly heterodox inclinations that erupted sporadically throughout Spain and Spanish America, led to a robust book trade in New Spain. It appears that even books banned by Inquisitorial and Jesuit censors made their way into the viceroyalty.[56] Finally, New Spain found itself at the end of the seventeenth century in a particularly vulnerable geopolitical position. As a conduit for Spanish galleon trade from Asia and the recipient of the annual fleet from Spain, the viceroyalty directly experienced British, French, and Dutch attacks on Asian and Caribbean trade routes. Meanwhile, French advances into Florida and Louisiana, along with the difficult evangelical project of Franciscans and Jesuits among the indigenous nations on the northern frontier, led to a renewed sense of insecurity in the viceregal capital of Mexico even as the Crown's fiscal crisis prohibited any strong centralized action.[57]

These conditions all contributed to the emergence of a vocal elite in late seventeenth-century New Spain, particularly in the viceregal capital and environs.[58] Although the "flowering" of Creole letters is best seen in the superior works of Sor Juana Inés de la Cruz, it was her contemporary, Carlos de Sigüenza y Góngora, who was responsible for the most impassioned defense of a local patria.[59] Born in Mexico City in 1645, Sigüenza y Góngora was the son of two Spanish immigrants. Before immigrating to New Spain his father had worked in the Spanish court, where he claimed to have taught the young prince Carlos Baltasar to read and write. His mother was a native of Seville and a distant relative of the famed Spanish poet Luis de Góngora, a relationship that Sigüenza emphasized in his own surname.[60] As a youth, Sigüenza completed the novitiate and took his vows at the Jesuit college at Tepotzotlán, moving to the Colegio del Espíritu Santo in Puebla to finish his training for the priesthood. Before he could do so, however, he was expelled, apparently for infractions of the college's rules. Despite several attempts, Sigüenza was never readmitted to the Jesuit order and instead became a secular priest in 1673.[61]

Because he lacked an institutional position, Sigüenza was more autonomous than most Spanish American authors of this period, who wrote for specific corporate interests. Yet he also complained bitterly about the financial insecurity that accompanied this autonomy and constantly searched for sources of steady income. In 1672 he won a competition for the open chair of mathematics in Mexico's university but was forced to augment the meager salary by writing commissioned works and selling yearly astrological almanacs, a requirement of the position but one that contradicted his skeptical position on astrology.[62] He also accepted several other positions, including chaplain of the Hospital del Amor de Dios and, in the last year of his life, Inquisitorial censor.[63] Although he was never completely dependent on viceregal court patronage systems, as was his contemporary Sor Juana Inés de la Cruz,

Sigüenza's commissions and publications required a network of sponsors culled from both the Creole and peninsular viceregal elite. Indeed, in 1680 he was named royal cosmographer, a position that carried with it obligations to advise the Novohispanic viceroys on such subjects as the *desagüe* project, the draining of the lake on which Mexico City was built, and to provide general information on local hydrography and cartography.[64] In this capacity, Sigüenza assiduously collected maps and he was reputed to have created the first locally produced general map of New Spain.[65] His cartographic skills also led to his only trip outside of central Mexico when, following reports of French presence in the region, in 1689 he uncharacteristically accompanied an expedition to map and secure Pensacola Bay.[66]

Often referred to as a Baroque polymath, in the tradition of European counterparts such as the Jesuit Athanasius Kircher of the Collegio Romano, Sigüenza y Góngora was certainly a wide-ranging intellectual. Yet his works do not harbor the type of universal project for which the Austrian Jesuit was famed.[67] Uneven and disparate, they instead reflect the hazards of a career cobbled together on the periphery of the Spanish Empire. Despite being relatively prolific as a writer, throughout his life Sigüenza was plagued by half-finished and unpublished projects.[68] Indeed, many of the works he was reputed to have written exist only as lists compiled by Sigüenza and his friends during his lifetime. Those of his writings that were published have been subject to changing perspectives on the late Baroque style common to his period. Whereas in the eighteenth century the Creole encyclopedist Juan José de Eguiara y Eguren praised Sigüenza's youthful Gongoresque poem to the Virgin of Guadalupe, for instance, in his 1929 biography Irving Leonard characterized this as one of the "earlier and lighter writings" and preferred the clearer style of Sigüenza's later texts.[69] The mid-twentieth-century historian Ernest Burrus was more disdainful, noting that with the exception of his astronomical treatise the *Libra astronómica* (Astronomical Balance), Sigüenza's published writings offered very little.[70] Even historians tracing the development of Creole politics have seen Sigüenza as a central but disappointing figure.[71] In Mexican intellectual history, Sigüenza has been most enthusiastically received as the first local antiquarian, the loss of whose patrimony has been lamented as a national tragedy.[72]

Despite this appreciation of Sigüenza as a historical figure, the aesthetically uneven and generic nature of his works has made it difficult to canonize him as a "classic" Latin American author. It is perhaps for this reason that there has been little systematic analysis of his writings. Although in his 1957 manifesto *La expresión americana* Lezama Lima referred to Sigüenza as "el señor barroco" and claimed that his titles alone merited appreciation for their Baroque exuberance,[73] most full-length studies have focused on his biographical and intellectual trajectory while describing his works in much more general terms. These studies have been crucial to unearthing documents on Sigüenza's life and writings and to reconstructing the context in which he wrote. The most important of these, Francisco Pérez Salazar's 1928 biography and Irving Leonard's 1929 monograph, *Don Carlos de Sigüenza y Góngora: A Mexican Savant*, together still provide the definitive reconstruction of the circumstances of his authorship. Since Leonard's work, several additional biographies have been published and a wealth of studies have considered individual works.[74] Despite regular scholarship on Sigüenza as an intellectual figure, however, few scholars have analyzed the most striking rhetorical aspects of his works themselves. Kathleen Ross's recent analyses of Sigüenza y Góngora's texts have been a notable exception to this rule. Through close readings of several texts, she has made key observations about the nature of his writings. First of all, she has argued that Sigüenza's "passion for history" was the basis for a secondary phase of colonization in Spanish America in which Creoles "rewrote" the chronicles of conquest.[75] Second, in her monograph on Sigüenza's 1684 history of the Real Convento de Jesús María, Ross shows that the Creole author incorporated heavily edited versions of the writings of the convent's nuns. She concludes that in the case of writing "about women for women" Sigüenza was both patriarchal and patrimonial, disciplining and patronizing.[76]

If we extend Ross's observations to what were arguably the most central motifs in Sigüenza's writings—his concern with local history, imperial politics, and, above all, his obsessive patriotism—it becomes clear that he approached the social concerns of late seventeenth-century New Spain with the same patriarchal attitudes. To analyze Sigüenza's writings from this perspective, it is necessary to resist the expectations of unity and coherence that underlie the idea of authorship in traditional literary and intellectual history. Sigüenza wrote all of his works, even his most personal and unpublished, to meet the generic and institutional expectations that governed authorship in seventeenth-century New Spain. Throughout his writings, however, he attempted to adapt these rhetorical expectations to a project that had no institutional basis at the time: the delineation and defense of a local homeland or patria.

LIBRA
ASTRONOMICA,
Y PHILOSOPHICA
EN QUE

D. Carlos de Sigüenza y Góngora
Cosmographo, y Mathematico Regio en la
Academia Mexicana,

EXAMINA
no solo lo que à su MANIFIESTO PHILOSOPHICO
contra los Cometas opuso
el R. P. EUSEBIO FRANCISCO KINO de la Compañia de
JESUS; sino lo que el mismo R. P. opinò, y pretendio haver
demostrado en su EXPOSICION ASTRONOMICA
del Cometa del año de 1681.

Sacala à luz D. SEBASTIAN DE GVZMAN Y CORDOVA,
Fator, Veedor, Proveedor, Iuez Oficial de la Real Hazienda
de su Magestad en la Caxa desta Corte.

En Mexico: por los Herederos de la Viuda de Bernardo Calderon
IXI. DC. XC.

Figure 2. The title page of Carlos de Sigüenza y Góngora's *Libra astronómica* (1690) showing his personal device, Pegasus, with the banner citing Virgil's *The Aeneid:* "sic itur ad astra" [thus you shall go to the stars]. Courtesy of the Bancroft Library, Berkeley, California.

The extent to which Sigüenza identified his writing with this idealized figure may be seen in his choice of a personal insignia, printed on the title pages of all of his published works (Figure 2). In this, Pegasus leaps into the air toward a banner containing a phrase from Virgil's Aeneid: "thus you shall go to the stars" (sic itur ad astra). In his 1680 *Theatro de virtudes* (Theater of Virtues), Sigüenza explains the significance of this personal device:

> the Impresse, or Hieroglyph, to which I turned to publish my Humble works [has] the composition and epigraph of the Pegasus, because, as is well known from Vincencio Ruscelo who states in explaining Jacobo Foscarini's insignia, both of which are cited by Brixiano in the *Commentaria Symbolica*, Verb. Pegas number 14, "[Pegasus] signifies the man who demonstrates a soul always focused on the sublime for the benefit of his *patria*."

> (la Empressa, ò Hieroglyphico, que para publicar mis Humildes obras discurri, del *Pegaso* con la disposicion, y epigraphe, que es notorio por saber lo que explicando la de Jacobo Foscarini dixo Vincencio Ruscelo referido de Brixiano en los Coment. Symbol. Verb. Pegas num. 14 y es que *Significat hominem, qui demonstrat animum suum semper ad sublima fere intentum pro beneficio suae PATRIAE.*)[77]

Not only does the citation provide an excellent example of the tortured hyperbaton that marks Sigüenza's prose in the *Theatro*, but it also underlines the limits of analyzing Baroque authorship in postromantic terms of authorial originality. The insignia is itself a composite of other works: the phrase is taken from Virgil while the Pegasus is found in Antonio Ricciardi's 1591 *Commentaria symbolica*, a storehouse of Renaissance iconography. Through this insignia Sigüenza dedicated his "humble works" to the higher cause of a patria, which he defines in the manner of Cicero as a transcendental ideal organizing and directing the actions of its citizens' souls.

Given the composite and citational nature of Sigüenza's authorship, it is not difficult to see the relationship between Sigüenza's writing and another project that paralleled his career of commissioned works and unpublished manuscripts. By the end of the seventeenth century Sigüenza had amassed what he himself qualified as one of the largest private libraries in the Spanish viceroyalties. Sigüenza's collection included both published works, many specifically related to what he called "things of the Indies" (cosas de Yndias), as well as unique manuscripts documenting the history of Spain's American territories.[78] This collection is clearly central to Sigüenza's writings.

Not only did it provide his historical perspective on the region but it also formed the material and intellectual basis for his relations with other authors, both previous and contemporary. As an assiduous collector of information on the history of New Spain, for instance, Sigüenza often looked to the written record of indigenous, clerical, and mestizo historians, particularly the early seventeenth-century Franciscan chronicler Juan de Torquemada and the mestizo historian Fernando de Alva Ixtlilxochitl, a descendent of the royal family of Texcoco. His relations with Ixtlilxochitl's nephew, Juan de Alva Ixtlilxochitl, led to his greatest coup: the collection of manuscripts and codices that had been the basis of Ixtlilxochitl's histories.[79]

Sigüenza's own unpublished manuscripts circulated among the small erudite elite of New Spain and probably influenced contemporary histories such as Fray Agustín Ventancurt's *Teatro mexicano* (Mexican Theater) (1698), which celebrates Sigüenza as a "curious investigator of ancient works, anxious that the greatness of this new world be discovered and published" (curioso investigador de papeles antiguos, y desseoso de que se descubran, y publiquen las grandezas deste nuevo mundo) and lists a number of Sigüenza's works in its sources.[80] Sigüenza also benefited from others' works: a manuscript that he received from the Jesuit missionary Manuel Duarte documenting the presence of Saint Thomas the Apostle in the Americas, for instance, possibly served as inspiration for his now lost text on the subject.[81] Nor were Sigüenza's relations limited to New Spain: in 1691 Sigüenza offered to exchange his astronomical observations with other scientists from abroad, and in 1697 the Neapolitan traveler Gemelli Careri copied several of Sigüenza's codices and later published them in his account of his stay in Mexico City.[82] Indeed, according to a declaration he made in the last year of his life, Sigüenza corresponded with many of the leading members of the Habsburg circle and beyond, a broadly cosmopolitan group that included Athanasius Kircher, Juan Caramuel, Giovanni Domenico Cassini, John Flamsteed, José Zaragoza, the Duke of Jovenazzo, and Pieter van Hamme.[83]

This network of scholars, while not unusual in the early modern period, was even more crucial for Sigüenza, considering his isolation from any one institution that would patronize his authorship. His apparently compensatory dedication to imagining a local homeland depended, in the first place, on an archive of local artifacts. In fact, there is good reason to believe that the core of Sigüenza's project was not authorship, understood as the source of original and creative production, but rather collection itself. Not only did Sigüenza spend most of his life gathering books, manuscripts, and objects that he understood to be broadly relevant to the regional context of New Spain, but he also employed these to bend the institutional discourse of the late Baroque to his project of delineating a local homeland. One of the most notable aspects of Sigüenza's public writings, for instance, is his extreme penchant for citation. This has most often been interpreted as the reflection of a peripheral scholar's need to justify himself through established authorities and thus a limitation on Sigüenza's intellectual autonomy.[84] Yet this explanation does not account for the types of citations Sigüenza chose nor for their appearance in the context of specific arguments in his works. More accurately, Sigüenza's citations should be linked to the method and rhetoric of Jesuit dispute, which sought not to celebrate juxtaposition and contradiction for its own sake but rather as a means to find a way out of conceptual binds. Reflecting this method, his compositions courted incoherence in order to overcome limits dialectically, through appeal to a higher plane of meaning. As the sublime point to which Sigüenza's ideal citizen dedicated his actions, the delineation of a local patria appears to have been just such a conceptual bind for Sigüenza and what has been glossed as the Baroque aspects of his writing, including its contradictory citations, a means to arrive at a solution.

Sigüenza's writings and his collection were therefore not two separate projects but part of one overarching impulse to store, record, and utilize a library of sources, to sift through them and to animate them in order to find a point of transcendence. In this sense, they paralleled a general practice of collecting in seventeenth-century European court culture, especially that of the Habsburg empire.[85] Like many of his contemporaries, for instance, Sigüenza followed the work of the Jesuit polymath Athanasius Kircher, whose collection of artifacts attracted visitors to the Collegio Romano, where it was housed.[86] Other collections, less systematic and public, were gained through pirate raids with strongly national interests in what has been called "epistemological mercantilism."[87] Indeed, Sigüenza's collection shares traits of each and thus has often been referred to as a "museum," a reference to the cabinets of curiosities that housed the exotica of seventeenth-century European collectors. Like many others imported from a European context, however, this term does not accurately describe Sigüenza's archive. Rather than a collection of exotica or an encyclopedic project aimed at finding universal order among variety, Sigüenza's collection had the specific purpose of articulating a local homeland. Accordingly, Sigüenza sought knowledge that was relevant to local conditions rather than for its own sake, out of "curiosity." And since the truth imparted by the objects he collected was only fully intelligible in a local context, to become "universal" it demanded the mediation of Creole scholarship. Sigüenza further stressed the need for collection in light of the destruction of the original contexts for his artifacts, whether these were classical authorities or indigenous codices. By collecting and safeguarding documents relevant to local conditions, Sigüenza thus provided an archive of authority and knowledge at a moment of Spanish imperial crisis.

Beginning with this archival function of Sigüenza's writings, it is therefore possible to analyze late seventeenth-century Creole politics in New Spain as a response to the loss and limitation of the basis for Spanish imperial sovereignty. Yet while the archive embedded in Sigüenza's writings reaches beyond his immediate context into general problems of seventeenth-century Spanish imperialism, it is important to note the ways in which his texts also uniquely reflect this context. It is, above all, in the strange and unresolved images in Sigüenza's texts that the contradictions of forming a political community in the wake of Spanish imperialism become the clearest. These images can be understood only through close readings of textual passages that might otherwise be glossed as contradictory, obtuse, or even illogical. Paradoxical or uncanny moments might be common to all documents that engage the political project of colonization and its aftermath, but the ironic, grotesque, or idealized figures that interrupt institutional discourse in Sigüenza's writings were determined by the specific conditions of Spanish imperialism.[88] In a sense, they are the true register of the emergence of a Creole regionalism, which sought not only to create an illustrious past for a local elite but also warned of immediate threats to Spanish sovereignty in the viceroyalty. In Sigüenza's mature writings, indeed, local history became the key to coalescing and guiding a Creole citizenry capable of defending the expansive territory of New Spain.

By relating Spanish imperial politics to Sigüenza's writings, this study thus takes up and revises several themes that have been central to scholarship on seventeenth-century Spanish American letters.

t place, it avoids the interpretation of Creole politics as
sness or identity by placing the images, arguments, and
Creole writings within the context of Spanish imperial
...gy rather than Creole subjectivity. By doing so, it also combats the perception that the seventeenth century was a stagnant period of Creole politics, a perception that follows the definition of politics as the desire for political autonomy from Spain.[89] Finally, it reorients arguments on the Spanish American Baroque by focusing on an author who has often been seen to harbor a pre-Enlightenment rationalism. Rather than seeing Sigüenza as a rationalist caught in a period of rhetorical obscurity, this study emphasizes the critical strain, best exemplified in New Spain in the works of Sigüenza and Sor Juana, embedded in the late Spanish American Baroque.[90] Above all, it turns to the contradictions of Spanish imperial sovereignty, which justified its possession of oversees territories in terms of Christian evangelization, to explain the specific political imaginary that emerged among Creoles in seventeenth-century New Spain. Arguably these contradictions intensified as Spanish American territories moved further away from the first stages of evangelization and new interethnic corporate identities formed in urban areas. In these areas Creoles began to promote the idea of a local patria to fill the vacuum in governance created by a sixteenth-century Spanish imperial model unable to account for seventeenth-century viceregal society. Rather than a natural instinct among seventeenth-century Creoles, patria was the figurative ideal that bridged the universal pretensions of Spanish imperialism and the local politics that had to contend with its consequences.

Precisely because they are eclectic and incomplete, Sigüenza's works expose the way in which the invention of a patria in Spanish America occurred in several discursive genres and combined various local themes: history, chronology, mathematics, regional cults, and racialized portraits of viceregal society. Yet while fragmented, his texts constantly returned to the two central tasks that had to be accomplished for any regional polity to be imagined: on the one hand the establishment of a sense of historical continuity that could overcome the interruption of the Spanish conquest and on the other a notion of local citizenship extracted from the totality of the viceroyalties' inhabitants. If a polymath like Athanasius Kircher in Europe could aspire to universalism, his equivalent in Spanish

America couched his regional focus in cosmopolitan pretensions. This dual responsibility to local conditions and global geopolitics meant that Sigüenza and other Creoles had to confront not only the legacy of Spanish imperial categories, such as the innocent indigenous neophyte or the perverse apostate, but also competing notions of society emerging among an ethnically mixed urban populace and the encroachment of competing European powers on the viceroyalty's frontiers. The particular value of Sigüenza's writings is that they show, like Benjamin's ruins, both the ideals of a Creole patria and its constitutional limitations. Above all, they expose the particular conditions, both regional and global, that favored the emergence of such a figure at the end of the seventeenth century in New Spain.

It is perhaps tempting to locate this untimely notion of a Creole patria, with all of its limitations and contradictions, within a teleology that leads to the triumph of political independence from Spain. To do so, however, would obscure the particular way in which Spanish imperialism has shaped Spanish American political ideas and ideals, especially the genesis of an exclusive notion of citizenship. And although these imaginary political projects depended greatly on the ideological fantasies of a small political and economic elite, many of their suppositions have had enormous consequences for regional politics. Reading these fantasies against the grain, moreover, exposes the threat that alternative versions of society and community posed to Habsburg governance. Indeed, the strong sense among Creoles that New Spain found itself in crisis at end of the seventeenth century lent a distinct aura of urgency to their writings. The sense of crisis also points to the exact place in which the notion of a Creole patria attempted to overcome the contradictions of Spanish imperialism. But if patria could be considered a need, in an ideological rather than psychological sense, it had to be invented in Spanish America from the material at hand precisely by consigning artifacts to the interior of an archive. Thus, while inspired by classical notions, the seventeenth-century Creole patria was an *ars inveniendi* based on the composition and arrangement of artifacts, an inventory and invention in the classical rhetorical sense. Rather than an expression of ambivalence, the late Creole Baroque attempted to animate these artifacts by finding their relevance to regional conditions at a time when the Spanish imperial project was faltering. Yet the Creole impulse to archive, which ranged from the physical protection of material objects such as indigenous codices to the metaphorical salvaging of pertinent citations for a regional imaginary, also moved beyond a simple reconstitution of Spanish imperialism. Ironically, it was in order to save Spanish imperialism from its own contradictions that a Creole patria first became an autonomous political figure.

CHAPTER I
Allegory, Archives, and Creole Sovereignty

In what was the most important seventeenth-century summary of Spanish colonial legislation, *Política indiana* (Indian Politics) (1648), the Spanish jurist Juan Solórzano Pereyra ends his discussion of legislation on indigenous subjects with the juridical problem of new lineages in the Americas. Considering first the case of Creoles, he asserts: "There can be no doubt that those who are born in the Indies of Spanish parents, commonly referred to there as 'Creoles,' are true Spaniards and as such should enjoy all corresponding rights, honors and privileges, and be judged as Spaniards, given that the provinces of the Indies are replicas of Spain and united with and incorporated in them as accessories" (Los que nacen en las Indias de padres españoles, que allí vulgarmente los llaman 'criollos,' no se puede dudar que sean verdaderos españoles y como tales han de gozar sus derechos, honras y privilegios, y ser juzgados por ellos, supuesto que las provincias de las Indias son como auctuario de las de España y acesoriamente unidas e incorporadas en ellas).[1] Thus, despite a history of Spanish and Amerindian intermarriage, Solórzano defines Creoles as fully Spanish and declares that their rights "in accordance with other rules of the same law, do not follow their place of residence but rather the natural origin of their parents" (conforme otras reglas del mismo derecho, no siguen el domicilio sino el origen natural de sus padres).[2] These rights were not so easily extended to subjects who mixed Spanish and non-Spanish lineage, however. Even as he all but dismisses the neologism "Creole," calling it a "common" (vulgar) term used to describe Spaniards born in the Americas, Solórzano readily accepts mestizo and *mulato* as accurate names for racially mixed colonial subjects. The first "received the name of 'mestizos' because of the mixture of blood and nations that combined to engender them, for which reason the Latins called them 'divergent' and 'hybrids'" (tomaron el nombre de mestizos por la mixtura de sangre y naciones que se juntó a engendrarlos, por donde los latinos los llamaron 'varios' e 'híbridas'). *Mulatos*, on the other hand, derived their name from mules "because this mixture is thought to be uglier and stranger and one understands by this name that they are compared to the nature of a mule" (por tenerse esta mezcla por más fea y extraordinaria y dar a entender con tal nombre que le comparan a la naturaleza del mulo).[3]

Solórzano's discussion of lineage exposes the challenge that new colonial subjects presented to the sixteenth-century political fiction that the American territories contained two separate "republics," one Indian and the other Spanish.[4] In accordance with over a century of Spanish imperial jurisprudence, Solórzano defines indigenous subjects as innocent neophytes. Writing in the middle of the seventeenth century, however, the Spanish jurist was forced to negotiate changing demographics unforeseen by early colonial legislation. By the end of the sixteenth century, many areas under Spanish control had witnessed a sharp demographic decline as epidemics and labor conditions decimated indigenous populations. Recovery in the seventeenth century presented a distinct social and economic picture. Rather than a conceptually unified "republic," indigenous subjects were effectively subdivided between Christianized and Hispanicized central regions and frontier territories where Spanish missionary and military advances continued to meet with armed resistance. In urban centers, moreover, ethnic mixture and social exchange had created new subjects not easily categorized by the binary colonial code.[5] Initially considered nonindigenous and therefore Spanish, mixed-race subjects or castas soon became subject to many of the same types of restrictions that had been applied to indigenous subjects with few of the protections.[6]

Indeed, even as new social categories emerged, the model of two republics contributed to a hypertrophied emphasis on lineage in Spanish America in a discourse of "purity of blood" that adapted language originally linked to Spanish anti-Semitism to the colonial context while limiting newer and more suspicious converts to Christianity to the bottom of the social and economic hierarchy.[7] Traveling between Spanish America and Madrid, Solórzano attempted to resolve the fundamental contradiction between the concept of two separate republics that continued to dictate Spanish imperial law and the fluctuations of American societies. Incorporating language from the legal tradition of the *Siete Partidas*, for instance, his 1648 *Política indiana* inaugurated a new juridical figure that deemphasized the ideal of full conversion that had dominated sixteenth-century debates on the "nature of the Indian." His notion that Indians were "miserable" subjects designated them to a special category of care and abridged rights.[8] "Miserable persons" (miserables personas), he writes, are those "for whom we naturally feel compassion because of their state, nature and travails" (de quien naturalmente nos compadecemos por su estado, calidad y trabajos). Indigenous subjects fit this definition well "because of their humble, servile, and submissive condition" (por su humilde, servil y rendida condición) and "even if Indians cannot be defined as miserable people for these reasons, it is sufficient that they are recently converted to our Faith" (aun cuando no concurrieran en los indios estas causas para deber ser contados entre las personas miserables, les bastara ser recién convertidos a la fe).[9] The terms "nature" (*calidad*) and "condition" (*condición*) in these definitions also imply that indigenous humility and servility were innate qualities, rather than temporary social conditions. As a counterpart to his argument in favor of the terms "mestizo" and "mulato," Solórzano's juridical treatise thus also employed the budding language of colonial race to support the idea that indigenous subjects were permanent neophytes.[10]

Solórzano's treatise shows the extent to which seventeenth-century jurisprudence had turned to racialized notions of "blood" in order to protect the hierarchy of estates crucial to Spanish colonial law.[11] The jurist's particularly negative assessment of subjects of mixed lineage paralleled a general decline in their social status since the early years of the Spanish conquest, when the offspring of Spanish migrants and indigenous noblewomen were often incorporated into the Spanish republic.[12] Solórzano reflects this legacy when he insists that mestizos and mulattoes who were legitimately conceived should be considered Spaniards with full rights.[13] He asserts that the majority of mestizos and mulattoes were illegitimate offspring, however, whose mixture already placed them outside of the law "because there are few honorable Spaniards who will marry Indians or blacks" (porque pocos españoles de honra hay que casen con indias o negras).[14] Solórzano goes on to characterize mixed subjects as those "bad castes, races, and conditions" (malas castas, razas y condiciones) who haunted the highways as thieves and vagabonds and argues that they should be sent to labor in the mines in place of innocent indigenous subjects.[15] If in Solórzano's treatise, purity of lineage allowed the Creole elite to continue juridically as Spanish subjects, despite having been born in the Americas, mixed blood became a sign of moral degeneration that condemned mestizos and mulattoes to what was recognized even at that time to have been a virtual death sentence.[16] And even if the persistent idea of indigenous innocence, humility, and servility protected them from the same fate, the idea that indigenous subjects were "miserable" placed them in a state of permanent welfare that widened the breach between indigenous commoners and nobility, virtue, and citizenship.[17]

THE CRISIS OF SOVEREIGNTY IN SPANISH AMERICA

The seventeenth-century developments in racial status and nomenclature showed the cracks in one of the most central tenets of sixteenth-century Spanish colonization: that the Spanish Empire was built on the voluntary and peaceful conversion of non-Christians and their subsequent inclusion into a Christian polity. The emphasis on voluntarism in Spanish imperialism reflected the particular historical juncture of initial conquests and the subsequent attempts to justify and legitimize these in accordance with the Thomistic precepts that came to dominate peninsular theology.[18] Carried out in the wake of the Reconquest of the Iberian peninsula, Spanish colonization of the Americas had been easily grafted onto the goal of creating a universal Christian monarchy.[19] The occupation of territories outside the context of war, however, had demanded some justification of Spain's sovereignty (*imperium*), or right to rule over native subjects, and property rights (*dominium*), or right to profit from land, labor, and minerals. Spanish sovereignty over the Americas had initially relied on Alexander VI's papal bull of 1493, which granted Spain and Portugal joint custodianship over a globe divided the following year in the Treaty of Tordesillas.[20] However, it was not until the spectacular conquests of the Mexica and Inca Empires in 1521 and 1535, respectively, that a more developed narrative of Spanish imperial sovereignty emerged. Given the complexity of the Mexica and Inca polities, which more closely resembled European monarchies than had the polities of the circum-Caribbean, Hernán Cortés was able to announce in his second letter to the newly crowned Habsburg emperor Carlos V that "one might call oneself Emperor of this kingdom with no less glory than of Germany which by the grace of God Your Highness possesses" (se puede intitular de nuevo Emperador della y con título y no menos mérito que el de Alemaña que por la gracia de Dios Vuestra Sacra Majestad posee).[21] Conquerors' reports represented the conquests that established what would later become the two major viceroyalties of Spanish America, New Spain and Peru, as either the peaceful donation of the Mexica and Inca empires by their sovereign rulers in the tradition of *translatio imperii* or as wars justly waged in the defense of Christianity.[22]

This notion that the American territories had been annexed by contract or just war rather than "conquered" agreed well with the sixteenth-century consolidation of the Spanish state as a "composite monarchy" formed of semiautonomous kingdoms.[23] Technically, the administrative territories of Spanish America, or viceroyalties, had the same political status as Aragon or Naples in what came to be known as the greater "Spanish monarchy." Yet this theoretical principle of equality between kingdoms within one overarching monarchy could never fully erase the anomalous manner by which the American territories and subjects had been incorporated into the Castilian Crown through the twin process of conquest and conversion.[24] Nor did it clarify the manner in which Spain would oversee and manage its newly acquired American territories. Early in the sixteenth century, therefore, the Crown began adapting Spanish institutions to the particular context of an overseas territory. One of the earliest was the House of Trade (Casa de Contratación), established in 1503 on the heels of Spanish settlement in the Caribbean in order to oversee trade and commerce, principally the movement of gold. Following a strong conciliar tradition in Spanish administration, in 1523 the group of advisors who had been instrumental in shaping Crown policy in the Americas became formalized as the Council of Indies (Consejo de Indias) and was given responsibility for all administrative aspects of the overseas territories. *Audiencias*, or high courts, were assigned judicial oversight and in 1542 the two major viceroyalties were established with viceroys named as the king's substitutes.[25] Throughout the long period of Spanish rule over the Americas, all administrative representatives in high positions and all legislation emanated from Spain itself, a policy that increasingly played into tensions between the locally born colonial elite and peninsular bureaucrats.[26]

Thus, despite the language of equal and autonomous kingdoms of the Spanish monarchy, and the practice of respecting native political and juridical structures in other regions of the Spanish Empire, by the end of the sixteenth century the centralizing institutions of Spanish viceregal administration had created what was de facto a Spanish colonial state in the Americas.[27] Even so, the difficulties involved in sending word back and forth between the Crown and the viceroyalties meant that effective political control by the Spanish Crown was never possible. Instead, governance was achieved by means of numerous negotiations at all levels without for that reason overturning the fundamental notion that the Spanish monarch was the sole repository of the law.[28] In an attempt to further centralize administration, Carlos V and his successors distanced Spanish colonial sovereignty from the authority of the 1493 papal bull.[29] The earliest extensive consideration of Spanish sovereignty came from the Dominican Francisco de Vitoria, the central figure in the revival of Thomism among Spanish theologians, in a *relectio* delivered in 1539 and subsequently published based on student notes as *De indiis* [On the Indians] (1557).[30] Drawing on the Thomist tradition of natural law, Vitoria effectively reduced the legitimacy of Spanish colonial sovereignty to Amerindians' voluntary submission to the Spanish monarch and conversion to the Catholic Church. Thus, Vitoria's Thomist theology provided Carlos V and his successors with a renewed language of *imperium* that replaced the papal decree with a more contractual and evangelical language of conversion.[31]

The Thomist obsession with voluntary conversion did face a strong counterargument that property rights (*dominium*) were conferred by civilization and not by natural law; thus, the relevant question was whether Amerindians pertained to recognizable societies. These contrasting views paralleled debates between mendicants and settlers on the Crown's practice of distributing the spoils of conquest in the form of *encomiendas*, a practice by which the Crown ceded to designated Spanish settlers a number of indigenous subjects in trusteeship provided that they oversee and encourage their evangelization and integration into a Spanish-style society. Although in theory the *encomienda* was intended to promote both settlement and evangelization of indigenous subjects, without granting to the Spanish settlers more permanent rights, in practice the system quickly established a class of settlers, known as *encomenderos*, who had virtually unfettered use of indigenous land and labor.[32] These abuses quickly gained the attention of clergy and some, such as the Dominican las Casas, became prominently involved in denouncing the situation.[33] Constantly reminded of their obligations to convert indigenous subjects to Christianity and concerned about the increasingly autonomous power of the Spanish settlers in the Americas, the Spanish Crown repeatedly attempted to rein in the encomenderos. The most drastic measures were the 1542 New Laws, which restricted the inheritance of the encomiendas and reinstated Crown ownership over those whose current holder had died. These laws prompted immediate and in some cases violent responses from the settlers and were difficult if not impossible to put into effect on the ground.[34]

Although the Crown soon lifted the most severe restrictions on the encomiendas, continued abuses prompted the Council of Indies to suspend all conquests until the issue of indigenous rights and settler obligations had been resolved by a theological junta. The resulting 1550–51 debate between the Dominican Bartolomé de Las Casas and the emperor's chaplain, Ginés de Sepúlveda, focused on the underlying question of whether war could justly be waged against indigenous subjects who resisted Spanish sovereignty. In lengthy arguments, Sepúlveda famously argued that indigenous Americans fell under the Aristotelian category of slaves by nature and therefore were not in possession of true sovereignty while Las Casas defended the rights of indigenous subjects to convert voluntarily and peacefully.[35] Ultimately, the Spanish Crown took the middle ground, opting both to curtail the establishment of a strong Spanish settler class, particularly by limiting the rights of the encomenderos, while at the same time maintaining indigenous subjects in a position of perpetual tutelage subject to a tribute tax and community labor requirements.[36] Meanwhile, the cumulative effects of war, Spanish labor practices, and epidemic diseases had led to such a disastrous population decline of Amerindians that by the end of the sixteenth century the theoretical issues arising from early colonization were rendered increasingly irrelevant. Reorganized administratively into new Spanish-style towns and neighborhoods, the indigenous survivors of the first decades of Spanish conquest were in the anomalous position of being subjects whose status as Christian neophytes and lack of recognizable Spanish cultural traits (*policía*) meant that they were easily assigned to a permanently inferior status in colonial society. Although this subordination did not on the surface contradict early modern notions of a stratified hierarchy of estates, indigenous subjects were in a unique position, caught between the Christianizing and profiteering motives of Spanish imperial expansion.[37]

Writing nearly a century after these sixteenth-century debates, Solórzano inherited Spain's justification of sovereignty by evangelization in an increasingly complex geopolitical context. During this time, a weakened Spanish monarchy oversaw a far-flung empire that was politically and fiscally impossible to administer. The crisis of the Habsburg monarchy opened the door for rebellions in the Low Countries, Portugal, and Catalonia and strengthened regional oligarchies in Spain itself. In addition to the piecemeal disintegration of the empire's territories, the second half of the century saw a drop in silver revenue from the Americas, further depleting a Spanish treasury already saddled by the debt incurred in maintaining its fragmented empire intact.[38] Finally, commercial competition, pirate attacks, and the encroachment of other European powers into what Spain considered its territories was taking a toll on the empire. From the first decades of the seventeenth century, both official and unofficial publications outlined possible responses to what was perceived by many to be a decline in Spanish power.[39] By the end of the century, it became increasingly difficult to contradict the perception among Spaniards and non-Spaniards alike that the empire was spiraling downward.[40] Embattled on several geographic fronts, in 1670 Spain conceded British sovereignty over several Caribbean islands, for the first time publicly recognizing the impossibility of the pretension of a universal Christian monarchy.[41] As the century drew to a close, most Spaniards had accepted the fact that Habsburg rule had come to an end and were most concerned with what would replace it.[42]

The language of Solórzano's midcentury treatise reflects the increasing defensiveness of the Spanish monarchy as it responded to physical and ideological attacks by other European states in expansion. Writers interested in promoting the rights of other states to trade and conquest had appropriated Francisco de Vitoria's discussion of natural rights and the lurid representation of Spanish atrocities in Las Casas's polemical *Brevísima relación de la destrucción de las indias* (Very Brief Account of the Destruction of the Indies) (1552) to question the justification of the exclusive sovereignty of Spain over its empire.[43] Given this context, Solórzano chose to avoid entirely the discussion of legitimacy that had been of central concern in the sixteenth century and instead addressed the pragmatics of Spanish colonial jurisprudence.[44] The quarrels of other European states were unfounded, he argues, "since the acquisition, as we have stated, was undertaken with titles and in good faith and such circumstances, over the long run, make it irrevocable" (pues la adquisición, como habemos dicho, se hizo con título y buena fe y tales circustancias que, acompañadas con el transcurso de largo tiempo, le hacen irretractable).[45] If he did take up the issue again at all, he writes, it is not "because it is necessary to go around inquiring into and questioning the justice of kingdoms acquired and entered into so long ago . . . but rather to satisfy so many heretics and writers badly inclined toward our nation" (porque sea necesario andar inquiriendo y calificando la justicia de los reinos ya de antiguo adquiridos y entablados . . . si no por satisfacer a tantos herejes y escritores mal afectos a nuestra nación).[46] Finally, if even the Roman Empire had had salutary effects on the peoples it had conquered, "I don't know why envy can cast doubt on the justification of ours by the same title since it has surpassed the Roman to such an extent, both because of the greater number of barbarous territories that we have brought to order and because of the improved education we have imparted, since aside from political life we have also granted the light of eternity" (no sé por qué la envidia puede hacer dudosa la justificación del mismo título a los nuestros, que tanto en esta parte se han aventajado a los romanos, así en ser muchas más las provincias bárbaras que han reducido, como en su mejor enseñanza, pues demás de la vida política se les ha dado la luz de la eterna).[47]

Solórzano's treatise thus outlined a justification of the Spanish Empire that coincided with Spain's self-presentation, from the end of the sixteenth century onward, as the embattled defender of Counter-Reformation Catholicism on both European and non-European fronts. While this defense still conceived of Spanish imperialism as a force for Christianization, the seventeenth-century focus was not on expansion through conversion but rather on the conservation of an empire that was beginning to show signs of fragility.[48] Given this context, Solórzano advises the king in his preface that "it is better to anticipate the ends than find the origins, that conserving kingdoms does not require less care than acquiring them, and that only [kingdoms] that are protected and defended with the prudence and caution of the princes that govern them are secure and lasting" (es más prevenir los fines que hallar los principios y que no se requiere menor recato en conservar los reinos que en adquirirlos, y ser sólo firmes y durables aquellos que guarda y defiende la prudencia y cuidado de los príncipes que los rigen).[49] For this reason, argues Solórzano, the law was the prince's "strongest bulwark" (mas seguras murallas)[50] and the only means to rein in Spain's far-flung empire, especially its American polities, where "the king's orders usually arrive late, feeble, or in vain, and those that live or pass through find ample space to judge and consider licit whatever their appetites deem fit" (los mandatos de los reyes suelen ser tardos o vanos o llegan flojos y se descubre más ancho campo a los que las habitan o biernan para juzgar y tener por lícito todo lo que les pide o persuade su antojo).[51] While he admits that Spanish colonization at times had resulted in excessive violence, he attributes this to the passions of renegade soldiers and finds in it one more reason to fortify the colonial state by means of "goodly and saintly laws" (buenas y santas leyes).[52] Rather than returning to the vexed question of the right of Spanish sovereignty, then, Solórzano proposes the practical and urgent task of sorting through and organizing the colonial legislation that had accumulated chaotically over the past century.

Solórzano's project for reorganizing Spanish imperial jurisprudence reflected the combination of pragmatism and idealism by which seventeenth-century Habsburg rule responded to its perceived decline.[53] Indeed, Solórzano's 1629 *De Indiarum iure* (On the Laws of the Indies) and its revised Spanish version, the 1648 *Política indiana*, were distillations of the larger task of compiling and ordering Spanish colonial legislation to which he had been assigned together with Antonio León Pinelo, a rationalization intended to tighten Crown control over the territories. Still incomplete at the time of its authors' deaths, the *Recopilación de leyes de los reynos de las Indias* is an apt reflection of the crisis of the Spanish monarchy in the seventeenth century. When the compendium was finally published in 1680 under Carlos II, its juridical language showed the extent to which the ideology of Spanish imperialism had stagnated since the end of the sixteenth century. Rather than adapting to the changing geopolitical situation of Spain and its empire, the *Recopilación* was by nature a conservative document that reiterated the principles of Spanish imperialism through a summary of what was by then almost two centuries of Spanish colonial legislation.[54] Above all, the *Recopilación* continued to emphasize the paternalistic protection of indigenous subjects through an alliance between clerics and the Crown and the centralized coordination of viceregal governance.[55] Thus, under the strong influence of Solórzano's pen, the Spanish Crown greeted what by all accounts was an irreversible decline in its imperial power by reinforcing the constitutional fictions of its early colonial period.

THE RISE OF CREOLE PATRIMONIALISM

The political and fiscal crisis of the Habsburg monarchy in the second half of the seventeenth century not only strengthened regional oligarchies in Spain but also contributed to the autonomy of local elites in the viceroyalties. Although the situation was far from homogeneous across the extended territory of the Spanish Empire, local forms of governance often filled the vacuum created by the divided court of Felipe IV and the instability of the extended reign of his invalid son Carlos II.[56] This relative triumph of the Spanish American elite in the late seventeenth century capped a period of more contentious competition between the local and viceregal governments. During the first two-thirds of the seventeenth century, Spanish bureaucrats had been able to skirt the restrictions on marrying into local families, thus creating a limited sphere of mutual influence among peninsular and Creole elites.[57] And yet the town councils (*cabildos*), the most representative body for the Creole elites, were shorn of any direct political power on the viceregal level, instead limited to negotiations with the top echelon of royal officials, even in some cases on matters of municipal and provincial taxes.[58] The only other avenue to administrative autonomy that might have been open to Creoles, the higher posts of the mendicant orders, was likewise closed off to them early in the seventeenth century through the piecemeal enactment of the *alternativa*, a policy that guaranteed the succession of Spanish friars to the top ranks. Thereafter, although Creoles became numerous in the secular priesthood, their aspirations to higher office in the mendicant orders were actively curtailed.[59] By the last third of the seventeenth century, however, the tide appeared to shift slightly in Creole favor, enhanced by a combination of improved economic conditions in the viceroyalties and the disarray of the Habsburg monarchy. While the enforcement in the mendicant orders of the alternativa continued to provoke flare-ups between Creole and peninsular friars, the Crown's fiscal problems and inability to take an active role in imperial politics led to increased Creole autonomy in local politics, even including the sale of higher posts that had been previously reserved for peninsular officials.[60] Despite these material changes, Creoles continued to be viewed with suspicion by peninsular administrators, not the least on questions of their ultimate loyalty.⁶¹

Solórzano's juridical works, inspired in part by his participation in the Audiencia of Peru, reflected not only a desire to aid imperial administration but also an active sympathy for the situation of the Creole elite in the American viceroyalties.⁶² Solórzano was particularly sensitive to the accusation that climate had had a detrimental effect on those born in the Americas: "we need to take note of the [royal decrees] in order to disabuse the ignorance or ill will of those who, not wishing that Creoles participate in the rights and respect awarded to Spaniards, hardly judge them worthy of the name of rational beings, under the pretext that because of the stars and climate of those provinces [Creoles] degenerate to such a degree that they lose any benefit that Spanish blood could contribute" (Conviene notarlas para convencer la ignorancia o mala intención de los que no quieren que los criollos participen del derecho y estimación de españoles, tomando por achaque que degeneran tanto con el cielo y temperamento de aquellas provincias que pierden cuanto bueno les pudo influir la sangre de España, y apenas los quieren juzgar dignos del nombre de racionales).⁶³ While he admitted that climate could affect nature, Solórzano argued that many American regions were actually quite temperate and that even in those that were not, Creoles' lineage and descent were strong enough to ward off any noxious elements as "the good blood from which they descend ensures that theirs loses part if not all of the harm from the stars and land it passes through" (la sangre buena que se va derivando hace que pierda en todo o en parte la suya lo nocivo del cielo y suelo adonde se pasa).⁶⁴ Finally, Solórzano finds precedents for Creole claims to local administrative posts, asserting that in the Christian world it is custom and law that offices should be reserved for natives (*naturales*).⁶⁵ In the case of the American viceroyalties, he adds further reasons that Creoles should be considered worthy of higher office: "the great love that they hold for their land and birthplace" (el mayor amor que tendrían a la tierra y patria donde nacieron) and "their command of the language or tongue of the Indians of the same land, which those born there suckle along with mother's milk and that foreigners learn slowly and badly" (la pericia del idioma o lengua que hablan los indios de la misma tierra, la cual maman en la leche los nacidos en ella y la aprenden tarde y mal los que vienen de fuera). Finally, Solórzano ominously predicts that if Creoles were not rewarded they might "fall into such a state of desperation that they come to hate virtue and studies" (venir a caer en tal género de desesperación que aborreciesen la virtud y los estudios).[66]

Yet although Solórzano has been seen as a defender of the Spanish American elite, his solution of increased juridical oversight and centralization was not necessarily the one favored by Creoles themselves.[67] By the time Solórzano published his treatise in 1648, the American-born viceregal elite were already thinking of themselves in terms of regional polities with their own customs and peculiarities. Not only had many begun to appropriate what Solórzano characterizes as the "common" term *criollo* to distinguish themselves from peninsular Spaniards but they had also begun to speak of nebulous regional territories—at times restricted to a local birthplace and at others referring to a broader transregional area—as their homelands or patria*s*. Reflecting the provincial nature of experience during the period, patria most commonly referred to a local birthplace. It was thus intimately related to notions of community obligations and an emotive link to a local landscape as opposed to legal and administrative relations with a greater kingdom or state.[68] Yet the classical sources of Renaissance humanism, which often spoke of Rome as the *communis patria*, also created a precedent for the application of patria to an abstract metropolitan community.[69] Other classical sources provided the emotive and moral contours of the notion of patria, from Ciceronian ideals that placed loyalty to country above familial bonds to the Horatian topic that led seventeenth-century Spanish authors to refer to patria as *la dulce patria*.[70] Thus, even in its reference to local birthplace, patria often evoked a nostalgic yearning for communal unity that made it possible to transfer the notion to nongeographic and abstract entities.[71] With the hardening of national borders and the consolidation of centralized states, therefore, patria easily became employed to refer to supralocal regions and state territories, particularly when under attack.[72]

To these common uses of the term patria in early modern Europe, Creoles added the idea of an exclusive citizenship selected by lineage. For this reason, when speaking of a political community, Creole texts often invoked patria together with *nación*, a term that emphasized lineage rather than territory.[73] In this sense, the concept of patria that emerged in the writings of the seventeenth-century Creole elite referred not only to a local birthplace but also to a community of citizens defined by the confluence of Spanish descent and an emotive connection to the American land. It has been difficult to relate this seventeenth-century concept of a Creole patria to later ideas of republican nationalism, however, especially that which resulted from the historical trajectory of nineteenth-century movements of independence in Spanish America.[74] One approach to early Creole patriotism is to understand it as a version of what Benedict Anderson has called an "imagined community." Indeed, the late seventeenth-century Creole concept of a patria agrees with many aspects that Anderson attributes to later national communities: it was imagined to the extent that it was composed of persons outside of face-to-face contact, it was a community to the extent that it was forced to delineate horizontal membership often defined through the term "citizen," and it was limited to the extent that it did not aspire to universal membership and indeed shunned the concept. In fact, the only term from Anderson's analysis of national imagined communities that clearly does not fit the seventeenth-century Creole notion of patria is that of "sovereignty," as it suggests that the nation was conceived in opposition to monarchical absolutism.[75]

In his critique of Anderson's thesis that nationalism was a European invention transported in "modular" form to regions that had been colonized by European states, however, Partha Chatterjee has recently decoupled "sovereignty" from political independence. In colonial contexts such as British India, Chatterjee argues, "anticolonial nationalism creates *its own domain of sovereignty* within colonial society well before it begins its political battle with the imperial power."[76] As Chatterjee's argument suggests, imperial sovereignty presupposes an inherent gap between a preexisting sovereignty, with its local elite, and a justified occupation. But any similar analysis of the position of the Creole elite in Spanish America must begin with the fact that Spanish sovereignty in the Americas itself was divided. On the one hand, the viceroyalties were understood to be "kingdoms" in a confederated monarchy and thus were subject to the commonplace Thomistic ideas of a society of estates headed by a monarch. In this sense, as Solórzano asserted, Creoles nominally had the same status as Spanish subjects, a fact that fed resentment at their unequal treatment in administration. On the other hand, subjects of non-Spanish descent were held under a more contractual version of sovereignty, having in official accounts submitted to the Castilian monarch and converted to Catholicism of their own volition. As long as these two forms of sovereignty could be kept separate it was possible to speak of two distinct republics within the American viceroyalties. In practice, however, they were difficult if not impossible to discern, especially as the viceroyalties moved farther away from their apostolic beginnings.

The problem of sovereignty in the Spanish Americas also blurred the distinction between vassalage and citizenship. While republican patriotism might have encouraged an idea of citizenship, Spanish notions of rights, obligations, and honor continued to follow the language of early modern vassalage. Without a notion of fraternal universalism, citizenship was limited to those of Spanish descent. Amerindians, who might be considered citizens of their own republics, had the additional problem of a pagan past. Although from the beginning of the Spanish colonization of the Americas a major theoretical question had been whether the civilizing force of Spanish institutions (*policía*) should precede or follow conversion, by the seventeenth century it is quite clear that the scales had been tipped in favor of institutional forms of policía not only as a requisite for conversion but, in a population of now converted indigenous and mixed subjects, as a guarantor against backsliding or apostasy.[77] Despite the fact that the distinct lineages that made up the urban centers of viceregal society were often imagined as corporate identities, represented through such institutions as guilds and visually displayed in the numerous public processions that marked urban life, they also continued to carry with them juridical and social markers of an origin outside of the Spanish social body. Thus, by the seventeenth century the everyday language of castes in the viceroyalties had adapted the Thomistic idea of a harmoniously ordered society of estates to the political theology of Spanish imperialism, which maintained distinctions among subjects according to their lineage and religious descent.[78]

As viceregal societies moved further away from their apostolic origins, moreover, Creoles' bid for greater administrative influence focused increasingly on governance rather than evangelization. In this sense, late seventeenth-century Creoles harkened back to a line of reasoning that had underwritten much of the nonvoluntarist readings of Spanish sovereignty, especially evident in Ginés de Sepúlveda's arguments, by which indigenous subjects were naturally subordinated to a superior civilization. Whereas even Sepúlveda saw this as a temporary rather than permanent condition, however, by the middle of the seventeenth century, ideas of natural order had taken on stronger racial connotations.[79] In concert with this reasoning, Creoles suggested that their role in Spanish imperialism would be to act as magistrates of local patrimonial orders that, through a combination of lineage and local knowledge, could govern more effectively than peninsular administrators. Released from the obligation to convert non-Christians, Creoles increasingly proposed their combination of virtue, descent, and local knowledge as the only antidote to what they presented as an unruly popular culture.[80] Their relationship to non-Spanish subjects, therefore, held none of the horizontal fraternalism associated with republican citizenship, nor the alliance between native elites and commoners that Chatterjee suggests existed in British Bengal, but rather carried forward the paternalism implicit in Spanish imperial sovereignty.[81] Unlike the anticolonial nationalism that Chatterjee studies in India, then, Creole patrimonialism created a "domain of sovereignty" not to confront the Spanish state but rather to overcome the paradoxes of Spanish imperialism itself.

PATRIMONIALISM AND THE CREOLE ARCHIVE

Patrimonialism, in Max Weber's definition, is a traditional form of authority of the "pure type" in which "obedience is owed not to enacted rules but to the person who occupies the position of authority by tradition or who has been chosen for it by the traditional master."[82] Patrimonial authority is both discretionary and limited, underwritten "partly in terms of traditions which themselves directly determine the content of the command" and "partly in terms of the master's discretion in that sphere which tradition leaves open to him."[83] Following the work of Richard Morse, scholars have applied Weber's notion of patrimonialism to the Spanish imperial state, especially to the figure of the Spanish monarch. Yet whereas Weber explicitly distinguishes patrimonialism from bureaucracy, which he saw as a faceless and rule-driven apparatus, Morse argues that Spanish governance in the Americas was both "patrimonial and bureaucratic."[84] Indeed, colonial governance was in fact an interplay between distinct types of authority, not always harmoniously coordinated. It is even possible to argue that rather than diminishing its patrimonial character, the bureaucratic distance of the Spanish monarch led to a fragmentation of patrimonialism into ad hoc areas of discretion, a logic enshrined in the well-known formula of Spanish law *obedezco, pero no cumplo* (I obey, but don't comply).[85] In this sense, the patrimonial character of viceregal society followed from a combination of factors that do not fit neatly into Weber's definition. Although one of the more decisive influences was the pastoral model of the mendicant orders, the seigniorial authority of landowners, urban employers, and indigenous nobles was also structured on paternalistic models.[86] The tensions involved in juggling these positions meant that, while following an overall Thomistic logic of social hierarchy in which "all parts of society were ordered to the whole as the imperfect to the perfect," actual governance in Spanish America was carried out through a combination of internal dispute and, as a last resort, appeal to the king or viceroy as the ultimate source of mediation.[87]

The emergence of a distinctly Creole patrimonial discourse in the Spanish viceroyalties coincided with the crisis and decline of several forms of authority upon which colonial governance had relied in the sixteenth and early seventeenth centuries. Reflecting the actual practices of governance in late seventeenth-century Habsburg rule, Creoles often voiced worries about the vacuum in traditional authority in indigenous communities and the rise of an urban casta population entirely free of all traditional structures of authority. To offset this loss, Creoles added to the pastoral model of care implicit in the 1681 *Recopilación* their privileged access to local knowledge for governance.[88] As Weber notes, patrimonial authority implies the notion of a tradition: "Rules which are in fact innovations can be legitimized only by the claim that they have been 'valid of yore' but have only now been recognized by means of 'wisdom.'"[89] Yet local forms of patrimonialism in the Spanish viceroyalties could not rely on the simple recuperation or recognition of rules "valid of yore." Rather, these rules had to be invented by combining traditions that Spanish colonization had interrupted. As historians such as Anthony Pagden have noted, during the seventeenth century Creoles began to appropriate local history, including the past of those "their ancestors had conquered."[90] But whereas European historiography of the same era documented the continuous authority of a dynasty or kingdom, Creoles emphasized the sutured and artificial nature of their traditions by describing paradisiacal local landscapes imbued with a providentialist aura or by cultivating an antiquarian interest in the pre-Columbian past.[91] These local archives, understood as both material collection and epistemological privilege, proved the best and perhaps only way to overcome the historical interruption of the conquest.

The ability of the archive to delineate a tradition in the wake of colonial disruption derives from what Jacques Derrida has called its "topo-nomological" structure. According to Derrida, the most basic function of the archive, to gather together or collect documents, unites two distinct principles: the sequential, that of "commencement," and the jussive, that of "commandment."[92] The archive's documents, not necessarily written, are external marks, traces, or signs that recall an origin. In Derrida's terms, the process of archiving "consigns" these documents to a place and an order in which "there should not be any absolute dissociation, any heterogeneity or secret which could separate [secernere], or partition, in an absolute manner."[93] The concept of an archive is therefore intimately related to a hermeneutic power that bridges origin and artifice by interpreting relations among objects and ordering them accordingly. Further, as Derrida notes, the Greek term *arkheion* referred to the residence of the *archons*, the magistrates or those who commanded. In consigning documents to the residence of those who command, the archive creates a force of law that is also "economic," related to the *oikos* or "house" as a place, domicile, family, lineage, or institution. To do so, it retrieves documents from previous locations and regroups them in filial relations: it is a "domiciliation" of the law, its "house arrest." The topo-nomological function of the archive, its combination of place and of law, thus creates a patriarchical or patrimonial law, publicly relevant but privately administered.[94] Derrida's emphasis on this archival constitution of patriarchical law thus denaturalizes what might otherwise be seen as an anterior and original law, the law of the fathers or the community.

Although the archive has been employed as a metaphor for analyzing the formation of a Latin American literary tradition, its power to constitute a domestic or patriarchical law has not been explicitly addressed. Rather, two very distinct studies of the formation of intellectuals and letters in Latin America have drawn from Michel Foucault's earlier definition of the archive as a "system of enunciability."[95] The first of these, Roberto González Echevarría's *Myth and Archive*, is a sustained meditation on the meaning of origins in Latin American literature. González Echevarría sees literature, broadly defined as an imaginative discourse released from the constraints of veracity, as an attempt to disrupt hegemonic discursive systems that create the repository of Latin American identity: law in the colonial period, science in the nineteenth century and anthropology in the twentieth.[96] In his posterior study, *Constructing the Criollo Archive*, Antony Higgins focuses on two neo-Latin authors from eighteenth-century Mexico to argue that the formation of regional archives was essential to the creation of Creole class identification at a moment when the Spanish imperial state began instituting effective centralizing reforms. Higgins chooses a period in which literature was limited to the colonial elite to show how authors worked to institutionalize and codify a collective Creole subjectivity: Juan José de Eguiara y Eguren through his midcentury encyclopedic archive of Mexican authors and Rafael Landívar through a bucolic version of the Mexican landscape in his poem the *Rusticatio* (Country Life) (1782). Although like González Echevarría, Higgins invokes Foucault's notion of the archive as a system of enunciability, he emphasizes literature's regulatory rather than liberating properties.[97]

These contradictory interpretations of the site and function of the Latin American "archive" reflect very distinct concepts of the politics of literature, concepts that in turn orient these studies' empirical examples. Perhaps because they understand the archive as *either* liberating or regulatory, neither González Echevarría nor Higgins include the seventeenth-century Baroque in their discussions. Instead, both studies focus on periods defined by classical humanism: González Echevarría on what he defines as the "crepuscular humanism" of the Inca Garcilaso de la Vega, in whose 1609 *Comentarios reales* [Royal Commentaries] he finds the disassembling of the colonial archive of law, and Higgins on the renewed humanism of eighteenth-century Neoclassicism that provided the foundation for a local epistemology.[98] The period between these, roughly the second quarter of the seventeenth century through the end of the century, has been difficult to equate with the foundation of institutional archives. Nonetheless, it is clear that Baroque systems of knowledge encompassed an impulse to safeguard and house objects, as may be seen in the antiquarian collections or cabinets of curiosity that were common to the period in Europe.[99] These collections reflected, and in some cases instigated, the material consequences of the tectonic geopolitical shifts of the period: imperialist competition and the rise of mercantilist capitalism, the dissolution and reconfiguration of absolutist monarchies, religious wars waged over the nature of signs, empirical and new philosophical approaches to nature.[100] In fact, Baroque collections might indeed be considered properly "archival," in Derrida's sense, since by placing objects in physical proximity with one another they reacted to the breakdown of previous archives by searching for alternative points of unity. The Baroque is thus a compelling place to relate archival innovation to conservation. Indeed, scholarship on European collections has done much to show the relationship between collection and such phenomena as new forms of scientific authority.[101]

Beyond focusing on the greater European impulse to collect during this period, however, any consideration of archival practices in the Spanish American Baroque must also address the complex politics of memory in regions in which the process of evangelization often entailed attempts to "erase" the memory of a pagan past. In another recent investigation, Diana Taylor has addressed the interplay and competition among memory systems in Latin America by pairing the idea of the archive with that of "repertoire." According to Taylor, Spanish colonization should be understood not as the imposition of the written word on primarily oral cultures but rather as the constitution of archives and the deauthorization of other forms of memory and knowledge: "what changed with the Conquest was not that writing displaced embodied practice (we need only remember that the friars brought their own embodied practices) but the degree of legitimization of writing over other epistemic and mnemonic systems."[102] Indeed, as Taylor goes on to argue, the archive of written materials and the repertoire of embodied practices often coexisted in Spanish missionary practices. As sixteenth-century missionaries quickly discovered, the "repertoire" of embodied practices and rituals was a possible, and perhaps the only, means to transform indigenous belief into Catholicism. By the end of the sixteenth century, however, the inclusion of indigenous practices in Christian ritual led missionaries to suspect that these forms of worship could themselves provide a medium for old beliefs to be carried forward.[103]

Taylor's emphasis on the dialectical tensions between the ephemeral, oral sphere of performance and the written corpus of the archive in early Spanish imperialism is an important prelude to understanding the archival principle of the seventeenth-century Baroque. Indeed, from the widespread dissemination of Ignacio de Loyola's *Spiritual Exercises* to public festivities, the emphasis on corporeal practice in seventeenth-century Counter-Reformation theology both augmented and fine-tuned the embodied practices of the early missionaries.[104] In a sense, the early Counter-Reformation collapsed the distinction that Taylor makes between the archive and the repertoire by assuming that "pagan" memory could be fully eliminated by directing embodied signs toward the Spanish church and state. For this reason, at the same time that Counter-Reformation rituals and public acts such as processions sought to channel memory, campaigns in both Mexico and Peru attempted to eradicate what they presented as perverse repositories of non-Christian belief.[105] The early Baroque might therefore be considered "antiarchival" in its attempts to dissipate indigenous "pagan" memory. By the end of the seventeenth century, however, the Counter-Reformation illusion that non-Christian elements could be either fully eliminated or fully absorbed into Catholic rites came under renewed scrutiny and suspicion as the body was increasingly seen as the site of irredeemable and uncontrollable passions, now equated with popular plebeian culture.[106] With the return of the fear that the body could be an archive for alternative memory even within Catholic ritual, there was also a decisive return to written documents as sources of knowledge and memory.

Many of the texts most closely associated with the Spanish American Baroque were written in the latter half of the seventeenth century, well after the height of the European Baroque. This fact does not simply reflect the belatedness of Spanish American cultural practice, since Baroque aesthetics was imported together with the Counter-Reformation reforms and courtly culture. In fact, it is possible to speak of at least two major currents in the seventeenth-century Spanish American Baroque. One was the poetics and rhetoric institutionalized at the beginning of the seventeenth century, largely by the Jesuits and in accordance with the practice of Habsburg rule. The other emerged at the end of the seventeenth century with the crisis of this institutionalized form. Although these stages each witnessed innovations and regional variations, as well as hybrid and even heterodox forms, the late Baroque generally evinced cynicism toward the transcendental and symbolic unity of the earlier Baroque forms. These formal shifts paralleled the politics of memory in Spanish imperialism. During the seventeenth century, as mendicant friars and indigenous nobility lost their place in colonial governance, the institutions that had previously preserved the indigenous past were also weakened. At the same time, popular culture in Spanish America increasingly called into question the official narrative of Spanish conquest in the Americas. Although the emergence of Creole patrimonialism during this same period was thus a reaction to the weakening of previous paradigms of meaning and governance, including that of Spanish law, it did not institute a revolutionary break with these paradigms. The late seventeenth-century Creole project was foremost an attempt to invent a local origin by reassembling elements from previous projects, including classical, indigenous, and Spanish ones, into regional archives. Against the growing specter of popular culture, Creoles founded colonial authority on an archaic past accessible through an intricate web of signs that only they could fully interpret.

ALLEGORY AND THE CREOLE BAROQUE

Understanding late seventeenth-century Creole writings as a specific phase of the Spanish American Baroque provides a third approach to a debate that has been dominated by two general tendencies. Whether implicitly or explicitly, analyses of the Spanish American Baroque have often drawn on José Antonio Maravall's seminal 1975 study, *Culture of the Baroque* (*Cultura del barroco*). Combining historical and formal analyses, Maravall argued that the Spanish Baroque was a conservative style that directed a mobile society of individuals toward centralizing points of transcendence.[107] Harnessed by the post-Tridentine church and absolutist state, Baroque aesthetics contributed to creating a new urban culture that was, in Maravall's terms, "massive," "directed," and "conservative."[108] Against the idea that the Baroque was a repressive arm of the absolutist state, a second approach has emphasized the syncretism of the Iberian American Baroque as a liberating aesthetic that overcame the normative closure of its Iberian models. The earliest version of this argument may be found in José Lezama Lima's playful assertion that the Iberian American Baroque was an aesthetic of "counterconquest" able to express a distinctly American ontology.[109] Noting that the Baroque provided a formal expression for cultural hybridity that undermined as much as it served hegemonic colonial institutions, critics have employed variations of Lezama's argument to question the applicability of European models such as Maravall's to Spanish America.[110] Yet while touting the liberating properties of the Latin American Baroque, these critiques have not succeeded in dislodging Maravall's fundamental assertion that the seventeenth-century Spanish state was a centralizing force for control and subordination. Even appropriations of Gilles Deleuze's undulating "fold" as a formal model for the "concept-style" of the Baroque have taken this as a trope for a mobile aesthetic impossible to center and contain in transcendental structures, and thus have inadvertently supported the idea of a singular and unifying state.[111]

These theoretical approaches do not take into account multiple points of authority, nor do they address the fact that Spanish American Creoles more often than not supported the viceregal state. Indeed, the question that was most central to much viceregal art was not freedom *per se* but to which point of transcendence, or ultimate source of authority, would Baroque art and rhetoric be directed. Although it is not often applied to the Iberian American context, Walter Benjamin's early study of Baroque drama, *Origins of German Tragic Drama* (*Ursprung des deutschen Trauerspiel*) (1929), provides a distinct approach to the relationship between material culture and theological transcendence in the Baroque.[112] Benjamin's study centers on his theory of allegory, through which he relates the formal characteristics of Baroque drama to the theological crisis of seventeenth-century Europe. For Benjamin, the Baroque marked a secularizing threshold of doubt in which objects and humans, irrevocably stripped of any transcendental release from their earthly condition, still acted within the "dim light of redemption." In a world in which the theological symbol had become relativized, and thus displaced, allegory compensated for the loss of eschatological clarity with the artifice of an *ars inveniendi*. In a structure that Benjamin likens to alchemy, allegory was an art of "arranging" profane objects in the attempt to create the spark of redemption: "For it is common practice in the literature of the Baroque to pile up fragments ceaselessly, without any strict idea of a goal, and in the unremitting expectation of a miracle, to take the repetition of stereotypes for just such a miracle."[113] As opposed to the common understanding of allegory as an extended metaphor, Benjamin reads Baroque allegory as a dialectic of scrambled signs.[114]

Benjamin further links the theological crisis of the seventeenth century to a breach in the medieval Christian concept of sovereignty. Whereas in Christian political theology the sovereign was a conduit for providence, the theological crisis of the Baroque left fate entirely in the hands of human agents. Just as profane objects were simultaneously debased and elevated, the humanized sovereign became the sole source of redemption in a world devoid of eschatological teleology.[115] The result is a melancholic circle in which redemption depends on a sovereign incapable of decision: "the prince, who is responsible for making the decision to proclaim the state of emergency, reveals, at the first opportunity, that he is almost incapable of making a decision."[116] From this shared basis, Benjamin argues, German and Spanish Baroque theater diverged. In Catholic Spain, "the Baroque features unfold much more brilliantly, clearly and successfully" as "the conflicts of a state of creation without grace are resolved, by a kind of playful reduction, within the sphere of the court, whose king proves to be a secularized redemptive power."[117] In Lutheran Germany, by contrast, sovereign action was reduced to two equally unsatisfactory outcomes: on the one hand the Machiavellian machinations of schemers and on the other the passive martyrdom of a stoic monarch.[118]

Whereas in the German *Trauerspiel* this temporality of hesitation becomes eternally repeated, in Spanish drama the monarch is able to save the appearance of transcendence in spectacular eschatological resolutions.[119]

In the Spanish viceroyalties, however, the viceroy was a simulacrum of monarchical power with none of the bodily mysticism attributed to the king's person. Indeed, Spanish imperial sovereignty rested as much on the conversion of non-Christian subjects as it did on the figurehead of the monarch. Because of the peculiar mixture of an absent monarch and a contractual sovereignty in Spanish imperialism, the two versions of the Baroque that Benjamin outlines for seventeenth-century Europe coexisted in the Spanish American Baroque. On the one hand, the colonial state attempted through spectacular public displays to produce a form of "secular redemption" all the more specular and illusionary as they centered on the viceroy, the king's substitute.[120] On the other hand, a more pessimistic current interpreted the proliferation of hybrid forms of Christianity as a reversal of the contract of Spanish sovereignty in the Americas.[121] Although the figure of the Amerindian neophyte continued to play an important role in colonial texts, by the end of the seventeenth century renewed pessimism among the colonial elite also contributed to numerous accusations of indigenous idolatry, drunkenness, and rebellion as well as suspicions about plebeian casta culture.[122] Rather than placing hope in the eschatological end that underwrote initial Spanish imperialism, seventeenth-century Creoles substituted allegorical descriptions of landscape, history, and local objects for the mystical substrate of the Spanish monarchy. In a context in which the king's body was absent, they sought to supplement this absence with an authority that rested on artifice, Baroque hermeneutics, and, ultimately, on their unique possession of a local archive. It was this deep historical consciousness, made necessary by colonialism, that provided a form of secular redemption absent from Benjamin's European Baroque.

It has often been noted that Creole patriotism appropriated regional history on both sides of the colonial divide by imbuing Amerindian artifacts with antiquarian meaning.[123] And yet the Baroque aesthetics of the same period has been touted as an antihistorical style in which visual immediacy took precedence over historical narrative. In the most complete account of Spanish American historiography to date, for instance, Jorge Cañizares-Esguerra depicts the seventeenth century as a lull between the grand histories of the sixteenth and eighteenth centuries: "With the exception of Carlos Sigüenza y Góngora, who devoted much energy to the elucidation of Mesoamerican calendars and chronologies, the seventeenth-century clergy had better things to do. In the intervening years between the publication of Torquemada's *Monarquía indiana* (Indian Monarchy) (1615) and Eguiara y Eguren's *Bibliotheca mexicana* (Mexican Library) (1756), the clerical elites of New Spain are remarkable for their silence concerning the study of the Amerindian past."[124] Citing Kenneth Mills and William Taylor, Cañizares-Esguerra argues that during the seventeenth century the Baroque style encouraged an "escape from history."[125] When eighteenth-century clerics and scholars did return to Amerindian history, Cañizares-Esguerra asserts, their interpretations continued to consist of the "hairsplitting etymologies and allegorical interpretations of images" typical of Baroque Neo-scholasticism. Nonetheless, quite in contrast to the assumption that the Baroque was a conservative style that attempted to shore up traditional authority in the face of cultural change, Cañizares-Esguerra provocatively argues that these later scholars showed "reckless modernity, [when] they brushed aside all traditional colonial historiography." He closes his book with a call to revisit the "radical modernity of the Spanish American Baroque in the same critical spirit of the patriotic epistemologists reviewed in this book."[126]

Although accurately noting the importance of the Baroque in a long transitional period, Cañizares-Esguerra's contrast between an "antihistorical" clerical tradition of the Counter-Reformation Baroque and the work of individual scholars such as Sigüenza y Góngora risks obscuring their shared relationship to the problem of historical time. After the collapse of the eschatological and providential narratives that had dominated sixteenth-century Spanish historiography, seventeenth-century Spanish American authors employed various approaches to the problem of local history. Indeed, as Cañizares-Esguerra suggests, the ostentatious and spectacular visual displays of public processions and the exuberant church interiors engaged the emotions of participants by drawing the spectator into an ulterior world outside everyday life. These manifestations of Baroque culture may certainly be considered an "escape from history," if what is meant by history is written historiography intended to link the present with the past in a continuous teleology. Yet the posttridentine Church was not for this reason entirely antihistorical. Rather, the dialectics

[...]rmation spirituality attempted to reduce history to [narr]atives of redemption. From sermons to ecclesiasti[cal histories] such as Antonio de la Calancha's *Crónica moralizada* [(Moralized Chro]nicle), individual examples became substitutes for [the epic of] Spanish imperialism.¹²⁷ Neoplatonic interpretations of the American landscape as a web of hidden signs allowed others to write local into universal history and thus to minimize the importance of the conquest as the origin of Spanish American societies. Those authors who did return to the conquest itself, such as Antonio de Solís and Agustín Vetancurt, subtly rewrote the providentialist narratives of sixteenth-century Spanish historiography in terms of lineages of local rule. As Solís wrote, defending his decision to focus exclusively on the conquest of New Spain, past historians of the Spanish Empire had been unable to rein in its regional variations into one all-encompassing story. More prudent, he concludes, is to describe the particular merits of its most exemplary and glorious conquest.¹²⁸

These histories were all allegorical, in Benjamin's sense of the term, in that they eschewed the eschatological epic for the fragment while still maintaining the desire for a transcendental basis for Spanish imperialism. While turning to profane objects, including those that had previously been tinged with demonic powers, seventeenth-century authors in urban Spanish America embraced the profane as a threshold of redemption. But the "redemption" they favored was sharply divided between a continuing narrative of evangelical salvation and a more secular focus on administration and governance. While in Benjamin's account of the European Baroque "death" is the favored motif of this threshold, "because death digs most deeply the jagged line of demarcation between physical nature and significance,"¹²⁹ in the Spanish American Baroque, corpses were more likely to be found in depictions of missionaries martyred on the frontier than as a motif that leveled difference to a common human condition.¹³⁰ The epidemics and cultural disarticulation of indigenous communities at the end of the sixteenth century that led to what Serge Gruzinski has called the "torn net" of indigenous memory, meant that in the seventeenth century, figures of guilt and redemption were increasingly woven together in mixed objects rather than in the abject figure of the corpse.¹³¹ From the auto-da-fes of the Peruvian campaigns of extirpation to the suspicion with which local healing practices were treated in Oaxaca, seventeenth-century clerics displaced indigenous guilt onto objects that could then be eliminated. And rather than the corpse, the natural landscape itself became a site of struggle between demonic and divine forces, in what Cañizares has called the "satanic epic."[132] At the same time, local cults of veneration incorporated a pagan past into sites of redemption.[133]

Baroque authors were thus more pessimistic about the possibilities of the complete conversion of pagan subjects than had been their earlier apostolic counterparts. While some seventeenth-century Spanish American clerics did not forgo their eschatological hope, they increasingly eschewed emphasis on individual conversion in favor of the administration, arrangement, and containment of indigenous communities. The history that they attempted to "escape" was the greater picture of cultural continuity that cast a shadow over all things American and that they feared provided a subterfuge for paganism. It was the task of allegory, as a hermeneutic structure, to eliminate or absorb these untimely remnants of pagan guilt in spectacular holocausts or Baroque analogies. By the middle of the seventeenth century, the proliferation of these mixed objects, persons, and practices had moved beyond the juridical problem that it had been for Solórzano. For many Creoles, these hybrid forms signaled the degradation of traditional authority, both Spanish and indigenous, and therefore exposed a problem of governance. Through formal rhetorical arrangements that can be likened to Benjamin's notion of allegory, Creoles discerned the phantasmagoric threats to Spanish imperialism and reordered its objects in new constellations for regional governance. But above all, seventeenth-century Creole authors were conscious of the fault lines and open-ended histories created by Spanish imperialism. Rather than presenting signs of an ambivalent quest for identity, their striking images, grotesque figures, and paradoxes embedded this unresolved historical consciousness.

The seventeenth-century Creole invention of an archaic past suggests a variant of one of the central metaphors of Benjamin's study of Baroque drama. In Benjamin's conceptual vocabulary, allegories are ruins of transcendental forms: "in the spirit of allegory [the German *Trauerspiel*] is conceived from the outset as a ruin, a fragment. Others may shine resplendently on the first day; this form preserves the image of beauty to the very last."[134] As Beatrice Hanssen has argued, what appears most important for Benjamin is not the success of allegorical redemption itself but the resistance of the ruin to an inauthentic secular time associated with Romanticism even as it also exposed the impossibility of a return to past eschatological transcendence.[135]

These reflections are helpful for understanding the significance of ruins for the late Creole Baroque. In the early seventeenth-century Spanish America, the ruins of Amerindian polities still signaled a triumph of Spanish imperialism and nostalgia of indigenous nobility.[136] With the crisis of Spanish imperialism itself at the end of the seventeenth century, however, Creoles began to look to Amerindian ruins as repositories of a hidden past.[137] In fact, perhaps the most important function of ruins was to segregate the deep past from the present and thus to establish the latter as inauthentic. By appropriating artifacts from the past, Creoles were able to ward off entrance into an "inauthentic" posteschatological time in which hybrid objects, mixed lineages, and partial conversions had proliferated. They are emblems, in this sense, of the gap that Creole antiquarians sought to represent between a glorious, even if pagan, past and the decayed state of the present indigenous populations.[138]

In this sense, the idea of ruins in the Spanish American Baroque can be extended to include all types of Amerindian artifacts that had been previously incorporated in postconquest genealogies of the indigenous nobility, clerical demonology, and European *exotica*. Whereas in all of these forms, indigenous artifacts preserved the essence of alterity, ruins for Creoles, whether in the form of codices thought to be pre-Columbian or the pre-Aztec pyramids at Teotihuacan, signified a unifying ancient and esoteric law that had been lost in Spanish imperial time. But ruins themselves were only invented when they were collected, archived, and interpreted as such. The task of the Creole archive was therefore as much to create ruins as it was to save them from destruction. As in Benjamin's interpretation, Creole interest in ruins turned on the ability to redeem the profane depredation of the present through a return to a hermetic law that could define a new community of citizens. At once the sign of a fallen indigenous and casta population, now a people without history, and the key to a lost law that could restore order, Amerindian history provided this esoteric origin. While the gap between present and past was thus essential for their authority, Creoles avoided the grand narratives of Spanish imperialism. Rather, it was the archive itself, collections of disperse fragments from a century and a half of Spanish colonialism, that authorized local forms of patrimonial right.

CHAPTER 2

"Nostra Academia in Barbara..."

Building an Archive on the Imperial Frontier

In 1682 and 1683 the Royal University of Mexico celebrated the doctrine of the Immaculate Conception with an array of festivities, including a procession and an *auto* (mystery play), an atrium decorated with altars, and two poetic jousts (*certámenes*). Carlos de Sigüenza y Góngora, since 1672 a professor of mathematics at the university, was entrusted with describing the events and publishing the winning entries for the poetic competitions. Printed in 1683 under the title of *Triunfo parthénico* (Parthenic Triumph), the resulting catalogue is one of the most complete collections of Baroque poetry in viceregal Mexico.[1] Most of the work reproduces the winning poems for the two poetic jousts, for which poets had been asked to follow specific guidelines. The first joust required poets to compose verses in designated meters, often by incorporating fragments of the Cordoban poet Luis de Góngora's poems. The second asked poets to elaborate on emblems characterizing the Virgin Mary's virtues. The winning poems were a decisive display of the viceroyalty's talents in composing acrostics, anagrams, and sonnets indebted to Góngora's complex style. Yet Góngora's influence was not limited to the poems themselves. As one twentieth-century scholar has noted, despite his explicit renunciation of Gongorism in his *Parayso occidental* (Western Paradise) published the following year, Sigüenza's own prose introduction employed all the rhetorical flourishes associated with Góngora's style, including severe hyperbaton, Latinisms, and ornate analogies.[2]

Twentieth-century criticism of Sigüenza's *Triunfo parthénico* has focused heavily on the issue of its style. Even after the poets of the

Spanish Generation of 1927 revived Góngora's poetics, critics continued to question the aesthetic value of the belated and often mechanical imitation of Góngora in the Spanish American viceroyalties. Writing in 1929 from an anti-Gongoresque perspective, for instance, Irving Leonard argued of the *certámenes* in general that "it is not startling to observe that they were the fruitful inspiration of much poor verse" and, after giving a sample drawn from the *Triunfo* of the "verbal patch-work quilt" of Góngora's poems, declared "it would be difficult to find more convincing evidence of the blind, almost unreasoning cult of Góngora in seventeenth-century Mexico than is displayed in such laborious compositions as we have here viewed."[3] Even those critics favorable toward the *Triunfo parthénico* have left aside its aesthetic value. Rather, they have taken the poetic jousts as evidence that by the end of the seventeenth century New Spain's literary culture was flourishing.[4] Indeed, if the playwright Pedro Calderón de la Barca's death in 1681 has been assumed to mark the end of Spain's "Golden Age" of letters, the poetic competitions in Mexico the following year might be considered the high mark of the Baroque in the American viceroyalties. Yet despite the diligence of historians of Mexican literature, the only poet in the *Triunfo's* ranks to have been elevated to anything near a canonical status is Sor Juana Inés de la Cruz, who entered the competition under a pseudonym.[5]

In focusing so heavily on the issue of poetic style in the *Triunfo parthénico's* poetry, studies have all but ignored Sigüenza y Góngora's lengthy preface to the catalogue in which he takes the opportunity to reflect on the difficulty the university has faced in garnering a reputation in Europe. After dedicating the first chapter to a defense of the doctrine of the Immaculate Conception, Sigüenza opens the second chapter with a citation from Justus Lipsius, who, following the sixteenth-century court historian Francisco López de Gómara, had remarked that "although located in the far West, where reason was entombed due to the unfortunate barbarism of its inhabitants, Mexico produced civilized schools in its venerable antiquity" (aun siendo en el retirado ocaso, en que por la perjudicada barbaridad de sus habitadores se sepultó la razón, gozó México de políticas escuelas en su venerable antigüedad).[6] It is clear that for Sigüenza, these remarks by a central figure of the late sixteenth-century Republic of Letters indicate that even well after the foundation of Mexico's university, Europeans still associated the viceroyalty with a barbarous past. Indeed, Sigüenza goes on to note that a later commentator, influenced by Lipsius's words, still "only spoke ... of the heathen schools that the Indians possessed" (sólo habló ... de las Escuelas gentílicas que poseyeron los indios).[7] Responding to this continued association between New Spain and paganism, Sigüenza turns to descriptions of the university by two local authors, Francisco Cervantes de Salazar and Bernardo de Balbuena. In Francisco Cervantes de Salazar's 1554 dialogues on Mexico City, written to celebrate the inauguration of the university in the previous year,[8] a local subject describes the city to a visiting Spaniard. Sigüenza chooses two citations from the dialogue to illustrate the importance of the university for the foundation of a European-style political society after the conquest. In the first, the Novohispanic subject informs his Spanish visitor that the university's instructors are "by no means ordinary men, and Spain has few like them" (minime vulgares & quales paucos habet Hispania).[9] In the second, the now-convinced Spaniard predicts that "your university, still in its infancy and situated in a region up until now barbarous and uncivilized, has been established with such beginnings that, in my belief, New Spain hitherto known for its supply of silver, will be celebrated among the other nations in the future for the multitude of its learned men" (vostra Academia in barbara & ante hac inculta regione posita, modo etiam eiusmodi est inchoata principiis, ut brevi credam futurum Novam Hispaniam, ut hactenus argenti copia, ita in posterum sapientium multitudine apud caeteras nationes optime audituram).[10]

Sigüenza follows these Cervantes de Salazar citations with verses from Bernardo de Balbuena's 1604 poem, *Grandeza mexicana* (Mexican Grandeur), which praises the city's erudite subjects as preternatural "monsters of perfection in [their] abilities" (monstruos en perfección de habilidades). If held up against the best of Spanish schools and universal human understanding, Balbuena concludes, "the elegant wits of this land / equal, polish and comprehend it / in sweet peace or friendly war" (Los gallardos ingenios de esta tierra / lo alcanzan, sutilizan y perciben / en dulce paz o en amigable guerra).[11] Yet while both Cervantes and Balbuena argue that Mexican erudition was equivalent to that of Europe, Sigüenza himself goes on to imply that it was only by adopting the oath to defend the Immaculate Conception that the university had finally achieved chronological parity with its European counterparts. "Although not as ancient as those of Europe in its foundation" (Aunque menos antigua que otras de la Europa en el tiempo de su erección), he argues, the University of Mexico is nonetheless "contemporary to almost all in [its] sincere affection for the Holy Virgin" (coetánea a casi todas en el cordial afecto a la Santísima Virgen).[12] Despite this achievement, Sigüenza notes, the University of Mexico had still been omitted from the Franciscan order's 1649 list of universities that had agreed to defend the Immaculate Conception. Rather than find in this omission one more example of European prejudice, however, Sigüenza argues that Mexicans themselves had not sufficiently publicized their own achievements: "And if, lacking plumes, not even fame itself could spread across the globe, how then could distant nations know how high those [plumes] of Mexico have flown since they are so lacking in translation to print?" (Y si ni aún la misma fama pudiera espaciarse por el orbe, si le faltasen las plumas, escaseando tanto las mexicanas el trasladarse a los moldes, ¿cómo pueden saber las naciones distantes a dónde llega su vuelo?).[13]

With this, Sigüenza turns away from the problem of European recognition that had implicitly structured Cervantes's and Balbuena's descriptions and toward the internal problem of the Mexican archive. It is this missing archive documenting the university that Sigüenza proposes to remedy through the *Triunfo parthénico*. Given his argument that the defense of the Immaculate Conception had put the Mexican university on a par with European universities, for instance, Sigüenza takes pains to document its adoption in Mexico. In 1618, the same year that Felipe III had officially embraced the doctrine of the Immaculate Conception, he begins, Mexico City had celebrated with processions and festivities. Yet, Sigüenza notes, these had only been registered in the "book of common memory" (libro de la común memoria), which had "already begun to be consumed by the moths of time" (ya comenzado a carcomer de la polilla del tiempo).[14] Documentation of the university's adoption of the oath to the Immaculate Conception was likewise missing. While it had been adopted well beforehand, proof of the oath could now be found only in the university constitutions, themselves belatedly published in 1668 after a lengthy bureaucratic process.[15] Meanwhile, although the university had continuously conducted the oath to the Immaculate Conception, Sigüenza could not find "this oath among the papers of the archive, nor a record of it in the books of the cloister's decisions, not because it had not been performed, but because of a lack of interest in preserving its elegant and zealous clauses for the sake of its perpetual memory" (entre los papeles del Archivo este juramento, ni en los libros de las determinaciones de los Claustros su testimonio, no porque no se hiciese sino por haber faltado la curiosidad que conservase para la perpetuidad de su memoria las fervorosas y elegantes cláusulas que lo formaban).[16] Exasperated, Sigüenza concludes that the missing archive reflects "how little all that begins big in our America endures" (la poca duración de todo lo que en nuestra América se empieza grande).[17] Sigüenza's invocation of print as a bulwark against amnesia employs language common to European Neostoicism, and indeed he goes on to cite Seneca on the brevity of life to support his argument. Yet he also clearly relates the destruction "of everything that begins with greatness" to a specifically American trait and suggests that this lack of permanence itself threatens to continue New Spain's barbarous reputation.

With this conclusion, Sigüenza suggests that the inability of the university to realize Cervantes' optimistic 1554 prediction is not a problem of foundation but rather of conservation. The *Triunfo parthénico* will remedy this problem not only by publishing the academy's present talents but also by serving as an archive for an event that might otherwise be lost to the "violence of time" (la violencia del tiempo).[18] Noting that European institutions had done the same, for instance, Sigüenza includes in his already bloated introduction the oath to the Immaculate Conception established by the university constitution.[19] Indeed, in Sigüenza's argument, it is the Immaculate Conception itself that has finally sealed a transition from barbarism to civilization by confirming the purity of Mexican knowledge:

> Since the declaration of the Immaculate Conception of Mary is the basis from which the possession of knowledge can be legitimately deduced, o thee thousand times blessed imperial, pontifical, Parthenic Mexican Academy, whose lights transform the Western twilight where less than two centuries ago reason was entombed in the shadows of impiety, into erudition of the East!

> (Con que siendo la propugnación de la Concepción Purísima de María premisas de que legítimamente se deduce la posesión de las ciencias, oh tú mil veces dichosa Imperial, Pontificia, Parténica Academia Mexicana, cuyas luces trasforman en Oriente de erudición el Ocaso en que no ha dos siglos se sepultaba la razón en sombras de la impiedad.)[20]

But if the university's oath to the Immaculate Conception draws it toward Europe, the local archive establishes a distinct hi͏͏ the viceroyalty and thus a measure of cultural autonomy. archive can establish cultural autonomy from Europe by c barbarism in a distant past. This logic is reflected in a sub͏ nificant change that Sigüenza makes in the second citation from Cervantes's dialogues. Whereas in the original the Spanish visitor recognizes "Your academy" (Vostra Academia), Sigüenza replaces the "your" (vostra) with "our" (nostra). The phrase, as he cites it, "Our academy in a region up until now barbarous and uncivilized" (Nostra Academia in barbara & ante hac inculta regione) incorporates the history of the university's origin in a local present and thus displaces the foreigner as the point of judgment. With this, Sigüenza redirects the problem that had framed early descriptions of the university from one of recognition to one of both instituting and conserving a temporal divide. He thus imagines the university not as a medium for transforming the region but rather as the site of a mystical break with a barbarous past.

OPENING THE BAROQUE CIRCLE

Sigüenza's insistence in the *Triunfo parthénico* on the necessity of a continuous local archive shows the extent to which cultural autonomy in seventeenth-century Spanish America depended on structures of temporality. While Spanish American Creoles' interest in local history has often been linked to the origins of a distinct identity or consciousness, the Baroque style of their texts has not been considered a temporal structure. Rather, Creole writings have most often been associated with space.[21] By understanding identity in spatial terms, whether geopolitical, social, or aesthetic, contemporary criticism has underemphasized the importance of time and historicity in the Spanish American Baroque. It is true that throughout the *Triunfo*, Sigüenza presents the university as an enclosed circle, an idealized sphere or "literary republic" protected from worldly concerns.[22] Indeed, Sigüenza continually returns to the symbolism of the circle, which he argues aptly represents the Immaculate Conception of the Virgin Mary: "since because of her purity and the extension of her grace she was that new circle of Jeremiah who contained all of God in its center" (pues por su pureza y amplitud de su gracia fué aquel nuevo círculo de Jeremías que contuvo a todo Dios en su centro).[23] The university's oath to uphold the doctrine of the Immaculate Conception, in Sigüenza's argument, is precisely an emulation of the mystical purity of knowledge in Mary:

> This then was the Immaculate Mary and that the immaculate instant which, free from sin, was the moment of knowledge now celebrated,

applauded, eulogized and praised in these blessed times by all those
in the universities where letters triumph or the studious dedicate
themselves to the pursuit of knowledge or doctors are privileged to
extol her doctrine. And it is not too much to demand that all engage
in such glorious toils, if the essence of wisdom that separates them
from the commoners likewise earns them a title in the catalogue of
this Most Pure Mother's sons.

(Esto era entonces la Inmaculada María, y ese inmaculado instante
de entonces en que por no ser posesión de la culpa era desempeño
de la sabiduría es el que ahora en la felicidad de estos siglos cel-
ebran, aplaudan panegirizan, elogian cuántos en las Universidades,
en donde triunfan las letras o se matriculan estudiosos para lograr la
enseñanza o se privilegian doctores para ensalzar su doctrina. Y no
es mucho se empleen todos en tan gloriosas fatigas, si el carácter de
sabios que los separa del vulgo los rotula en el catálogo de los hijos de
tan Purísima Madre.)[24]

By emphasizing the mystical time of knowledge, Sigüenza rewrites
the division between the *doctos* (educated) inside and the *vulgo* (commoners) outside of the university walls as a temporal break. This mystical threshold of purity, which establishes a spatial segregation of
the university from its surroundings, is the key to the permanence of
knowledge in New Spain.

Sigüenza's description of the university's atrium, decorated with
altars dedicated to the Virgin, further relates purity to a temporal
break. Sigüenza carefully narrates the twelve altars in a stunning
example of Gongoresque poetics applied to Baroque ornamentation.
His ecphrasis of the exuberant decoration of the atrium's interior is
typical:

> There, in crafted bouquets, the embellished Almathea spilled her
> cornucopia, while fertile Arabia trafficked her perfumes in fragrant
> flasks, admiring that Hybla donated her golden hives in tribute to
> the torches and that the veins of this septentrional America spilled
> forth into silver for the candlesticks. The interior of the ceiling was
> adorned with tapestries and velvets, the latter crimson and the former
> executed by an eminent hand, and all garnished by the most silvery
> lace produced in France and sent to us by Milan.

(Allí, en artificiados ramilletes, vertía su cornucopia la matizada
Amaltea, mientras en fragantes pebetes comerciaba sus olores la Ara-
bia fértil, admirada de que para antorchas le tributase el Hibla sus
colmenas rubias, y que para candeleros, las venas de esta septentrional América se desatasen en plata. Lo interior del techo se adornó
con entretejidos de pinturas y terciopelos, éstos carmesíes y aquellos

ideados de valiente mano, y todo ello guarnecido de las más argenta-
das puntas que labra Francia y que Milán nos envía.)²⁵

Sigüenza punctuates descriptions such as these with a narration of the viewer's passage around the atrium, which he describes as a state of contemplation marked by the contradictory desire to contemplate further and to move on to the next:

> This rapturous display, to whose height the eyes were elevated until reaching the vanishing point, warranted the total suspension of the senses, for vainly hoping to find port in that immense gulf, they swim on to navigate its expanses, just as a burning thirst tends to drain the refreshing spirits, tilting the glass further back the more it holds.
>
> (Merecióse por largo rato la común suspensión este aparatoso embeleso de los sentidos, en cuya celsitud se elevaron los ojos hasta perderlo de vista, porque mal sufrida la esperanza de tomar puerto en tan dilatado golfo, se aletaba a navegar lo que le restaba, como cuando la ardiente sed suele agotar el licor frígido, empeñándose más mientras más comprende el espacioso vaso.)²⁶

Again, Sigüenza describes this movement as circular, this time adding the sacred dimension of circularity itself: "If this constant, circular movement was mysterious or fortuitous, I cannot say; I only know that, even among the vain and superstitious rites of the gentiles it was the solemn custom to venerate circles at their altars" (Si este circular, sucesivo movimiento, fue misterioso o casual no lo averiguo: solo sé que, aun entre los vanos y supersticiosos ritos de los gentiles, era solemne costumbre el adorar en círculo sus altares).²⁷ Although Sigüenza's description is quite typical of Baroque rhetoric, in which the energetic tension between exuberance and limitation depends on a temporal sensation of constant interruption, what is most remarkable in these metaphors is the correlation they establish between interiority and purity. The exuberance of the university's atrium does not appear to fear emptiness, as in the trope of *horror vacui* often associated with the Baroque, but rather contamination.²⁸

But what here is considered to be impure? The altars' adornments—"all the precious stones that Asia exchanges for the refined silver of America" (cuantas preciosas piedras le permuta la Asia a la América por su copelada plata), "oriental pearls" (orientales perlas), "in tribute for her religious devotion: gold from our Potosí; mother of pearl from the shells of the South; rubies from Ceylon; diamonds from Cathay; and emeralds from Muso" (por tributarles para su religioso culto las venas de nuestro Potosí, el oro; las conchas del sur, el nácar; Ceilán, rubiés, el Catay, diamantes, y sus esmeraldas, Muso)—contribute to the sensation that the atrium contains the world. This exuberant exoticism is quite similar to that of Balbuena's 1604 poem *Grandeza mexicana*, whose nine chapters in verse anticipate many of the tropes and rhetorical structures of Gongorism.[29] As John Beverley has noted, Balbuena's poem is a "festival of commodity fetishism ... in which the goods that 'the Mexican spring' offers to the colonizers are 'gifts'" but "the figure of the 'ugly Indian'—the actual source of this wealth—necessarily remains unrepresented until the final verses."[30] Yet it is not clear why this source of labor appears at all at the end of the poem after having been so systematically erased through references to the "sovereign hand" (soberana mano) ordering the mercantilist movement. In fact, for Balbuena, Mexico City's opulence is based more on its geographical relationship to the Asian-Pacific and American commercial routes than on internal productivity. As Octavio Paz notes, the motor in the *Grandeza mexicana* is "interest," a feverish movement that must be adequately reined in by the viceregal administration.[31]

For this reason, Balbuena reads production as "tribute" of which the "ugly Indian" (indio feo) of the final verses is the source ("fills your fleet with his tribute" [por tributo dél tus flotas llena]). The gratuitous adjective "ugly" by which Balbuena qualifies "Indian" echoes his earlier claim that "the theater of fortune is to be admired / since only one hundred years have passed since one saw here / humble huts, mud, and marshes" (y admírese el teatro de fortuna / pues no ha cien años que miraba en esto / chozas humildes, lama, y laguna).[32] In Balbuena's poem the Spanish have literally built Mexico City from the ground up into an emporium of the world. In this sense, the "ugly Indian" stands for the local substrate that cannot be translated into a mercantilist vision of objects coursing across the globe; it must be remarked in order to emphasize its elimination in the rest of the poem. The *Triunfo parthénico* employs a similar trope. While the altars adorned with luxurious objects are symbolic of the world's tribute to the Virgin Mary, the Gongoresque language of the poetry competitions is punctuated only once by a local object: the prize for worst poem in one competition is a *chilacayote*, which Sigüenza explains is a type of "squash" (*calabaza*).[33] This exclusion of local objects must be made momentarily visible in order to give value to a distinct space: one that combines artifice, exchange, and luxury. Similarly, in Balbuena's *Grandeza mexicana*, the local is negatively defined by its inability to participate in mercantilist exchange. Instead, the motor behind Mexico City's grandeur is controlled activity that overcomes a barbaric and provincial past by extracting a surplus value and turning it over to the Spanish monarch as tribute. As opposed to Balbuena's tribute to an imperial center, however, Sigüenza's late seventeenth-century *Triunfo parthénico* dedicates surplus to what he has posited as the source of Novohispanic autonomy: the Virgin Mary's Immaculate Conception.

A similar distinction may be made between the early and late seventeenth-century treatment of another common trope: Mexico as a spring-like paradise. Although earthly paradise had been invoked together with the invention of the "New World" itself, Balbuena may well have been the first author to use this image to praise Mexico City.[34] In Balbuena's version, the city and its environs enjoyed an "eternal spring" cultivated by divine dispensation: "Here, my lady, Heaven / appears to have selected beautiful gardens by hand / and also wished to be the gardener" (Aquí, señora, el cielo de su mano / parece que escogió huertos pensiles, / y quiso él mismo ser el hortelano).[35] Rather than the earthly paradise that marked early colonial texts, however, Balbuena compares Mexico to "that human paradise / so celebrated by Greek eloquence" (aqueste humano paraíso / tan celebrado en la elocuencia griega) of which he asserts "although it is much, it is a cipher, compendium, and accent / for the florid Mexican environs" (aunque lo es mucho, es cifra, es suma, es tilde, / del florido contorno mexicano).[36] As Jorge Cañizares-Esguerra has noted, the Creole metaphor of paradise emphasized the idea of cultivation, rather than natural landscape, in a pastoral trope of gardens and gardening. As Cañizares-Esguerra also points out, however, this metaphor was often paired with the Creole understanding of the uncultivated wilderness as the realm of the "demonic epic."[37] Rather than a return to paradise, Creole authors took paradise metaphorically to signify their intervention in and control of what otherwise might be an untamed or barbaric wilderness in which demons actively sought to continue a pagan past.

In this sense, the Creole trope of paradise emphasized artifice and renewal, a break with a pagan past, rather than nature as a pristine prelapsarian state. Walter Benjamin addressed this tension between history and timelessness in Baroque motifs of paradise when he wrote of the pastoral: "the decisive factor in the escapism of the Baroque is not the antithesis of history and nature but the comprehensive secularization of the historical in the state of creation. It is not eternity that is opposed to the disconsolate chronicle of world-history, but the restoration of the timelessness of paradise."[38] By the early seventeenth century, it was the Creole "demonic epic" that was beginning to look like Benjamin's "disconsolate chronicle of world-history" as the millennial utopianism of the first century of colonization faded. For this reason, when the *Triunfo parthénico* constructs purity by shutting out the local it also distinguishes the university from the evangelical battles of the wilderness. Likewise the motif of a cultivated paradise in Balbuena's poem transformed the epic battle of colonization into a tale of urban luxury and misery that breaks entirely with the past.[39] Just as he characterizes Tenochtitlan as a city of shacks built in the mud and reeds of the lake, the "ugly Indian" of Balbuena's poem is stripped of history. In both cases, what Ángel Rama has called the "lettered city" was conceived of as a mystical break from the depressing chronicle of indigenous conversion after the collapse of Spanish providentialism.[40] Whereas Balbuena conceived of this break as itself a tribute to Spanish imperial sovereignty, Sigüenza eulogizes the university as an autonomous center of erudition. As much as a spatial division, Sigüenza's *Triunfo parthénico* institutes a new time in which Creoles would become the agents of history.

This emphasis on artifice as renewal in Creole writings contrasts with the image of American nature found in contemporary imperial writings such as those of Juan Eusebio Nieremberg, the most influential natural historian of seventeenth-century Habsburg Spain. Raised in the Spanish court, in 1625 Nieremberg became a professor in the Colegio Imperial, the Jesuit college in Madrid. Drawing on his lectures at the Colegio Imperial, Nieremberg wrote two widely disseminated books of natural history, an erudite treatise in Latin titled *Historia naturae, maxime peregrinae* (Natural History, Especially Foreign) (1635) and a popular tome in Spanish titled *Curiosa y oculta filosofía* (Curious and Occult Philosophy) (1634). A theologian of Neoplatonic instincts, Nieremberg emphasized the study of nature's marvels as a means to venerate God's creation. Although he included American natural wonders, culled for the most part from the writings of Francisco Hernández, his works were not limited to the Spanish Empire but intended to be a comprehensive survey of natural wonders.[41] Nonetheless, as Juan Pimentel has argued, America figures heavily in Nieremberg's works as a landscape of renewal. In the bird of paradise, in Pimentel's words, Nieremberg found a basis for arguing that "America would be the new paradise, a promised land for the future, more than the true and biblical paradise of the past."[42] In what Pimentel has called a "preterimperial science" Nieremberg raised America above a regional or even imperial possession to a divine and providential landscape.[43] As Pimentel further notes, Nieremberg's focus on nature as a divinely orchestrated landscape led him to a problem of time. Arguing against the possibility of generation independent of God's design, in his 1634 *Curiosa oculta filosofía* Nieremberg defended the constancy and stasis of the natural landscape.[44] Cañizares-Esguerra has also noted that whereas his predecessor Francisco Hernández wrote of demonic plants, Nieremberg limited demonism to cause and analogy, preferring instead to emphasize preternatural marvels in the American landscape.[45]

In Creole writings, by contrast, the trope of paradise as renewal necessarily contained a relationship to history. Although primarily dedicated to the history of the conquest and description of Mexico City, for instance, Augustín Vetancurt's 1698 *Teatro mexicano* also includes an initial summary of the "common fertility and wealth of this New World" (fertilidad y riqueza en comun de este Nuevo Mundo). Vetancurt follows Balbuena's example by describing Mexico City as a labyrinth of streets with the tree-lined alameda and an environs of "orchards, gardens, and olive groves with country houses that the wealthy of the city have built for their recreation" (huertas, jardines, y olivares con casas de campo que los ricos de la Ciudad han edificado para su recreo).[46] The landscape surrounding the city, however, also suggests that the Creole notion of cultivation extended into the wilderness. Like Nieremberg, Vetancurt draws on the works of Francisco Hernández, the late sixteenth-century botanist who compiled an encyclopedia of plants from the Americas in 1571.[47] Yet gone are any references to demonic activity. Neither does Vetancurt's summary propose to be a survey of the marvelous extremes of divine dispensation. Rather, he associates the fertility of the land with a favorable climate that affects not only plants but also its inhabitants: "those born here are intelligent and learned in all types of sciences" (los que nacen acá son agudos, y profundos en todo genero de ciencias).[48] This pastoral motif of cultivation in Creole writings, in which a civilizing force masters the natural landscape, is a local rather than imperial phenomenon. As in both Balbuena's 1604 *Grandeza mexicana* and Sigüenza's 1683 *Triunfo parthénico*, in Vetancurt's text the wilderness outside the city becomes a receding frontier. In the process, nature itself becomes yet another repository of Creole knowledge.

Throughout the seventeenth century, the frontier served as a metaphor for unredeemed and demonically inspired indigenous paganism. The title page of the Augustinian missionary Antonio de Calancha's 1639 *Crónica moralizada* clearly shows the metaphorical value that Creole authors attached to cultivation as a mystical transformation of a barbaric wilderness. As Jorge Cañizares-Esguerra notes, the frontispiece depicts bucolic scenes of missionaries "harvesting" the souls of indigenous subjects (Figure 3). Yet, he notes, the chronicle itself represents nature as the domain of demonic agents who spur indigenous subjects to resist Christian evangelization in a clear message that this pastoral landscape was an ideal still to be achieved.[49] As Creole texts moved outward from urban enclaves, the struggle became one of incorporating local knowledge into a paradigm that avoided demonism. While Calancha leaned heavily on miracles to support his narrative of Augustinian evangelization, demonic forces still appear frequently in his chronicle in representations of idolatrous communities under the sway of local shamans. Yet he also added a new element that tipped the scales in favor of Christian evangelization: widespread evidence that St. Thomas the Apostle had evangelized the Americas well before the Spanish conquest. With this story, indigenous conversion became linked to the recuperation of an archaic past. For Calancha, the American wilderness recorded this lost Christianity in a labyrinth of decayed signs. The counterpart to the mystical break between the university and its surroundings was this natural archive that Creoles were uniquely positioned to interpret.

ST. THOMAS: FOOTSTEPS IN THE LANDSCAPE

Calancha was not the first to have argued that the Apostle St. Thomas had evangelized the Americas long before Europeans arrived. From the early years of Iberian colonization, chroniclers had found signs of prior Christianization in the Americas. Inspired by evidence that St. Thomas had been in India, in 1549 the Jesuit Manuel de Nóbrega, stationed in Brazil, was the first to suggest that he had also visited the Americas and thus that the indigenous had been preevangelized. As evidence, he noted human footprints in stone and indigenous accounts of a bearded white man named "Zomé" whom he interpreted to be St. Thomas.[50] While Nóbrega's account inspired other

Figure 3. Antonio de la Calancha, frontispiece of the *Crónica moralizada* (1639) with detail showing evangelization as a bucolic activity. Courtesy of the John Carter Brown Library at Brown University.

sixteenth-century missionaries to seek similar proof that St. Thomas had visited the Americas, support for the idea was far from unanimous. Competing theories included las Casas's thesis that analogies between indigenous and Christian customs were providentialist signs, rather than decayed Christian forms, and José de Acosta's argument that they were the work of the devil.[51] The debate gained prominence in 1625 when Gregorio García, author of a widely disseminated 1606 tract on the origin of indigenous Americans, published his own consideration of the argument.[52] In his 1648 *Política indiana* Juan de Solórzano mentioned the polemic and, citing Acosta, added that "it would not be unreasonable to give little weight to such stories of the Indians . . . because, even if they are true, it is possible that the devil, as one who is always trying to ape and imitate Christ, suggested them to these barbarians to further trick them and be worshipped by them by mixing many errors and superstitions in figures that are themselves so saintly" (no será mucho exceso dar poco crédito a tales relaciones de indios . . . porque, caso que sean ciertos, pudo el diablo sugerirlas a estos bárbaros para más iludirlos y hacerse adorar de ellos con mezcla de muchos errores y supersticiones en figuras que en sí son tan santas, como quien siempre procura hacerse simia y remedo de Cristo).[53]

As Solórzano suggests, the proof for St. Thomas's passage through the Americas depended greatly on oral accounts that could confirm the meaning of otherwise enigmatic signs. The debate thus presupposed the more basic question of the reliability of indigenous artifacts and oral histories. Indeed, Calancha's argument in favor of St. Thomas's presence in the Americas explicitly refutes positions such as Acosta's. Marshalling nearly a century of accumulated evidence to affirm St. Thomas's presence, Calancha also provided an aggressive attack on all those who would doubt the story:

> Those who cannot be convinced that the Apostle preached in this New World go against natural, divine, and positive laws and insult the compassion and justice of God; they go against natural law, since they wish upon these lands the misfortune of having no Apostle to preach the word of God, something that no European would wish for himself, as if evangelization were only partial or universal redemption limited.
>
> (Los que no se persuaden que predicó el Apóstol en este nuevo mundo, van contra las leyes natural, Divina i positiva, i agravían a la misericordia i a la justicia de Dios; van contra la natural, pues quieren para estas tierras las desdicha de no averse predicado la Fe

por Apóstol. Cosa que los Europeos no quisieran para sí, como si la predicación fuese parcial o se limitase la universal redención.)[54]

In his fundamental study of the myth of St. Thomas's evangelizing of the Americas, Jacques Lafaye writes that with this argument Calancha transformed the debate from one of missionary hermeneutics to a Creole desire for inclusion into a universal order.[55] Certainly, the geographic scope of Calancha's argument overcame the spotty regionalism of previous accounts. Calancha even ventures the route that St. Thomas took through the Americas, arguing that he had begun there before moving on to India. Yet his search for multiple sources of evidence also established a new hermeneutics of indigenous sources. Rather than documenting isolated observations, Calancha's account depends on the accumulation and repetition of fragmented signs that point toward a hidden truth: "if a singular sign does not qualify as evidence, then many singularities prove a truth" (si algo singular con indicios no califica probança, muchas singularidades conprueva una verdad).[56]

Thus, to show evidence of St. Thomas's presence, Creoles such as Calancha were forced to defend indigenous records against attacks such as Acosta's that attributed indigenous artifacts to diabolic imitations. Yet it was still up to these authors to archive and interpret these obscure signs in light of a lost unitary truth. Calancha himself often returns to the primary evidence for the Apostle's visit: the stones that bore the saint's footprints were complemented, as in Nóbrega's account, by oral tradition. These oral traditions, which Calancha argues were corrupted by indigenous pronunciation and faulty memory, repeatedly told the story of a white bearded man who had passed through the region, preaching against incest and polygamy. Calancha attributes the variations in the story, particularly the regional differences in St. Thomas's name, to difficulties in preserving the story in oral tradition: "the lack of letters, or the passage of time, wreaks woeful havoc on the certainty of events and on the integrity of antiquities" (la falta de las letras, o la sobra de los tiempos, aze lastimosos estragos en la certeza de los acaecimientos, i en la integridad de las antiguedades). Those regions with better memory systems preserved the clearest versions of the story. In Peru, he argues, where the story had been preserved through the Andean knotted cords (*quipus*) that recorded oral histories, it was clearest in provinces near Cuzco and Chuquiabo since "that was where the quipus were housed and the quipucamayos [cord readers] lived in the court, just as the king's councilors and secretaries live in Madrid, Granada, and Valladolid and the Spanish archives in Simancas and those of Portugal in the Tower of the Tomb" (allí se gardavan los Quipos, i residían como en la Corte los Quipocamayos, como en Madrid, Granada i Valladolid, los Consejos i Secretarios del Rey, i los archivos de España en Simancas, i los de Portugal en la torre del Tanbo).[57] But equally, he argues, "among Indians with neither letters nor universities of learning it is more remarkable that they preserved anything over such a long period of time than that they would fall into the idiocy of hellish discord over a thousand and five hundred years, trading the articles and precepts of Christ for superstitions" (entre Indios sin letras, ni universidad de ciencias cayese en el idiotismo de la cizaña del infierno en mil i quinientos años, trocando en superstición los artículos i preceptos de Christo, antes fue mucho retener algo en tanta dilatación de tiempos).[58]

In Calancha's account, the *quipus* are an inferior system of record keeping that nonetheless preserve the record of the saint's passage and are analogous to another cryptic record left in the Peruvian landscape. As Calancha recounts, a Dominican priest in Calango, a town in the mountains south of Lima, learned of a stone (Figure 4) on which there was a footprint "impressed in it as if it were soft wax and on one part many letters in lines, some Greek and others Hebrew; in Greek characters I only recognized X and Y" (undida como si fuera en blanda cera, i a una parte muchas letras en renglones, unas Griegas i otras Ebreas, en el carácter Griego, sólo conocí la X, i la Y). Taking a copy of the inscriptions on the rock around to convents, Calancha found a priest with knowledge of Greek who could not make out the meaning "because some of the letters were not very clear and were confusing in parts" (por estar no muy señaladas algunas letras i confusos algunos puntos). After citing the Dominican, Calancha reproduces the symbols and interprets them in this way:

> The Indians were unfamiliar with this image of two keys, one larger than the other, nor did not use them in their houses, nor had they seen anchors until the Spanish came, nor did they know about characters or letters; the anchor was in the Hebrew and Latin nations a symbol of hope.... So perhaps it means that they should wait, that in the time to come the keys of the Church of Saint Peter would enter this land where he left his footprints and could not establish his faith.
>
> (las dos llaves una mayor que otra, no las conocieron, ni usaron los Indios en sus casas, ni asta que vinieron españoles vieron anclas, ni

Figure 4. Insignia with letters etched in a stone in Peru. Reproduced from Antonio de la Calancha, *Crónica moralizada*, 6 vols. (Lima: Universidad Nacional Mayor de San Marcos, 1981), 743.

supieron de caracteres ni letras; el áncora fue en las naciones Ebreas i Latinas sínbolo de la esperança. . . . Si a caso quiso significar, que esperasen, que en los venideros tienpos entrarían las llaves de la Iglesia de San Pedro en estas tierras, donde él dejó sus pisadas, i no pudo introducirse su Fe.)[59]

Because the region was still idolatrous, the *visitador* Duarte Fernández ordered that the figures be chipped away. Calancha goes on to comment that "he did not do well in erasing a sign so worthy of veneration" (no izo bien en borrar una huella tan digna de veneración), but notes that other stones in the region also show signs of the saint's passage. St. Thomas had chosen to leave his mark on stones, Calancha argues, in order to suggest the "hardness" (*dureza*) of Amerindian resistance to evangelization.[60] Through this interpretation Calancha implicitly answers the question as to why, after this apostolic evangelization, Christianity had not taken hold in the Americas as it had in India. But the passage also suggests that the stones themselves could miraculously resist both superstitious interpretations and physical aggression.[61]

After Calancha's chronicle, clerics who took up the question of St. Thomas's evangelizing went further in their defense of indigenous records. In his 1662 *Noticias Curiosas e Necessárias das Cousas do Brasil* (Curious and Necessary Notices of the Things of Brazil), the Jesuit Simão de Vasconcelos more explicitly defends the accuracy of oral narrative as a historical source. After recounting numerous other relics, especially footprints, that had been collected by Calancha and others, Vasconcelos provocatively equates indigenous oral narratives with sources of classical histories in Europe: "just as letters are printed on paper, why can the likeness of memorable things not be printed as well in memories?" (assim como no papel as letras, por que não se imprimirão também nas memórias, as espécies das coisas memoráveis?).⁶² Vasconcelos then gives a striking example of the accuracy of indigenous record keeping. Citing the Jesuit Alonso de Ovalle's 1646 *Histórica relación de Chile* (Historical Account of Chile), he recounts a story in which another Jesuit missionary had witnessed an elderly man walking in a valley near Quito beating a drum and singing "certain tales in his tongue" (em sua lingua certas histórias). The priest asked the crowd of youths who were attentively listening what ceremony he was witnessing, and one of the youths responded:

> that Indian who was singing was the archivist of the village and had the obligation to appear in that place on all holy days and repeat the traditions and memorable deeds of their ancestors by singing them in the presence of those who were chosen to take his place after his death because, since the Indians did not have books, they used this method to conserve the ancient histories in their memory.
>
> (aquele índio que cantava, era o Arquivista da aldeia, a quem corria obrigação de sair àquele lugar todos os dias santos, e repetir cantando as tradições, e coisas memoráveis de seus antepassados, em presença dos que ali estavam que por morte dele, estavam destinados para ficar em seu lugar; porque como os índios não tinham livros, usavam desta diligência para conservar nas memórias as histórias antigas.)

The youth went on to explain that he sang about a flood that had happened in antiquity and about a white man named Tomé who had preached a new law "never heard in those lands" (nunca ouvida naquelas regiões). Vasconcelos concludes that "this is an example that provides evidence of the credence that we should give to the traditions of the people, even if they are still barbarous" (Exemplo é este, que mostra com evidência a fé que devemos dar às tradições das gentes, ainda que bárbaras).⁶³

The reliance of these clerics on indigenous record keeping to prove that St. Thomas had evangelized the Americas is not in itself a novelty. Jorge Cañizares-Esguerra has called attention to the fact that from the sixteenth century onward Europeans had turned to indigenous record keeping to reconstruct pre-Columbian history.[64] Yet the seventeenth-century search for signs of St. Thomas's evangelizing was antiquarian in a way that previous European uses of indigenous record keeping had not been. Arnaldo Momigliano has defined early modern European antiquarianism as a collector's craft distinct from historiography. In fact, as Momigliano suggests, the authority of an archaic past seemed to depend precisely on an eclecticism that defied orderly narrative. It was this collection of fragments that lent an aura of hermetic truth to ancient history: "The antiquarians loved disparate and obscure facts. But behind the individual, seemingly unrelated items there was Antiquity, mysterious and august."[65] As Momigliano notes, early modern antiquarians such as Nicolas Fabri de Peiresc sought out physical objects as the only reliable record of antiquity precisely because they resisted narrative interference.[66] Even Francis Bacon, who in 1605 defined antiquarianism as "defaced history or some remnants of history which have casually escaped the shipwreck of time," admitted that its legitimate goal was not to create what he terms a "perfect history."[67] Like the antiquarian relics in Europe, the fragmented, rune-like quality of the relics of St. Thomas's evangelizing was a testament to defaced permanence. But rather than being defaced by the ravages of time, the relics of St. Thomas had resisted a diabolic interregnum between Christian periods precisely through their mysterious symbolism. The possibility of diabolic interference between the period of St. Thomas's apostolic journey and the arrival of the Spanish thus demanded an allegorical hermeneutics that classical antiquities did not.

In the Mexican version of the story of St. Thomas's evangelizing, the Creole contention that the indigenous record was a hermetic script that documented this archaic truth was facilitated by the existence of the pre-Columbian tradition of pictographic glyphs. The primary source for this variant is a manuscript apparently penned by Manuel Duarte, a Portuguese Jesuit who spent fourteen years in New Spain before being sent to the Philippines, where he died in 1689. Duarte's manuscript, titled *Pluma rica* by the nineteenth-century Mexican antiquarian José Ramírez, is a rambling compendium of all the evidence that had been gathered on the apostle's presence throughout the Americas. Although the majority of the work focuses on New Spain, Duarte includes sources for St. Thomas's evangelizing of Brazil,

Paraguay, and Peru, drawn primarily from Vasconcelos, Calancha, and Ovalle, grounding his assertions in the previous evidence of the apostle's presence in Goa (Figure 5). Duarte's purpose, as he states it, is to add the Mexican case to the list of evidence that the Apostle had preached in the Americas. Although he admits that his accumulated evidence is still a loose collection of documents without any style, he insists that he must write the history so that it will not die with him.[68] The manuscript appears to be an elaboration of an earlier description of evidence of St. Thomas's presence in New Spain, since Duarte declares that upon leaving New Spain for the Philippines in 1680 he had left with Carlos de Sigüenza y Góngora a codex and fifty-two pages of "news that Saint Thomas had preached in New Spain" (noticias de aver predicado en N. España Santo Tomas). This lost manuscript, it is now assumed, was the basis for Sigüenza's own work on St. Thomas, "El fenix del occidente" ("The Phoenix of the West"), which, if ever written, has never been located.[69]

As in other regions in which St. Thomas had been associated with local deities, Duarte argued that the Mexica god remembered as Quetzalcoatl was none other than St. Thomas himself. Some of his evidence for this association parallels that found in Brazil, Paraguay, and Peru. Just as St. Thomas's name had been corrupted by pronunciation and time in other areas, for instance, he points out that *coatl* in Nahuatl and *Thomé* in Greek share an etymological reference to twins.[70] Likewise, Duarte finds the saint's handprints on a stone in Tlalnepantla in central Mexico.[71] As Lafaye shows, the merging of the story of Quetzalcoatl with that of St. Thomas's evangelizing of the Americas drew on a previous effort to Christianize the god, primarily by the late sixteenth-century missionary Diego de Durán.[72] Yet the clarity of the story of St. Thomas allowed Duarte to go further than Durán in reading pictorial records as hieroglyphs endowed with hermetic significance. Because the Spanish could not understand their significance, he claims, many destroyed the very codices that proved that St. Thomas had evangelized the region. He goes on to insist that the remaining indigenous records should be taken as reliable documents:

> they are the ones who knew [the stories] and placed them in a history of origins, at first in figures and characters and afterwards, when a few of the most able of them learned alphabetic script, in [writings which] I possess; and I am so envious of the language and style in which they are written that I would love to be able to translate

Figure 5. Drawing of a cross in Goa proving St. Thomas's presence in the region. From Manuel Duarte, *Pluma rica* (ca. 1680). Courtesy of the Bancroft Library, University of California, Berkeley.

into Castilian the elegance and grace of the Mexican language; and because it was a pure and true history I will follow it to the letter; and if those who read it feel that these are fabrications, I assure you that they are not, but rather the true history that occurred but which has not been written until now because the few that chronicled the events of the Indies did not know about this, nor was there anyone to tell them about it.

(son los que muy bien las supieron y las pusieron en historia a los principios por sus figuras y caracteres, y despues que supieron escribir algunos curiosos de ellos las escribieron las cuales tengo en mi poder; y tengo tanta envidia al lenguaje y estilo con que estan escritas, que me holgara saberlas traducir en castellano con la elegancia y gracia que en su lengua mexicana se dicen; y por ser historia pura y verdadera la sigo en todo; y sí a los que las leyeren pareciesen novedades digo que no lo son, sino la pura verdad sucedida; pero que no se han escrito hasta agora, porque los pocos que han escrito los sucesos de las indias, no las supieron, ni hubo quien se las dijese.)[73]

Although he goes on to praise Bernardino de Sahagún for having preserved much of the evidence relating to Quetzalcoatl, he disagrees with the diabolic interpretation of Quetzalcoatl espoused by the sixteenth-century Franciscan.[74] Instead, Duarte relates the elegance of the Nahuatl transcriptions to the purity of a first law preserved by the "elegance and grace" of Nahuatl (*lengua mexicana*). If for Calancha *quipus* had been a decayed but sufficient form of record keeping, under Duarte's pen indigenous glyphs became a pristine language of origins.

Duarte's most important source of evidence for these claims is the very codex that he supposedly left with Sigüenza y Góngora upon his return to the Philippines. Although this codex was in his possession for fourteen years while he was in Mexico, he relates, he didn't "understand it completely until I was able to read this copy by Herrera, from Cealcoquin" (entenderla de todo, hasta llegué a leerlo aquí copiado, de Herrera de Cealcoquin).[75] The images on the map, he argues, must be interpreted allegorically in order to find the references to St. Thomas: "one must assume that most of this painting signifies spiritual and religious things through metaphors and allegories, as when one says sun for justice, lion for Judas, male for strong, etc." (se ha de suponer que lo mas de esta pintura tiene su sentido como el de cosas espirituales, y de Religion en metaphoras, y alegoricas [sic], como quando se dice Sol de Justicia, Leon de Iuda, Varon fuerte &a).[76] When interpreted in this way, he argues, the figures depict both the presence of St. Thomas in the region and the content of his evangelizing. Later Creole authors who wrote on St. Thomas's evangelizing, such as the eighteenth-century Mariano Fernández de Echeverría y Veytia, would scoff at Duarte's allegorical reading, asserting that the codex appeared nothing more than a register of a local township dispute in Oaxaca.[77] Yet Duarte's reading established an antiquarian authority for Creoles in a manner that previous readings of Quetzalcoatl had not. One of the most striking aspects of the Quetzalcoatl legend was his association with Tula, the obscure civilization of the Toltecs whom the Mexica revered as their own antiquity. While through his interpretation of Quetzalcoatl Duran had appropriated the Toltec Empire for Christianity, his reading had depended on the indigenous memory of the god. Duarte, a Portuguese Jesuit who had resided only fourteen years in Mexico, turned the codices into hermetic keepers of an ancient Christian law, rather than indigenous. Although his evidence is strikingly distinct from that which authors in other regions had found for St. Thomas's evangelizing, the logic is quite similar. That which could be the basis for indigenous cultural continuity, the web of meaning embedded in the natural landscape, oral traditions, or material sign carriers, was resignified as an allegory of archaic Christianization.

THE VIRGIN OF GUADALUPE: IMAGE AND ARCHIVE

Walter Benjamin's 1929 *Origin of German Tragic Drama* is one of the few theories of the Baroque to take into account its temporal structure. For Benjamin, after the decay of the theological symbol, the Baroque turned to a dialectical form of allegory that froze and rearranged human history in order to find redemption: "Whereas in the symbol destruction is idealized and the transfigured face of nature is fleetingly revealed in the light of redemption, in allegory the observer is confronted with the *facies hippocratica* of history as a petrified, primordial landscape."[78] While conceived in reference to the theological battles of seventeenth-century Europe, Benjamin's theory also provides an approach to the late Baroque in Spanish America. After early utopian models of evangelization, seventeenth-century Spanish jurisprudence was forced to address a society composed of partially converted indigenous subjects. Again, the jurist Solórzano Pereyra provides the clearest synthesis of figures that appeared repeatedly in early seventeenth-century theological writings. For Solórzano, Christianity among indigenous subjects was a precarious and reversible state even where it had been achieved. It was important, he warned, to eliminate anything in indigenous communities that "could revive the memory of and desire for their infidelity or suggest that they were not altogether beyond it" (les pudiese avivar la memoria y deseo de su infidelidad, o dar indicio de que no estaban bien apartados de ella).[79] As Woodrow Borah has argued, by drawing on Spanish legal tradition to define indigenous subjects as "miserable," Solórzano established a juridical precedent for the tutelary relationship between the Spanish Crown and indigenous neophytes.[80] When applied to indigenous Christianity, "misery" was a positive category that placed indigenous subjects in permanent transition: freed from the memory of pagan customs but not yet fully Christian.

Whereas jurists such as Solórzano Pereyra continued to rely on concepts of tutelary segregation to address incomplete conversion, Creoles approached the problem through time. As in the *Triunfo parthénico*, they envisioned a clean break between Mexica and Creole institutions or, as in the story of St. Thomas, enshrouded indigenous objects in the allegorical language of Neoplatonic hermeticism. Thus Creoles exiled the pagan past to either anachronism or archaic obscurity. Yet although the story of St. Thomas appropriated artifacts of indigenous culture, it did not solve the problem that indigenous conversion in the present continued to appear partial, decayed, or even resistant. The Creole solution to the problem of indigenous Christianity was the story of the Virgin of Guadalupe. As opposed to Solórzano's fickle neophyte, whose categorization as "miserable" demanded oversight and vigilance, the narrative of the sixteenth-century apparition of the Virgin of Guadalupe to the neophyte Juan Diego identified indigenous Christians as humble and devout, part of a brotherhood already confirmed by a miracle. The counterpart, as Jacques Lafaye famously showed, to the story of St. Thomas's preevangelizing of the Americas was the transformation of the pagan landscape after the conquest through the Virgin's appearance to Juan Diego. Although Lafaye does not make this explicit, both the story of a Christianized past and the confirmation of a Christian present avoid the issue of historical and human time.[81]

One of the problems that has consumed studies of the Virgin of Guadalupe is the fact that, although it set the appearance in 1531, the first written testimony of the apparition appeared only in 1648. In that year, Miguel Sánchez published a long treatise on the apparition under the title *La imagen de la Virgen María de Dios de Guadalupe* (The Image of the Virgin Mary of God of Guadalupe) (Figure 6). According to Sánchez, in a narrative that was repeated with only slight differences in all subsequent versions, the Indian neophyte Juan Diego was walking on the barren hillside of Tepeyac outside Mexico City in December, ten years after the Spanish conquest, when he heard a celestial music distinct from the songs of any birds he knew. He then heard a voice call his name and turning, he discovered a woman who beckoned him to come further. She had "a beauty that enchanted him without danger, a light that shone without blinding him" (una hermosura que lo enamora sin peligro, una luz que lo alumbra sin deslumbrarlo), and "a graciousness that captivated him without flattery" (un agrado que lo cautiva sin lisonja). She asked

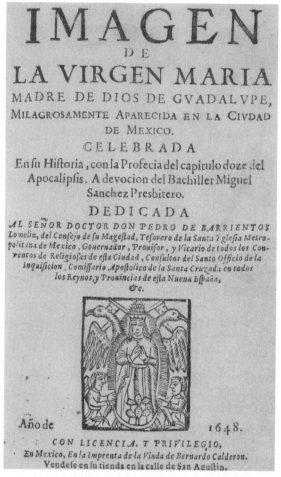

Figure 6. Frontispiece from Miguel Sánchez, *La imagen de la Virgen María de Dios de Guadalupe* (1648). Courtesy of the John Carter Brown Library at Brown University.

him, "My son, Juan, where doest thou go?" (Hijo, Juan, ¿adónde vas?). He replied that he was going to Tlatelolco for the "teachings and obedience of the religious fathers" (doctrina y obediencia de los padres religiosos). Sánchez narrates that Mary then told Juan Diego that she was the Mother of God and that she would like him to go to the palace of the bishop Juan de Zumárraga in Mexico City to carry the message that "I have a particular desire that he design and build a temple for me in this site" (tengo particular voluntad de que me labre y edifique un templo en este sitio).⁸²

Returning the next day to the same spot, Juan Diego again found the Virgin and told her that he had carried out her request but that the bishop had thought that the request "was born of my own imagination and not of your command" (nacía de mi propia imaginación y no de tu mandato). He begged the Virgin to give the task to someone "who has more credence" (a quien se dé más crédito). The Virgin insisted that he take the message to the bishop again and, after doing so, Juan Diego returned to the hillside the next day to find the Virgin waiting for him. He recounted that this time the prelate had responded, "apparently somewhat angry" (al parecer algo desabrido), that "if only my words, reports and person were to convince him to undertake such an important task" (si solamente mis palabras, informes y persona habían de moverle a negocio tan grave) he would also need a sign "that certifies your will" (que certificase tu voluntad). This time the Virgin told him to return the following day so she could provide him with such a sign, Sánchez recounts that Juan Diego left without realizing that Bishop Zumárraga had sent his own pages to investigate the account. Yet although they followed him to the spot where he spoke with the Virgin, they lost sight of him just as he had rounded the hill and thus returned to the bishop reporting that the Indian's claim was an "illusion, fiction, or dream" (engaño, ficción, o sueño).⁸³

Meanwhile, upon arriving in his village, Juan Diego discovered that his uncle was sick with *cocoliztli*, the Nahuatl term for the epidemics that had decimated the indigenous population of New Spain throughout the sixteenth century. Instead of returning the next day to Tepeyac as the Virgin had requested, Juan Diego stayed in town to search for a doctor for his sick uncle. Returning to his accustomed route to the city the following morning, he attempted to avoid the spot where the Virgin had met him previously. But, all-seeing, she noticed him and appeared once again. Juan Diego, embarrassed and distressed, knelt to tell her that he had intended to return to carry out her request. Believing his sincerity, the Virgin told him not to worry as his uncle would be cured. Then she told him to return to the spot where he had first seen her and to cut the roses that he found there. "Without pausing to note that it was frozen and wintry December" (Sin replicar el tiempo, era diciembre helado invierno), Juan Diego climbed to the spot to find "various flowers, miraculously in bloom" (diversas flores, brotadas a milagro), which he cut and carried back to the Virgin in his "rough, poor and humble cape" (tosca, pobre y humilde manta), which, as Sánchez comments, was "the common style and clothes of the Indians" (el común estilo y traje de los indios). The Virgin took the flowers in her arms and then returned them to him, telling him not to open his cape until he was in the presence of the bishop. This time, when Juan Diego returned to the palace, the pages were intrigued by his bulky cape and gave him an audience with the bishop. When Juan Diego opened his cape to present the bishop with the flowers, they fell to the ground. In their place, his cape was imprinted with a portrait of the Virgin herself "in her saintly image that today is conserved, protected, and venerated in the sanctuary of the Mexican Guadalupe" (en su santa imagen que hoy se conserva, guarda y venera en santuario de Guadalupe de México).[84]

As in all early modern apparition narratives, Sánchez's account of the Virgin of Guadalupe at Tepeyac revolves around confirmation by a sign.[85] Yet as Stafford Poole has recently pointed out, the image of the Virgin imprinted on Juan Diego's rough cape (Figure 7) also served as a relic of her presence.[86] The miracle is thus formed around a specular object: not the apparition itself, but the imprint of the image that reproduced the Virgin's beauty on the indigenous *tilma*. Indeed, Sánchez dedicates most of his treatise, written in a hyperbolic language of "mystery" that has often been described as "Baroque" or "Gongoresque,"[87] to an exegesis of this miraculous image. Sánchez emphasizes the limitations of words for describing the visual image: "If we wish to understand miracles, they have their own language, logic, and words because since they are created by Christ, who is the divine word, they are formed of that word which is worth more than all other words, and we must read attentively" (Que si queremos entenderlos, tienen los milagros sus lenguas, razones y palabras, porque como son obrados por Cristo, que es la divina palabra, quedan ellos con aquesta palabra, que vale por todas las palabras, y atentos leamos).[88] The image "will make the paintbrush that imitates it form a concept" (formarán un concepto al pincel que retoca) to "speak" the mysteries of its cause.[89] He also claims that the meaning of the image itself had come to him miraculously when he was contemplating the figure of the Apocalypse and realized that the latter was a commentary on Mexico's conquest of pagan idolatry.[90] If John's vision at Patmos could be read as a commentary on signs leading up to the Spanish conquest, he asserts, the image of the Virgin is the

Figure 7. The reflection of the Virgin of Guadalupe on Juan Diego's *tilma*. Luis Becerra Tanco, *Felicidad de México* (1675). Courtesy of the John Carter Brown Library at Brown University.

seal of a "new paradise" in the form of a woman. If the seven-headed dragon in Revelation is the seven caves that gave origin to the Mexica, and the crown of twelve stars represent their idols, the stars on the Virgin of Guadalupe's cape are the conquistadors who make way for Mary's appearance.[91] While the Guadalupan narrative thus adds to the European apparition tradition the potential confusion of Juan Diego's neophyte "imagination,"[92] Sánchez offsets this with a biblical hermeneutics and a providential reading of the Spanish conquest.

At the same time, the image draws the meaning of indigenous conquest and conversion out of history and into a symbolic language. The apparition is a confirmation of a conversion that occurs ten years after "the City of Mexico had been conquered and had surrendered to peace" (habiéndose conquistado, y dádose de paz esta ciudad de México).[93] The image thus serves as a symbolic bridge over a period of transition. As if to emphasize the resistance of the image to historical chronology, Sánchez explains that he turns to the image only after having searched in vain for documentation of the apparition:

Determined, willing, and diligent, I searched among papers and writings regarding the saintly image and her miracle and did not find them, and although I combed all the archives where it might have been kept, I learned that due to the vicissitudes of history those that had existed had been lost. I appealed to the providence of the ancients' curiosity in which I found some, in truth many, [records], and not satisfied, I examined these in all of their details, at times comparing them with the chronicles of the conquest and other times turning to the oldest and most reputable people of the city, still other times searching for the owners from whence the papers were said to originate and I confess that lacking all of this, I would not have suspended my search except for the fact that I had on my side the customary, grave and venerable law of the tradition of that ancient, invariable and universal miracle.

(Determinado, gustoso y diligente busqué papeles y escritos tocantes a la santa imagen y su milagro, no los hallé, aunque recorrí los archivos donde podían guardarse, supe que por accidentes del tiempo y ocasiones se habían perdido los que hubo. Apelé a la providencia de la curiosidad de los antiguos en que hallé unos, bastantes a la verdad, y no contento los examiné en todas sus circunstancias, ya confrontando las crónicas de la conquista, ya informándome de las más antiguas personas y fidedignas de la ciudad, ya buscando los dueños que decían ser originarios de estos papeles, y confieso que aunque todo me hubiera faltado, no había de desistir de mi propósito, cuando tenía de mi parte el derecho común, grave y venerado de la tradición, en aqueste milagro, antigua, uniforme y general.)[94]

Upon finding no document for the image, he concludes by citing Luis de Cisneros's text on the Virgin of Remedios that "when there is tradition, there is no need to search further" (en habiendo tradición, no hay más que buscar).[95] What has often been characterized as Sánchez's excessive biblical commentary and "Baroque" language, then, supplements a historical lacuna. In Sánchez's argument, it is the exegesis of the image itself that becomes the historical record.

David Brading has noted that the numerous Guadalupan sermons from the seventeenth century, for the most part preached by Creole members of the secular clergy, almost unanimously adopted Sánchez's allegorical reading of the Guadalupan image as the basis for their interpretations.[96] Yet as the demands to authenticate the cult of the Virgin of Guadalupe grew, the missing archive of the apparition forced Creole prose of the same period to return to the question of the narrative's historicity. Following Sánchez's 1648 treatise, the shrine's chaplain, Luis Lasso de la Vega, published a Nahuatl version of the apparition narrative titled *Huei tlamahuiçoltica* (The Great Event).[97]

It was not until Mateo de la Cruz's 1660 popularized version of Sánchez's treatise, however, that new elements were added to the apparition narrative, including a date of 1531 for the events.[98] On the heels of this publication, several of the most fervent supporters of the tradition sought Vatican approval for a special feast day on December 12. The petition was returned for insufficient evidence but with the promise that the Vatican would send an inquiry. Rather than wait for this envoy, in 1666 the petitioners initiated their own investigation in which they interviewed a variety of witnesses, principally from the town of Cuauhtitlan, where they argued Juan Diego had lived. Although there were no remaining direct witnesses to the events of the apparition, several indigenous interviewees said to be 112 years old confirmed that their parents or other relatives had personally known Juan Diego and heard about the apparitions from him. Another woman from a principal family of the town spoke of papers that detailed the apparition but which had gone missing. Drawn from indigenous, mestizo, and Spanish sources, the testimonies minimized the issues of reliability of indigenous testimony that had been the center of the apparition narrative itself and provided important details about the image, such as the history of its installation in the chapel at Tepeyac.[99]

Of all the testimonies taken in 1666, however, perhaps the most important for the development of the cult was that given by a Creole, Luis Becerra Tanco. A secular priest and professor of mathematics at the Royal University, Becerra Tanco largely repeated his testimony to the commission in his own treatise on the Virgin of Guadalupe, published posthumously in 1675. In what became one of the principal sources for later Guadalupan texts, Becerra begins by noting that the 1666 testimonies were taken in the absence of a written record of the apparitions. He then argues that other narratives

> have not been sufficiently exacting in their inquiry into this story as to avoid omissions due to lack of sources and informants from whom to cull this information, and thus the history's progress remained deficient; likewise because they did not fully understand the Mexican language in which the circumstances of the origin of this miraculous and blessed image of Our Most Holy Virgin Lady were written and painted by the hand of the natives who immediately chronicled and recorded it as a special prodigy.
>
> (no han sido tan exactos en el escrutinio de esta historia, que no se les haya quedado algo por falta de noticias, y por no haber tenido de quién poderlas saber radicalmente, con que el progreso de lo historial quedó diminuto; y así mismo por no haber tenido entera comprensión

de la lengua mexicana, en que se escribió y pintó lo acaecido en este milagroso principio de la bendita imagen de la Virgen Santísima Señora Nuestra, por mano y letra de los naturales que lo pintaron y escribieron luego, como prodigio memorable.)[100]

Becerra further characterizes his version of the story as the most closely related to the indigenous account "because in my adolescence I set myself to the task of acquiring knowledge of the Mexican language and of the ancient characters and paintings with which the competent Indians recorded the events of their ancestors before the Spanish had arrived to these provinces as well as those which occurred during the first century of their incorporation into the Spanish monarchy" (por el que yo puse en mi adolescencia en adquirir la inteligencia del idioma mexicano, y de los antiguos caracteres y pinturas con que historiaron los indios hábiles los progresos de sus antepasados, antes que viniesen los españoles o [sic] estas provincias, y lo que sucedió en aquel primer siglo de su agregación a la monarquía de España).[101]

Whereas Sánchez's dense reading of the image had replaced a missing historical record, Becerra defends his choice of a more Spartan style as a reflection of empirical truth: "I deemed it unbecoming of the truth to clothe it in wordy apparel when one's purpose is to lay it bare; and I judged superfluous the affectation of stylistic elegance and polish because the refinement and beauty of discourse is proper to those who seldom harvest any other fruit from their writings than sweetness" (tuve por indecoroso a la verdad el buscarle ornato de palabras con que vestirla, cuando se trata de hallarla desnuda: juzgando por superfluo el afectar gallardía y suavidad de estilo, porque el culto y hermosura de las razones es muy propio de aquellos que no suelen coger de sus escritos otro fruto que su dulzura).[102] The apparition, he argues, is best preserved by the indigenous record "since it appeared to Indians" (por haber sido indios a los que se apareció). Yet in order to proceed with this evidence, he continues, it is necessary to "establish first what faith and credence should be given to their writings and memories" (establecer primero la fe y crédito que debe darse a sus escritos y memorias).[103] Indigenous documents, he goes on, are as reliable as those written by Spanish notaries

> because they did not entrust [these] to ignorant plebeians but rather only to grave priests who were the historians and whose authority and eminence were highly regarded in the heathen times; and therefore these characters and paintings are free from suspicion . . . ; excepting, of course, the superstitious rites by which they worshipped

their false gods to whom they attributed any prosperous or unhappy events, the narrative itself is authentic and truthful.

> (porque no se fiaban de la plebe ignorante, sino de los sacerdotes solamente, que eran los historiadores, cuya autoridad y crédito era muy venerable en el tiempo del gentilismo: y así no padecen duda estos caracteres y pinturas ... quitando, pues, lo supersticioso que toca a los ritos, con que daban culto a sus falsos dioses, a quien aplicaban algunos sucesos prósperos o infelices, lo historial es auténtico y verídico).[104]

Becerra asserts that although indigenous records are the most reliable, "that which the Indians today affirm about their antiquity contains many errors and is muddled and without order" (lo que hoy afirman los indios de su antigüedad, es con muchos errores, y confuso y sin orden). Rather, it is clerics—"those evangelical ministers who focused their attention on examining maps and paintings" (aquellos ministros evangélicos que se aplicaron a escudriñar los mapas y pinturas)—who are best equipped to read the documents critically. Among these, Becerra includes himself: "I have taken great pains to correlate their calendar to ours and to separate that which is superstitious from that which is natural" (Y a mí me costó mucho desvelo el ajustar su cómputo al nuestro, y apartar o supersticioso de lo natural).[105]

Interestingly enough, in his 1675 revision of his Guadalupan treatise, Becerra Tanco also provided one of the earliest notices of St. Thomas's evangelizing in Mexico. In this, as Duarte later would note, he claimed that the Mexica calendrical tradition corresponded to the Julian calendar and that it had been St. Thomas himself who "taught them the calendar with the year count" (les enseñó el calendario con la cuenta del año).[106] Becerra's intervention in the Guadalupan tradition follows a similar logic. In all accounts of the Guadalupan apparition, the image had not only confirmed Juan Diego's Christianity but had also mediated the cultural gulf that divided the neophyte indigenous subject from the Spanish bishop. Becerra goes further, however, when he credits the indigenous accounts as the most accurate for authenticating the event of the apparition. These had been previously disregarded, he argues, because Spanish held "Indians to be beasts incapable of reason, as our historians affirm" (a los indios por bestias e incapaces de razón, como afirman nuestros historiadores).[107] Becerra's was also the first account to deal explicitly with the question of translation in both the narrative and its historical record.[108]

By emphasizing the inability of Spaniards to understand indigenous documents of the apparition, Becerra thus drove a wedge between the indigenous and Spanish communication that the image itself miraculously established. At the same time, however, he sealed these documents into an archive that no indigenous commoner could access. If the growth of the Guadalupan cult in the seventeenth century has been attributed in part to the power of the image to overcome linguistic and cultural barriers, Becerra isolates the historicity of the apparition in written documentation that only Creoles could accurately interpret.[109] Although they were ostensibly the subject of the seventeenth-century Guadalupan cult, contemporary indigenous subjects were thus alienated both from Sánchez's allegorical interpretation and from Becerra's archival hermeneutics.

THE TIME OF CREOLE PARADISE

Given the paucity of historical documentation for a sixteenth-century cult, twentieth-century Guadalupan scholarship has focused heavily on the writings of seventeenth-century Creoles whom Francisco de la Maza has ingeniously labeled the "four evangelists": Sánchez, Lasso de la Vega, Becerra Tanco, and Francisco de Florencia, the author of a 1688 encyclopedic account of the Guadalupan tradition.[110] Beyond this elite record, however, it has been hard to ascertain how widespread the cult was during this period. Popular devotion to the Virgin of Guadalupe clearly predated Miguel Sánchez's 1648 treatise. A copy of the image was created as early as 1606 and in 1615, to raise funds for the first chapel to the Virgin at Tepeyac, Archbishop Juan de la Serna published an engraving depicting Guadalupan miracles. During the floods of 1629 the image was carried to Mexico City, where it stayed until 1634, thus increasing its visibility.[111] There are fewer indications that the cult was active in the sixteenth century. One of the earliest, and clearest, records of the image is Francisco de Bustamante's negation of a sermon preached by Alonso de Montufar in 1556. In this, he claims that the image had been painted by an Indian named Marcos but makes no mention of the apparition to Juan Diego.[112] Following this statement, and the dearth of any other information on the existence of a sixteenth-century cult, it is possible to conclude that the image was painted around 1556 and only later became the object of veneration associated with a miraculous imprint. Whatever the extent of the popular cult to the Virgin of Guadalupe in the seventeenth century, it is clear that its initial geography of devotion centered around the environs of Tepeyac and Mexico City. Only after 1648 was it carried by parish priests to what William Taylor has called the "urban-network" of small satellite cities in central Mexico.[113]

It seems reasonable, in this sense, to speak of a seventeenth-century Creole invention of the cult of the Virgin of Guadalupe. One of the most significant aspects of seventeenth-century Creole writings was the mystification of the image. Following Sánchez, commentators stressed its beauty, arguing that it would have been impossible for any human hand to have created it.[114] The fact that the image had been imprinted on a tilma, the dress of indigenous commoners, was another source of its power. From Sánchez onward, the tilma was a material reminder of Juan Diego's humble station.[115] Commentators also argued that the fabric's resistance to decay was proof of its sacred origin, all the more notable since the material of the tilma was known to be fragile and its location particularly close to the saline humidity of the lake. In 1666 a commission of "royal physicians" (*protomédicos*) examined the tilma and confirmed that its resistance to decay was miraculous.[116] Yet while the tilma was closely associated with indigenous daily life, the image of the Virgin of Guadalupe was clearly of European provenance. As Jeanette Peterson has recently written, the image has clear affinities to the Immaculate Conception, itself often read as an allegory of the Apocalypse. Given the millennial aspirations of the early Franciscans, she writes, it is not surprising that the Immaculate Conception found its way to New Spain, where it might have served as an inspiration for the painter of the Guadalupan image.[117] Peterson concludes that the artist of the image was most likely Marcos de Aquino, an indigenous painter trained at the Franciscan Colegio de Santa Cruz in Tlatelolco, who drew upon the largely Flemish influenced visual materials of the Franciscans.[118]

Again, however, the seventeenth-century Creole tradition obscures any genealogy of the image. Although Sánchez's allegorical reading of the Guadalupan image draws on the tradition of reading the Immaculate Conception as an allegory of the Apocalypse, he does not make explicit this European prototype. In another striking omission, given the association between the two images and his own Guadalupan devotion, Sigüenza y Góngora hardly mentions the Virgin of Guadalupe in the *Triunfo parthénico*. When he does, in the context of an altar representing the Immaculate Conception through apocalyptic imagery, he simply directs the reader to Sánchez's treatise.[119]

separation of the two images suggests that, while related, distinct symbolic roles in Creole theology and politics. In *parthénico* the oath to uphold the doctrine of the Immaculate Conception had sealed the Creole break with indigenous institutions by showing that the Mexican university was now on a par with its European counterparts. By contrast, the Guadalupan apparition acted as a medium by which to transform an allegorical "barren landscape" into a "flowered paradise." The significance of Juan Diego's path through the barren and rocky hillsides, "after the wars of conquest had ceased," is clear. Just as the hillside miraculously bloomed, whether with Castilian roses or indigenous flowers, Juan Diego is received in brotherhood by Zumárraga. If the Immaculate Conception signified a pure knowledge in the interior of the Creole university, the Virgin of Guadalupe thus developed the Creole motif of paradise into an allegory for the incorporation of indigenous neophytes into Christian society.

Indeed, beginning with Sánchez, the Virgin of Guadalupe was often referred to as a "Creole" (*criolla*) image to emphasize its local rather than European identity.[120] While the Creole appropriation of the image could be understood to be an attempt to find a providential blessing to compete with European saints, it is important to understand the peculiarities of the Guadalupan story. Unlike Spanish apparition narratives, the story of Juan Diego touched upon the historically difficult process of indigenous conversion. The narrative recalls the discontinuity of the period after the conquest, which it reduces to only ten years, as a period of confusion. Although the story of Juan Diego's uncle's sickness has been seen as a digression in the narrative, it is integral to the apparition's symbolic meaning.[121] The narrative looks past the older generation, represented by Juan Diego's uncle, toward the new generation of indigenous Christians. The subtle break between generations parallels the broken chain of documentation of the apparition. The humble innocence of Juan Diego, symbolic of a discontinuity with pre-Columbian customs, parallels the historical record of interrupted oral testimonies from Cuauhtitlan. The written documentation that Creoles reportedly held, while providing a bridge between the periods before and after the conquest, was the product of a fragmented tradition that had to be recuperated after the demise of the original indigenous participants. Whether through a symbolic reading of the image as a mystical confirmation of indigenous conversion or through an antiquarian archive of its historicity, Creoles called attention to the discontinuity created by the Spanish conquest by stressing a fragmented and hermetic record.

Carlos de Sigüenza y Góngora's diverse writings on the Virgin of Guadalupe have not received the same attention as the texts of the apparition's four "evangelists."[122] Yet beginning with his 1668 Gongoresque poem *Primavera indiana* (Indian Spring), the young Creole scholar made the most concerted attempt to develop the symbolism of the Virgin of Guadalupe into an allegory of postconquest social cohesion. Twentieth-century critics have generally concurred with Irving Leonard's assessment that Sigüenza's poem drew directly on the symbolic meanings that Miguel Sánchez had attributed to the apparition. He develops this symbolism through a literary chiaroscuro contrasting the Mexican landscape before and after the apparition:

> Mexico was left by this immense glory
> just as a traveler whom, in a shaded
> deep valley, the winter cold assailed
> with a dense blanket of fog.
> This lifted instantly, with an intense light,
> a tortuous serpent, with such ready verve
> that the traveler is left in neutral calm
> the body dead and the soul throbbing.
>
> (Quedó México de esta gloria inmensa,
> cual queda el caminante, que en sombrío,
> profundo valle, le asaltó con densa
> manga de nubes el invierno frío.
> Voló de fuego, con la luz intensa,
> tortuosa sierpe, con tan presto brío,
> que deja al caminante en neutral calma
> difunto el cuerpo, y palpitante el alma).[123]

The poem describes the hillside of Tepeyac as a rocky barren landscape "whose cliffs / are the rigid dread of uncultivated brambles" (cuyas peñas / rígido asombro son de incultas breñas), a reflection of the state of Mexico.[124] The Virgin is variously described as a light source that dispels the shadows—"homeland fortress of the dawning light" (alcázar patrio de la luz naciente)[125]— and a composition of flowers that brings a permanent springtime—"the immortal spring of a rose" (la inmortal primavera de una rosa).[126] Juan Diego is a "pauper" (pobre) who listens to her in a state of suspended attention: "the attentive Indian has his soul in suspense" (tiene el alma supensa al indio atento).[127] The poem thus describes a state of transition that ends in the flowering exuberance of the Guadalupan image.

Once the apparition has been confirmed by the miraculous image on Juan Diego's tilma, the poem ends quickly, claiming that the image itself cannot be scrutinized: "Enough my plume! restrain the passionate / and heroic impulse of your ardent flight.... Since if you wish irreverently to investigate /this beautiful prodigy you will be / wishing to scrutinize the gold its veins / the heavens their lightning and the sea its sands" (Basta pluma, reprime el afectuoso / conato heróico de tu vuelo ardiente.... Pues será si pretendes, este hermoso / prodigio, investigar irreverente / querer escudriñarle al oro venas / al cielo rayos o a la mar arenas).[128] But while in 1662 Sigüenza thus declared that the image resists "scrutiny," as his antiquarian interests grew he took a decisive stand on the apparition's historicity. In his history of the Hospital de la Inmaculada Concepción de Nuestra Señora, written sometime between 1691 and 1693,[129] Sigüenza challenged Francisco de Florencia's attribution of the Nahuatl version of the apparition to Jerónimo de Mendieta. Instead, he asserted that the author was none other than Antonio Valeriano, the famous indigenous scribe of the Franciscan Colegio de Santa Cruz in Tlatelolco, thus giving the narrative a verifiable authorship for the first time.[130]

If Sigüenza thus blended Sánchez's apparitionist tradition with Becerra Tanco's antiquarian empiricism, he also provided one of the best examples of the Guadalupan cult as the center of a postconquest community. Between the 1662 publication of *Primavera indiana* and his later stance on the apparition's documentation, Sigüenza was commissioned to write a description of the festivities accompanying the new Guadalupan chapel of Querétaro. *Glorias de Querétaro* (Glories of Querétaro) (1680) is in many ways typical of the festival literature that proliferated in seventeenth-century Mexico. But it also uniquely promotes the Virgin of Guadalupe as a symbol of social renewal after a frontier conquest. The text begins by praising the small city of Querétaro in terms that evoke the Creole theme of a paradisiacal landscape:

> never in that site did the earth tremble, nor did the mountains shudder; and if from there one gazes upon the heavens, never will one see these horrified by black billowing storms but rather with beautiful clouds, which dissolving into soft rains fertilize the earth, which is ignorant of the insults of thunderous lightning and the dissembled burn of harsh frost.
>
> (jamás en aquel sitio tembló la tierra, ni se estremecieron los montes; y si desde allí miramos el cielo, nunca se verá horrorizado con rumazones

negras, sino apacibles con celajes hermosos, que liquidados en suavísimas lluvias fecundan la tierra, que ignora los insultos de los estruendosos rayos, y los disimulados incendios de los yelos desabridos.)[131]

Sigüenza explicitly associates the paradisiacal qualities of Querétaro with the cultivation of fruits and vegetables catering to both "Creole" (*criollo*) and "Spanish" (*gachupín*) tastes:

> in any of the gardens of the city the Creole may find custard apples, avocados, white sapodillas, bananas, guavas, bilberry cacti, pitayas, plums, diverse prickly pears; and the Spaniard will not be without his celebrated and desired peaches, pomegranates, quinces, figs, apricots, pears, oranges, and lemons of various types.
>
> (en cualquier huerta de la ciudad hallará el criollo, chirimoyas, aguacates, zapotes blancos, plátanos, guayabas, garambullos, pitayas, ciruelas, tunas diferentísimas; y no echará menos el gachupín sus celebrados y suspirados duraznos, granadas, membrillos, brevas, albérchigos, chabacanos, manzanas, peras, naranjas y limones de varias especies).[132]

Sigüenza relates this mixed cultivation to the growth of the city: "this serving as an effective medium for Querétaro to grow imperceptibly from not a very large town to a magnificent and populous city" (sirviendo esto de medio eficaz para que insensiblemente pasase Querétaro de pueblo no muy grande a ser ciudad magnífica y numerosa).

Once again, however, this cultivated paradise exists in explicit tension with history. Sigüenza uses an organic metaphor to argue that Querétaro's development from humble beginnings opposes a trajectory of decay and decline:

> Meager beginnings have always been adequate means for great ends; because that which is exalted at its origin will tend to suffer a decline and that which is born small never fails to climb to the eminent throne of its potential. Such is the dictate of nature in the continual vicissitude of her progress, and even God observes it in the admirable regularity of his actions, since the Sun does not rise to the height of its meridian without passing through the depressions of the horizon and those perfections that adorn the admirable extension of the universe were first unkempt shadows amid the horrors of chaos, from which I infer that for this reason the greatness of the Congregation of the Most Holy Mary of Guadalupe that I celebrate and the majestic temple whose dedication is my topic may be admired on their high throne since they begin in humble minuteness.
>
> (Principios cortos siempre fueron proporcionados medios para fines grandes; porque lo que en el origen fue excelso desde luego se inclina

a padecer el destrozo, y lo que nace pequeño jamás deja de remontarse al eminente trono de lo máximo, dictamen es de la naturaleza en la continua vicisitud de sus procederes, y aun Dios lo observa en la regularidad admirable de sus acciones, supuesto pue [sic] el Sol no llega a lo excelso del meridiano, sin pasar por las depresiones del horizonte, y cuantas perfecciones adornan la amplitud admirable del universo, primero fueron desaliñadas sombras entre los horrores del caos, de que infiero, que la grandeza de la Congregación de María Santísima de Guadalupe que celebro, y el Templo majestuouso cuya dedicación es mi asunto, por eso se admira en el trono de la eminencia, porque se cimentaron en la pequeñez humilde.)[133]

This mention of the region's humble beginnings and the analogy of pre-Edenic chaos only obliquely refers to the violent origins of Querétaro as a frontier of Mexican colonization. Rather, Sigüenza emphasizes a city peacefully divided among its current residents: "the lower part being that of the community of the Indians and the superior part being that of the Spanish, whose population distributed among neighborhoods and hearths is around five hundred without counting the Indians, blacks, mulattoes, and mestizos, who are many" (siendo la parte inferior la comunidad de los indios, y la superior el lugar de los españoles, cuyo número distribuído por las vecindades y humenos llegará a quinientos, no comprendiendo los indios, negros, mulatos y mestizos, que son muchos).[134] Just as cultivation provides a metaphor of natural renewal, the city's urban divisions reflect a postconquest social order that sublimates the history of violent conquest.

Sigüenza's description of the processions celebrating the inauguration of the chapel continue in a similar vein. The procession features an orderly hierarchy of confraternities, floats, and members of the local elite, whom Sigüenza names and personally acknowledges. The procession begins with the "the blacks of Saint Benedict of Palermo, luminous honor of Ethiopia and brightness of the Seraphic religion" (Negros de San Benito de Palermo, honor resplandeciente de la Etiopía y lustre de la Religión Seráfica). A confraternity of "Otomite Indians" (indios otomites), another of "Tarascans" (tarascos), and a third of mulattoes follows. "Following these, either because they were the most venerable or the most qualified" (Seguíanse, o por más antigua o más calificadas), were the confraternities "all of Spaniards, and all numerous and exceedingly devoted" (todas de españoles, y todas devotísimas y numerosas).[135] Sigüenza's description of the procession is generically panegyric, employing tropes of abundance, celebration, and wonder.[136] It not until the description of a specially orchestrated procession to show "the singular affection that the natives have for this Lady" (el singular cariño que a esta Señora tienen los naturales) that this generically Baroque façade cracks to expose the social violence of the region's origins. After describing in detail the site of Querétaro, the events leading up to the construction of the Guadalupan chapel, and finally the architectonic details of the chapel itself, Sigüenza turns to this procession, organized by the indigenous governor Don Diego de Salazar.

The first group in the indigenous procession is composed of "Chichimec" Indians, a generic title often given to nomadic nations on the viceregal frontier. Sigüenza describes this as a

> motley crowd of savage Chichimecs, wearing barely enough to respect common decency and with no other adornment than the earthly colors with which they paint their bodies, their unkempt hair made uglier by vile and decomposed feathers and, as almost an imitation of the imaginary Satyrs, or of dreamt up monsters, they horrified all [in attendance] with their cries and uproar and, while gesturing with their bows and clubs, gave reason for fright with the barbarous spectacle of their disorderly and fearful skirmishes.
>
> (desordenada confusión de montaraces chichimecos, que sin otra ropa que la que permitió la decencia y sin más adorno, que los colores terrizos con que se embijan los cuerpos, afeadas las desgreñadas cabezas con descompuestas soeces plumas, y casi remedo de sátiros, fingidos, o de los soñados vestiglos, horrorizaban a todos con algazaras y estruendos, mientras jugando de los arcos, de las macanas, daban motivo de espanto con el bárbaro especimen de sus irregulares y temerosas peleas.)[137]

This spectacle of barbarism is followed by the elegant order of a Hispanicized "company of infantry" (compañía de infantería). While Sigüenza aestheticizes the fright and admiration for these opposed groups, the contrast goes beyond antithesis, as he also comments that the precision of the second group suggests "that they are not incapable of discipline should it be necessary to introduce them to martial studies" (no ser incapaces de disciplina, si acaso fuera necesario introducirlos en los marciales estudios).[138]

If the first two groups of the procession thus recall the Chichimec wars that marked the region's colonization, the third group profiles the genealogy of the Texcocan and Mexica nobility, led by the conquistador of the region, Diego de Tapia, and closed by Carlos V. Sigüenza praises this group as "the third and most principal piece of the impressive masquerade which, while heathen and barbarous, was composed with greatness and warranted the title of Augustan, after the manner in which its scepter ruled the extensive Septentrional Empire of the West" (tercero y más principal trozo de la lucida máscara que se compuso de grandeza, que aunque gentílica y bárbara mereció las aclamaciones de Augusta, a beneficio del Cetro que rigió el dilatado Septentrional Imperio del occidente). Not only does Sigüenza defend the grandeur of the display of indigenous kingship, but he even suggests that it is the only means to produce an authentic indigenous celebration: "And of course it would be a reprehensible monstrosity if the Indians, to display their joy, turned to foreign ideas when in their emperors and kings there was enough material for splendor" (Y claro está, que fuera monstruosidad censurable, el que para manifestar su regocijo los indios, se valiesen de extrañas ideas, cuando en la de sus Emperadores y Reyes, les sobró asunto para el lucimiento).[139]

But in addition to this moral apology and commentary, Sigüenza also evaluates the accuracy of the representation of pre-Columbian dress: "and the elegance with which all were dressed was the ancient style displayed in their paintings and preserved by memory, as all were so uniformly garbed and with such rich and elegant compositions of their extraordinary adornments" (y la gala la que todos vestían era la antigua, que en las pinturas se manifiesta, y que en la memoria se perpetúa, siendo en todos tan uniforme el traje, como rica y galante la contextura de sus extraordinarios adornos).[140] As if to confirm his competence in this evaluation, Sigüenza names each of the kings represented and comments on the imperial relations between the Texcocan and Mexica lineages. He ends the passage with an extensive description of their adornments in a cascade of Nahuatl terms:

> The heads of all were adorned with the *xiuhzolli*, which was the very sign of lordship, each of them a noble deposit of howsoever many of the most precious stones had traveled from the East, to which they owed their luster, to these Western provinces to display their karats; nor were they lacking the headdresses that perfected their elegance, such as the *malacaquetzalli, tlauquecholtontec*, and *aztatzontli*, all uniform in the preciousness of their feathers and singular in the exquisiteness of their composition; their hands and feet were admirably decorated with the *iexiteceuceuexli icxipepetlchtli*, and *matzopetzli* and their most expensive blankets, that they called *xiuhtlapiltilmatli y netlaquechilloni*, and which only served for the majesty of the throne; but why do I tire myself with the particulars of their adornments when referring to them in the originality of their elegant tongue may irritate those who do not know the Mexican language?

(Adornábanse las cabezas de todos con el *xiuhzolli*, que era divisa propia del Señorío, siendo cada uno de ellos noble depósito de cuantas riquísimas piedras desde el oriente a que debieron sus brillos pasaron a estas provincias del ocaso a manifestar sus quilates, no faltándole la estimable trenzadora, en que se primorizaba su gala, como son el *malacaquetzalli, tlauquecholtontec* y *aztatzontli*, todos uniformes en la preciosidad de las plumas y singulares todos en lo exquisito de su disposición admirable lucieron en pies y manos, el *iexiteceuceuexli icxipepetlchtli* y *matzopetzli* y sobresalieron las extraordinarias costosísimas mantas, que sólo servían a la majestad en el trono, que llamaban *xiuhtlapiltilmatli* y *netlaquechilloni;* pero para qué me canso en particularizar sus aliños, cuando por referirlos en la propiedad de la elegante lengua, puede ser que fastidie a quien ignora el mexicano idioma?)[141]

Sigüenza makes no effort to translate the Nahuatl terms in this description and even emphasizes the opacity of these terms for "those who do not know the Mexican language." The value of the words in Nahuatl does not seem to lie in their ability to signify, although they clearly do for those familiar with Mexica regal attire, but in the fact that they retain "the originality of the elegant tongue" (la propiedad de la elegante lengua) that mimics the nobility represented. It is their very resistance to translation, in fact, that defines the "barbarous grandeur" of the pre-Columbian kings.

In contrast to the extremes of indigenous barbarism and Hispanic order represented by the first two groups in the procession, the third epitomizes the ideal of a syncretic, postconquest alliance between Creoles and indigenous nobility. Sigüenza himself explains the meaning of this third group's display by recounting the story of the colonization of the region. Having seen the Spanish overwhelm the Mexica Empire, he writes, a group of Otomís fled into the Chichimec regions north of Mexico City. Led by Conín, a "rich merchant" (mercader rico), they settled in Querétaro, under the encomienda of Juan Pérez de Bocanegra. Together with the friar of the region, the encomendero convinced Conín to be baptized and with his help in turn "many were converted" (se convirtieron muchos).[142] After attributing the conversions to the linguistic prowess of the friar, who "achieved an astounding command of the Otomite language, despite its difficulty, as well as that of the neighboring Chichimecs" (el que siendo dificultosa en extremo la lengua otomí, la aprendió maravillosamente, como también la de sus vecinos los chichimecas).[143] Sigüenza ends by declaring: "This very ancient debt was repaid on this occasion by the Indians of Querétaro through the generous demonstrations of their affection which amazed all" (Esta tan antigua deuda fue la que pagaron en esta ocasión los indios de Querétaro, con las generosas demostraciones de su cariño, que suspendieron a todos).[144] The two terms that structure Sigüenza's commentary, "conversion" and "debt," recall the economy of exchange that justified indigenous tribute after the conquest.[145] But if indigenous tribute was conceived of as a compensation to Spanish administrators for the benefits of conversion, here it is remarkable that the gift is one that resists Spanish comprehension. In Sigüenza's description, the gift of "antiquarian" artifacts thus avoids the violence of the conquest while nonetheless conserving the memory of past pagan difference.

Indeed, any remaining difference that could irritate present social relations is sublimated by the Virgin of Guadalupe, as shown by the anecdote that closes his narration. Climbing the tower of the new chapel to view the procession, a relative of the Caballero y Ocio family that had sponsored the construction of the chapel slips and falls. Sigüenza provides the gory details of how the man's body hit the sides of the tower on the way down:

> he fell from the bell tower with all the precipitous violence of the human body in free fall; the descent was not so straight to keep him from hitting his head several times on the walls over the distance of almost eight yards to the first spiral stairs, which number twenty-three and descend to the door that opens upon the choir; he tumbled down all of these with the misfortune that they were made of unhewn rock, so that, still unpolished, they were covered with sharp edges. After this immeasurable and horrific fall he was left senseless with blood streaming from all of the orifices of his body and with all the symptoms that one recognizes on these occasions to be of mortal wounds.

> (cayó por el cubo de la torre con tan arrebatada violencia, cuanta es la gravedad descuidada de un cuerpo humano, no fue el descenso tan recto, que dejase de dar una y otra vez con la cabeza, y otro por las paredes en distancia de casi ocho varas, que había hasta los primeros escalones del caracol que son veinte y tres para coger la puerta que desemboca en el coro: por todos ellos rodó con circunstancia de formarse piedras brutas, que por faltarles todavía la perfección sobresalen con penetrantes puntas. A lo horroroso y desmesurado del golpe, quedó sin sentido arrojando sangre por todos los orificios del cuerpo, y con cuantos síntomas en estas ocasiones se reconocen mortales.)[146]

Miraculously, the fallen man is revived from his bloody stupor and in three days is perfectly well. While Sigüenza attributes this miracle to the fact that the man's family had sponsored the chapel's construction, the violence of his fall also prompts a reflection on the materiality of monuments:

> Rome owes its venerable perpetuity more to its civilized laws than to the ostentatious construction of magnificent palaces, for the latter, at last, have fallen into ruin and are decayed and moth-ridden by time, while the former were made eternal in the prolific reaches of memory, serving as a pleasant reminder for piety of that which was forged by the proper dictates of reason.
>
> (Mas le debe Roma la perpetuidad venerable a sus políticas leyes, que a la soberbia fábrica de sus palacios magníficos, que estos al fin se desmoronaron caducos con la polilla del tiempo, y aquellas se eternizaron en las duraciones prolijas de la memoria: sirviendo de recuerdo agradable de la piedad lo que se forjó en el acertado dictamen de la razón.)[147]

Glorias de Querétaro offers two alternatives to imperial monuments, subject to what in the *Triunfo parthénico* Sigüenza calls the "violence of time." If the display orchestrated by the indigenous governor turns any remaining indigenous resistance into antiquarian artifacts, the Virgin's miraculous cure seals the postconquest social order. While not the most prominent promoter of the Guadalupan tradition, or even of the story of St. Thomas's evangelizing of Mexico, Sigüenza y Góngora most clearly saw the distinction and interplay between the two forms of allegory represented by the miraculous image and the antiquarian archive. It is clear that in Sigüenza's text these are the only foundations upon which a postconquest society can be built.

In the years after he published *Glorias de Querétaro*, Sigüenza was involved in two further writings on the Virgin of Guadalupe. The first was the major compendium of the tradition written by his friend Francisco de Florencia, the last of the "four evangelists," who has also been called the "great orchestrator" of the tradition.[148] Florencia's work, *La estrella de el norte de México* (The Pole Star of Mexico) (1688), for which Sigüenza served as censor, was an encyclopedic attempt to unite all aspects of the Guadalupan tradition. But the work also marked a new moment in the Creole promotion of the cult. After the intense worries about historicity that marked midcentury texts, Florencia moved away from an investigation of the apparition itself, focusing instead on the Guadalupan miracles. These, he argues, are the best evidence for the apparition's historicity: "the Castillos and Torquemadas may remain as silent as they wish about all that they, whether through neglect or caution, failed to say, for I trust more in the testimony of the many miracles that God has bestowed and continues to perform every day for the Saintly Image of Guadalupe in confirmation of our pious devotion to her" (callen los Castillos, y Torquemadas, lo que dexaron de decir, o por cautos o por omissos, que para mi pesa mas el testimonio de tantos milagros, como ha hecho, y cada dia hace Dios por la Santa Imagen de Guadalupe en confirmacion de la piadosa fe, que tiene de ella).[149] Although he gives a detailed account of his personal experience of the problematic petition to Rome, as well as the testimonies taken in 1666 in its wake, Florencia dismisses the importance of the question of historicity that plagued this effort. Instead he asserts that the continuity of Guadalupan miracles overcame the need for historical evidence: "conservation, as the philosophers say, should not be distinguished from action itself, which they call production; and thus, if the conservation is miraculous so will the production be miraculous" (La conservacion, dicen los Philosophos, no se distingue de la propria accion, que llaman produccion; con que si la conservacion es milagrosa, sera milagrosa la producción).[150] On this basis he concludes that the permanence of the image and the repetition of miracles have the same validity as the original apparition.

Despite his dismissal of the need for historical documentation of the apparition, Florencia does cite the indigenous record of the miracle. Summarizing Becerra Tanco, he suggests that the absence of a written account in Spanish resulted from a lack of paper in the early years of colonization. But he also defends the omission on the grounds that early missionaries were more concerned with conversion than documentation.[151] Finally he declares that God "wished to work such a rare marvel, using as his medium and instrument an Indian to so glorify his Mother, likewise determined that while the first Spaniards would forget to write it down, but not to celebrate [this miracle], it would be the Indians who would preserve it in their own writings" (quiso obrar este tan raro prodigio, tomando por medio, y como por instrumento a un Indio, para tanta gloria de su Madre, assi determinó que olvidándose los primeros Españoles de escribirlo, aunque no de celebrarlo; fuessen los Indios los que conservassen en sus escriptos proprios).[152] In Florencia's version of Becerra Tanco's argument all forms of indigenous memory were equally capable of preserving the tradition:

> By leaving to posterity the memory of this immortal omen, the Mexican Indians (although believed to have been barbarous) showed themselves to be more civilized and more grateful than the Spaniards. . . . Not only did they write this history in prose, but also recounted it in verse, and not only in their hieroglyphic figures, which they used instead of characters, but also with the letters of our alphabet after they had learned them only a few years after this apparition; and if there had been any further ways of disseminating it to future generations they would have used all of them to make their noble gratitude and attentive providence known to her.
>
> (Los Indios Mexicanos (aunque los tengan por barbaros) en dexar la posteridad de los siglos memoria inmortal deste portento, se mostraron mas politicos, y mas agradecidos, que los Españoles. . . . No solo escribieron esta Historia en prossa, sino que la contaron en metros, ni solo con sus figuras hierogliphicas, de que usaban en lugar de caracteres; sino tambien con las letras de nuestro Alphabeto, luego que las aprendieron, que fue pocos años despues desta Aparicion: y si mas modos huvieron tenido de hacerla notoria a las edades futuras, de todos huvieron usado, para darla conocer su noble gratitud, y atenta providencia).[153]

Indeed, he argues, indigenous painters are still the most adept at reproducing the painting. Thus although Florencia integrates several of Becerra Tanco's arguments, including the nobility of indigenous record keeping, which was assigned to "the most capable of the natives who, because of their nobility and authority, had the responsibility of being chroniclers" (los Naturales mas capaces, en quienes por su nobleza, y Authoridad, recayó la obligación de Chronistas), he does not present indigenous tradition as a hermetic archive. Indeed, by noting the indigenous adoption of alphabetic script, Florencia emphasizes the transparency, rather than hermetic closure, of the Guadalupan tradition.

At the same time that he strenuously argues that the apparition was Creole and not Spanish, as a sermon in Madrid had claimed, Florencia avoids the Creole hermeneutics of Sánchez and Becerra Tanco. Rather, he presents widespread indigenous devotion, for which Juan Diego becomes a model, as the most important effect of the miraculous image. Florencia's emphasis on the clarity of indigenous memory parallels his argument that the apparition was directed toward indigenous commoners, whom he presents as humble and devoted Christians. Although, he says, the Virgin "appeared and remained as an image for all, Spanish and Indians, blacks, and whites" (se apareció, y quedó en retrato, para todos, Españoles, e Indios, negros, y blancos) the miracle was "more for the Indians" (más para los Indios).[154] In enumerating the variants of current veneration he writes: "Let us begin with the Indians as the miraculous favor of the Virgin began with them. They have such singular and superlative affection for this Venerable Virgin that it is impossible to find a house or Indian shack, however poor it may be, without her; and not only in Mexico but in the entire kingdom" (Empezemos por los Indios, pues empezo por ellos el milagroso favor de la Virgen. En ellos es tanto, y tan singular el afecto a esta Venerable Virgen, que no se hallará casa, o choza de Indio, por pobre que sea, sin ella: y esto no solo en Mexico, sino en casi todo el Reino).[155] Whereas previous authors had called the Virgin's skin color "olive," perhaps associating her with a Mediterranean origin, Florencia is the first to give the skin tone of the image an indigenous pigment: "I cannot help but admire and venerate the discretion of the Lady of Guadalupe who, since she came to win over the will of the natives to the devotion of God, wished to resemble them in her dress and countenance, esteeming their skin and golden hue in order to win them over and move them to devotion through resemblance" (no puedo dejar de admirar, y venerar la discreción de la Señora de Guadalupe, que como venia a aficionar las voluntades de los Naturales, para ganarlos con su devocion para Dios; quiso parecer, y aparecer en su trage preciandose de su tez, y color trigueño; para conciliarles con la semejanza la aficion, y atraerles las voluntades).[156] Finally, whereas previous commentators had downplayed the role of Juan Diego, describing him simply as a "humble Indian," Florencia investigates the details of his life, including the argument that Juan Diego had remained celibate, despite the fact that he was married.[157]

Although he was involved in Florencia's work, for which he wrote the approval, Sigüenza approached the historicity of the apparition from a distinct angle. In his introductory approval of the work, just as in the *Triunfo parthénico*, he attributes a lack of documentation to Creole negligence.[158] Florencia himself acknowledges Sigüenza several times in his work, most prominently as the owner of a "select library" (selecta librería) that contributed a key manuscript containing the Spanish translation of a Nahuatl version of the apparition.[159]

Both Florencia and Sigüenza attribute this document to the early seventeenth-century mestizo author Fernando de Alva Itlilxochitl, a descendent of the Texcoco kings. Yet as his criticism of Florencia in his later *Piedad heroyca* (Heroic Piety) (c. 1691–93) indicates, Sigüenza differed vigorously with Florencia on the authorship of the Nahuatl original. While Florencia declared the author to be Jerónimo de Mendieta, a sixteenth-century Franciscan friar, Sigüenza scoffed at this notion.[160] As noted earlier, he insisted that the author was Antonio Valeriano, one of the most prominent of the sixteenth-century indigenous scribes.[161] The difference between their theories is significant. Florencia, in keeping with his emphasis on the miraculous confirmation of indigenous conversion, lent relatively little weight to written documentation of the Guadalupan tradition. By contrast, Sigüenza sought to link the written trail as closely to the events of the apparition as possible.

If what has been cited as his final writing on the Virgin of Guadalupe is correctly attributed, Sigüenza further attempted to remedy the lack of documentation in the final year of his life. The manuscript, which has been given the title "Critical Annotations" ("Anotaciones críticas") appears to have been written in 1699 and was likely written by Siguënza.[162] Indeed, the author does adopt a version of the empirical stance that Sigüenza had taken in his poem *Primavera indiana*: "there is nothing else possible to investigate beyond the historical circumstances that preceded it and the steps by which this sovereign portent arrived to us" (no ay en el otra cosa capaz de inquisicion sino es la serie historial de las circunstancias, que precedieron, y los pasos, por donde se nos encaminô este soberano Portento).[163] While Sigüenza's early poem focused on the mystical transition effected by the image, however, the "Critical Annotations" reconstructs the history of events leading up to the apparition. With this, the manuscript attempts to overcome the discontinuous archive by providing a bridge between the violence of the conquest and the mystical foundation of a new society.

The author begins by explaining the significance of the site of the apparition: "in the most fruitless, arid, and least privileged place in New Spain, there God planted the new paradise of his pleasures and the Viridiarium of his delights. Today that which is Catholic Guadalupe before was heathen Tepeyacac" (en el mas inutil, mas arido, y menos gracioso puesto de nueva españa, alli planto Dios el nuevo paraiso de sus plazeres, y el Viridiario de sus delicias. El que hoy es el catolico Guadalupe fue antes el gentilico Tepeiacac).[164] The meaning of this site, the author argues, may be found in the Nahuatl etymology of Tepeyac as "Nose-Hill" (Nariz de Cerro): "they called it thus to signify a point and sharp extremity at whose cragged peaks the mountains that come from the north and stretched to midday ended . . . and whose tip pointed toward the great temple, or shrine, that was in the main square, that they called Tlatelolco, today Tlatilulco" (llamaronle assi, para significar una punta, y extremidad sobresaliente, en cuya desigualdad rematan los cerros, que vienen de norte a medio dia. . . . Y a la quenta apuntaba al gran Cu, o adoratorio, que estaba en la plaza mayor, que llamaban el Tlatelolco, hoy Tlatilulco).[165] The hillside was a perfect vantage point from which to witness the sacrifices to Huitzilopochtli, the Mexican god of war with whom the Spanish had associated the most excessive cruelty of pagan idolatry.[166] The apparition of the Virgin, "the Tower of Purity" (la Torre de la pureza), thus counteracted the pinnacle of idolatry. On Tepeyac, moreover, the Virgin appeared "together, at the foot of a particular tree, which has in front of it a spring of mineral water" (junto, y al pie de cierto arbol, que tiene de frente el manatial de agua de alumbre).[167] The Virgin's apparition transformed the barren landscape and highest point of idolatry to a sealed and protected spring: "Thus they questioned the hardness of rocks and the softness of a spring answered" (Preguntaban pues a la dureza de las piedras; y respondiales la blandura del manatial).[168] Indeed, following an image from the Song of Songs, the Virgin's image acted as a seal that enclosed its purity: "the venerable place put a fence, roof, and seal on the image, converting it into a eulogy to the songs in which the Virgin is called 'sealed or enclosed fountain,' *Fons, signatus*" (Puso dentro de la Imagen, cercô, techo, y sello con llave el venerable lugar, reduciendo a practica un elogio de los Cantares en que se llama la Virgen Fuente sellada, o cerrada, Fons, signatus).[169]

After detailing the mystical power of the apparition, the author turns to the prehistory of the site. Unlike other accounts that elide the violence of the conquest, the "Critical Annotations" links the apparition directly to the actions of the conquistadors. Drawing on Bernal Díaz del Castillo's chronicle of the Mexican conquest, the author argues that in preparation for the apparition, the Spanish conquistador Gonzálo de Sandoval destroyed the idol found at Tepeyac.[170] If the Spanish chronicles preserve a record of the destruction of the Tepeyac idol, however, it is the "heathen books of the Indians" (libros gentílicos de los indios)[171] that best preserve the events of the apparition itself. Indeed, the manuscript provides the most complete description of the map that Becerra claims to have seen in the possession of Alva Ixtlilxochitl. Although a representation of Moctezuma allows the author to confirm the map's antiquity,[172] the most telling aspect of his discussion is his explanation of indigenous script itself. Taking issue with Florencia's comparison of indigenous glyphs to Chinese characters, he finds instead that they are closer to Egyptian hieroglyphs because of their use of "images" (imágenes).[173] He also notes that the Mexican calendar is a "most noble thing" (cosa nobilissima) because of "the regularity with which they computed their ages" (la regularidad, que tenian en la computacion de sus edades). Citing Becerra, he argues that "Indians so savage in other ways could not have such an exact count of their years except through another medium, which was that of the Apostle Saint Thomas" (esta quenta tan firme de los años no la pudieron tener estos Indios tan incultos por otro medio, que por el de el Apostol Santo Tomas) but adds that "I am of the opinion that he also taught them the characters with which they were to record the year counts" (discurro yo que tambien les enseñaria los caracteres, con que havian de notar essos mismos años, y quentas).[174] The author thus makes explicit an assumption that pervaded Creole antiquarianism: that "Indians so savage" could not have invented their own writing and calendrical systems. The archive, in this sense, most naturally pertains to the Creoles, who possessed the skills to interpret its hermetic truth.

From the beginning of the century, the Creole promotion of the stories of St. Thomas's evangelizing and the apparition of the Virgin of Guadalupe provided alternative perspectives on the status of recently converted indigenous subjects. Whereas Solórzano's 1648 definition of indigenous subjects as "miserable" gave juridical weight to continued indigenous tutelage, during the seventeenth century the Virgin of Guadalupe instituted a new figure for indigenous faith, the prototype for which was the humble and devout Juan Diego. The distinction between these two versions of indigenous subjects may be seen in the divergent uses of the term "miserable" in seventeenth-century texts. Nearly contemporaneously with Solórzano's juridical treatise, the powerful Bishop Juan de Palafox wrote that the job of priests was "to show compassion to the miserable and afflicted" (compadecerse de los miserables, y afligidos).[175] But by the end of the seventeenth century, Florencia applied the term "miserable" only to preconquest commoners, writing, for instance, that the purpose of the Virgin's apparition was to redeem the "miserable Indians sacrificed to the devil" (miserables Indios sacrificados al Demonio).[176] Once their Christianity had been confirmed, indigenous subjects became cleansed of this source of their "misery:" the Virgin of Guadalupe was a "counterpoison of the Poisons" (contraveneno de los Toxicos) and an "antidote to Idolatries" (antidoto de las Idolatrías).[177] Florencia takes both Juan Diego and his uncle as a prototype for this renewed indigenous innocence: "the little Indian, to whom this occurred, is not less worthy because he is an Indian; since Juan Diego and Juan Bernardino were also Indians and were given credence by the archbishop and visited by the Sovereign Queen of Angels who does not attend to the rank of her subjects but rather to the innocence and candor of their souls" (El Indiecito, a quien sucedió, no desmerece el credito por ser Indio; pues Juan Diego lo era, y Juan Bernardino, y merecieron ser creidos del Arzobispo, y visitados de la Soberana Reina de los Angeles, que no ira a la condicion de las personas, sino a la innocencia y candidez de las almas).[178] The apparition, in Florencia's account, thus redeemed indigenous subjects from the permanent state of "misery" they had held in the midcentury works of Solórzano and Palafox.

If in Creole accounts the Virgin of Guadalupe thus confirmed indigenous separation from idolatry, the break in indigenous memory also allowed Creoles to appropriate artifacts from the pre-Columbian past. In order to authorize indigenous documents, Creoles emphasized the nobility of the indigenous scribes. Yet while members of the indigenous elite, such as Alva Ixtlilxochitl, might have contributed to preserving this archival record, nobles were only a midway point in the recovery of an apostolic Christianity that pervaded all forms of indigenous memory in the Creole archive. If St. Thomas did not succeed in converting indigenous subjects in Becerra's account, in the late seventeenth-century "Critical Annotations" the apostle did provide the origin of indigenous computation and writing, which, in the Neoplatonic tradition, denoted an archaic and even Adamic script. It was not the violence of the Spanish conquest that could unleash the potential of indigenous documents, but rather the scholarship of later Creoles who could interpret them allegorically. As in Sigüenza y Góngora's *Glorias de Querétaro*, Creole antiquarianism envisioned the passage of visual artifacts from the indigenous elite to Creole society as a repayment for the benefits of conquest. For Creoles such as Sigüenza it was only this permanence of an archaic past that could overcome the violent divisions of imperial time.

CHAPTER 3

Mexican Hieroglyphics

Creole Antiquarianism and the Politics of Empire

Throughout the seventeenth-century Habsburg world, highly orchestrated urban spectacles provided one of the most public faces of political and ecclesiastical power. Combining parades, theater, music, and ephemeral visual art, including elaborate allegorical floats and firework displays, Baroque festivals broke the routine of daily life by providing mass entertainment in a carnivalesque atmosphere.[1] In the urban centers in Spanish America, as in Madrid, public festivals commemorated religious and state celebrations throughout the year. The extent to which these spectacles dominated urban life is nothing less than astounding: it has been estimated that at the height of spectacle culture in Mexico there were ninety processions or celebrations of some kind a year.[2] Printed accounts (*relaciones*) recounting the details of festivities held for religious and state celebrations such as Corpus Christi, *autos-da-fe*, and the entrance of church and state officials give a clear picture of the organizational intent behind these events. Replete with tropes of excess intended to add grandeur to the celebration, the accounts also provide details about the ephemeral art, processions, and social circumstances of each festival. Central to many descriptions were the representations of the urban populace. Coordinated around confraternities defined by ethnic and pre-Columbian political divisions, the procession itself provided a visualization of the groups that made up urban society. Meanwhile, the crowds that thronged the streets added support to the idea that the city as a whole was unified around the motive at hand.

But although the participation of confraternities in official festivities was enforced through penalties for no-shows,[3] the highly encomiastic nature of the relaciones has made it difficult to generalize from the descriptions about the actual effect of processions on popular culture. According to José Antonio Maravall's well-known thesis, Baroque festivals in Spain created a state of awe (*asombro*) among spectators.[4] In this passive state, he argued, the crowd was particularly susceptible to associations between festive artifice and divine power.[5] Maravall concludes that the Spanish absolutist state used this visual staging to direct the passions of the crowd toward affective adherence to figures of power.[6] Although it continues to dominate much of the scholarly literature on festivals, Maravall's theory has been critiqued for assigning too much power and unity to the early modern Spanish state and too little agency to spectators.[7] In the case of Spanish American festivities, the additional factor of the geographical distance between viceregal subjects and the Spanish Crown must be posited. Not only was the viceregal polity itself divided juridically and socially, but the presence of the Creole elite, who identified racially with peninsular subjects but was formally excluded from holding the higher viceregal offices, created an additional layer of mediation between the local populace and metropolitan governance. In this context, part of the task of the accounts was to distinguish among these different social categories while also giving the appearance of a unified polity homologous to its transatlantic counterpart.

Nowhere was this complex political relationship addressed more publicly than in the entrance of church and state officials into viceregal cities. The viceregal entrance was a highly ritualized affair that drew from the Roman tradition of the triumph, in which the emperor crossed the threshold of the welcoming city. The Renaissance version of this ritual increasingly emphasized the symbolic unity of the early modern state through a web of visual signs and theatrical performances.[8] In Spanish America, the ritual of the viceroy's entrance into the city thus provided an ideal platform for the local elite to pay homage before the official representative of the Crown.[9] As in European counterparts, some of the most impressive structures marking the entrance of the viceroy into Spanish American cities were triumphal arches. As opposed to the stone monuments of the Roman triumph, the early modern adaptations were ephemeral structures built of wood, carton, and paper and ornately painted with emblems, decorative motifs, and poetry. Placed at pivotal points along the viceroy's route through the city, they were meant to symbolize the meaning accorded to the viceroy's entrance. City councils (*cabildos*), responsible for receiving the viceroys, bestowed the task of creating the arches on members of the Creole elite who were charged with finding adequate allegories to symbolize and honor arriving officials.[10] An exercise in decorum, the theme of each arch had both an encomiastic and a jussive role, simultaneously lauding the official and challenging him to carry out his mandate in accordance with early modern political values.[11]

Towering over the plaza where they were erected, the arches themselves were undoubtedly visually impressive; but their central attraction was surely the emblems that adorned their façades and provided the visual code for the festivities in a mysterious and hermetic political language. By no means limited to processions, early modern emblems were an extensive iconographic system common to humanists in Europe and the Americas. Invented in the sixteenth century, Renaissance emblems drew on the Neoplatonic fascination with Egyptian hieroglyphs. Following the 1419 rediscovery of a manuscript mistakenly attributed to the Egyptian priest Horapollo, Renaissance humanists such as Marsilio Ficino turned their attention to hieroglyphics in the belief that their exegesis would uncover pre-Edenic divine knowledge. Horapollo's manuscript also provided the model for Andrea Alciato's 1577 invention of emblems, visual enigmas that drew heavily on classical and hermetic iconography.[12] Together with handbooks of symbols such as Piero Valeriano's *Hieroglyphica* (Hieroglyphics) (1556) and Cesare Ripa's *Iconologia* (Iconology) (1593), Alciato's emblems influenced almost all areas of cultural production of the Spanish American elite, from poetry and theater to painting, iconographic illustrations of moral lessons, sermons, and other visual and verbal artifacts.[13] The basic structure of the emblem combined an iconographic visual icon with a verbal text, usually in the form of a poem, adage, or short title. Each of these components partially expressed the emblem's hidden meaning, which the reader was challenged to decipher.[14] In the case of the emblems that adorned the triumphal arches of viceregal entrances, the printed accounts of the event often specified the meaning of each emblem in an extensive *explicatio*. Written in an obtuse and dense prose, the accounts continued to imbue emblems with mystery even as they exposed their hidden allegorical meanings. While this rhetoric of mysterious instruction created the possibility that their authors might use the triumphal arches to veil political critique as well as praise, the allegories themselves were invariably quite tame, intended to produce panegyric and laudatory reflections of the new official based on common iconographic and mythological themes drawn from the manuals.

For the most part, any direct political message was limited to the figuration of ideal governance often through the advocacy of virtuous rule in the tradition of the "mirror of princes."[15]

In one of the best known viceregal entrances in the colonial period, in 1680 the Mexico City *cabildo* and cathedral chapter chose Carlos de Sigüenza y Góngora and Sor Juana Inés de la Cruz to create dual triumphal arches to celebrate the arrival of the new viceroy, Don Tomás Antonio de la Cerda, Marqués de la Laguna. The commissions provided the two young members of the Creole elite an unparalleled public forum to make their names. The allegories they chose for their respective arches, however, betray a marked discrepancy in their political stances toward viceregal authority. For her arch, *Neptuno alegórico* (Allegorical Neptune), Sor Juana created emblems based on the resonances between the title of the entering viceroy, "Laguna," and the lake on which Mexico City was built. This witty pun provided the extensive mythological motif for her arch: Neptune, of whom she claimed the viceroy was a modern avatar. Through the emblems that adorned her arch, Sor Juana allegorized the feats of the mythical god as analogies for the viceroy's own virtues even as she played on the metaphor of the ocean for the lake to call attention to the perennial problem of flooding in the city.[16] As has often been noted, Sigüenza's arch was strikingly distinct from Sor Juana's. Rather than adopting a classical myth for his allegory, Sigüenza based his emblems on the lineage of Mexica kings who had ruled Tenochtitlan before the arrival of the Spanish. Each of the twelve emblems that adorned the arch linked a Mexica monarch to a political virtue necessary for "good governance:" "my intention being," as he explains in his accompanying text, "to exalt imperial virtues, so that these may serve as an example" (siendo mi fin hazer alarde de las *virtudes imperiales*, para que sirvan de *exemplo*).[17]

The novelty of Sigüenza's arch should not be underestimated. From the time of the conquest, indigenous cultural artifacts, especially those of the Mexica, had appeared in spectacles, art, and architecture in both Europe and the Americas.[18] Yet these appearances were inevitably remembrances of political subjugation or decorative interpretations of American barbarism, as in the 1637 celebrations held at the Buen Retiro in Spain in which Indians were represented by forty participants "dressed as savages" (con disfraz de salvajes).[19] When Mexica leaders were portrayed, these representations always included a gesture of submission, as in the 1677 celebrations of Carlos II's coronation held in Mexico City. In these, the representation of Amerindian subjects who as "sons of our America ... came forth dressed following the example and prestige of the memorable Moctezuma" (hijos de nuestra América ... iban vestidos a ejemplo y gala del memorable Moctezuma) was balanced by Moctezuma's own gesture of subjugation to the Spanish monarchy. "Aside from the crown, which splendidly ennobled his brow" (Demás de la corona, que lucidamente ennoblecía sus sienes), the text notes that a footman carried another "with a gesture offering it to our majesty the king, Carlos II" (con ademán de rendirla a nuestro rey y señor Carlos Segundo).[20] Sigüenza's arch thus breaks with the convention of public spectacles in New Spain in two ways: first, by electing to allegorize through local figures, rather than those common to the pan-European iconographic repertoire, and second, by presenting pre-Columbian kingship as a model for viceregal governance, rather than touting indigenous submission to the Spanish Crown. Indeed, Sigüenza opens his text by defending the "risky" novelty of his arch: "One could judge the unusual idea for the design of my arch as a dangerous reef upon which good sense risked running aground, as if leaving the well trodden paths of the ancients were tantamount to drawing near the precipice and danger" (Escollo en que peligrase el acierto pudiera jusgarse de mi idea en la disposicion formal del *Arco*, que aqui descrivo lo extraordinario, como si apartarse de las trilladas veredas de los Antiguos fuera acercarse al precipicio, y al riesgo).[21]

Despite Sigüenza's own emphasis on its riskiness, his arch has for the most part been interpreted as a relatively staid political intervention. Most readers have focused on the fact that while he introduces the pre-Columbian kings as models for viceregal governance, the virtues he draws from their examples are quite common in the European literature of statecraft.[22] Historians in search of the roots of Creole patriotism have also been frustrated by Sigüenza's florid Gongoresque prose style, with its dense hyperbata and labyrinth of citations drawn from classical and modern authorities.[23] For the most part, this style has been interpreted as an impediment to a clear political program in a version of the long-standing association between Gongorism and obscurity.[24] David Brading comments, for instance, that "such a maze of conflicting opinions served more to magnify Sigüenza's erudition than to expose his own sentiments. Nevertheless, he reached to the same sources to justify his innermost convictions."[25] Anthony Pagden echoes this idea when he writes, "Sigüenza y Góngora's arch was an opportunity to press home, in as direct a manner as was available to him ... a striking if still confused political message."[26] Others have assumed that the text, like the arch itself, was purposely convoluted and obscurantist. The triumphal arch, argues Serge Gruzinski, "was a game of scholars for an intellectual public, those *erúditos* [sic] whose approval Sigüenza y Góngora was seeking."[27] Meanwhile, defenders of Gongoresque aesthetics such as Roberto González Echevarría have celebrated this same quality of Sigüenza's text: "the Colonial Baroque is surface, festival, mask.... The culmination of this tendency can perhaps be found, like an emblem, in Carlos de Sigüenza y Góngora's *Theatro de virtudes políticas.*"[28]

Yet although the arch cannot be equated with a clear political program as such, neither should it be considered a mere repetition of the literature of European statecraft. Sigüenza's lengthy and convoluted explanation suggests instead that the display and defense of the arch were two moments of a political speech act. The value of the Mexica kings lay not only in their examples of political virtues but also in their ability to bridge the distance between a local polity and the Spanish monarch: "And clearly, if the intention is to propose examples for imitation, it would be an insult to one's PATRIA to scavenge for foreign heroes among those from whom the Romans learned to exercise their virtues, and all the more so since even among peoples reputed to be barbarous there are more than enough precepts upon which to found a civil order" (Y claro está que si era el intento proponer para la imitacion exemplares, era agraviar a su PATRIA mendigar estrangeros heroes de quienes aprendiesen los Romanos á exercitar las virtudes, y mas quando sobran preceptos para asentar la politica aun entre las gentes que se reputan por barbaras).[29] Rather than simply salvaging the reputation of the Mexica, Sigüenza seems to equate the redemption of present Mexico as a whole with the recognition of its civilized past. It is this redemptive function that is missing from "foreign" models such as the mythological deities that guided Roman governance.

As Sigüenza goes on to argue, however, patriotic representation is not only valuable for those who govern but also for those governed. Citing Isaac Papin, he argues the benefit of "patria" for the "souls" of its subjects: "the beautiful love of virtue should not be sought in foreign models; domestic praise moves souls and it is better to know of local triumphs" (*Neque enim externo monitore petendus / Virtutis tibi pulcher amor, cognata ministret. / Laus animos*, praestat que domi novisse triumphos).[30] Patriotic examples thus appear to have an almost physiological effect upon citizens, in turn defined as those who "live" through its force:

"Whoever is a citizen lives not for himself, but rather for his patria," as Farnesio says in his *de Simulacro Reip.* book I. fol. 51. Even if there is no one to promote [the patria], it lacks nothing that is admired in other cities. And even lacking these circumstances, we should never falter in our efforts when the motive remains constant. "Therefore the PATRIA is salutary," continues Farnesio, "a sweet name [and] nobody dedicates himself to it because it is illustrious or magnificent, but rather because it is the PATRIA."

(*Qui civis est non sibi, sed* PATRIAE *vivit*, que dixo Farnesio de Simulacro Reip. lib. I. fol. 51. como falta quien la promueva, y mas no faltando en ella quanto en todas las lineas puede afrontarse con lo que en otras se admira grande. Y aun quando le faltara esta circunstancia nunca se havia de perdonar al conato por estar siempre tan persistente el motivo. *Res est igitur salutaris* PATRIA, prosigue Farnesio, *nomen suave, nec id circo quis quam est studiosus quia aut praeclara aut magna est, sed quia* PATRIA *est*.)[31]

In Sigüenza's description the arch provides not only a model for governance for the new viceroy but also a means to transmit a local past. The emblems must mirror the grandeur of the viceroy but, perhaps more importantly, they must also create citizens by moving and directing their "souls" toward the patria.

The challenge that Sigüenza faced, then, was to find an appropriate medium that would simultaneously accomplish these two goals. His solution was the emblematic form itself. As opposed to Sor Juana's definition of her emblems as "hieroglyphs" that will protect the mystery of the viceroy's power, Sigüenza cites another common definition that emphasizes the balance between the iconographic and literary components of the emblem through the metaphor of the "body" and the "soul."[32] As Sigüenza writes of his arch, it is the viceroy who will provide the "spirit" to animate the "body" of the emblems: "And if it was fortune that determined that at some point the Mexican monarchs were to emerge from the ashes of oblivion so that like phoenixes of the West they could be consecrated to immortal fame, then there was never a better time than the present since it is Your Excellency who will infuse them with spirit" (Y si era destino de la Fortuna el q' en alguna ocasión renaciesen los Mexicanos Monarcas de entre las cenizas en que los tiene el olvido, para que como Fenizes del Occidente los inmortalizase la Fama: nunca mejor pudieron obtenerlo, que en la presente, por haver de ser V. Ex[a] quien les infundiese el espíritu.)[33] Thus, if Sigüenza defines patria as that which "moves the soul" of its citizens, it appears that Mexica history cannot do this on its own but must rely on an infusion of "spirit" from outside.

Mexican Hieroglyphics

Although Sigüenza employs local history in the interest of delineating a Mexican patria, then, he does not imagine his arch to be an autonomous structure, nor to overcome the need for the representative of the monarch. The viceroy's role, however, is limited to a specific function: he will "animate" the "body" of the emblems so that the Mexica kings may be reborn as the foundation of New Spain's governance.

Sigüenza's closing remarks, in the final lines of his treatise, suggest that he has understood his task as one of balancing his debt to both a Novohispanic patria and Spanish governance. This debt has put him in a difficult position, which he has overcome through the symbolic form of the emblem:

> In this way I fulfilled (as well as I could) the duty bestowed upon me by my PATRIA on such a grand occasion, observing Casan's remarks on Plato, book *de Amore*, in *Cathal.* part I. consid. 50, "The perfect praise is that which describes the origins of things, narrates the present form, and shows future events." Thus the description of this arch contains the origin of the Mexican government, and all else that I hope to see fulfilled.
>
> (De esta manera sali (como pude) del empeño en que me puso mi Patria, en ocasion tan grande, observando lo que de Platon, lib. de Amore, dize Casan, in Cathal. parte I. Consid. 50. *Perfecta laudatio est, quae precedentem rei recenset originem, praesentem formam narrat, sequentes ostendit eventus.* Pues en la descripcion de este Arco se halla el principio del Mexicano govierno, y lo demas que me prometo muy cierto.)[34]

It is clear from Sigüenza's remarks that the fusion of local history and viceregal governance in the emblems of the Mexica kings, if unwieldy and enigmatic, is nonetheless the only foundation of governance that will respond to the dual demands placed on local citizens. Sigüenza's citation further indicates that the future governance of New Spain depends on recuperating the history of its "origins." Indeed, the emblems are an allegorical form of history that will collapse the time of patria into one figure: the "perfect praise" that "describes the origins of a thing, narrates the present form, and shows future events." The arch as a whole, therefore, becomes a cipher for the foundation of good governance by providing a link between origin and future.

THE BROKEN MIRROR OF THE SPANISH MONARCHY

The play of mirrors in Sigüenza's arch was itself an extreme reflection of the peculiar structure of Spanish imperial administration. As J. H.

Elliott notes, the fact that the Spanish-held territories were referred to as the *monarquía española*, rather than "empire," shows the extent to which the king served as a reference of indivisibility. The emphasis on symbolic unity in Spanish imperialism thus produced a particular version of what Ernst Kantorowicz has called the doctrine of the "king's two bodies": one natural and subject to death and the other mystical and eternal.[35] Indeed, in the Spanish monarchy the natural body of the king appears to have absorbed the mystical element of medieval kingship. Elliott notes that, as opposed to the monarchs of other European states, "at the end of the sixteenth century, the kings of Spain apparently had no official throne, no sceptre, no crown" and held no coronation ceremony.[36] The most powerful of European monarchs was represented instead by the spartan and almost homely images of his official portraiture, an austerity that was further epitomized by the stripped-down palace of the Escorial, designed and built by Felipe II at the height of Spanish power. Thus, the king's body itself became closely tied to an image of moral rectitude, the representation of which was more important than the divine aura surrounding the throne.[37] In her study of the representation of kingship in early modern Spanish theater, Dian Fox cites an example in which the king and queen, attending a theatrical performance, sat facing their own portraits. She concludes that "only portraits permitted everyone in the hall to see the king and queen, present both as part of the audience and as part of the staging. As many Spanish dramatists of the period insist, in order to be loved, the king must be seen."[38]

This unifying concept, however, was a necessary compensation for what was actually a loosely articulated political network composed of distant polities with little in common with one another. Actual administration depended on an extensive bureaucracy established during the reigns of Carlos V and Felipe II.[39] The problem became how to multiply the king's body in the extensive overseas monarchy, and the solution was the viceroy. Literally conceived of as the king's substitute, the viceroy denied the problem of the absence of the king's natural body in such an extensive empire by maintaining the "fiction central to the structure of the Spanish Monarchy—the fiction that the king was personally present in each of his territories."[40] The practice of substituting the viceroy for the king's physical presence was derived from Aragonese rule. While Castilian unification was carried out through law, in Aragon the customary legal code was left intact in each of the provinces. To preserve the unity of the kingdom, a substitute for the king, known as the *vice gerens* and usually a member of the royal family, was sent to every province. The constant fear of Creole political power and the specter of insurrection by dispossessed colonial subjects meant that the principle of loose constitutionalism underlying governance in Aragon was not recognized in the Americas.[41] Instead, the viceroy was the image and executor of the monarch and the Consejo de Indias. Other restrictions were aimed at preventing the viceroy from forming permanent ties to the American territories. The viceroy's tenure was limited and although he was allowed to take his family with him, his children could not marry Americans. Thus, rather than a system directly structured on negotiation with a native elite, as in Aragon, the regulation of the American viceroy was aimed at preventing the Creolization of viceregal administration.[42]

Diego de Saavedra Fajardo's emblem 33, contained in the collection of emblems he created for Prince Carlos Baltasar and published as *Idea de un príncipe político-cristiano* (Idea of a Political Christian Prince) (1633), best illustrates the principle of unity in Spanish kingship. In the emblem (Figure 8) a lion faces a mirror cracked down the middle. The broken halves of the mirror reflect his figure in two identical shadowy images. The motto above the image reads, "Always the Same" (Siempre el mismo) and the *explicatio* develops this adage:

> that which the mirror represents in its entirety, it also represents in each of its parts after having been broken; in this manner, one sees the lion in the two pieces of mirror of this impresse, thus signifying the fortitude and generous constancy that the prince must conserve at all times. The mirror is the public in which the world is seen; thus stated King Don Alonso the Wise, referring to the actions of kings and recommending caution so that men will follow the example of what they see them do, and this is why it is said of [kings] that they are like mirrors in which men will see their likeness as comely or deformed. For this reason, whether prosperous fortune has kept it whole, or adversity has broken it, the mirror must always show the same appearance.
>
> (lo que representa el espejo en todo su espacio, representa también despues de quebrado en cada una de sus partes; así se ve el Leon en los dos pedazos del espejo desta empresa, significando la fortaleza, i generosa constancia, que en todos tiempos ha de conservar el Príncipe. Espejo es público, en quien se mira el mundo; así lo dijo el Rey Don Alonso el Sabio tratando de las acciones de los Reyes, i encargando el cuidado en ellas. Porque los Omes tomen exemplo dellos, de lo que les ven fazer; e sobre esto dijeron por ellos, que son como espejo, en que los Omes ven su semejanza de apostura, o de anatieza. Por tanto, o ya

Figure 8. "Always the Same" ("Siempre el mismo") from Diego de Saavedra Fajardo, *Idea de un príncipe político-christiano* (Valencia, 1655). Courtesy of the Bancroft Library, University of California, Berkeley.

sea que le mantenga entero la fortuna próspera, o ya que le rompa la adversa, siempre en él ha de ver un mismo semblante.)[43]

Although Saavedra's emblem represents the desirability of the Neostoic trait of constancy in the monarch,[44] it also suggests the paradox of the geographical extension of a kingship constructed on mimesis. If in Spain the simultaneous presence of the king and his mirror image enhanced the illusion that his natural body had absorbed the mystical properties of divine kingship, the office of the viceroy was an empty simulacrum that could not hold the mystical spirit of kingship. This explains the fact that although, as Elliott claims, Spanish kingship became stripped of ceremonial rites, these were celebrated with particular intensity in the Americas. In the absence of the original, only allegory could give meaning to the blank space of the simulacra. It also ensured that the king's alter ego remained tied symbolically to a role of reflection.[45]

In this play of mirrors, the most important aspect of processional allegories was that they not deviate from the ideal image of the absent king. For this reason, the vast majority of arches were based on conservative commonplaces of moral governance argued through a shared European language of classical mythology. Sigüenza's arch breaks with one side of this play of resemblances. Although he maintains the language of governance based on classical virtues, the content of the allegory has changed from the abstract figures of classical myth to the bodies of the Mexica kings. In the absence of the Spanish king's body from the American colonies, Sigüenza infuses the alternative "body" of Mexica kingship with the spirit of monarchy, refracted through the viceroy. By doing so, he divides the spiritual amalgam of kingship that Elliott finds in the Spanish model and returns to what Kantorowicz proposed was the metaphysical basis of kingship, albeit through the back door. The viceroy is now not the "image" but the conduit for the "spirit" of the Spanish monarch who will animate the bodies of the dead Mexica kings, themselves representative of a local patria. The spirit of patria is not divine in itself, however, but borrowed from the already mystified Spanish kingship. Thus if patria is divinely consecrated, it is not autonomous: its body and history must be continually reinfused with spirit from the outside. If this is the function that Sigüenza assigns to the person of the viceroy, the arch is the means to capture or contain the spirit of patria in an allegorical figure. Sigüenza's arch may be understood, therefore, as a "writing of history" that couples the dead matter of local history with Christian theopolitics.

Sigüenza's turn toward local history also challenged the commonly held idea that emblems in processions signified on two levels, one for the vulgo and the other for the docto. For example, in *Neptuno alegórico* Sor Juana defends the mystery of her emblems by citing Cicero's dictum that "familiarity breeds contempt" (*Nimia familiaritas contemptum parit*) and Piero Valeriano's definition of hieroglyphics as a script used to protect Egyptian gods from the common people, "so as not to vulgarize their mysteries for the ignorant commoners" (por no vulgarizar sus misterios a la gente común e ignorante).[46] Although Sigüenza's arch remains enigmatic, this is not to veil the viceroy in mystery, as in Sor Juana's definition of hieroglyphs. Instead, Sigüenza equates the historical nature of the Mexica kings with a form of local truth. Rather than an attempt to differentiate between doctos and vulgo, emblems provide a means to gain access to and communicate this elusive truth. In an argument diametrically opposed to Sor Juana's, for instance, Sigüenza cites the inappropriateness of celebrating the king's representative through "fables." Although he acknowledges that "it has been the common style among American wits to adorn the majority of triumphal portals that have been erected to receive our princes with mythological ideas from deceitful fables ... who does not see that truths revealed through a fog cannot represent themselves to the eyes but with black stains" (Estilo comun á sido de los *Americanos* Ingenios hermosear con mithologicas ideas de mentirosas fabulas las mas de las *portadas triumphales* que se han erigido para recevir á los Principes ... quien no vé que verdades que se traslucen entre neblinas no pueden representarse á la vista sino con negras manchas).[47] These "deceitful fables" are thus an inappropriate adornment for princes who are the "representatives of God" (vicarios de Dios).[48] In fact, Sigüenza ominously argues, the enigmatic form of mythological figures could as easily hide a demonic power as adorn a theocratic sovereign.[49]

Ironically, then, Sigüenza argues that the historical lineage of Mexica kings—despite its association with the pre-Columbian pagan past—is a more appropriate mirror for Spanish kingship than is classical mythology. If Sigüenza's emblems maintain enigma and obscurity, it is only in order to find an adequate ground to represent the paired "truths" of local history and a distant monarch. Thus, although he argues against basing emblems on classical mythology, he does not argue against the emblematic form itself as a medium for historiography. In his closing remarks, in fact, Sigüenza paradoxically defends the presentation of truth through enigmas and parables even as he argues against the use of fables to adorn the arch. Quoting the commentaries on Exodus by the sixteenth-century Portuguese tridentine theologian and Inquisitor, Jeronimo de Azambuja, he notes that Christ often spoke in parables since it was so difficult for kings and crowds to hear unadorned truth:

> "the saints used to keep in mind men's anxiety at hearing the truth: with what averted face and rude countenance they look upon her and with what joyful countenance they embrace falsehoods, and so considering how necessary it is for men to hear the truth, the [saints] accustomed to surround and veil the truth with parables and likenesses so that those who loathed the naked truth and whose ears were ready to hear lies, would at least hear her dressed with artifice."
>
> (*Considerabant sancti quam aegre ferrent veritatem audire: quam torvo vultu, et hirtoso naso eam aspicerent, et quam hilari facie mendacia amplexarentur et considerantes quam necessarium foret hominibus veritatem audire: veritatem parabolis, et similtudinus involvebant et velabant, ut qui veritatem nudam fastidiebat, et ad mendacia arrectas haberent aures, veritatem saltem fictis vestibus tectam audirent.*)[50]

The "naked truth" (*veritatem nudam*) that Sigüenza wished to communicate through his arch was the analogy between the spirit of the Spanish monarch and that of the pre-Columbian kings. The emblems were the "parabolic" form of transmitting this truth in a way that would move the souls of the citizens gathered to receive the official.

HUITZILOPOCHTLI AND EMBLEMATIC TRUTH

The novelty of Sigüenza's 1680 arch was this ingenious use of emblems to spiritualize what he presented as the dead matter of pre-Columbian kingship. The form that he chose for this purpose is not surprising, however. Since the sixteenth century, the combination of emblems and arches in public spectacles had been used to lend a transcendental aura to secular power.[51] By their own claims, the Jesuits were the first to introduce triumphal arches into public spectacles in colonial Mexico in their 1572 inaugural procession celebrating the numerous relics sent from Spain to adorn their churches.[52] The procession and the arch clearly indicate the Jesuits' imperial designs, as Solange Alberro has suggested, but the use of emblems to decorate the arch also marks a more subtle turn in the visual culture of the colonial religious orders.[53] As opposed to the Franciscans' use of didactic images to convert and proselytize neophytes, the Jesuit order was founded on a meditative technique in which the image itself became a route to spiritual consciousness. This sensorial technology gave a new life to visual iconography among the Creole elite schooled at Jesuit institutions, where emblems were often used for moral instruction. As the design of triumphal arches proliferated and passed into the hands of Creoles, the adaptation of emblems for state functions rested on the tension created by their panegyric analogies in which the greater the obscurity of the analogy, the more impressive its solution. Thus while the obscurity served a gatekeeper function, the shared moment of solution between author and the selected readership of the printed explanations provided a bond between their Creole authors and the arriving official. This bond suppressed, at least on an official level, any actual tensions between the colonial administration and the local elite.

A spiritual technology—"machine" (*máquina*) as Sigüenza calls it—the triumphal arch was thus a natural medium for what Jean Seznec called the "survival of the pagan gods." In his foundational study of the allegorization of classical mythology in the Renaissance, Seznec cites reference manuals of the period as the culmination of a moralizing and didactic allegory in which the pagan gods were forced to "[proclaim] philosophical truths and moral concepts" to the detriment of classical aesthetics.[54] By contrast, Walter Benjamin associated emblems with the dialectics of Baroque allegory in which the pagan gods never shed their associations with the demonic occult. Rather than consummating their transformation, allegory was a battleground for a militant Christianity on the cusp of a secular age.[55] It is notable, in this sense, that in 1680 Sigüenza remembered the pagan origins of emblems and proposed the lineage of Mexica kings as an antidote to these "deceitful fables." Emblems, he argues, are the ideal structure for attaining this historical truth since, according to Farnesio and Kircher, they have "knowledge," "virtue," and "intelligence" as their end and history as their means:

> And although I could have turned to more eccentric ideas, I thought it better not to neglect that of impresses and hieroglyphs, remembering what Farnesio wrote in his *Simulacr. Reip.*, book 1, p. 59: "Just as rivers flow toward the sea in a precipitous and headlong course, in this way hieroglyphics are hastening, by their art, to knowledge; virtue and intelligence are their ends," and furthermore knowing that these allow for historical truth as context, as the ancient Mor Issac Syro affirmed in his *Theolog. Philosoph.*, cited by Kircher, as I have already said: "The discipline of symbols (in which we include impresses, hieroglyphs, and emblems) is the science by which we express notable things, that are sometimes mysterious, with brief and compendious words variously taken at times from the sayings of wise men and at others from history."

> (Y aunque pude tambien desempeñarme con mas extraordinarias ideas, jusgue mejor no desamparar la de las Empresas, y Hieoglyphicos, acordandome lo que escrivió Farnes. de Simulacr. Reip. lib. I. pag. 59. *Nam ut flumina ferruntur ad mare praepeti et prono cursu; sic hieroglyphica sua arte rapiuntur in sapientam: meta eorum virtus est, et intelligentia,* y mas sabiendo que admiten estos la verdad de la historia, para su contexto, como afirmó el antiguo Mor Isaac Syro en su Theolog. Philosoph. citado de Kirchero donde yá dixe: *Symbolica doctrina* (en que se comprehenden Empressas, Hieroglyphicos, Emblemas) *est scientia que brevibus et compendiossis verbis insignia quaedam misteria significamus est que varia, alia ex dictis sapientum sumitur ... alia ex historiis.*)[56]

Thus, if Mexica history retains any aura of the demonic, from the perspective of the European viewer, the hieroglyphic form of the emblem transforms this resistance into a hidden "truth." By pairing this truth with the spirit of the arriving viceroy, Sigüenza's emblems exorcise a pagan residue and bind it to Christian theopolitics.

The arch's secularization of a potentially demonic resistance is underscored by its most ingenious aspect. Mexica kingship provides not only the theme of the arch but also the basis for its iconography, which is drawn from the kings' name glyphs. Sigüenza's emblems, essentially, are a translation of pre-Columbian iconographic writing into European emblems. As no visual reproduction of the arch exists, this aspect of the arch must be understood from the description of the emblems themselves and from Sigüenza's own declaration: "the impresse, or hieroglyphic, was deduced from the name of the emperor or the manner in which the Mexicans signified it in their paintings" (del nombre del Emperador, o del modo con que lo significavan los Mexicanos por sus pinturas se dedujo la Empressa, ó Hieroglyphico).[57] Name glyphs were at once one of the clearest and most symbolic aspects of pre-Columbian iconographic writing, as they were often composed of elements signifying attributes of the person described. Indeed, in their combination of contradictory symbols unified through an anthropomorphic form, name glyphs were perhaps the closest analogy to Renaissance emblems. And yet, for Sigüenza's contemporary Athanasius Kircher, Mexica glyphs also held an exotic and even occult meaning that allowed the Jesuit polymath to associate them with Egyptian hieroglyphs. By converting the name glyphs of Mexica emperors into emblems, then, Sigüenza reduces and concentrates these enigmatic qualities in a controlled iconography that accords with European visual language. After carefully detailing the twelve emblems that decorate the arch's façade, each of which is a symbolic representation of a Mexica king based on his name glyph, Sigüenza links the symbolism of each king's name to a historical anecdote from which he derives a moral lesson for leadership.

The translation of the enigma of Mexica glyphs into a transcendental political foundation may be seen most clearly in one of the strangest anomalies of Sigüenza's arch: only eleven of the twelve emblems are true Mexica monarchs. To the lineage of eleven pre-Columbian kings Sigüenza adds a surprising twelfth: not a monarch but Huitzilopochtli, the Mexica deity most demonized by the Spanish after the conquest. Although Sigüenza suggests that he includes Huitzilopochtli to give the arch numerological harmony, he also defends the importance of the deity as originator of the Mexica migration from Aztlan to Tenochtitlan:

This most beautiful machine of colors was animated, for the reasons that I have written in the second prelude, by the fiery spirit of the Mexica emperors, from Acamapich to Cuahtemoc, accompanied by Huitzilopochtli, not so much in order to complete the number of panels, but rather because he is justly deserving of praise for having led them from their patria, until now unknown, to these provinces, called in antiquity Anahuac.

(Animóse esta hermossisima maquina de colores, por las razones que dexo escritas en el Preludio 2. con el ardiente espiritu de los Mexicanos Emperadores desde ACAMAPICH, hasta QVAVHTEMOC, á quienes no tanto para llenar el numero de tableros, quanto por dignamente merecedor del elogio acompañó HUITZILOPOCHTLI, que fue el que los condujo de su Patria, hasta aora incognita, á estas Provincias, que llamó la antiguedad *Anahuac*.)[58]

Sigüenza's defense of Huitzilopochtli's historical role thus may itself be taken as a metaphor for the process of allegorization that the arch will effect, from an enigmatic and obscure origin to the clarity of historical time. This metaphor becomes clearer in Sigüenza's description of the emblem based on the glyph of Huitzilopochtli's name:

Amid clouds was painted a left arm gripping a fiery torch and accompanied by a leafy branch on which a hummingbird [*Huitzilin*] was perched, for which Virgil's *Aeneid* provided the phrase: "God is my guide." In the background, represented in the attire proper to the ancient Chichimecs [was] the valiant Huitzilopochtli, who, gesturing to the various people that which was seen in the clouds, exhorted them to migrate by proposing the destination and prize with the phrase from Genesis, chapter 43, "into a great nation." It was my intention to make understood the need for princes to begin their actions with God, so that these might excel in greatness and be venerated as heroic.

(Pintóse entre las nubes un brazo siniestro empuñando una luciente antorcha acompañada de un florido ramo en que descansaba el Pájaro *Huitzilin* á que dió mote Virgilio, 2 AEneid. *Ducente Deo*. En el Payz se representó en el trage proprio de los Antiguos *Chichimecas* el valeroso *Huitzilopochtli*, que mostrando â diferentes personas lo que en las nubes se via los exhortava al viage proponiendoles el fin, y el premio con las palabras del Genes. cap. 43. *In gentem magnam*, fue mi intento dar a entender la necesidad que tienen los Principes de principiar con Dios sus acciones, para que descuellen grandes, y se veneren heroycas).[59]

The emblem is the centerpiece of Sigüenza's argument that, rather than a god, Huitzilopochtli was a secular leader of the Mexica. Employing what Seznec argues is one of the oldest strategies for the secularization of pagan gods, euhemerism,[60] Sigüenza goes on to argue that if the Mexica mistakenly thought that Huitzilopochtli was a deity, it was because "this action [was] so well considered in their ignorant barbarism that they did not know how to repay him except through apotheosis, and so after his death they venerated him as a god" (accion tan estimada de su barbaridad ignorante, que no supieron pagarla sino con la Apotheosis, conque despues de su muerte lo veneraron por Dios).[61]

Although this argument would be novel for any of the Mexica gods, Huitzilopochtli's infamy as the war god who received copious and bloody sacrifices makes Sigüenza's apology all the more striking. Indeed, as Sigüenza goes on to argue, early Spanish chroniclers followed the Mexica deification of Huitzilopochtli unquestioningly, thus turning a historical figure into an idol. The mispronunciation of Huitzilopochtli's name in Spanish historiography reflects this misunderstanding of his true nature: "Because they were ignorant of the Mexican tongue" (Por ignorar la lengua Mexicana), he writes, the historians Antonio de Herrera, José de Acosta, Enrico Martínez, and Gregorio Garcia "called him Uitzilipuztli" (lo llamaron Uitzilipuztli).[62] And "worst of all was Bernal Díaz del Castillo in the *History of the Conquest of Mexico* who calls him Huichilobos, and whom Bartolomé de Góngora in his Octava Maravilla ms. imitates" (peor que todos Bernal Díaz del Castillo en la *Historia de la Conquista de Mexico* lo nombra *Huichilobos*, â quien en esto imita Bartholome de Gongora en su Octava Maravilla. M. S.).[63] Even the late sixteenth-century Franciscan friar Juan de Torquemada, whom Sigüenza openly admires in other writings, "declares that he was called Huitziton, even though this contradicts all the original histories of the Mexicans that are preserved today on their paper, made from the branches of the *amacuahuitl* tree and which they call *texamatl*" (dice haverse llamado *Huitziton*, siendo assi que consta lo contrario de quantas Historias de los Mexicanos se conservan oy originales pintadas en su papel, fabricado de varas del Arbol *Amacuahuitl*, que ellos llaman *Texamatl*).[64] Indeed, of Spanish historians of the Indies, only Torquemada has approached the truth when later in the *Monarquía indiana* he "gave Huitzilopochtli his true name, stating (and very well) that it is deduced from Huitzilin, which is the little bird that we call hummingbird, and from Tlahuipochtli, which means necromancer or witch doctor who throws fire, or, as others think, [from] Opochtli, which means left hand" (le dió su verdadero nombre de *Huitzilopochtli*, diziendo (y muy bien) que se deduce de Huitzilin, que es el pajarito que llamamos: Chupa-flores, y de Tlahuipochtli, que significa Nigromantico o

Hechicero, que arroja fuego; ó como quieren otros Opochtli, que es mano siniestra).[65]

The key to Sigüenza's historical interpretation of Huitzilopochtli is thus the phoneticism of the Mexica name glyphs. Even if the phonetics of the name Huitzilopochtli permits two interpretations—Opochtli or Tlahuipochtli—Sigüenza argues that these are not contradictory meanings. Although he favors Opochtli or "left hand" for his emblem, he admits that Tlahuipochtli or witch doctor (hechicero) may also be correct as long as the term *hechicero* is interpreted, as it is in Antonio de Calancha's chronicle of Peru, as "admirable, miraculous man, worker of prodigies" (hombre admirable, milagroso, obrador de prodigios) in the same sense as "magician, which in antiquity did not only include wise men . . . but also the masters and kings" (Mago, que no solo comprehendia en la Antigüedad a los Sabios . . . . sino tambien â los Superiores y Reyes).[66] A knowledge of Nahuatl and the correct pronunciation of Huitzilopochtli's name thus transforms the Spanish pronunciation from a demonic cacophony—and even the suggestion of a "wolf man" in Bernal Diaz's deformation "Huichilobos"—into a series of legible symbols indicating secular leadership inspired by a divine spirit.

To offset the demonization of Huitzilopochtli, the emblem's spiritual symbolics appropriate the huitzilin, or hummingbird, closely associated with the god. Sigüenza follows Torquemada's interpretation of the importance of the huitzilin in the migration of the Aztecs, differing only in one important respect. Both agree that the Aztecs were inspired to migrate by the repeated song of a bird, *tihui, tihui*. Indeed, this sound was hardly in need of interpretation since it is a homonym for the Nahuatl word meaning "let's go, let's go." In his *Monarquía indiana*, however, Torquemada insists that the secular leader who interpreted this sign was Huitziton and that the god Huitzilopochtli appeared only later in the migration as "the devil disguised as an idol and telling them that he was the one that had brought them out of the land of Aztlan and that they should carry him with them, that he wished to be their god and to favor them in all things and they should know that his name was Huitzilopuchtli (which in another part we have said is the same as that which the pagans called Mars, god of battles)" (el demonio en la representación de un ídolo y diciéndoles que él era el que los había sacado de la tierra de Aztlan y que le llevasen consigo, que quería ser su dios y favorecerles en todas las cosas y supiesen que su nombre era Huitzilopuchtli (que como en otra parte decimos es el que los gentiles llamaban Marte, dios de las batallas)).[67]

Repeating his argument that Huitzilopochtli was a historical leader, Sigüenza streamlines his version of the story:

> He did not earn his place among the Mexican Emperors which adorn this triumphal Portal because he was their progenitor and head, but rather because he was their guide and leader, who, inspired by the song of a bird which repeated *tihui, tihui*, which is the same in the Mexican Dialect as "let's go, let's go," persuaded the numerous Aztec peoples that they should leave their birthplace and pursue what that birdsong foresaw, which was taken as a joyous premonition of their fortunes.
>
> (Lo que le consiguió colocarle entre los Mexicanos Emperadores, conque se hermoseó la *triumphal Portada*, no tanto fue su progenitor, y Cabeza; quanto por haver sido su Conductor y Caudillo, quando, movido del canto de un pajaro, que repetía: *tihui, tihui*, que es lo mismo en el Dialecto Mexicano, que *vamos, vamos*, persuadió al numeroso Pueblo de los *Aztecas* el que dexando el lugar de su nacimiento, peregrinase en demanda del que les pronosticava aquel canto, que tenia por feliz prenuncio de su Fortuna.)[68]

By omitting the division that Torquemada makes between Huitziton and Huitzilopochtli, Sigüenza supports the dual symbolic elements of Huitzilopochtli's name: the left hand meaning "leadership" and the huitzilin signifying both a spiritual origin and direction for the Mexica journey. The unknown patria from which the Mexicas descend, therefore, is itself a hieroglyph and foreshadowing of their divine destiny: "From this fanciful illusion of a noble origin emerged the greatness and sovereignty to which the Mexicans would rise, for which they earned the generous epithet of *Great Nation*, a title that could be proven by many pages, if there were not already so many histories of their deeds, albeit seldom read" (Desta imaginada sombra de buen principio se originó la grandeza, y soberanía á que se encumbraron los Mexicanos mereciendo la denominacion generosa de *Gente grande* titulo que pudiera comprobar por muchas planas, si no huviera de sus hechos tantas historias, aunque poco leidas).[69]

MEXICA MIGRATION AND CREOLE PATRIA

It is probable that the display of Sigüenza's arch marked the first time since the conquest of Mexico that the most demonized god of the Mexica pantheon had been redeemed for use in an official public spectacle. The closest precedent for Sigüenza's interpretation was Juan de Torquemada's *Monarquía indiana* in which, as Serge Gruzinski has argued, the Franciscan read the glyph of Huitzilopochtli as an emblem that hid

Figure 9. Huitzilopochtli with a hummingbird headdress. From Juan de Tovar, *Historia de la benida de los yndios apoblar a Mexico de las partes remotas de Occidente* (ca. 1585). Courtesy of the John Carter Brown Library at Brown University.

the deity's demonic origins: "he had a golden mask . . . since divinity is hidden from the eyes of men, who cannot see it" (tenía una máscara de oro . . . por ser la divinidad oculta de los ojos de los hombres, los cuales no pueden verla).[70] According to Gruzinski, Torquemada's ability to "read" the glyphs as emblems simply gave the Franciscan a more precise vocabulary for finding the demonic power behind Aztec symbols.[71] Yet whereas the pre-Columbian glyph for Huitzilopochtli emphasized his symbolic attributes, as in the image from Juan de Tovar's sixteenth-century codex (Figure 9), Sigüenza most likely followed the westernized depictions of the Texcoco kings found in the Codex Ixtlilxochitl (Figure 10), a manuscript in his possession. By adorning a classical body with Huitzilopochtli's symbolism, Sigüenza transformed what Torquemada had interpreted as a "mask" into allegorical accoutrements symbolizing the feats of a historical figure.[72]

Rather than a demonized deity, Huitzilopochtli thus becomes both interpreter and diviner of the sign by which the Aztecs would know to found their city: the eagle perched on a nopal and eating a serpent. In

Figure 10. Texcoco kings reproduced from the Codex Ixtlilxochitl. In Giovanni Gemelli Careri, *A Collection of Voyages and Travels* (London, 1704). Courtesy of the John Carter Brown Library, Providence, Rhode Island.

indigenous codices Huitzilopochtli is depicted alternately as a leader who points the Aztecs on their way in their migration from Aztlan to Tenochtitlan or as a deified mummy, carried by the group in a shapeless bundle. In several codices, Huitzilpochtli dies and is then carried in a shapeless mummy "bundle," identified only by the huitzilin glyph attached to it.[73] Thus, along the journey Huitzilopochtli is transformed into the spirit that will be realized with arrival at Tenochtitlan. By presenting Huitzilopochtli as a leader by virtue of his ability to interpret enigmatic signs, the emblem condenses the process of emergence that the arch itself hopes to effect: the migration from the unknown to the known. Significantly, this physical movement from Aztlan to Tenochtitlan also inscribes this enigmatic origin in time, as a shadowy past, and the present as a place of historical possibility.

But if Sigüenza's interpretation translates pre-Columbian glyphs into the language of European iconography, his emblems nonetheless retain an element of impermeability. The huitzilin's call is an example of this resistance to translation. A mere bird's song for those who don't speak Nahuatl, it has meaning for those who understand the wordplay, *tihui, tihui*. A charged symbol of origin and future, it is this bird's song that holds the key to unifying the pre-Columbian past and viceregal present. By basing the solution to his emblems on Nahuatl wordplays, Sigüenza creates a new kind of enigmatic writing: a "Creole hieroglyphics." For it is only the Creole who speaks both languages, indigenous and European, and is thus able to defuse the demonic power of indigenous cultural forms by reinterpreting these in the language of Christian theopolitics. Yet whereas in the European emblematic form, wit and analogy suggest the necessity of the emblem's moral sentence, Sigüenza solves the enigma of his emblems by reading the meaning of the name glyphs in historical anecdotes. Sigüenza's arch, which presents historical development in a visual tableau, might thus be likened to the process of allegory itself, in which as Walter Benjamin asserts time becomes spatially displayed.[74] And yet, unlike the purely dialectical movement of the European allegories that Benjamin studies, the migration of the Mexica provides Sigüenza with a motif of temporal progress toward a moment of allegorical solution, or *allegoresis*. For this reason, the first emblem on Sigüenza's arch may stand in for the process that the arch itself is intended to achieve: the conversion of a pagan past into the metaphysical basis for historical continuity.

What meaning is realized in this journey? Here Sigüenza gives a twist on the common allegorization of the Aztec migration. In the pre-Columbian narrative, the meaning of the journey was the fulfillment of the prophecy and the foundation of Tenochtitlan. The Mexica vision of the symbol for Tenochtitlan fulfilled the prophecy and gave a mystical aura to the foundation of the city that allowed Spanish historians to extend the allegory, postponing its fulfillment until the arrival of the Spanish. But whereas Torquemada's reading of the same scene interprets the bird's call that incites the Aztecs to leave Aztlan in search of Tenochtitlan as a sign from the Christian God, to be fulfilled with the arrival of the Spanish, Sigüenza's emblem allows him to move beyond even this allegorization of a Christian destiny. In fact, Sigüenza does not represent the Spanish arrival as a moment of redemption, but rather as a moment of displacement and loss that necessitated the recuperation of the emperors from "the ashes of oblivion where they lie" (las cenizas en que los tiene el olvido), as he proposes that his arch will achieve. Likewise, the explanation of the emblem for the last emperor, Cuauhtemoc, represents the arrival of the Spanish as tragic, if inevitable, rather than victorious. Citations sprinkled throughout the explanation emphasize the Neostoic fortitude of the last ruler in the face of the loss of his empire and Sigüenza includes in his description the infamous anecdote of the conquest "when with unconquerable patience he suffered the torture to which the Spaniards subjected him when they burned his feet so that he would reveal the location of his treasure" (quando con invictissima paciencia sufrió el tormento, que para que por él les retornase sus tesoros le dieron los Españoles quemandole los pies).[75]

In Sigüenza's history of the migration, the allegorical end is neither the Mexica arrival in Tenochtitlan nor the Spanish conquest but rather the arrival of the viceroy. The principal passage through the arch passed beneath a plaque that, written in Latin, underlined the allegorical importance of the event by writing the year 1680 in roman numerals hidden in the marques's name (Figure 11). Below, the same year is represented as the "353rd" year after the foundation of Mexico City, a count that does not begin with the Spanish foundation but rather with the Mexica arrival at Tenochtitlan (Figure 12). Here, however, we return to the question of the image of the viceroy, whose portrait, along with the portrait of his wife, Sigüenza places amid the emblems of the emperors. As opposed to the allegorical depictions of the Aztec rulers, Sigüenza describes the portraits of the viceroys as painted so realistically that "it is possible that someone might greet them, confusing [the portrait] for the original of his acquaintance" (no aya faltado quien tal vez los salude teniendolos por el original que conoce).[76] Yet the

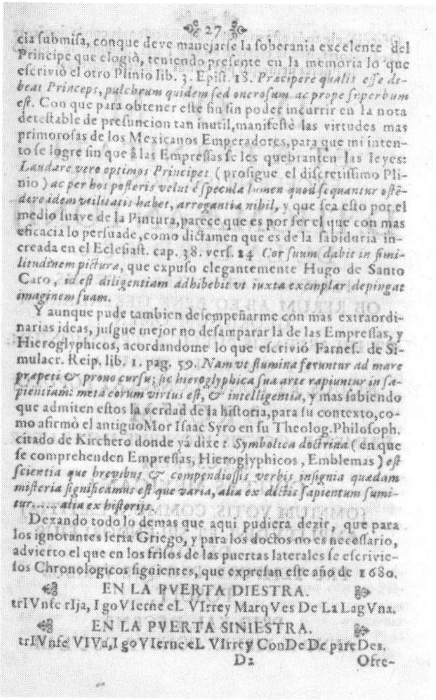

27

cia ſubmiſa, conque deve manejarſe la ſoberania excelente del Principe que elogiò, teniendo preſente en la memoria lo que eſcriviò el otro Plinio lib. 3. Epiſt. 18. *Præcipere qualis eſſe debeat Princeps, pulchrum quidem ſed onerosum ac prope ſuperbum eſt.* Con que para obtener eſte fin ſin poder incurrir en la nota deteſtable de preſuncion tan inutil, manifeſtè las virtudes mas primoroſas de los Mexicanos Emperadores, para que mi intento ſe logre ſin que à las Empreſſas ſe les quebranten las leyes: *Laudare vero optimos Principes* (proſigue el diſcretiſſimo Plinio) *ac per hos poſteris velut è ſpecula lumen quod ſequantur oſtēdere idem vtilitatis habet, arrogantia nihil*, y que ſea eſto por el medio ſuave de la Pintura, parece que es por ſer el que con mas eficacia lo perſuade, como dictamen que es de la ſabiduria increada en el Eccleſiaſt. cap. 38. verſ. 24 *Cor ſuum dabit in ſimilitudinem picturæ*, que expuſo elegantemente Hugo de Santo Caro, *id eſt diligentiam adhibebit vt iuxta exemplar depingat imaginem ſuam.*

Y aunque pude tambien deſempeñarme con mas extraordinarias ideas, juſguè mejor no deſamparar la de las Empreſſas, y Hieroglyphicos, acordandome lo que eſcriviò Farneſ. de Simulacr. Reip. lib. 1. pag. 59. *Nam vt flumina feruntur ad mare præpeti & prono curſu; ſic hieroglyphica ſua arte rapiuntur in ſapientiam: meta eorum virtus eſt, & intelligentia*, y mas ſabiendo que admiten eſtos la verdad de la hiſtoria, para ſu contexto, como afirmò el antiguo Mor Iſaac Syro en ſu Theolog. Philoſoph. citado de Kirchero donde yá dixe: *Symbolica doctrina* (en que ſe comprehenden Empreſſas, Hieroglyphicos, Emblemas) *eſt ſcientia que brevibus & compendioſſis verbis inſignia quædam miſteria ſignificamus eſt que varia, alia ex dictis ſapientum ſumitur..... alia ex hiſtorijs.*

Dexando todo lo demas que aqui pudiera dezir, que para los ignorantes ſeria Griego, y para los doctos no es neceſſario, advierto el que en los friſos de las puertas laterales ſe eſcrivieſos Chronologicos ſiguientes, que expreſan eſte año de 1680.

EN LA PVERTA DIESTRA.

trIVnfe rIja, I goVIerne eL VIrrey MarqVes De La LagVna.

EN LA PVERTA SINIESTRA.

trIVnfe VIVa, I goVIerne eL VIrrey ConDe De pareDes.

D2 Ofre-

Figure 11. The year 1680 in roman numerals incorporated into the Marqués de la Laguna's name. Carlos de Sigüenza y Góngora, *Theatro de virtudes* (Mexico, 1680), 27. Courtesy of the Nettie Lee Benson Latin American Collection, University of Texas Libraries, The University of Texas at Austin.

portraits of the viceroy and his wife are nonetheless buried in the allegory of the arch itself. Neither these portraits nor the arch's emblems can stand on their own. The entrance of the viceroy is therefore the moment of *allegoresis* in which the meaning of the allegorical fragments will be realized: "By entering the triumphal Portal on November 30 at 4:15 in the afternoon, his excellency provided the complement for this entire machine" (Diósele complemento á toda esta maquina entrando su Excelencia por la triumphal Portada á treinta de Noviembre a las quatro horas, y un quarto de la tarde).[77] At this moment, the viceroy himself united all twelve Aztec leaders into one figure: "All of the rays from the Princes were unified in his Excellency, as one can read in this

Mexican Hieroglyphics

> Ofreciòcele toda esta grandeza à su Excelencia con la siguiente Dedicatoria, que se escrivió en vna Tarja, conque se coronò la Puerta principal por donde se hizo la entrada.
>
> **D. O. M.**
> ET ÆTERNITATI
> EXCELENTISS. PRINCIPIS
> **D. THOMÆ ANTONIJ**
> DE LA CERDA, &c.
> FELICISS. PAT. PATRIÆ FORTISS.
> OB RERUM AB EO BENE GERENDARUM
> GLORIOSUM OMEN,
> ET HILARITATIS PUBLICÆ TESTIMONIUM:
> UT OMNIA, ET SINGULA
> ÆQUUS, ET BONUS CONSULAT POPULO,
> **ARCUM**
> PRIMEVÆ GENTIS ICONIBUS IMPERATOR.
> ILLUSTREM
> **CIVITAS MEXICANA**
> (OMNIUM VOTIS, COMMUNI LÆTITIA)
> AMPLITVDINI, ET SPLENDORI EIUS
> DEUOTA
> PRO TEMPORE, PROQUE VIRIBUS
> POSUIT.
> PRID. KAL. DECEMB.
> ANNO A. MEXIC. CONDIT. CCC L III.

Figure 12. Reproduction of the plaque from the 1680 triumphal arch, including the Marqués de la Laguna's name in Latin and the statement: "353rd year of the foundation of Mexico City." Carlos de Sigüenza y Góngora, *Theatro de virtudes* (Mexico, 1680), 28. Courtesy of the Nettie Lee Benson Latin American Collection, University of Texas Libraries, The University of Texas at Austin.

oracle and which experience shows to be true: 'that which has divided the blessed, you will bring together'" (Unianse todos los rayos de los Principes en su Excelencia, y alli se leía este oraculo: *Et quae divissa beatos efficiunt, collecta tenes*, demuestranos la experiencia el que es verdad).[78]

It is not at all clear, therefore, whether the Mexica kings are subordinate to the the viceroy and his wife or whether the viceroy is merely an excuse for their "reanimation": whether he lends his spirit to them or they to him.[79] This dialectical tension is paralleled by the physical position of the viceregal portraits, which, although central, are engulfed not only by the emblems of the Aztec leaders but also by other decorative details. The portraits of the viceroy and his wife, for instance, are carried by Mercury and Venus respectively. Although Sigüenza acknowledges, "I am aware that it is not licit to add to princes' portraits traits they do not possess" (no ignoro el que no es licito añadir â los retratos de los Principes lo que no tienen), he defends these allegorical details by noting that Mercury and Venus always appear together with the sun, a fitting analogy for the viceroys because of their relation to the monarch.[80] Even more surprising is an allegory for Mexico City, represented by "an Indian woman in her proper attire" (una *India* con su trage propio) sitting on a nopal cactus and placed above the portraits of the viceroy and his wife. Sigüenza defends the allegory in the following manner: "And because those who saw this understood that the arch was of the kings and the Mexican emperors and that the flower of the Tuna represents a crown, they were not surprised to see the phrase from Virgil's 3rd Eclogue crowning the nopal, 'Flowers are born with the names of Kings inscribed'" (Y sabiendo quantos lo vian, ser el Arco de los Reyes y Emperadores Mexicanos, y que la flor de la *Tuna* tiene representacion de corona, no extrañavan el mote Virgilio Eclog. 3. que coronaba al Nopal *Inscripti nomina Regum nascuntur Flores*).[81] While the viceroy's arrival is that which lends meaning to Mexica history, Sigüenza seems to equate his mystical spirit with the enigmatic local meaning contained in these vertiginous symbolic hieroglyphs.

What then is the arch that Sigüenza creates? The arch has usually been interpreted as a paradoxical mixture of bold innovation and conservative mirroring that introduces the Mexica lineage as a model but equates this with political virtues common to the literature of European statecraft. According to this reading, the only way that Creoles could appropriate the pre-Columbian past was to translate its difference into a trite political language. And yet the arch is not only a monument to remember the past but indeed projects the arrival of the viceroy as the moment when the Aztec lineage will be revived. The viceroy is only a means to unite the details of Sigüenza's triumphal arch, which will then form a "mirror" for his person and governance. The arch consecrates local sovereignty by means of a spirit that seems to be contained, as in hieroglyphs, in the mysterious details of local history. Here it is perhaps not too far-fetched to remember that the huitzilin had first appeared in postconquest symbolism as the glyph for the Holy Spirit in Pedro de Gante's pictographic catechism in the sixteenth century.[82] But what meaning does the huitzilin give to the arch? As there is no

Mexican Hieroglyphics 137

internal symbolic closure, and the symbol of the viceroy is merely a mirror reflection of the allegorical arch itself, there is no way of determining the meaning of the huitzilin's call, nor the direction and final resting place of the Mexica migration. This is the power that the migration and allegory have for Creole sovereignty. Rather than spirit and consecration from outside, Sigüenza's argument is for the foundation of governance in local history, whose enigmas will point the direction for the future patria. Sigüenza's coup is to recast the direction of this mirror image, which will now point not toward the Spanish monarch but toward the history of Mexico City, from which it will receive its spiritual power.

VIOLENCE AND THE POLITICS OF EMPIRE

While the arch could thus be understood to be a self-sufficient "machine," its significance for governance could hardly have been clear to the incoming viceroy and local political elite. Sigüenza employed his accompanying textual description to establish a context of governmental crisis and implicitly proposes the arch as a symbolic solution. Yet this is not to say that the text was intended to clarify the enigma of the arch. Rather, its juxtaposed fragments, citations, and hyperbata themselves imitate the spiritual technology of the emblems. One of the most striking aspects of the *Theatro de virtudes* is the labyrinth of citations forming the majority of the text, a practice common to the Neo-scholastic argument style in which Sigüenza was trained. Although at times contradictory in their content, as David Brading has pointed out,[83] the citations might better be understood as a second "textual" hieroglyph that places the theme of local governance in the nexus between classical precedent and political modernity. Sigüenza first introduces the theme of governance in the preface to the *Theatro* in which he argues against calling his arch "triumphal." After recognizing the Roman origin of triumphal arches, Sigüenza distinguishes Spanish governance in the Americas from Roman imperialism:

> The triumphal arch was the glorious prize of military successes that, in memory of these, consecrated the immortality of those who spilled their blood in this pursuit. In his description of Rome, chapter 15, Georg. Fabric. [writes]: "At another time arches were erected in the name of the virtue and honor of those who, having subjugated foreign nations, gave signal victories to the patria." In this, Europe has sufficient reason to occupy itself, just as we Americans can boast of no need to aspire to such glories.

Thus if we have no such motives, then who would doubt the impropriety of this name? A triumphal ARCH was the memory of a triumph and as such, derived from the battles of bloody invasions; it was never erected to anyone who had not taken the life of at least five thousand enemies.... And if we have always experienced the Princes that have governed us without bloodshed, how can we then describe as *triumphal* the pomp with which Mexico receives those to whom it offers its love?

(Era el *triumpho* premio glorioso de felicidades Marciales, como memoria de estas, los Arcos en que se consagravan á la immortalidad los que â costa de su sangre las conseguían. Georg. Fabric. en la descripcion de Roma cap. 15. *Arcus olim honoris virtutisque causa erecti sunt iis, qui externis gentibus domitis singulares victorias patriae pepererunt.* En esto bien tiene en que ocuparse la Europa, como gloriarnos los *Americanos* de no necesitar de conseguir estas dichas. Conque si la razón no subsiste quien pondrá duda en la impropriedad deste nombre? ARCO triumphal era memoria del *triumpho*, como este illacion, que se deduxo de las invasiones sangrientas de las Batallas, pues nunca se erigió á aquel aquien por lo menos no huviesse despojado de vida á cinco mil enemigos.... Y si siempre hemos experimentado á los Principes, que nos han governado nada sangrientos, como puede tener denominacion de triumphal la pompa con que Mexico recive á los que ofrece su amor?)[84]

Although in his reading of the twin triumphal arches of 1680 Octavio Paz declares that it is "curious" that in this passage Sigüenza does not take into account the violent colonization of Mexico,[85] the passage's intention is not so much to accurately depict the violence of conquest as it is to delineate a theoretical division that will underlie Sigüenza's argument for "good governance." Sigüenza presents imperial governance as a choice between two models: one Christian, based on love, and the other Roman, based on violence.

This theoretical division, common to Spanish imperial political theology,[86] provides the framework for Sigüenza's proposal for local governance. Citing classical and modern sources, Sigüenza suggests several alternative interpretations for triumphal arches. First, although monuments to war, Roman arches were also magnificent: "it appeared that a city should celebrate the laudable entrance of a new and worthy prince only with such a magnificent representation" (parece que solo con un remedo de tanta magnificencia se deve festejar en una Ciudad la plausible entrada en ella de un nuevo Principe merecedor).[87] Second, in Hebrew the word "arch" is associated with the word "manus," indicating that arches were "mirrors" for princes and "from there, their hands would take their example" (de alli sus *manos* tomen exemplo).[88] Finally Sigüenza proposes that arches are not monuments but gates to the city: "in my own judgment, these structures are not imitations of the ARCHES that commemorated triumph, but rather the *Doors* that gave access to the city" (en mi sentencia mas proprio, no son estas fabricas remedo de los ARCOS que se consagravan al Triumpho, sino de las *Puertas* por donde la Ciudad se franquea).[89] He goes on to say that portals were often decorated with emblems and symbols to guide governance, and it was there that governors would gather to make decisions. Instead of monuments, therefore, Sigüenza finally arrives at a definition of arches as places of passage, liminal points that symbolically define the entrance into the polis: "so that the litigants would end their disputes and enter into the city calmly and peacefully: 'so that with minimal discord they would enter into the city, where it is best to live in concord'" (porque terminandose alli las controversias los litigantes, entrasen en la Ciudad con tranquilidad, y quietud: *Ut urbem in qua concorditer oporteret vivere discordes minime intrarent*).[90]

Although he declares that of these possible interpretations of arches "each one should choose that which appears most appropriate" (elija cada uno la que le pareciere adequada),[91] Sigüenza clearly wishes to emphasize that his arch was a structure for peaceful governance. What is novel in Sigüenza's argument is not this distinction itself, which was fundamental to Spanish sovereignty in the Americas, but rather his use of the distinction to defend the Mexica theme of his arch. If, etymologically, violence is the artificial bond between two terms, the imposition of "fables" foreign to New Spain would be tantamount to allegorical discord.[92] This violence may be opposed to the "natural" correspondence that Sigüenza suggests exists between Mexica rulers and peaceful governance, a coherence that also corresponds to history as a restoration of a natural truth. For this reason, as an assurance of peaceful governance, Sigüenza proposes the truth of local history rather than the mythological fables that would interpret Spanish imperialism in terms of Roman precedent. By turning to history, Sigüenza avoids the voluntarism of Spanish imperial sovereignty, but in order to argue that this is a natural order, he must also avoid the idea of allegory as a violent binding of two dissimilar terms. For this reason, Sigüenza reads his arch not as the imposition of one form over another but as a liminal point for the meeting of inside and outside, a discussion and resolution of differences in the polis.

The key to nonviolence is the harmonious unification of voices in the city, as Sigüenza argues in a further etymological analysis of the term "triumph":

And even if only because of the origin of this term, we should avoid using "triumph" to describe this ceremony: not because it is derived from TRIAMBOS, the name of Bacchus, for having been the first to triumph, as asserted in Diod. Sicul. book 4, Bibliot., chapter 2, Varro book 5 of Latin language whose authority is referred to by Rosin book 10, antiquit. Romanar., chapter 19, the aforementioned Mendoza, and many others, but rather because, as stated by Balthasar Bonifacio in book 5 of his Hist. Ludic. chapter 15, "triumph" is derived from *Thriambos* in the Greek dialect: *Apotu throineae iambizin*, which is to say praising and insulting. An indecent affront indeed to equate satyrs with princes, who should be solicitously attended and venerated with esteem.

(Y aun por lo que significa el vocablo devieramos evitar el que con el de triumpho se mencionase esta pompa: no porque de TRIAMBOS, nombre de *Baccho*, se denomine *triumpho*, por haver sido, el primero que triumphó, como afirma Diod. Sicul. lib. 4, Bibliot. cap. 2. V Varr. lib. 5 de ling. lat. de cuya autoridad lo refiere Rosin lib. 10 antiquit. Romanar. cap. 19, el yá citado Mendoza, y otros muchos, sino porque como dize Balthasar Bonifacio lib. 5. Histor. Ludic. cap. 15. se denominó el triumpho en el dialecto Griego *Thriambos: Apotu throineae iambizin. Hoc est ab aclamando & maledicendo*. Indignidad nada decente cortejar con Satyras á los Principes á quienes solo se deven sacrificar atenciones, y venerar con aprecios.)[93]

Through this etymology, Sigüenza suggests that "triumphal" displays create the possibility of a double voice: "praising and insulting." Although the arch is ostensibly an encomiastic structure, intended to praise the incoming viceroy, Sigüenza suggests that arches interpreted through the lens of Roman imperialism lead to a dissonant and discordant voice. The threat of allegory, as the binding of dissimilar terms, was that it might indeed allow this "other" to speak, as its etymology suggests.[94] Sigüenza's arch thus treats with caution the division between docto and vulgo that Sor Juana proposed as the purpose of allegorical emblems, and which was conventional in literature on arches. Only by creating a common subject of patria would true praise, that is, univocal praise, of the viceroy be possible.

Sigüenza furthers these associations between violence and the specter of a double voice through an anecdote that stresses the vulnerability of the sovereign's natural body. After describing the arch, Sigüenza adds a note of tragedy: the life of one of its principal engineers ended before he could witness the celebration of the viceroy's entrance. A propos of this death, Sigüenza adds the following:

> Some would say that this fatality was the typical trial by which pleasures are ordinarily tempered by sadness, as Lucrecio said in book 3

of *Natura Rerum*. . . . But I would assert that this was a sign of good fortune, so that the triumph with which his excellency the Marquis de la Laguna entered Mexico would be no less than those that glorified Rome, given that, as is known to all, from the very chariot in which the emperor paraded he heard voices that reminded him of his mortality: "from atop his high car the triumphant emperor was reminded that he was human and from behind his back came the suggestion: look back and remember that you are human," as written in Tertuliano's description. And even if this were not the case, no one would deny that one can predict with certainty the success of the principate, or government, that begins within sight of a tomb, as this is a sign that this office comes only from God, who intervenes in such circumstances.

(Algunos discurrirán haver sido esta fatalidad, pension comun conque se alternan los gustos, que de ordinario se desazonan con aquel dolor que dixo Lucrec. lib. 3 de Nat. Rer. . . . Pero yo afirmara el que fue disposicion de la Fortuna, para que el triumpho conque el Excelentissimo Señor Marques de la Laguna havia de entrar en Mexico, no fuesse nada inferior á los que engrandecieron á Roma, supuesto que nadie ignora el que desde el mismo Carro en que triumphava el Emperador se oían las vozes que le avisaban su mortalidad: *Hominem esse etiam triumphans Imperator in illo sublimi curru admonetur; suggeritur enim ei á terge: respice post te, hominem memento te;* dexó escrito Tertul. in Apologet. Y si no es esto, nadie me negará, que al Principado, ó Govierno que se principia á vista de los horrores de un tumulo, desde luego se le puede pronosticar con seguridad el acierto, por ser indicio de que proviene de solo Dios aquel cargo en que semejantes circunstancias intervinieron.)[95]

Through this example, the voice of the people reminds the emperor of his natural state and, in Sigüenza's reading, his dependence on divine providence. As Sigüenza argues, only governance based on Christian theopolitics will rein in this threatening spirit that haunts emperors. By extension, the "truth" of patria, animated by the viceroy's arrival, will unify dangerous divisions among the viceregal populace.

In accordance with his own definition of emblems, in which there is to be a "just analogy" between the spirit and the body, Sigüenza must still defend the appropriateness of the viceroy as a complement to the Mexica kings. This he does through an ingenious interpretation of Sor Juana's analogy between the viceroy and Neptune. In apparent contradiction to his argument against the use of mythological figures, he begins the third prelude to the description of his arch, titled "Neptune is not a false deity" (Neptuno no es fingido dios), by defending Sor Juana's comparison of the incoming viceroy to Neptune. Through a series of tortuous etymologies, analogies, and citations, Sigüenza creates an argument similar to the one he makes in favor of Huitzilopochtli. By citing sources that link Neptune to Carthage, the origin in several theories of the time of the predecessors of the Indians, he argues that Neptune was not a god but indeed the long-forgotten forefather of the American Indians. Just as classical authors had no knowledge of the American Indians, so too is nothing known about the sons of Neptune:

> Of the peoples and descendents of Neptune nothing is known except that they existed: Joseph, book 1, Antiq. chapter 7 of Nepthemis (which is Nepthuim or Neptune) "we know nothing except his name." This appears to be a paraphrase of the peoples of this new world, news of whom (I determine) the [following] had: Plato in Tim. Elian. book 3 and Var. Historia chapter 18, Pompon. Mela book 1, chapter 5, and above all Seneca in Hippolit. act. 3: "Fugitive, you must pass through unknown faraway nations; even though a land located at the ends of the earth, separated by the tracts of the Ocean, keeps you away, and you inhabit the region of the world opposite our feet." But "except their name we know nothing," they had such a perplexing name that it only survived in signs, which do not indicate certainties but rather originate confusions, since they did not determine with any certainty the place that they inhabited.
>
> (De las Poblaciones, y descendientes de Neptuno no se sabe otra cosa sino que solo las huvo. Joseph. lib. I. antiq. cap. 7. *Nephthemi* (que es Nephthuim, ó Neptuno) *praeter nomina nihil scimus*. Perifrasi parece este de las gentes deste nuevo mundo: noticia (jusgo) tuvieron de ellas Plat. in Tim. Elian. lib. 3. de Var. Hist. cap. 18. Pompon. Mela lib. I. cap. 5. y mas que todos Senec. in Hippolit. Act. 3,
>
>> .... *Profugus ignotas procul*
>> *Percurre gentes: te licet terra, ultimo*
>> *Summota mundo, dirimat Oceani plagis*
>> *Orbem que nostris pedibus obversum colos.*
>
> Pero *praeter nomina nihil scimus*, tenian un nombre tan confusso, que solo se quedava en señas, no que indicassen certidumbres, sino que originassen confussiones, pues no determinaban con fijeza el lugar de su habitacion.)[96]

The argument has much in common with the story of Saint Thomas's preevangelizing of the Americas in which the isolation of the American Indians led to confused signs and forgetting.[97] In this case, however, it is not conversion to Christianity but the name of their forefather that the Indians have forgotten. By turning the story of St. Thomas's evangelizing into one of paternity, Sigüenza subtly transforms its fulfillment from one of conversion to the return of governance by a lost father.

Sigüenza's interest in this secular version of the myth of Saint Thomas may be seen in the proofs that he offers as evidence of the link between Neptune and the American Indians. Not only are the pre-Columbian glyphs similar to those of the Egyptians, as Athanasius Kircher had already pointed out, but furthermore, according to Sigüenza, Indians are the very image of a wandering, migratory people who have forgotten the name of their father:

> Read with attention the versions that Puente gives in the *Conven. de las Monarquias*, book 3, and you will see how much more these apply to the miserable Indians than to the Spanish, and if any in particular those of Mexico: people uprooted from their lands, strangers in their own provinces, peoples torn to pieces in defense of their patria, crushed by poverty, a people made terrible by their sufferings and, after all is done, one will not find another that suffers with such patience, a people that always expects a remedy for their misery and is always trampled upon by all, whose land is afflicted by repeated flooding.
>
> (Leanse con atencion quantas versiones trae Puente en la Conuen. de las Monarquias lib. 3 y se verá quanto mas se ajustan á los miserables Indios, que á los Españoles, y si algunos en particular á los de México gente arrancada de sus Pueblos, por ser los mas estraños de su Provincia, gente despedazada por defender su Patria, y hecha pedazos por su pobreza, Pueblo terrible en el sufrir, y despues del qual no se hallara otro tan paciente en el padecer, gente que siempre aguarda el remedio en sus miserias, y siempre se halla pisada de todos, cuya tierra padece trabajos en repetidas inundaciones.)[98]

Beginning with Antonio de la Puente's discussion of the origin of the Spaniards, Sigüenza interprets the source of indigenous "misery" as a loss of place.[99] Rather than the providential myth of Mexica migration, Sigüenza describes a wandering people whose uprootedness has created the conditions for their forgetting.

Implicitly, it is the return of this memory that will redeem the Amerindian condition. Again, Sigüenza turns a common trope of Spanish providentialism, that the Amerindians had received signs of the immanent arrival of the Spanish, into an open-ended sign to be fulfilled in the present:

> A curious thought occurred to me and it is that these Indians were expectant people, *gentem expectatem*, and that they were expectant is certain since they had a prophecy that he who was truly their King would be coming to govern them, and therefore those who led in their

Empire were only his substitutes, and [they were] waiting for proper dominion by their legitimate master.

(Pasavaseme una singularidad curiosa, y es que eran estos Indios gente que esperava, *gentem expectatem*, y que esperasen es cierto, pues tuvieron profesia que havia de venir á governarlos el que propriamente era su Rey, conque los que arbitravan en el Imperio eran solo sus substitutos, esperando con la propriedad del dominio á su legítimo dueño.)[100]

He concludes that the "king in truth could be no other than Neptune" (Rey en propriedad no podia ser otro que Neptuno).[101] The arrival of the reincarnation of Neptune, the Marqués de la Laguna, will therefore be the return of a long-lost father of the American Indians.

But if Neptune himself is behind this lineage, it is not only as forefather but as the spirit that guides the Mexica patriarchs to their final destination: "and with Neptune as a guide, the first founders of Mexico could easily leave the discomfort of a lake in favor of the security of a strong city" (y teniendo los primeros fundadores de México á Neptuno por guia, pudieron facilmente salir de las incomodidades de una laguna á las seguridades de una fuerte Ciudad).[102] It is now clear that the voice of the huitzilin that had guided Huitzilopochtli toward Tenochtitlan is the spirit of Neptune and that the prophecy of the Mexica is fulfilled only with Neptune's return in 1680. Thus, if Sigüenza's arch provides a narrative of providential redemption, it is a redemption quite distinct from the providentialism of Spanish imperialism, which read the sixteenth-century Spanish conquest as the beginning of a Christian world order. For although the new viceroy plays the role of redeemer, Sigüenza also reduces him to a mirror reflection of the patriarch of the Indians, whose historical narrative will be clarified and completed upon the arrival of the Spanish governor. History itself, therefore, provides the basis for the redemption of a patria plagued by internal division and migration. If the viceroy infuses the parts of the arch with spirit, it is not in the sense of a symbol, a spirit that is immanent in both object and his person, but a spirit that had been buried and forgotten in the hieroglyph of local history. Not only was this secret awaiting the arrival of the long-lost father but also the Creole interpreter who could connect the parts of the puzzle and make whole what had been rent during years of separation.

Sigüenza's pairing of the dignity of the Mexica emperors with the miserable state of present Indians echoes his representation of the divided procession in Querétaro earlier that year.[103] Yet *Theatro de virtudes* makes several key changes to the formulaic contrast between the grotesque Chichimec processioners and the dignified parade of Texcoco monarchs by suggesting that the lineage of monarchs will go beyond "repayment" for Christianity to redeem the viceroyalty's subjects from their miserable and uprooted state. What is even more striking, however, is Sigüenza's repetition and inversion of the same phrase with which he closes his account of the indigenous procession in Querétaro. Whereas in *Glorias de Querétaro*, Sigüenza declares that with the procession "this very ancient debt was repaid on this occasion by the Indians of Querétaro through the generous demonstrations of their affection which amazed all" (Esta tan antigua deuda fue la que pagaron en esta ocasión los indios de Querétaro, con las generosas demostraciones de su cariño, que suspendieron a todos),[104] in the *Theatro* he reverses the debt. Citing the Creole Augustinian missionary Padre Calancha of Peru, he asserts: "I will end by saying, along with the erudite Calancha, who was faced with a similar task in his *Coronica de San Augustín del Perú*, book 1, chapter 7, number 7, that 'with these paragraphs I have repaid the Indians for the patria that they gave us and in which the heavens give us so many favors and the earth gives us tribute'" (concluyeré diziendo con el docto Calancha estando en semejante empeño en la Coronica de S. Augustin del Perú, lib. I., cap. 7., num. 7, que *con estos Parrafos les he pagado á los Indios la Patria, que nos dieron, y en que tantos favores nos haze el Cielo, y nos tributa la tierra*).[105]

Thus, if Sigüenza interpreted the Querétaro procession as payment by the Otomís for their conversion, here it is the Creole scholar that repays the American Indians for their gift of a local patria. The arch, therefore, will serve a double purpose. First, it will link a local polity to a distant monarch. As he declares in the opening lines of the *Theatro*, the arch is a gift of natural inferiors to the "political souls that continue their life" (estas almas politicas, que les continuan la vida).[106] But the arch that Sigüenza erects in the name of the Mexican populace is also the foundation of good governance. Whereas *Glorias de Querétaro* projects the danger of divisions among Indians, the arch goes further by linking subjects divided by the violence of conquest. On a larger scale, this is the purpose of Sigüenza's 1680 triumphal arch for the new viceroy. The importance of the arch is not its content, per se, but its writing of a shared history whose "spirit" is nonetheless tied up in hieroglyphs. Only these emblematic allegories are able to integrate voice and body to create a common ground for the Creole and non-Creole subject.

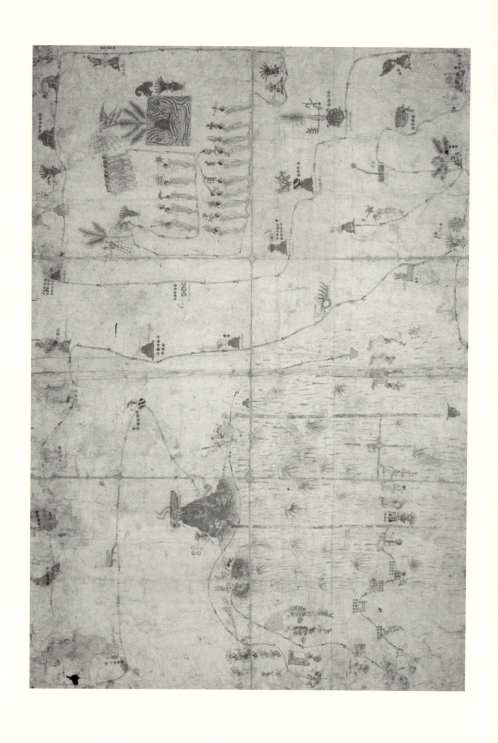

Because these visual icons are still fragmented, however, the Creole is a key magistrate of this new local polity. For only the Creole savant can successfully interpret the glyphs within the language of European governance and thus defuse the remnants of pagan resistance.

The hermeneutic authority of Sigüenza's arch was closely linked to his possession of indigenous codices. Although little is known about the exact contents of his "Indian museum," it is possible that by 1680 Sigüenza already possessed a manuscript that since the eighteenth century has borne his name and that this served as one source for his arch. One of the most complete chronological maps of the Mexica pilgrimage from Aztlan to Tenochtitlan, the "Mapa de Sigüenza" has certain characteristics that distinguish it from other Mexica pilgrimage codices (Figure 13). Three of these accord with Sigüenza's understanding of the Mexica pilgrimage in the *Theatro*: the displacement of Chicomoztoc from the origin to the middle of the Mexica's journey, the focus on Chapultepec as a point of arrival in the central valley, and the historical division between Tlatelolco and Tenochtitlan.[107] Also notable are the overly large bird who speaks to the assembled pilgrims, which is closer to Christian iconography of a dove than to the huitzilin or hummingbird commonly represented as the origin of the Mexica prophecy, and the absence of sacred bundles carried by the leaders along the journey.[108] These peculiarities all suggest a dissident Tenochca version of the pilgrimage that transformed Huitzilopochtli's role as sacred guide into an iconography more amenable to postconquest Christianity.[109]

Since the manuscripts on pre-Columbian history and calendrics that Sigüenza claimed to have written have never been located, it is difficult to know how he interpreted this particular codex. The best approximation may the reproduction of the map and commentary made by the Italian traveler Gemelli Careri in his 1699 travel narrative *Giro al mondo* (Tour of the World). María Castañeda de la Paz has noted that Gemelli provides toponyms for several glyphs not glossed in the original codex as well as translations of many others, such as those for Papantla and Xaltepzaucan. As these are remarkably accurate, she argues, it is likely that Sigüenza provided Gemelli with this information.[110] Additionally,

Figure 13 (opposite page). "Mapa de Sigüenza." A sixteenth-century codex depicting the Mexica pilgrimage from Aztlan to Tenochtitlan. Amate paper (sixteenth c.). Courtesy of the Biblioteca Nacional de Antropología e Historia, Mexico City.

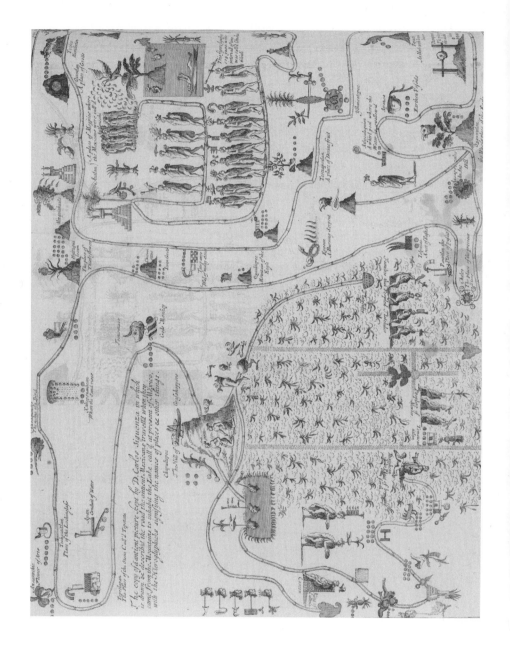

the copy of the map included in the English translation of Gemelli's travels contains the following description (Figure 14): "The copy of an antient picture kept by D. Carlos Siguenza in which is drawn & described the road the antient Mexicans travell'd when they came from the Mounts to inhabit the Lake, call'd at present Mexico with Hieroglyphicks signifying the names of places & other things." From this it appears that Gemelli consciously added translations of glyphs for a European readership.

While Gemelli's reproduction of the "Mapa de Sigüenza" favors translation over Creole hermeticism, in his comments on Sigüenza's unpublished "Ciclografía" ("Cyclography") the Neapolitan traveler alludes to a more antiquarian explanation for Mexica writing and calendrics. In reference to the Mexica calendar wheel, a copy of which he includes in his text (Figure 15), he writes:

> Those who are familiar with the errors of the Eastern nations in this matter will understand how worthy of praise and esteem is the intelligence of the Mexicans who invented such an ingenious and accurate circle. This accolade is not meant for contemporary Mexicans, who would never be mistaken for astronomers or mathematicians and whose ignorance would soon enough prove me to be a liar, but rather for their gentile ancestors, as I have already argued, and for their ancient teacher Netuin, as Carlos Sigüenza y Góngora, professor and chair of mathematics at the University of Mexico, has eruditely shown in his "Cyclography."
>
> (Or quanto degno di laude, e di stima sia l'ingegno de'Mexicani, inventando tal artificioso, e regolatissimo circolo, potran giudicare coloro, i quali sanno quanto errore, in questa materia, presero quasi tutte le nazioni Orientali. Questa lode però no si deve a'Mexicani d'oggidì, i quali certamente non sono nè Astronomi, nè Aritmetici: e colla loro ignoranza, mi convincerebbono di menzogna: ma a quelli della Gentilità, come abbiamo ragionato di sopra, e al loro antichissimo Maestro Neptuin: siccome eruditamente va divisando D. Carlos de Sigüenza, y Gongora, Cattedratico proprietario, e professore di Matematica nell'Università di Mexico, nella sua Cyclographia.)[111]

Gemelli's comments, some of the only evidence of the possible content of Sigüenza's "Ciclografía," suggest that Sigüenza adapted Becerra

Figure 14 (opposite page). "A Copy of an Antient Picture." Reproduction of the "Mapa de Sigüenza." Giovanni Gemelli Careri, *A Collection of Voyages and Travels* (London, 1704). Courtesy of the John Carter Brown Library at Brown University.

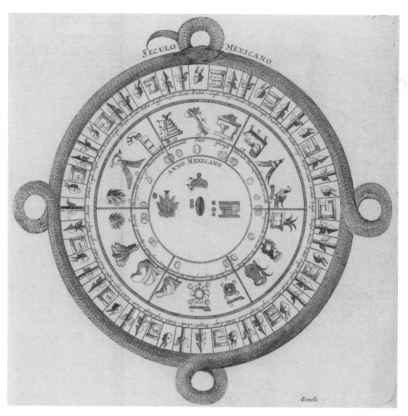

Figure 15. "Seculo mexicano." Reproduction of the Mexica calendar wheel. Giovanni Gemelli Careri, *A Collection of Voyages and Travels* (London, 1704). Courtesy of the John Carter Brown Library at Brown University.

Tanco's reading of St. Thomas as the origin of indigenous script and calendrics to his argument that Neptune was the progenitor of the Amerindians. Yet in his widely distributed travel narrative Gemelli himself does little to develop this idea of a hermetic truth in indigenous documents. The documents he includes from Sigüenza's archive, the pilgrimage map and the Mexica calendar wheel, are curiosities rather than sources of Creole antiquarianism.

Despite these differences in their interpretations, it is not at all clear that Sigüenza would have objected to Gemelli's representation. Gemelli recognizes the Creole scholar's generosity in sharing with him his codices, and his text surely established Sigüenza's name among a European reading public. Sigüenza was more critical of European authors who failed to acknowledge Creole interpretations of glyphs. Although he admiringly cited Athanasius Kircher in other instances, in the *Theatro* Sigüenza criticizes the inadequacy of the Roman-based scholar's reading of Mexica glyphs:

> In this chapter, as in chapter 4 of the "Hieroglyphic Theater" of volume 3 of the said work, in which he wishes to explain part of the ancient Mexican annals that are held in the Vatican, [Kircher] succumbs to many misreadings. He is not to be blamed, since it is true that in those parts so little traveled by our Creole nation he would lack someone to give him information or who could enlighten with erudition on matters that otherwise remained obscure; the defect is ours, since although all of us pride ourselves on being such lovers of our patrias, what we know of them we owe to foreign pens.

> (en este Capitulo como en el 4. del Theatro Hieroglyphico del tom. 3. de dicha obra, en que quiere explicar parte de los Annales antiguos Mexicanos, que se conservan en el Vaticano tiene muchissimas impropriedades no ay porque culparle, pues es cierto, que en aquellas partes tan poco cursadas de los de nuestra Nacion Criolla le faltaria quien le diesse alguna noticia, ó le ministrase luzes eruditas, para disolver las que juzgaria tinieblas; el defecto es nuestro, pues quando todos nos preciamos de tan amantes de nuestras Patrias, lo que de ellas se sabe se debe á estrangeras plumas.)

By contrast, Sigüenza praises the recognition of Mexica glyphs by the English collector Samuel Purchas, knowledge of which he surely received from Kircher's citation in the *Oedipus Aegyptiacus* (Egyptian Oedipus) (1652–54):

> This is a truth that all acknowledge, and that no one denies since the books that publicize it display it to the world. I am not speaking of the explanation of the characters, or Mexican hieroglyphs, that some would consider a contemptible triviality, and consequently an unworthy object of their sublime studies, because they judge the ancients' commonplace, "The eagle does not hunt flies," to apply, or because (to our embarrassment) it was the work of Samuel Purchas of the English nation in his *Peregrinaciones del Mundo*, volume 3, book 4, chapter 7, in which with singular and very select information the finest lover of our patria reiterated all that he could express on this topic.

> (Verdad es esta que reconocen todos, y que ninguno dismiente, porque son manifiestos al mundo los Libros que lo publican, no hablo de la explicacion de los Characteres, ó Hieroglyphicos Mexicanos, que algunos tendrán por trivialidad despreciable, y por el consiguiente indigno objeto de sus estudios sublimes, porque en ellos juzgan se verifica el *Aquila non captat muscas* de los antiguos, ó porque (con verguenza

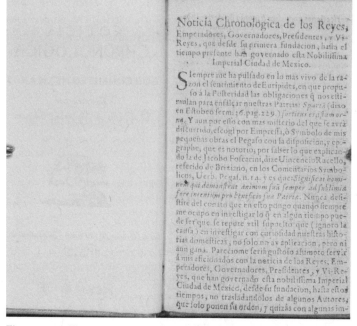

Figure 16. First manuscript page of Carlos de Sigüenza y Góngora's *Noticia chronológica de los reyes, emperadores, governadores, presidentes, y vir-reyes* (1681?). Courtesy of the Lilly Library, Indiana University, Bloomington.

nuestra) ya fue empeño de Samuel Purchas de nacion Ingles en sus Peregrinaciones del Mundo tom. 3. lib. 5. cap. 7. donde con individuas, y selectissimas noticias, recopiló quanto pudiera expressar en esta materia el amante mas fino de nuestra Patria.)[112]

From these passages it is clear that preservation and interpretation were not separable for Sigüenza. While he recognizes the efforts of both Kircher and Purchas, he appears to grant the heretical English collector more credence than the more contemporary Jesuit savant because the former copied ("recopiló") rather than interpreted the Mexica glyphs. This respect for the local source of knowledge even garnered Purchas the epithet of "finest lover of our patria," a distinction Sigüenza never awarded to the Roman Jesuit.

Sigüenza coupled his insistence that local scholars had special access to the pre-Columbian past with a notion that this past was of benefit to New Spain's citizens. Indeed, in the same year that he created his triumphal arch Sigüenza also published a short broadside (Figure 16) titled

Mexican Hieroglyphics

"Chronological Notice of the Kings, Emperors, Governors, Presidents, and Viceroys That Have Governed This Most Noble and Imperial City of Mexico from the Time of Its First Foundation until the Present" ("Noticia chronologica de los reyes, emperadores, governadores, presidentes, y vir-reyes, que desde su primera fundacion hasta el tiempo presente han governado esta nobilissima imperial ciudad de México"). In this, Sigüenza explicitly argues for the public relevance of local history:

> I will never desist in the effort I exert whenever I dedicate my energies to the study of this subject, which someday might be deemed useful, given that (I know not why) there is neither dedication nor interest in studying with curiosity our domestic histories. It seemed to me that it would be a pleasant topic to provide my readers with the news of the kings, emperors, governors, presidents, and viceroys that have governed this very noble imperial city of Mexico, from its foundation up to the present, without transcribing these from other authors, who only put them in order and at times with a few imperfections, as is the case of Antonio de Herrera, Henrico Martinez, Fr. Juan de Torquemada, Rodrigo Mendez de Silva, and others, but rather, specifying the day of their entrance into the empire or government and the entire span of their rule, for which I made use of several ancient annals of the Mexicans, which begin in the year 1402, and other paintings of theirs as well as the original books of the secretary of government and war of this New Spain, in which the titles of the most excellent and noble viceroys are noted. It is necessary to explain all of this so that my dedication can be appreciated and considered by those who have besmirched it. As for the adjustment to the days of our calendar so that they would correlate with those of the Mexican, more information is necessary which can only be found in my "Treatise of Mexican Cyclography," if it ever sees the light of day.

> (Nunca desistiré del conato que en esto pongo quando siempre me ocupo en investigar lo que en algun tiempo puede ser que se repute util supuesto que (ignoro la causa) en investigar con curiosidad nuestra historias domesticas, no solo no ay aplicacion, pero ni aun gana. Pareciome seria gustoso asumpto servir a mis aficionados con la noticia de los Reyes, Emperadores, Governadores, Presidentes, y Vir-Ryes, que han governado esta nobilissima Imperial Ciudad de Mexico, desde su fundacion hasta estos tiempos, no trasladandolos de algunos Autores, que solo ponen su orden, y quizas con algunas imperfecciones, como son Antonio de Herrera, Henrico Martinez, Fr. Juan de Torquemada, Rodrigo Mendez de Silva, y otros: sino especificando el dia de su entrada en el Imperio, o Govierno, y todo el tiempo de su mando; para lo qual me vali de unos Annales antiguos de los Mexicanos, que comiençan desde el año de 1402 y de otras pinturas suyas, como tambien de los libros originales de las Secretarias de la Governacion,

y Guerra, de esta Nueva-España, donde se asientan los títulos de los Excelentissimos Señores Vi-reyes. Todo lo qual es necessario expressar para que en ello se reconozca mi aplicacion, y se ocurra a los q[ue] en ello pusieron macula. En lo que toca al ajuste de los dias de nuestro Kalendario, que coinciden con los del Mexicano, es necesaria, mas noticia, que no se puede dar sino es en mi *Tratado de la Cyclographia Mexicana*, si alguna vez viere la luz.)[113]

This short text, most likely included in his almanac of the same year and thus aimed at a population otherwise characterized as "rustic" (*rústico*),[114] further elucidates Sigüenza's assumptions about the public function of local history: first, that he understands Mexican history as a seamless chronology, uninterrupted by the Spanish conquest; second, that to write this history accurately one must return to an archive that has been fragmented and misread; third, that this history pertains to a passion that links the historian to a public—Sigüenza's "readers" (*aficionados*); and finally, that the ultimate purpose of this archival record is a utility that may only be known in the future—"which someday might be deemed useful" (lo que en algun tiempo puede ser que se repute util).

Of Sigüenza's 1680 arch Jacques Lafaye has provocatively written that "[a] new era had opened in which the Indian past and the Indian beliefs had lost all their subversive potential in Mexico City; the time was ripe for a process of mythification of the Indian past."[115] And yet the public function that Sigüenza envisioned for the Creole archive is an even more decisive turn in the politics of indigenous history than Lafaye's comments would suggest. The events surrounding Sigüenza's acquisition of his collection are symbolic of this transformation of pre-Columbian genealogical documents into a public archive. While it is possible that he acquired individual artifacts separately, it appears that the majority of Sigüenza's indigenous manuscripts came from one source: Juan de Alva Ixtlilxochitl, son of the mestizo historian and descendant of the rulers of Texcoco, Fernando de Alva Ixtlilxochitl. Gemelli himself attributes the artifacts he reproduces from Sigüenza's collection to this origin and, just as in the arguments of early antiquarians such as Becerra Tanco and Duarte, heralds the Creole's preservation of indigenous artifacts as a reversal of the early years in which the Spanish had destroyed the codices. After summarizing its contents, Gemelli describes the now lost "Ciclografía":

> which makes use of passages from scripture, of Indian traditions, of very singular paintings and hieroglyphs that had been preserved by

Juan de Alba, the noble of the San Juan de Teotihuacán *cacicazgo*. He had inherited these from his elders who had been kings of Texcoco, from whom he descended in a direct mixed line, and left them in the hands of Don Carlos, executor of his will. It can surely be said that similar paintings cannot be found in all of New Spain, because when the Spanish arrived they threw them on the flames wherever they found them since, seeing them without letters and with very strange figures, they considered them superstitious. Monseñor Zumárraga, the first bishop of Mexico who also smashed many ancient idols, quickly exterminated them; in this way the figure of the Mexican calendar and other Indian antiquities that will be reproduced in this volume, are owed all to the diligence and courtesy of Sigüenza, who lent me such curious rarities.

(in cui si serve di luoghi della Sacra Scrittura, di tradizioni degl'Indiani, di carte dipinte, e di geroglifici singolarissimi, che erano stati serbati da D. Juan d'Alva, Signor del Catzicazgo, e di S. Juan Teotihuacan. Costui le avea ereditate da'suoi maggiori, che erano stati Re di Tescuco, da'quali per dritta linea mescolata, discendeva; e lasciò in mano di D. Carlo, suo esecutore testamentario. Certamente può dirsi, che simili nonsi trovano in tutta la Nuova Spagna; perocchè gli Spagnuoli, quando vi entrarono, ovunque ne trovavano, le davano alle fiamme; perche vedendole senza lettere, e con tante diverse figure, le stimavano superstiziose. Finì poi di sterminarle Monsignor Sumarica, primo Vescovo di Mexico, che fece anche rompere moltissimi antichi Idoli; sicchè la figura del secolo Mexicano, & altre antichità degli Indiani, che verranno appresso delineate in questo volume, si denno tutte alla diligenza, e alla cortesia del Siguenza, che me fece dono di sì pellegrine rarità.)[116]

Unlike European antiquities that had been salvaged from what Francis Bacon called the "shipwreck of time,"[117] the preservation of pre-Columbian artifacts had overcome an active attempt to "exterminate" them. And rather than objects gathered through commerce and exchange, as were collections of American artifacts in Europe, the origin of Sigüenza's collection was a "gift" that signified an alliance with New Spain's indigenous nobility at a particular juncture in viceregal history.

Sigüenza's collection, so often understood to be the beginning of Creole antiquarianism, therefore also marked a new time that broke with early imperial politics in New Spain. The transfer of the collection from the Ixtlilxochitl family to Sigüenza symbolizes this shift. Fernando de Alva Ixtlilxochitl, the early seventeenth-century mestizo historian who appears to have had the strongest hand in uniting what would become the basis of Sigüenza's collection, authored a genealogical history to support his claim to nobility. Although Fernando de Alva

Ixtlilxochitl's histories of the Texcoco line of rulers were never published in his lifetime, he was highly regarded by Creole authors. This is partly due to his position as a high-ranking mediator in Spanish and indigenous governance: Alva Ixtlilxochitl was not only a historian but also Indian governor and interpreter of the Indian court, positions that brought him into contact with peninsular and Creole elite. Through these positions he was ultimately able to win for his family the coveted cacicazgo of San Juan de Teotihuacán despite that fact that he was a mestizo and therefore juridically prohibited from holding the position. After his death, however, fights among factions of the Ixtlilxochitl family took the matter of its inheritance to court. When his son Juan de Alva died, Sigüenza y Góngora became a party in the dispute, aiding a second son and eventual victor, Diego de Alva Ixtlilxochitl, in his fight to retain control of the cacicazgo. The details of Sigüenza's relationship to the Ixtlilxochitl heirs remain murky, but what is clear is that sometime before his death Juan de Alva Ixtlilxochitl, Diego's brother, willed the family patrimony of codices and artifacts to Sigüenza sealing a bond of friendship that the Creole repaid when he defended Diego against legal attacks by the brothers' dispossessed relatives. In fact, it is quite possible that the transfer of the codices to Sigüenza's possession took place in the very year that he penned both *Glorias de Querétaro* and his triumphal arch.[118]

The alliance between Sigüenza and the Alva Ixtlilxochitl family was based partly on a distinction between viceregal nobility, whether Creole or indigenous, and indigenous commoners. The original dispute over the cacicazgo of San Juan de Teotihuacán, for instance, focused on the issue of whether or not the Alva Ixtlilxochitls were Indian enough to hold the position. In 1643 the town's commoners filed a petition claiming that all the Ixtlilxochitl heirs were *españoles* and none were *indios*, an accusation that implicated the actual *cacica*, Ana Cortés Ixtlilxochitl, mother of Fernando.[119] To this accusation, Fernando was obliged to show titles to the land, proving the hereditary line that linked Fernando Ixtlilxochitl, Cortés's ally and Fernando's great-grandfather, to the line of Texcoco kings. In the following generation, townspeople again disputed the right to succession of Fernando's son, Diego, favoring another faction of the Ixtlilxochitl family. This time, Sigüenza y Góngora came to the aid of the empowered faction of the family, providing the documentation that established that Diego had been designated heir by his uncle, Fernando's older brother Juan de Alva, who had succeeded Ana Cortés Ixtlilxochitl.[120]

Yet if in these legal battles the Ixtlilxochitl family documents were called upon to prove genealogy and merit, it is precisely this aspect of Fernando de Alva Ixtlilxochitl's history that Sigüenza himself called into question in order to legitimize his own archive. In a note on his copy of Ixtlilxochitl's manuscript Sigüenza wrote: "The author of this historical compendium of the kings of Texcoco is don Fernando Ixtlilxuchitl, who should be read with great care since in order to aggrandize his progenitor, don Fernando Cortés Ixtlilxuchitl, he left the truth out of many things" (El autor de este Compendio histórico de los reyes de Tetzcoco es don Fernando Ixtlilxúchitl, el cual se debe leer con grande cautela pues por engrandecer a su progenitor don Fernando Cortés Ixtlilxuchitl falta en muchas cosas a la verdad).[121] While fleeting, Sigüenza's comments suggest the way in which the Creole archive transformed indigenous documents. Whatever the reason the Ixtlilxochitl heirs donated their archive to Sigüenza, the Creole himself saw its possession as an opportunity to disseminate a publicly relevant truth. Although in his 1684 *Parayso occidental* he celebrated Fernando de Ixtlilxochitl as the "Cicero of the Mexican language" (el Ciceron de la lengua mexicana),[122] his interest in pre-Columbian history reflected the breakdown of the two-republic system that had organized New Spain socially and juridically for the first century and a half after the Spanish conquest. In this system, indigenous histories were one of the most essential proofs of nobility for an elite that had served as crucial mediators between the Crown and its Amerindian subjects.

Sigüenza's archive pointed toward a new social imaginary in which Creoles would conserve and interpret a hermetic indigenous past in the interest of forming citizens and educating Spanish governors. The specter that this alliance sought to overcome was the disappearance of the strong class of indigenous *caciques* that had dominated early viceregal politics and an increase of rootless indigenous commoners and urban castas who fit into neither of the binary republics of Spanish imperial jurisprudence. Although these subjects were surely the majority of the spectators of Sigüenza's 1680 arch, they were decidedly excluded from the concept of citizenship that animated his passionate espousal of local history for governance.

CHAPTER 4

Counterhistory and Creole Governance in the Riot of 1692

From the early sixteenth century onward, the specter of popular rebellion had haunted the colonial administration of New Spain. Although arguably in the years after the conquest the Crown feared an uprising by disgruntled *encomenderos* more than it did rebellion by indigenous subjects, as the viceroyalty matured the growth of a nonindigenous urban population fueled fears of a general plebeian revolt.[1] Yet although insurrections in rural and provincial areas occurred regularly during the seventeenth century, prior to 1692 Mexico City witnessed only one large-scale disturbance when in 1624, protestors sacked the viceregal palace and trampled the portrait of the viceroy, who barely escaped by disguising himself as a servant.[2] Another rebellion, supposedly planned by Africans and mulattoes in 1612, was violently aborted before it even began.[3] In the middle of the century, tensions between the viceroy and the powerful bishop of Puebla, Juan de Palafox, also created near-riot conditions among the bishop's supporters, for the most part drawn from the lower classes. Animosities continued, however, until Palafox was ultimately reined in after his confrontations with the following viceroy.[4] In fact, rather than the rebellious agitation projected by colonial policy and jurisprudence, the political history of seventeenth-century New Spain was dominated by intrigue between Creole and peninsular elites jockeying for positions within the lower echelons of viceregal administration.[5] Even the popular rebellion of 1624 was heightened by grievances of the local Creole elite and secular clergy against the viceroy.[6]

By contrast, the massive riot that broke out on June 8, 1692, uniquely mirrored elite fears of a general plebeian revolt. Although recent historiography has questioned the exact causes and political circumstances of the riot, official reports and testimony written afterward agree on the basic events. In the months leading up to the riot, an acute food shortage caused by heavy flooding and crop failure stirred panic in the city, especially among commoners. As a result, a crowd of indigenous women began gathering daily around the city's central warehouse, demanding access to the corn stores. One day a scuffle broke out and the warehouse guard attacked the crowd, injuring a woman. When the same scene occurred on the following day, this time possibly killing a woman, the crowd carried her body in protest to the archbishop's house. Receiving no response there, the crowd continued through the city streets, gathering participants as it went. Lower-class Spanish immigrants and Creoles joined indigenous and casta subjects and alongside cries and jeers in Nahuatl could be heard the familiar Spanish refrain: "Long live the king and death to bad government!" (¡Qué viva el rey y muera el mal gobierno!). Upon arriving at the zócalo, the central plaza that housed both the viceregal palace and the city's newly finished cathedral, the rioters attacked the palace itself, setting it aflame. Others turned to the central marketplace, looting merchandise and burning stalls while mocking Spanish luxuries. By the time the crowd had finally dispersed it had left the most spectacular scene of destruction since the Spanish conquest: the viceregal palace had been half burned to the ground and the central marketplace ransacked and destroyed.[7]

Recent work by social historians has done much to further understanding of the political context of the riot. While not as clearly as in the case of the 1624 riot, documents from 1692 suggest that social divisions within New Spain's elite were aggravated by a combination of Spain's precarious financial situation and the particular interventions of the viceroy Conde de Galve in the administrative structure of the viceroyalty. The reams of reports sent to the Council of Indies (Consejo de Indias) after the riot were for the most part intended to exculpate the viceroy from any wrongdoing. But amid these accolades and defenses were several letters from disgruntled members of the colonial elite who signed only as "loyal vassals" (vasallos leales).[8] Now identified as two peninsular bureaucrats with long careers in the Americas, the authors of these letters may have voiced a more generalized discontent with the Conde de Galve, whose governance had favored Creoles in administrative positions, initiated a program of moral reform, and reined in economic rewards that overstepped Spanish mercantilist policies.[9] While this intrigue does not fully explain the events of the riot, which in all versions was based primarily on massive participation by lower-class castas and indigenous subjects, it certainly provides a frame for understanding the written documentation sent afterward to the Crown. Questions remain, however, as to the exact relationship between elite politics and the motives that spurred the popular protests. Whereas the historian Douglas Cope interprets the riot as a moment of plebeian solidarity in reaction to a food shortage,[10] for instance, Natalia Silva Prada has recently argued that political circumstances were a much stronger factor than previously suspected. Indeed, according to Silva Prada, the riot might have even been part of a resurgence of indigenous millenarianism at the end of the seventeenth century.[11]

One of the obstacles to understanding the popular politics surrounding the riot has been that of documentation. The extensive records generated by the trials of participants, for instance, contain few indications that plebeian politics went beyond the political idiom of patrimonialism.[12] Surprisingly, it is Sigüenza y Góngora's letter to his friend Admiral Andrés de Pez that contains some of the most complex expressions of casta actions during the events. Composed several months after the disturbances and sent to Madrid, where the admiral was advocating for the fortification of Pensacola Bay in Florida, Sigüenza's letter was clearly intended to defend the viceroy Galve. The lengthy letter first describes the events leading up to the riot, emphasizing the viceroy's attempts to address the problems of flooding and distribution that led to the crisis in the city's corn supplies. Sigüenza goes on, however, to provide a detailed narrative of the riot itself, including the movements and cries of the crowd. Going well beyond a defense of the viceroy, Sigüenza offers his own causal explanation for the riot, repeatedly attributing the insurrection to indigenous subjects' innate hatred of Spaniards and desire to avenge the Spanish conquest. Whereas other descriptions tend to describe the mob in general terms, moreover, Sigüenza singles out what he calls the "ungrateful, treasonous mob of insolent Indian women" (ingratta, chusma traidora de las insolentas indias) for instigating the insurrection.[13]

In no small part due to Irving Leonard's early editions, Sigüenza's letter remains the most analyzed document of the riot. Yet while Leonard praised the letter's "scrupulous effort at accuracy and impartiality,"[14] most recent readers agree that it is a rhetorically charged description written from an elite Creole perspective. Kathleen Ross, for instance, has analyzed Sigüenza's self-aggrandizement as a strategy of Creole affirmation.[15] José Rabasa and Mabel Moraña have interpreted its sarcastic and grotesque representations of indigenous and casta rioters as a form of racism specific to an emergent Creole politics. Rather than attempting to filter these lenses, with the intention of reconstructing a plebeian perspective on the riot, these readers have made the letter's ideological perspective itself a focus of analysis.[16] But in order to elucidate how Sigüenza's racial diatribes intervened in late seventeenth-century Habsburg politics, the full rhetorical context of the letter must be taken into account. Writing months after the riot had taken place, and after numerous missives recounting the events had already arrived in Madrid, Sigüenza clearly wished to add his voice to discussions of imperial governance. Read in its full rhetorical context, his letter provides an unparalleled basis for understanding how racialized accusations were crucial for distinguishing Creole politics from the two traditional forms of political authority that had sustained the viceroyalty for the first century and a half of Spanish rule: the ecclesiastical pastorate and the viceroy. Without directly confronting either of these sources of political authority, Sigüenza paints the riot as a sign of crisis in these political structures and suggests that only local Creole insights into the causes and solutions of the disturbance can provide the correct antidote to viceregal insecurity.

Throughout his letter, Sigüenza establishes this particular perspective on viceregal governance through two interrelated themes. The first frames the riot within a general atmosphere of imperial insecurity, including indigenous uprisings in the north, pirate attacks on the coast, and, at the end of the letter, the disappearance of the indigenous nobility that had served as a stabilizing mediator between indigenous subjects and the Crown. And while this frame initially serves to highlight what Sigüenza presents as Conde de Galve's judicious actions to secure the viceroyalty from outside attacks, the riot itself provides evidence that the viceroy is unable to govern internally. Rather than blaming the internal insecurity on the viceroy, however, Sigüenza stresses ways in which the riot resisted the tools of traditional governance. The riot, he argues, is a result of indigenous subjects' "innate hatred" of those of Spanish descent. This motive, however, is hidden in a series of complex signs that can be unearthed only by an

Figure 17. The anamorphic skull in *The Ambassadors* (1533). Oil on panel by Hans Holbein the Younger (1497/8–1543). Courtesy of the National Gallery, London, UK / The Bridgeman Art Library.

observer with access to local "truths." While Sigüenza's grotesque representations of the rioters signify their distortions of viceregal rule, he places himself outside the frame of representation, at an autonomous point from which to uncover their hidden meaning. Like Hans Holbein's well-known use of anamorphosis (Figure 17) in his painting *The Ambassadors* (1533), Sigüenza represents the truth of the riot as a distorted object that must be seen from an awry angle. Rather than confirming the symbolism of viceregal rule, therefore, Sigüenza's account establishes what Gilles Deleuze has called a Baroque form of perspective in which truth is culled from the distortions themselves rather than from their correction.[17] It is the awry perspective of the Creole that sees "evidence" hidden to peninsular governors.

The combination of distortion and insight in Sigüenza's letter is a striking reflection of what Etienne Balibar has called racism's "violent desire for immediate knowledge of social relations."[18] Although Balibar analyzes the emergence of what he calls "neo-racism" in contemporary France after the demise of biological notions of race, he notes that "racism without race" also describes racism before the "reinscription of 'genealogy' into 'genetics.'" Race and racism in early modern Europe, he argues, already followed a "historiosophical" logic: "racism is a philosophy of history, or, more accurately, a historiosophy which makes history the consequence of a hidden secret revealed to men about their own nature and their own birth."[19] In the interest of purifying national communities, racism condenses history into "stigmata of otherness," ciphers that can only be interpreted by those who understand the "secret" knowledge contained in birth and lineage.[20] What Balibar calls "historiosophy" is therefore an allegory of history: rather than tracing historical variation and development, racism purports to uncover a stain of guilt that ties subjects to a transhistorical condition. In his iconoclastic genealogy of Western racial discourse, Michel Foucault further argues that seventeenth-century European notions of race were closely tied to battles over national origins and the internal divisions created by these.[21] While Spanish colonization instituted a singularly complex discourse of race that combined notions of purity of blood and benevolent Christianity in a constellation of guilt and obligation, the conquest undoubtedly served as a historical origin similar to that which Foucault finds for European polities. Inevitably, as viceregal society matured, the meaning of this historical origin became more frought, with perspectives more likely to reflect present social divisions than continuous genealogical lines.

Indeed, it has often been noted that Sigüenza's letter underlines the importance of history during the riot, including what he represents as his heroic efforts to save documents from the city's burning archives.[22] Yet Sigüenza's invocation of history goes well beyond this action to touch upon what he sees as the underlying cause of the riot. Against official versions of the conquest, monumentalized in a myriad of forms in viceregal culture, the rioters in Sigüenza's account recall the Spanish conquest as the origin of a present state of injustice, in what Foucault calls the discourse of "counterhistory."[23] Sigüenza presents the riot not merely as a reversal of the contractual version of Spanish sovereignty but as a fight over the occupation of urban space that pitted an elite identified by its Spanish descent against an alliance of the city's casta and indigenous subjects. If he paints the riot in a particularly excessive discourse, it is to convince the Spanish court that the protection of the viceroyalty from internal and external attacks depends on the perception and disarticulation of this interethnic alliance. The necessity of a Creole citizenry armed with knowledge of local conditions in turn reoriented notions of citizenship beyond the language of obligation, loyalty, and obedience. Governance, in Sigüenza's argument, depended not on the benevolence of the pastorate or the king as *pater familias*, but on the possession and interpretation of a local archive that could root out and neutralize a new plebeian politics.

THE SEVENTEENTH-CENTURY CRISIS OF PASTORAL CARE

The contrast between Sigüenza's discourse of citizenship and more traditional forms of colonial governance may best be appreciated by analyzing his participation in a committee of parish priests convened by Viceroy Galve several weeks after the riot. The viceroy asked each member of this committee to assess the "difficulties that result from Indians living in the center of the city" (los inconvientes que resultan de vivir los indios en el centro de la ciudad).[24] The intention was clearly more to solicit support for a foregone conclusion than to open debate. Indeed, the responses reflect the official conclusion that the riot had resulted from a dangerous mixture of indigenous and non-indigenous subjects in the *traza*, the area in the center of the city legally reserved for Spanish.[25] Indeed, the priests often simply reiterated the viceroy's own statement of the problem: "For some time the convenience or inconvenience of Indians living in the city center and in the shacks, lots, and houses that make up the primary Spanish neighborhood, has impeded the order of the city and governance of its natives" (por opuesto a la buena policía de esta ciudad y gobierno de sus naturales, de algún tiempo a esta parte se ha dificultado de la conveniencia o inconvenientes de que vivan dentro de ella, y en los jacales, solares y casas que componen su principal vecindad de españoles).[26] The viceroy's letter goes on to cite the relevant colonial legislation that had segregated the city soon after the conquest, as summarized in the 1681 *Recopilación de leyes de los reinos de las Indias*: "so that the Indians may best benefit from Christianity and civilized order, they should be required to live together and in an orderly fashion, since in this way their prelates will know them better and will have better knowledge for their good and indoctrination" (dispone que para que los indios aprovechen más en cristiandad y policía, se debe ordenar que vivan juntos y concertadamente, pues de esta forma los conocerán sus prelados y entenderán mejor a su bien y doctrina).[27]

Yet whereas early colonial law had attempted to defend Indian areas against the intrusion of non-Indians, in 1692 parish priests blamed Indians for deserting their own neighborhoods, wandering and even living in other areas of the city in "insolent freedom" (insolente libertad):[28] "Having infiltrated the city, [the Indians] do not want to go to Mass or to comply with the church in their parishes. Nor do they know how to pray, nor wish to be counted [in attendance rolls] on Sundays, nor to help in their neighborhoods with the duties and offices required for service to your majesty and the church" (metidos en la ciudad ni quieren oír misa ni cumplir con la iglesia en sus parroquias ni saben rezar, ni quieren acudir a la cuenta los domingos, ni ayudar a los de los barrios a los cargos y oficios necesarios del servicio de S. M. y de la iglesia).[29] The ambulatory parishioners also created problems for church records (*tablas*) "where their ministers can register, recognize, and easily direct them to the catechesis, mass, and sermon" (donde sus ministros los puedan registrar, reconocer, y conducir con facilidad a la doctrina, misa y sermón).[30] Rural Indian migrants, many of whom the friars claimed had deserted their own towns after having committed crimes, also lived throughout the city and further confused historically ethnic neighborhoods.[31] Santo Domingo, for instance, was a hodgepodge of ethnicities: "Mixtec, Zapotec, Mestitlán, and Creole natives, and other nations, [who are] residents in this city" (naturales mixtecos, zapotecos, mestitlán, criollos, y otras naciones, residentes en esta ciudad). The friar recording this complaint goes on to call these subjects "wanderers" (extravagantes) because they "have their livelihoods in diverse parts, neighborhoods, and encampments of this city" (tienen su asistencia en diversas partes, barrios y ranchos de esta ciudad).[32] Yet not only were Indians leaving their neighborhoods, but Spanish were also buying and renting land in the Indian parishes and entering Indian neighborhoods in search of labor.[33] One friar noted that the Spanish protectors of indigenous subjects actively opposed friars who sought to return them to their parishes.[34]

The picture that develops in the friars' complaints is thus one in which the lines of urban segregation were generally being ignored. The friars' primary concern is not racial mixing *per se*, however, but rather the loss of Indian identity. By leaving their neighborhoods, living and working in the houses of Spanish, Indians had "mixed with blacks, mulattoes, and all types of people" (revueltos con negros, mulatos y todo género de gente),[35] whose dress, clothes, and manner they had adopted. This confusion also affected "the priests of wandering and vagabond [subjects] who, diversely, confusedly and uncertainly administer the sacraments to all who request them" (los curas de vagos y extravagantes, que mezclada confusa e inciertamente administran los sacramentos a todos los que los piden).[36] By donning Spanish garb, Indians had blended with the non-Indian population, "becoming mestizos" (haciéndose mestizos) to avoid their obligations: "many of these don leggings and shoes and some [don] collars and grow their hair out, and the women don skirts, and turning into mestizos, they attend church at the Cathedral in order to desist from and avoid their obligations" (muchos de éstos se ponen medias y zapatos y algunos valonas, y se crían melenas, y ellas se ponen sayas, y haciéndose mestizos, se van a cumplir con la Iglesia a la Catedral, por desistirse y desquiciarse de estas obligaciones necesarias).[37] Another friar speaks more bluntly: "by donning a cape, shoes and leggings and growing out his hair, we now have a mestizo soon to be a Spaniard free from tribute, an enemy of God, his church, and his king" (en poniéndose el indio capote, zapatos y medias y criando melena, hételo mestizo y a pocos días español libre del tributo, enemigo de Dios, de su Iglesia y de su Rey).[38]

The friars' concerns derive from the mandate that they "know" their parishioners, a model of governance that Michel Foucault has named "pastoral care."[39] Repeating verbatim colonial legislation, one of the administrators argues that Indians "need to be required to live together in an orderly fashion so that their prelates can know them and they will have better knowledge for their good and indoctrination" (se debe ordenar que vivan juntos y concertadamente, pues de esta forma los conocerán sus prelados y entenderán mejor a su bien y doctrina).[40] Repeatedly, the friars refer to their charges as their "sheep" and themselves as "pastors."[41] Rather than being "known and examined," late seventeenth-century Indians had gone underground, escaping to the "most hidden and secret places in this city" (los parajes más escondidos y ocultos de esta ciudad)[42] where they associated with castas: "hidden in the back patios and recesses of these houses, where it is not easy to find them, these Indians live in the company of mestizos and vagabonds, secretly scheming such savage iniquities as those that been recently carried out" (escondidos en algunos trascorrales y retiros de dichas casas, donde no es fácil el descubrirlos, habitando estos indios mezclados con los mestizos y la gente ociosa, comunicándose secretamente y maquinando tanta fiereza de maldades, como las que han ejecutado estos días).[43] Thus it was not only that Indians were deserting their neighborhoods, dress, and language, but, against the model of individual sin and collective salvation, they now had "secret" communication with the "mulattoes, blacks, mestizos" (mulatos, negros, mestizos) and the "vile plebes, their equals" (ínfima plebe, su semejante).[44] As one friar puts it, the fact that this hidden or secret communication took place in plain view and with the tacit permission of authorities had created many "Trojan horses that shoot flames toward us, endangering the future of this faithful city" (muchos caballos griegos que nos arrojen fuego, que ponga en contingencia la permanencia de esta fidelísima ciudad).[45]

While in agreement with the friars' overall assessment, Sigüenza participated in the committee convened by the viceroy not as a parish priest who must account for his pastoral charges but as a cartographer asked to redraw the lines of the parish boundaries. He begins his letter by acknowledging the impossibility of designating one area of the city for all Indians "due to the interminable quarrels that would commence and persist among the religious that work in the [Indian] parishes, afraid they might lose their parishioners" (por los pleitos inacabables que entre los religiosos que ocupan sus parroquias se originarían y mantendrían con grande empeño, porque se les quitaban sus feligreses).[46] Instead, citing historical sources such as Herrera, Bernal Díaz, and Torquemada, he proposes a return to the city plan that guided Cortés's rebuilding of Mexico City after the conquest, one that called for its indigenous inhabitants to be moved to surrounding neighborhoods. Sigüenza notes that he is in a unique position to return the city to this early postconquest state having saved "the original charters of this city" (los primeros libros capitulares de esta ciudad) during the riot. These papers, he argues, show that the first governors requested that "the city be walled and fortified for no other reason than to ensure against some movement by the Indians, induced by their inconstancy in goodness, in which they are constant, and the innate maliciousness with which, hating the Spanish (even when they have most benefited) they always proceed" (se amurallase y fortaleciese esta ciudad de México no por otro motivo sino el de asegurarse de los indios en algún movimiento a que les indujese la inconstancia en lo bueno, en que son constantes, y la innata malicia con que aborreciendo a los españoles (aun cuando más los benefician) proceden siempre).[47]

In substance, Sigüenza's recommendations differ little from the priests' call to restrict the movement of Indians to the neighborhoods outside the city center. Yet Sigüenza supplements the priests' complaints that they were losing control over their Indian parishioners by remembering a long history of problems that had resulted from allowing Indians to live in the city's Spanish center:

> When Juan Román, cobbler by vocation, conspired to take over the city in 1549, he turned to the Indians who were living in the city. Indians were those that in the sedition of January 15, 1624, turned what was begun by youth into a gigantic body; and the same Indians who infiltrated the city, living in the majority of the Spanish houses and, worst of all, in the same plaza, in permanent squats that they had there and in the *pulquerías* where they may be counted by the hundreds, those that frequented there by day and night were those who executed the destruction that we are looking at today and will always lament.
>
> (De los indios avecindados en la ciudad se valía Juan Román, de oficio calcetero, cuando el año de 1549 maquinaba señorearse de ella. Indios fueron los que en la sedición de 15 de enero de 1624 dieron gigante cuerpo a lo que principiaron muchachos; y los mismos indios avecindados casi en todas las más casas de los españoles, y lo más ponderable, en la misma plaza, en ranchos estables que allí tenían, y en las pulquerías donde se contaban por centenares, los que de día y de noche las frequentaban, fueron los que ejecutaron el estrago que tenemos hoy a la vista, para llorarlo siempre.)[48]

While never denying the ecclesiastical and viceregal interest in segregation, Sigüenza uses the term "living in" (*avecindado*), etymologically related to the term for citizen (*vecino*), to emphasize the need to exclude non-Spaniards from the polis. Employing the metaphor of a distended and deformed body often used in the early modern period to describe plebeian multitudes, he suggests that these *indios avecindados* continually threatened to produce a "gigantic body" that could overwhelm the Spanish traza.

In Sigüenza's letter, history becomes not only a basis for overriding possible jurisdictional fights among parish priests but also a means to discover the "innate perversity" of the city's indigenous inhabitants. Rather than limiting his proposal to the model of pastoral care that had defined the reports of the parish priests, Sigüenza proposes governance based on knowledge drawn from an original moment of colonial law. The desire to return to this original moment that had established colonial governance to overcome the "innate" perversity of the city's indigenous inhabitants accords with the nonvoluntarist readings of sixteenth-century Spanish imperialism, such as that of the sixteenth-century humanist Ginés de Sepúlveda. But whereas even Sepúlveda held out the possibility that Indians would eventually mature to become adequate, if not full, Christian subjects, Sigüenza's language of citizenship understands alterity as a permanent state.[49] For Sigüenza, this alterity cannot be redeemed; it can only be known and controlled, restricted from contaminating the citizens of the city center.[50] Together with this racist specter he thus proposes a new form of administrative knowledge, disinterested in the ecclesiastical quarrels over jurisdiction. Only after walking the city streets as a mathematician and engineer does he advocate the removal of indigenous subjects from the Spanish center, thus "returning to practice once again what was done at its foundation" (reduciendo otra vez a práctica lo que en su fundación se hizo).[51] Significantly, Sigüenza uses the term *reduciendo*, which in colonial parlance suggested both a spatial and a subjective governance of a resistant subject (*reducción*),[52] to imply not the salvation of indigenous neophytes but a spatial occupation of the city by a community of Creole citizens.

BAROQUE PERSPECTIVE AND COLONIAL GOVERNANCE

Sigüenza's report to the viceroy was a rehearsal for his lengthier description of the riot sent two months later to his friend Admiral Pez. The letter is a highly rhetorical piece of writing and, as is clear from his closing remarks in which he all but invites Pez to publish the document on the condition that "no word be added or deleted from it" (no se le añada ni se le quite ni una palabra),[53] one that Sigüenza wished might go beyond the hands of the admiral. Because Sigüenza writes nearly three months after the events of the riot, by which time numerous other letters, including two by the viceroy himself, had already arrived at the court,[54] he begins by defending yet another version of events:

> In the new currency of our misfortunes I am repaying you with this letter (which will be quite long) for the extensive news of those of Europe that you sent me in yours; because no ships have sailed from these kingdoms to those until now I remain in debt to you and, since

nothing travels faster, even to distant regions, than bad news and this always marked by incompleteness in detail and monstrously distorted, our friendship and correspondence obliges and even demands that I summarize here for you all that has occurred, free of these vices, without saying anything that is not public and well known and, if by any chance any of the [news] lacks these qualities, you can be very certain that either I have proof that it took place or I was present myself.

(En moneda nueva de nros malos susessos pago de conttado a Vmd en estta cartta (que sera bien larga) lo que, de las muchas noticias que de los de la Europa me dio en la suia; por faltta de embarcasion que aya salido desttos para essos reynos hasta aquí le devo y, no habiendo cossa que mas presto llegue, aun a regiones muy aparttadas, que una mala nueva y siempre con la sircunstancia de diminuta en mucho y monstruossa en todo, me obliga y aun necesitta Nra amistad y correspondencia a que, sin estos vicios, le compendie aquí a Vmd cuanto nos ha pasado sin desir cossa que no sea publica y sabvidisima y, si acaso le falttare a alguna esta calidad, estte muy cierto de que o tengo rason del fundamentto con que se hiso, o que me hallé presentte.)[55]

The exordium skillfully combines a sense of the public importance of the events he describes with a personal tone of friendship. By referring to his information as a "new currency," for instance, Sigüenza promotes his description of the riot as at once "new" and part of a public exchange (in a play between novelty and newly minted specie). At the same time, the language of debt, exchange, and friendship between him and Admiral Pez stresses the uniqueness of his perspective. Sigüenza dismisses the other reports that had arrived before his, for instance, asserting that in their eagerness to tell bad news quickly they had either left out relevant information or distorted it. His letter, by contrast, will be both complete and based on unique but reputable evidence: either that which is "public and well known" or authorized by his observation, reason and judgment ("either I have proof that it took place or I was present myself").

Continuing his discussion, Sigüenza furthers the idea of his unique testimony on the riot through the metaphor of mediated sight:

> He who looks at an object through a green lens placed between it and his eyes, necessarily, since the qualities that an object sends are shaded in the color of the intervening glass, will see it green. The spectacles that I use are very clear because, living so far from pretensions and lacking nothing since I have nothing (as Abdolomino said to Alexander the Great), I could be criticized if this were not the case. And so, confirming that there are no intermediaries that color the

qualities that I have carefully observed and will recount here, I certainly expect that even those who pay for nothing and criticize everything will agree with my truthful words.

(El que mira vn objetto, interpuestto entre el y los ojos un vidrio verde, de nesesidad, por teñirse las espesies que el objetto enbia en el color del vidrio que esta intermedio, lo bera verde. Los antte ojos que yo vsso son mui diáfanos porque, viuiendo aparttadísimo de pretensiones y no faltándome nada, porque nada tengo (como dixo Abdolomino a Alejandro Magno), sería en mí muy culpable el que assí no fueran; conque asertando el que no hay medios que me tiñan las especies de lo que cuidadosamente he vistto y aquí diré, desde luego me prometo, aun de lo que de nada se pagan y lo sensuran todo, el que dara asenço a mis palabras veridicas.)[56]

It is hard to miss the sardonic reference to his own spectacles, rumored to have once been broken in rage by Archbishop Francisco de Aguiar y Seijas. Yet Sigüenza also plays on a common seventeenth-century metaphor, especially prevalent in Jesuit writings and pedagogy, in which tinted glasses represent reason clouded by passion. In fact, Sigüenza's text was quite possibly inspired by one of the emblems of Juan de Borja's *Empresas morales* (Moral Impresses) (1581) showing a pair of spectacles, hanging midair, with a *subscriptio* that reads: "Since to whoever looks through spectacles everything appears through their lenses and in this way things appear to him great and small according to their size, in the same way the passions and affectations of the soul make it subject to the passion that lords over it, interfering with the eyes of reason" (Porque como el que mira con antojos, todo lo que vee, le pareçe de la color que ellos son, y assi le parecen las cosas grandes, o pequeñas conforme a la hechura que ellos tienen: de la misma manera las passiones y afecciones del alma, hazen, que todo parezca conforme à la passion, que la señorea, poniendose delante de los ojos de la razon).[57] Sigüenza's clear spectacles, then, become a figure for mediation that allows him to approach the riot subjectively even while drawing him outside of its frame. Indeed, by calling attention to his spectacles while distancing himself from the distortion of tinted glasses, Sigüenza suggests that truth can be reached *only* through mediation. Like the anamorphic games common in Baroque court culture, distortion appears to lead to a hidden truth that exposes nondistortion as the illusion. As Gilles Deleuze has written, the Baroque will to distortion amounts to "perspectivism as a truth of relativity (and not a relativity of what is true)."[58]

In Sigüenza's representation of the riot, this perspectival point is the only way to arrest objects that evade governmental control. In continuation, he describes New Spain before the arrival of the viceroy Conde de Galve as a territory embattled by an anarchic mobility. On the coast pirates used bases they had established in Campeche "to rob our ships without opposition in such a way that they constantly weakened our commerce" (para robar sin oposicion las embarcasiones con que se enflaquesía por instantes nro comercio).[59] On land, the frontiers were under siege by "bellicose and indomitable Indians whose irrational movements never have a good effect on those that are [already] pacified" (indios belicosos y siempre indomittos y de cuios mouimienttos irrasionales jamas se siguen enttre los que esttan pacíficos efecttos buenos).[60] Sigüenza then recounts that the viceroy responded to these interruptions of movement and commerce in New Spain by sending garrisons to the northern presidios of Sonora and New Mexico and the Windward Fleet (Armada de Barlovento) to the Campeche coast, even while he completed the fortress of San Juan de Ulúa in the port of Veracruz, "until that time a fort only by name" (hastta este tiempo con sólo el nombre de forttaleza).[61] Finally, in agreement with what Lewis Mumford describes as the "Baroque" urban ideal of controlled movement,[62] not only did the viceroy secure the outposts of the viceregal territory, but he also shored up the center, finishing building projects so that no part of the city "would be left idle" (estubiese osiosso).[63]

In the case of Mexico City, however, a system of canals subject to constant floods challenged this ideal of orderly movement. In the year leading up to the riot, heavy rains had once again bloated the city's canals and blocked transportation into the city. In his letter, Sigüenza describes the consequences of a city submerged in water:

> no one entered the city as its roads and causeways were impassable; there was a lack of coal, wood, fruit, vegetables, birds, and everything that is brought in from outside every day both for the sustenance of the residents, and there are many of us, as well as the domestic animals, which are not few in number. Bread could not be baked on account of the heavy rain and accompanying cold; meat became lean and tasted exceedingly bad because the sheep and cattle had no place to pasture. And all that I have mentioned was being sold only at an exorbitant price.
>
> (nadie entraua en la ciudad por no esttar andables los caminos y las calsadas; faltto el carbón, la leña, la frutta, las horttalisas, las aves y

cuanto se condusse de afuera todos los días, asi para sustento de los vecinos, que somos muchos, como de los animales domesticos, que no son pocos; el pan no se sasonaba, por la mucha agua y consiguientte frío; la carne estaba flaca y desabridisima, por no tener los carneros y reses donde pastar, y nada se hallaua, de cuanto he dho, sino a esxesivo precio.)[64]

Despite the rains, Mexico City continued with festivities in honor of the marriage of the Spanish monarch Carlos II. At the height of his description of these, however, Sigüenza sounds a pessimistic note: "how true is the [phrase] from scripture that says that laughter accompanies tears and that sadness always follows the greatest happiness" (quanta verdad es la de la Escriptura que con la rissa se mescla el llanto y que a los maiores gustos es consiguientte el dolor!).[65]

Following this invocation of providence, Sigüenza describes how the viceroy attempted to correct a disordered system by establishing a somatic relationship with the city's commoners (*vulgo*). The latter registered the crisis in disembodied laments and cries: "a voice was heard from among those (I'm not sure whether to call them venerable or contemptible) of the commoners who attributed the storm in the countryside, the destruction of the fields, and the flooding of the outskirts to punishment for the recent festivals" (oiose por estte tiempo vna uos entre las (no se si las llame benerables o despreciables) del bulgo que atribuía a casttigo de las passadas fiesttas, de la tempesttad en el montte, el destrozo en los campos y la inundación de los arrauales).[66] To these laments the viceroy responds in compliance with the early modern model of good governance, listening and intervening with prudence by cutting short the festivities to celebrate the monarch's marriage.[67] The cries continue, however, when a plague of *chiahuixtle* causes the corn crop to fail:

> Reaching into what appeared to be full of grain and finding hardly any corn among the husk, they cursed the year, the water, the clouds, the fog, the lack of wind, the *chiahuixtle*, the eclipse of the sun, and their bad fortune, and raised such a painful howl that it reached Mexico and the minute it reached the city warehouse the corn price soared.

> (Al hechar mano de las que paresian muy bien granadas, hallando en ellas casi ningun mais entre muchas ojas, maldiciendo al año, a las aguas, a las nubes, a las neblinas, a la calma, al chiahuistli, al eclipse del sol y a su desgraciada fortuna, levantaron vna uos tan dolorosa y desentonada que llegó a México, y al instante que entró por su alhondiga, se levanto el mais.)[68]

With the failure of the corn crop in addition to the crisis in the countryside, the viceroy was forced to address a growing food shortage and price gouging in the city. Even as he ordered all the corn available in the countryside to be sent into the city and asked the clergy to pray in secret ("so as not to perturb the city with public outcries" [por no contristtar a la ciudad con clamores públicos])[69] the viceroy called a meeting to solicit advice from the principal figures of the colonial elite. In what Douglas Cope calls "one of the most impressive gatherings of its kind in the history of colonial Mexico" the committee decided that corn should continue to be traded freely in order to increase the supplies, with disastrous results since this action permitted prices to jump exorbitantly at a time when supplies were already short.[70]

While he provides the details of these governmental discussions in his letter, Sigüenza distinguishes his own perspective from that of other viceregal advisors by relating examples of his scientific curiosity during the events leading up to the riot. The first of these examples occurs during a solar eclipse that Sigüenza had predicted in his almanac for that year, but which was unexpected by most witnesses. Sigüenza describes the effect on a superstitious populace:

> Since all this was unanticipated, at the moment the light disappeared, birds fell to earth in midflight, dogs howled, women and children screamed, [and] Indian women abandoned the stalls in the plaza where they were selling fruit, vegetables, and other such trifles and took refuge in the Cathedral and since at the same time the prayer bells began to toll not only in [the Cathedral] but in all the churches of the city, there was such a sudden confusion and shock that it caused terror.
>
> (Como no se esperaua tantto como estto, al mismo instante que faltto la luz, cayéndose las aves que iban volando, aullando los perros, gritando las mugeres y los muchachos, desamparando las indias sus puestos en que vendían en la plaza fruta, verdura y otras menudencias por entrarse a toda carrera en la Catedral; y tocándose a rogativa al mismo instante, no solo en ella sino en las mas iglesias de la ciudad, se causó de todo tan repentina confucion y alboroto que caussaua grima.)[71]

Even as he relates the vulgo's panic, Sigüenza distances himself from this superstitious reaction by noting how he happily observed the eclipse through a telescope: "I, in the meantime, stood observing the sun with my quadrant and long-distance spyglass, exceedingly happy and repeatedly thanking God for having allowed me to see what happens only rarely in a given place and of which there are so few observations in the books"(Yo, en este interim, en estremo alegre y dandole a Dios gracias repetidas por hauerme concedido ver lo que susede en vn determinado lugar tan de tarde en tarde, y de que hay en los libros tan pocas oberuaciones, que estuue con mi quadrante y anttojo de larga vistta contemplando al Sol).[72] Similarly, after explaining that the *chiahuixtle* plague had infected the wheat crop, Sigüenza discovers with the help of a microscope a "swarm of tiny little brownish animals no larger than the tip of a thin needle and whose feet and body were like those of a flea but with covered wings like weevils, and, whether with wings of the latter or feet of the former, jumped about with curious lightness" (enjambre de animalillos de color musgo sin más corpulencia que la de una puntta de aguja y que sea sutil; tiraua su forma y la de sus pies a la de una pulga pero con alas cubiertas como los gorgojos, y ya fuesse con estas alas o con aquellos pies saltauan de una parte a otra con ligeressa estraña).[73]

As instruments that achieved empirical truth through distortion, the telescope and the microscope divided scientific from everyday sight. Sigüenza sets himself apart from other observers through the inclusion in his account of such novel devices, rare in the viceroyalty. These examples of Sigüenza's scientifically informed perspective set the tone for his self-presentation as an advisor guided by empirical observation rather than superstition. When the year's rains had still not commenced, for instance, the Virgin of Remedios was brought into the city in the hope that her intercession might initiate them. Sigüenza comments dryly that as this measure was not yet necessary her presence had little effect, although it did seem to calm the vulgo, who "distracted on such occasions, forget about eating in order to watch" (diuertida en semejanttes ocasiones, se oluida del comer por acudir a mirar).[74] Similarly, when greeted with a "barrage of proposals and advice" (tropel de proposiciones y arbitrios) on how to drain the lake, the viceroy prudently listens to all, even entertaining the possibility that the lake had a plug that could be opened in order to release the excess water.[75] Sigüenza all but scoffs at this suggestion and instead introduces his own interpretation, noting that in the past the accumulated garbage had simply been piled next to the canal, causing it to fall back into the water with the slightest rain. Given this situation, he advocates clearing the blockage not only from the canal but from the sides. Indeed, it is with satisfaction that Sigüenza reports that the viceroy paid particular attention to his advice and authorized his engineering project of cleaning and opening the city's canals in such a way that "[n]ot one skiff of sediment now remained (much less where it was deemed that a levy was in order), which was not carried away to a suitable site so that the benefits from the dredging would continue for many years" (No quedo aora ni una sola vattea de lodo (menos donde se reconosio que se necesitaua de terraplén) que no se llevase adonde paresio conbeniente, para que con esto mantuviesen el beneficio de estta limpiessa por muchos años).[76]

FETISHES IN THE CANALS

Beyond simply presenting a problem of engineering, Sigüenza's description of the garbage-filled canals becomes a symbolic turning point in his narrative when he recounts a series of strange objects that he had found while overseeing the cleaning of the canals:

> A while ago, before the new canal that I mentioned before had been opened up, a hoard of superstitious objects had been pulled out from under the Alvarado Bridge. A large number of little jars and pots that smelled like *pulque* were found, as well as an even larger number of dolls or little clay figures who were Spanish and all pierced with knives and lances that were formed of the same clay or with signs of blood on their necks, as if they had had their throats slit.
>
> (Mucho tiempo anttes de ir abriendo la asequia nueva, que dije anttes, se sacó deuajo de la puente de Aluarado infinidad de cosillas supersticiosas. Hallaronse muchissimos cantarillos y ollitas que olian a pulque, y mayor numero de muñecos o figurillas de varro y de españoles y ttodas atrauesadas con cuchillos y lansas que formaron del mismo varro o con señales de sangre en los cuellos, como degollados.)[77]

If the rains, the *chiahuixtle* plague and even the garbage could be considered natural and divine occurrences to which the viceroy had acted in accordance with the values of early modern governance, the violently maimed figurines and pulque jars indicated a human motive for the riot. Their importance in Sigüenza's narrative rests on their ability to condense the politics of the riot into threatening ciphers that the viceroy would be barely able to understand, let alone address.

As the figurines and pulque jars, as well as Sigüenza's subsequent comments on their meaning, do not appear in any other account, they have been interpreted as examples of the Creole scholar's racial paranoia.[78] Yet even if just for this reason, it is worth pausing for a moment on their symbolic meaning. Sigüenza calls the objects *supersticiosas*, a term employed from the beginning of the conquest to refer to objects that Spanish interpreted as instruments of indigenous idolatry.[79] While the term "superstition" has a long genealogy in colonial discourse, however, the anthropomorphic figurines and pulque jars Sigüenza finds in the canals are more legible to European eyes than the usual signs of seventeenth-century idolatry, such as the ancestor objects that Spanish Inquisitors referred to as "bundles" (*bultos*).[80] Their location below the Alvarado Bridge, furthermore, brings them into a well-known historical frame. The bridge marked the site of the "sad night" (*noche triste*) during Cortés's campaign to conquer Tenochtitlan. On that night, the Spanish were temporarily routed and died en masse in the canals while trying to escape the city. Even at the end of the seventeenth century the incident remained a contentious point in Spanish historiography. While anti-Spanish propaganda related the event to Alvarado's violent massacre of indigenous nobility, Spanish lore associated it with the excesses of the conquest, as the soldiers who drowned were apparently weighed down by the gold they attempted to carry with them in their retreat.[81] The site therefore served as a reminder of the fragility of the Spanish Empire: both a monument to a tragic loss and an ominous warning against the celebration of imperial triumph founded on greed and violence.

The "superstitious objects" (*cosillas supersticiosas*) that Sigüenza finds in the canals thus served as physical reminders of the violence of the Spanish conquest. As hermetic references to the battles of the noche triste, the objects could be understood as what Walter Benjamin called a "dialectical image," able to shatter the continuum of historical time by conjuring up the past in a charged symbolic constellation.[82] Yet as Michael Taussig writes in his analysis of remarkably similar figurines created by twentieth-century Cuna Indians, in a colonial context the momentary recognition of Benjamin's dialectical image contains the additional threat of alterity.[83] The power of the Cuna objects, Taussig argues, lies in their ability to break the spell of colonial myths in a form of sympathetic magic that captures the power of the other side through what he calls "mimetic excess." The inversion of colonial hierarchy reflected in these objects "tears at identity and proliferates associations of a self bound magically to an Other, too close to that Other to be but dimly recognizable, too much the self to allow for satisfying alterity."[84] By reflecting a version of colonial violence within a symbolic economy of magic, the anthropomorphic figures that Sigüenza introduces into his narrative are imbued with similar mimetic powers. Maimed and in close proximity to pulque objects, the latter a constant trope in colonial documents for indigenous excess and ungovernability, the small Spanish figures are at once recognizable and "other."

The location of these objects in the canals, moreover, suggests the ongoing problem of history and memory in seventeenth-century Mexico City. One of the only physical structures to have survived the conquest, the canals symbolized the continuity between an indigenous past and viceregal present. As opposed to the buildings of Tenochtitlan, razed to make way for the viceregal city built on their ruins, the canals were preserved by the Spanish as a pragmatic means to administer the city. Yet as Sigüenza's description of the effects of the rains and indeed the perennial project of the *desagüe* indicate, rather than delivering ordered movement, the canals had become blocked over the years with the residues of everyday plebeian life in a process of accumulation and sedimentation that paralleled the growth of the city above.[85] Dredged from the murky waters below Mexico City, then, the figurines negated the eschatological progress of Spanish imperial ideology so prominently displayed in its buildings above by suggesting an underground dissent to Spanish rule. The ominous figurines thus served as reminders that the viceroyalty's present was still haunted by the conquest in the form of unresolved and accumulated residues. Dredged from amid the garbage that was blocking the controlled movement necessary for mercantilist governance, the objects signify an invisible presence lurking under the feet of unsuspecting peninsular officials. It is this negative presence, made visible by the project to engineer and cleanse the city, that allows Sigüenza an opportunity to introduce his particular understanding of the riot's deep historical causes.

The appearance of these objects in Sigüenza's narrative, therefore, allows him to connect engineering to hermeneutics. When the archbishop and viceroy ask him for an explanation, Sigüenza interprets the figurines as premonitions of the riot:

> This occurred on the day that the viceroy came to inspect that canal and I showed the objects to him (and afterwards to the archbishop in his palace). First one and then the other prince asked me what these were. I responded that they were the positive proof of how much the Indians hate us and a sign of what they anxiously wish for the Spanish because, since in that very place the Marqués del Valle [Cortés] had been defeated when, the night of July 10, 1520, he left Mexico

and, as their histories clearly show, they dedicated this to their greatest god (which is the war god) as ominous for us and for them happy, not having forgotten their ancient superstitions even now, they jettison in effigy those that they hate so that just as so many Spanish perished in that canal at that time, the same will happen to those whom they curse.

(Fue estto en ocasion que llegó a ver aquella obra el señor virrey, a quien (y después al señor arçobispo en palacio) se los mostre. Preguntaronme vno y vtro príncipe que que era aquello; respondí ser prueua real de lo que en estremo nos aborresen los indios y muestra de lo que desean con ansia a los españoles por que, como en aquel lugar fue desuaratado el marques del Valle quando en la noche del día de (dies) de jullio del año de mill quinientos veintte se salio de Mexico y, segun consta de sus hystorias, se lo dedicaron a su mayor dios (que es el de las guerras) como ominoso para nosotros y para ellos felíz, no habiendoseles olvidado aún en esttos tiempos sus supersticiones antiguas, arrojan allí en su retrato a quien aborresen para que, como peresio en aquella asequia y en aquel tiempo tantto español, le suseda tambien a los que allí maldisen.)[86]

The questions of the viceroy and archbishop register the inability of the Spanish officials to comprehend the mixed forms of seventeenth-century viceregal society. As in Taussig's example, it is the combination of recognition and alterity, the "mimetic excess," that gives the figurines power over the men, who most likely would not have been stunned by the appearance of ancestor bundles (*bultos*) or other amorphous objects usually associated with idolatry in colonial writings. The fear these signs provoke goes beyond the recognizable figure of plebeian revolt as an inversion of governance to touch upon the very basis for colonial rule, supposedly sealed by a contractual benevolence. Sigüenza's response ("I responded that they were the positive proof of how much the Indians hate us and a sign of what they anxiously wish for the Spanish" [respondí ser prueua real de lo que en estremo nos aborresen los indios y muestra de lo que desean con ansia a los españoles]) plays on this fear by shattering any illusion that the Spanish Empire had been built on voluntary submission and sustained by love. It also suggests that the peninsular officials were unable to understand the historically entrenched nature of Novohispanic politics.

Sigüenza goes on to present himself as the one best able to decipher these signs because of his unique access to codices in his possession:

This I inferred was the meaning of those objects from what I have read in their histories and what they themselves have told me about these when I have brought them together; now I can add that, since the figurines were many and recent, throwing them there was nothing other than a declaration by that action of the depraved spirit with which they wished to end us all.

(Esto discurri qué significauan aquellos trasttes, por lo que he leído de sus hystorias y por lo que ellos mismos me han dicho de ellas cuando los he agregado; añado ahora que, siendo el número de aquellas figuras mucho y resientes, no fue otra cosa arrojarlas allí que declarar con aquel ensaye [sic] el deprauado animo con que se hallauan para acauar con todos.)[87]

Thrown under the bridge that marked the greatest defeat of the Spanish during the conquest, the figurines attempted to imitate Mexica warfare by actively remembering Huitzilopochtli. Yet while he argues that the figurines were an attempt to reopen the past, Sigüenza draws them back to the present: the objects, he asserts, were "many and recent." Sigüenza's possession of written documents as historical proof thus serves a double purpose in his account: at the same time that it associates the maimed figurines with the Mexica practice of human sacrifice, the epitome in Spanish historiography of indigenous barbarity, it also undercuts present indigenous belief by interpreting it as a degraded attempt to recover the lost powers of the Mexica gods.

Sigüenza's accusation thus confirms the perversity of indigenous political will even as it strips indigenous politics of the demonic power and, indeed, even the possession of manuscripts that were the tangible links to an idolatrous past.[88] The codices in Sigüenza's possession, in this case, confirm indigenous confessions ("what they themselves have told me" [lo que ellos mismos me han dicho]) and allow him to unravel the mystery of the mutilated Spanish figures thrown into the canals. By interpreting the figurines as an attempt to animate past idolatry, moreover, Sigüenza draws the objects into a wider circle of superstitious thinking that confused natural and divine agency. As Sigüenza has already shown, the viceregal elite was at least as vulnerable as were plebeian subjects to erroneous readings of eclipses, popular religiosity, and such far-fetched ideas as that of a drain hole in the lake. And as he had in the case of these other superstitious beliefs, Sigüenza situates himself at a point from which the figurines can be disenchanted of this superstitious value in what William Pietz calls the "discourse of the fetish."[89] But this does not mean that he posits his perspective as an encounter with universally accessible truth. Indeed, Sigüenza retains enough of the objects' distortion to threaten the Spanish officials even while he uncovers what Balibar calls the "historiosophical" truth that racist distortion exposes: in Sigüenza's words, "the depraved spirit with which they wished to end us all" (el deprauado animo con que se hallauan para acauar con todos). Unlike the viceroy's more generic response to the riot, Sigüenza presents his awry gaze as the only one capable of comprehending the magical hermeticism of the fetishes thrown into the canals. His interpretation does not deny the magic the objects possess, or the fear that they create in the Spanish officials, but rather forecloses their effect by dividing them from the indigenous archive now in his possession.

But what of the "little jars and pots that smelled like *pulque*" found together with the maimed figurines? While perhaps less immediately threatening to the Spanish officials than the blood-stained figurines, the pulque paraphernalia also drew on long-standing associations in Spanish writings between drinking, the release of bodily passions, and immorality.[90] By the end of the seventeenth century, moreover, pulquerías were increasingly associated with a plebeian sociability that threatened to undo the rigid divisions of viceregal society. Thus while the late seventeenth-century Franciscan friar Agustin Vetancurt calls the small taverns or stalls that sold pulque around the city "synagogues of vices" (sinagogas de vicios) where inversions of Christian morals of all types took place,[91] he also argues that pulque forged alliances among subjects who should be sworn enemies: "there is no neighborhood nor any street that does not have a public tavern where selling takes place to the music of guitars, harps, and other instruments with rooms where blacks, mulattoes, mestizos, and many Spaniards gather; Indians who were the enemies of blacks have become their friends through drink " (no ay barrio, ni calle que no tenga taberna publica, donde se vende con musica de guitarras, arpas, y otros instrumentos con aposentos donde se juntan Negros, y Mulatos, Mestisos, y muchos Españoles, los Indios que eran de los Negros enemigos se han hecho con la bebida camaradas).[92] Even more disturbing to moralists such as Vetancurt was the Crown's policy of taxing the pulque trade. Indeed, while pulque was banned several times during the colonial period, including in the period directly following the riot, these prohibitions had always been reversed as soon as it was politically feasible because of the revenue gained by the tax.[93] Again, Vetancurt gives an example of the constant moral criticism of this policy among colonists when he writes: "I declare that if this were to reach the ears of a Catholic monarch such as our king, he would prize the salvation of the souls of these poor people more than money" (yo digo que si esto llegara à los oydos de vn Catholico Monarca como nuestro Rey, estimara mas la salvacion de las almas de estos pobres que el dinero).[94]

In the wake of the riot, a manifesto against pulque composed by members of the university went even further, coining the term poliplebio to refer to the perverse relationship among pulque, plebeian sociability, and an underground economy protected by Crown interests: "all the laws prohibit unauthorized and unconfirmed congregations and bodies: this one of the drinkers, since it is not the entire city, is not a monopoly, but as it is all the plebes it is *poliplebeian*. What discussions will they not have in these gatherings? What robberies will they not plan? And what else?" (Las congregaciones, y cuerpos no authorizados, y confirmados, prohiben todos derechos: esta de bebedores, si porque no es de toda la Ciudad, no es monopolio, siendo de toda la pleba, será poliplebio. Que conferencias no se haran en estas concurrencias? Que robos no se concerterán? Y que que?).[95] The report explicitly compares the pulque gatherings to a monopoly, thus mixing two etymological meanings of "poli." On the one hand, "poli" is "many" as in the many adherents to pulque. Yet the similar suffix "polio" in "monopolio" is etymologically related to *polein*, "to sell."[96] Rather than a city centered around a unified accumulation, a mercantilist "monopoly," the multiplication of pulque stalls around the city thus appears in the report to be the center of a many-headed plebeian economy, or *poliplebio*. The context of urban congregations, moreover, brings to mind the root "polis." The ingeniously incendiary term *poliplebio*, therefore, perfectly condenses elite fears that the plebe would form an alternative economy within the city, a deformed polis sanctioned by corrupt officials.

The association of pulque, moral degradation, and idolatry was a topos that circulated in sermons, diatribes and public debates throughout the seventeenth century and Sigüenza's works are no exception. In the prologue to his 1684 *Parayso occidental*, Sigüenza had already blamed indigenous degeneracy on "despicable pulque" (detestable pulque). Going further than this in 1692, Sigüenza reads the proximity between the figurines and the pulque jars as proof that the sedition had been plotted in the city's pulquerías

> where, because of a wicked and ungodly agreement, the contractors do not police. What could result that would be of use to us? They [the pulquerías] were frequented not only by the usual Indians but also by

the infamous plebes and, the former hearing the latter, they decided to scare (as they say in their language) the Spaniards, to burn the Royal Palace and to kill, if possible, the viceroy and magistrate; and since with this situation those who heard these talks and who were not Indians would not lack the opportunity to rob during that conflict, I assume that they applauded [the idea] (as we later saw).

(donde por condicion iniqua y contra Dios que se le concedió al asenttistta no entra en justicia, ¿qué pudo resulttar que nos fuesse vtil? Acudian a ellas como siempre no solo indios sino la mas despresiable de nuestra infame pleue y, oiendoles a aquellos, se determinaba a espantar (como dicen en su lengua) a los españoles, a quemar el Palacio Real y matar, si pudiesen al señor virrey y al corregidor; como con esto no les falttaría a los demás, que asistian a aquellas platticas y que no heran indios, mucho que rouar en aquel conflicto; presumo que se lo aplaudieron (por lo que bimos despues).)⁹⁷

Sigüenza further supports his accusation that the conspiracy took shape in these underground plebeian sites by referring to the confession of a man named the "Mouse": "That this all took place before their sedition is not for me probable but rather evident. I am not obliged to state this by the one who declared this in his confession and whom they punished for this crime and whom all know by the name of the 'Mouse,' but rather because of what I saw with my own eyes and touched with my own hands" (Hauer presedido todo estto a su sedicion no es para mi probable sino ebidente, y no me obliga a que assi lo diga el que assi lo dijo en su confeccion [sic] uno que ajustisiaron por estte delicto y a quien, con nombre de Ratton, conosieron todos, sino lo que yo vi con mis ojos y ttoque con mis manos).⁹⁸ Drawing on the etymological root of "evidence" as "sight,"⁹⁹ Sigüenza suggests the objects found in the canal complement the law's reliance on the confessions of degraded subjects such as the "Mouse" (Ratton) by providing a deeper revenge motive for the riot.¹⁰⁰

The objects in the canals thus become an alternative source of evidence that exposes excesses beyond the idiom of pastoral care and patrimonial reciprocity. At the end of his letter Sigüenza returns to the theme of pulque, making more explicit the relationship between its abundance and a late seventeenth-century void in colonial authority:

> Since never (from the beginning of their pagan times) had Indian drunkenness reached greater excesses and licentiousness than in these times in which those who peddle it do so under the pretext that they are contributing to the king our lord, there is more pulque in Mexico City on a single day than during an entire year when it was governed

by idolaters. In respect to its abundance there is no corner, let me correct myself, no street in the entire [city] in which, openly and shamelessly many more souls are sacrificed to the devil through this vice than those bodies that were offered at their pagan temples in the past.

(Como nunca (entrando el tiempo de su gentilidad) llegó la vorrachera de los indios a mayor exceso y dissolucion que en aquestos tiempos en que, con pretestto de lo que contribuien al Rey Nro Señor los que condusen, abunda más el pulque en México en solo un día que en un año entero cuando la gobernaban idolattras. Al respecto de su abundancia no hauia rincon, muy mal he dicho, no hauia calles ni plassa publica enttoda ella donde, con descaro y con desverguensa, no se le sacrificasen al demonio muchas mas almas con estte vicio que cuerpos se le ofresieron en sus templos genttílicos en los passados tiempos.)[101]

In 1684 Sigüenza also claimed to come to his knowledge of the pernicious associations between pulque and idolatry through direct communication with indigenous subjects.[102] In 1692, however, he places a greater emphasis on the collapse of authority, including that of indigenous nobles, as the cause of the increase in pulque throughout the city. Noting that after the riot the viceroy had immediately banned the drink, Sigüenza lists those who approved of this measure, including "the very Indians, those few who preserve something of their ancient nobility" (los proprios indios los pocos que conservavan algo de noblessa anttigua).[103] Through absence or complicity, then, the collapse of traditional sources of authority had allowed pulque to prevail in the city, fueling a dangerous counterhistorical memory that led to the riot. Sigüenza ends his antipulque diatribe by warning that providence itself has sent a message by allowing the riot to occur: "if there is no reform, he will perfect his justice" (Si faltta enmienda, perfisionara su justicia).[104] Unlike the conventional discourse of Spanish imperial providentialism, however, in 1692 it is only Sigüenza's perspective that allows divine justice to be deciphered.

THE LIVING CORPSE: WOMEN, RACE, AND RIOT

Whereas it is quite possible that Sigüenza invented or exaggerated his description of the figurines and pulque jars found under the Alvarado Bridge, his account of the rioters' words and actions appears more probable. Although clearly an attempt to deauthorize the rioters within the logic of early modern notions of social order, Sigüenza's letter also contains some of the most intriguing descriptions of the riot's events. Whether or not he intended this to be the case, Sigüenza's inclusion of cries of revenge for the conquest, critiques of viceregal excesses, and identification among the city's ethnically and socially diverse inhabitants suggests a political consciousness among rioters that went beyond the terms of Spanish contractual sovereignty. One of the most striking characteristics of Sigüenza's narrative, for instance, is the centrality he ascribes to women. This is not, on the surface, a cause for surprise. In fact, one of the most notable aspects of popular disturbances in the colonial period is the relatively high numbers of women who participated in them. As William Taylor has written of popular disturbances in seventeenth-century Oaxaca, "in at least one-fourth of the cases women led the attacks and were visibly more aggressive, insulting and rebellious."[105] Following E. P. Thompson's seminal work on riots in early modern England, historians have often interpreted this gendered aspect of colonial protests as a sign of moral crisis within a patrimonial logic.[106] In her thorough study of the social and political context of the 1692 riot, however, Natalia Silva Prada has questioned the assumption that women were defined by domesticity, pointing out that in Mexico City women were often public vendors, especially of pulque.[107] Indeed, women's involvement in the sale of pulque has also long been recognized. In his study of colonial drinking, William Taylor calls the presence of women among pulque sellers "striking" and suggests that this may be due to the "close association between the maguey plant and femininity."[108]

Yet it is clear that the involvement of women in pulque selling is as much tied to the informality of the trade as it is to symbolic associations between women and the maguey plant. In fact, Taylor himself goes on to assert that "some of the so-called taverns in peasant communities amounted to nothing more than the doorstep of a householder who was known to be tapping a few magueyes at the time" and that the high number of pulque bars found in surveys in the eighteenth century has to do with the informal structure of the trade.[109] This fluidity between domestic and public spaces in early modern culture facilitated pulque's association with political and moral disorder. Diatribes such as the 1692 pulque tract written by the university committee after the riot, for instance, directly relate the wealth of the women who sold pulque to moral corruption: "and it is notable that the sellers are always female (a circumstance that the said Father pondered in Peru, because in order to sell more, they engage in more sin) and ordinarily these Indian women pulque sellers are rich" (y es de notar, que las vendedoras siempre son hembras (circunstancia, que ponderó dicho P. en el Peru, porque a trueque de que les compren mas, caen allà en mas pecados) y ordinariamente estas Indias pulqueras son ricas).[110] In his *Teatro mexicano*, Vetancurt depicts the pulquerías as close to brothels and suggests that the women pulque sellers exchanged gifts and favors with administrative officials: "their first care is to have powerful men and ministers of the justice as protectors who shower them with gifts of little value (which the women hold in high esteem) " (su primer diligencia es tener a hombres poderosos y ministros de justicia por compadres a quienes regalan con cosas de poca monta (de que hazen las comadres mucho aprecio)).[111]

Although Sigüenza does not assert that the pulquerías were run by Indian women, he does place women at the center of the social disorder leading up to the riot, blaming them especially for fomenting false information about the viceroy. Sigüenza writes that despite the viceroy's efforts to maintain the corn and wheat levels in the city, a rumor began "in secret" (en secreto)[112] that officials were hoarding the stores for their own benefit. The rumors went public, he goes on to argue, after a priest preached an incendiary sermon: "not that which was needed to console people in their need but rather that which imprudently served to provoke them" (no lo que se devía para consolar al pueblo en la carestía sino lo que se dicto por la imprudencia para irritarlo). This fissure in governance opened the door for public dissidence: "The wretched parishioners reacted to what the preacher said with benedictions and applause and a notable murmuring; and from that time onward, considering this to be a confirmation of their previous suspicions, they now spoke shamelessly even in public places" (Correspondió el auditorio ínfimo a lo que el predicador desía con bendisiones, con aplausos y con desentonado mormullo; y desde entonsses, teniendo por euidencias sus antesedenttes malicias, se hablava ya con desvergüença aun en parttes publicaz).[113] At the height of tensions, the viceroy attended a service and "when he entered the church a not very hidden murmur was heard among the women (if the gentlemen-in-waiting and pages who were attending heard it, how could his excellency not as well?) in which they insulted and cursed him hideously, attributing the shortage of corn and lack of bread to his faults" (al entrar por la iglesia se levanto vn mormullo no muy confusso entre las mugeres (pues lo oieron los genttiles hombres y paxes que le assistian, ¿cómo pudo su excelencia dejar de oirlo?) en que feamentte le exsecraban y mal desian, atribuiendo a sus omisiones y mal gouierno la faltta de maíz y la carestía de pan).¹¹⁴ Thus Sigüenza associates "murmuring," a common trope in the representation of popular dissent in early modern texts, with women.

This blatant inversion of a masculine public space leads to Sigüenza's main accusation: rather than government officials, it was Indian women who had been hoarding corn in order to drive up the price of tortillas. Because of the shortage of wheat, Sigüenza writes, not only Indians but

> very many Spaniards, and most of the blacks and free mulattoes and house servants all began eating tortillas; and these were not made by the servants, nor the mulattoes, nor the blacks, nor the Spanish, nor by their women, because the only ones who know how to make them are the Indian women who, in crowds in the plaza and groups in the streets, went around constantly selling them.
>
> (muchisimos españoles, los mas de los negros y mulattos libres y los siruienttes de las cassas todos comian tortillas y esttas ni las hacian los siruientes, ni los mulattos, ni los negros, ni los españoles, ni sus mugeres, porque no las sauen hacer sino las indias que, a montones en la plasa y a bandadas por las calles, las andauan bendiendo continuamentte.)¹¹⁵

To illustrate his point, Sigüenza tells of his own experience buying a tortilla at an inflated price. Calculating the gain that the Indian woman had made on the transaction, he declares,

> how could they be dying, as they yelled, when that which they pocketed from (the tortillas) was not only sufficient for their sustenance, for which they need little as all know, but left them with a surplus that they could save, and this above and beyond the constant odd jobs and wages of their husbands? Therefore, only this clear gain, and not hunger, brought them to the grain warehouse in such inflated numbers that they trampled each other in order to buy corn; therefore, no other year was better for them.
>
> (¿cómo podían pereser, como desian a grittos, quando de lo que grangeauan con ellas no sólo les sobraba para el sustento en que se gasta poco como todos saven sino para ir guardando, y esto prescindiendo del conttinuo de los oficios y jornales de sus maridos? Luego, sólo estta ganancia tan conosida, y no la hambre, las traia a la alondiga en tan cresido numero que unas a otras se atropellauan para comprar maís; luego, en ninguno otro año les fue mejor.)¹¹⁶

Finally, the money gained from tortillas directly instigated the Indian men to riot since "having learned from their women that by buying corn they had gotten the better even of the Spanish, they began to boast in the pulquerías that this was the effect of the fear we had of such an action on their part" (sabiendo de sus mugeres el que en la compra del maiz las anteponían aun a españoles, comensaron a presumir en las pulquerías ser efectto del miedo que les teníamos semejantte acsion).[117]

Sigüenza's accusation that Indian women were responsible for a general inversion of the social, economic, and gendered hierarchy culminates in his pointed attack on the symbol that had immediately sparked the riot: the body of an Indian woman killed by a guard at the city's corn warehouse. Sigüenza's narrative of events agrees with the basic outline given by another anonymous witness.[118] As rumors circulated that the viceroy was actively hoarding corn, a crowd of Indian women began to gather daily at the corn warehouse to demand access to its stores. On one day in particular, the rations were insufficient and a violent confrontation ensued. In the middle of this melee, Sigüenza writes, a guard began to whip the crowd to keep it back. One young woman was particularly insistent, and the guard, "becoming angry" (enfadado destto), whipped her ten to twelve times.[119] Infuriated, the women lifted the wounded girl over their heads and carried her through the city. Traveling first to the viceregal palace and then to the archbishop's house to protest, they were refused at each. Although the archbishop sent word to the warehouse "that the women be treated with compassion" (que mirassen aquellas indias con compacion), Sigüenza dryly comments that "they must have wished for more than this, since they returned to the Royal Palace in even larger numbers than before" (debía de ser más que estto lo que querían, pues se boluieron en mucha mayor tropa que anttes al Palacio Real).[120] The rioters then stormed the palace but were prevented by guards from entering the viceroy's chamber and soon afterward dispersed.

The following day, however, a similar scene occurred when another woman fell and was trampled by the crowd. This time Sigüenza introduces the possibility that the body itself was a ruse:

> and, after she was well trod upon, they lifted her almost lifeless body, as some claimed, or they persuaded an old woman who was there to pretend to be dead, as others affirm. That which is known without controversy is that an Indian man lifted an Indian woman over his shoulders and that the others that were there followed her with more commotion and uproar than the previous day, going off toward the marketplace.

(y después de muy bien pisada, la levantaron casi sin respiración, como dicen unos, o que persuadieron a una vieja que allí estaua el que se fingiese muerta, como afirman otros. Lo que si se sabe sin controbercia es que, hechandose un indio a una india sobre los hombros y siguiendola con mayor aluoroto y estruendo que el día anttes cuantas allí estauan, que eran muchissimas, se fueron saliendo hasta el Varattillo.)[121]

As Sigüenza follows the crowd's progress he narrates a scene that proves that the woman was indeed still alive:

> During the time of this struggle, which was not long, two students were hanging around there and, drawing close to the Indian woman who was being carried, one said to the other these exact words: "Look, man, how the poor dead woman is sweating!" The other one drew as close to her as possible and responded, "She's not very dead, because she is blinking and swallowing saliva!" "What do you know about dead people, you ignorant dogs of students?" an Indian woman who overheard the discussion asked them. "Now all of you in Mexico will die, just as she has!" The students did not wait for another word but, taking advantage of the horrific confusion around them, scampered off. I learned of this from an honorable man who was present and who assured me, under oath as I asked him, that not only was it true what the students had said, but that slightly beforehand he had heard the dead woman ask them to carry her carefully. There you have Indians.

> (Durante el tiempo desta contienda, que no fue mucho, estauan por allí dos estudiantillos y, asercandose a la india que traían cargada, le dijo el uno al otro estas formales palabras: "¡Mirad, hombre como está sudando la pobre muerta!" Allegose el otro a ella lo mas que pudo y respondiole assi: "¡No estta muy muertta, porque pestañea un poco y trago saliua!" "¿Qué sabeis vosotros de cómo están los muerttos, perros estudianttes de modorro?" les dijo una india que les oyó la plattica. "Aora morireis todo México, como ella estta." No aguardaron los muchachos otra razón y, entre la confucion horrorosa que alli hauía, se escabulleron. Refiriome estto un hombre honrrado que se hallo presente y me aseguro, con juramento que le pedí, no solo ser verdad lo que los estudianttes dijeron, sino el que poco antes le oio decir a la muerta que la cargaran bien. Esttos son los indios.)[122]

This passage, and especially Sigüenza's final verdict ("there you have Indians"), is certainly one of the strongest examples of racism in the letter. Just as the maimed figurines that "show how much the Indians hate us," Sigüenza here purports to know the inherently perverse nature of indigenous subjects. And once again, Sigüenza's own perspective strikingly mixes an intimate knowledge of the "other" with judgment supported by empirical distance.

In this case, moreover, Sigüenza's intimate and distanced perspective allows him to undermine the crowd's symbol of injustice, by reporting that the corpse continued in its base bodily functions—sweating, blinking, and swallowing saliva. Although the students' comments verge on puerile satire, the "honest man" adds authority when he notes that not only was the students' perception correct but that the corpse even asked to be carried more comfortably. The "oath" of the honest man, in this case, provides Sigüenza with authoritative evidence even as it allows him to remain outside the frame of the scene, at a disembodied point of judgment.[123] Indeed, it is the response of the Indian woman who has overheard the students that returns the scene to violence. And yet as opposed to the objects found in the canals, the Indian woman's retort establishes a contrary perspective on events that escapes Sigüenza's narrative control. While the issue of whether the corpse was dead or alive was crucial to justifying the rioters' actions, the woman's response does not defend the corpse in these terms. Rather, she attacks the students' ability to judge what constitutes death itself: "What do you know about dead people, you ignorant dogs of students?" Rather than acknowledging a common notion of death, the woman seems to suggest that what constitutes life and death is relative and that the students cannot hope to understand the way in which this Indian woman was dead.[124] In the context of Sigüenza's narrative this idea is patently absurd and only serves to deauthorize even further the crowd's position by exposing the intentions that lie behind the ruse of the fake corpse. Yet given the highly charged atmosphere around the body, it is worth asking whether the woman's statement could have further meaning than simply the reassertion of authority through violence.

Indeed, this was not the first time in colonial Mexico that the body of a violently mistreated casta woman had prompted a popular protest. In 1611 blacks and mulattoes in Mexico City had also rallied around the body of a slave woman killed by her owner, marching through the city with the corpse above their heads.[125] Although in both cases it is plausible to understand the political symbolism of a woman's body within the gendered semiotics of a moral economy, and thus as a sign of disorder that does not disrupt patrimonialist logic, it is also important to consider these gestures in light of the colonialist imaginary. From the well-known engraving of Vespucci discovering America to the decorative allegory of the four continents, the bodies of indigenous women had symbolized territorial and subjective possession within a highly sexualized idiom.[126] In the Spanish colonial imaginary African and mulatta women appeared to have been more closely related to luxury and surplus, as were, indeed, African slaves themselves in colonial Mexico.[127] In 1692, as in 1611, it is possible that the corpse of a mistreated woman formed something like a "counterallegory" to this colonialist imaginary. Rather than protesting a momentary failure of reciprocity, the power of these corpses might have resided in their ability to expose patrimonialism itself as a false reciprocity and thus to refuse its terms. The unsignifiable object that denied the boundary between life and death might have been the only way to disrupt the official narrative of patrimonialism in which injustice should be countered by better treatment. Although clearly not the intention of Sigüenza's narrative, the Indian woman's refusal to acknowledge a common understanding of life and death makes it possible to think of the living corpse as a mixed sign for injustice that went beyond the reciprocal terms of patrimonialism to question the very meaning of living in late seventeenth-century Mexico City.[128]

COLONIAL COUNTERHISTORY

In Sigüenza's account of the 1692 riot it is the very excess of these signifying objects that turns them into hermetic ciphers. Resting on the border of unintelligibility, the distorted objects challenge the basic premise of a contractual sovereignty: that indigenous and plebeian intentions were transparent and good-willed.[129] Similarly, the cries Sigüenza records among the rioters threaten precisely because they understand the Spanish presence in Mexico to be an occupation of territory rather than a contract: "'Eh señoras!' the Indian women said to one another in their language, 'let's go willingly to this war, and if God permits all Spaniards to die in it, it will not matter that we die without confession! Is this not our land? Well then, what do the Spanish want with it?'" ("Ea señoras!" se desian las indias en su lengua vnas a vtras, "¡vamos con alegría a estta guerra, y comoquiera Dios que se acaben en ella los españoles, no importa que muramos sin confession! ¿No es nra estta tierra? Pues, ¿que quieren en ella los españoles?).[130] Speaking in Nahuatl, which Sigüenza translates, the women invoke a Christian God even as they reject confession. And while claiming possession of the land in European terms they protest its occupation by Spaniards. As in the case of the maimed figurines, it is the very terms that make these cries legible for a peninsular audience, or in this case translatable, that make them threatening. And just as in the case of the corpse that straddled life and death, they produce what Taussig calls "mimetic excess" by suggesting that a racially mixed plebeian populace could find symbolic coherence in an incomplete colonial project.

Whether consciously or not, it appears that this is exactly the sensation that Sigüenza wishes to evoke in his metropolitan readers. While presenting objects and rioters as grotesque distortions he allows them enough agency to produce the haunting sensation of the abject: the fear that the other could stand in one's place.[131] Sigüenza plays on this fear in one of the most well-known passages of his letter:

> You will ask me how the plebeians were behaving during this time and I'll respond briefly that well and badly; well, because they are such extremely plebeian plebeians that they earn their reputation as the most infamous. Indeed, they are the most vile of all populaces as they are made up of Indians, of Creole and *bozal* blacks of different nations, of *chinos, mulatos, moriscos, mestizos,* and *zambaigos,* of *lobos* and also of Spaniards who, declaring themselves to be *zaramullos* (which is the same as saying rogues, rascals, and cape-snatchers) and degenerating in their obligations are the worst of such a despicable lot.
>
> (Pregunttarame Vmd como se portó la pleue en aqueste tiempo y respondo brevemente que bien y mal; bien, porque siendo pleue tan en extremo pleue, que solo ella lo puede sser de la que se reputtare la mas infame, y lo es de ttodas las pleues por componerse de Indios, de negros criollos y Vosales de diferentes naciones, de chinos, de mulattos, de moriscos, de mestissos, de Sambaigos, de lobos y tambien de españoles que, en declarandosse Saramullos (que es lo mismo que pícaros, chulos y arreuata capas) y degenerando de su [sic] obligaciones, son los peores entre tan ruin canalla.)[132]

The impression that Sigüenza clearly wishes to give to his metropolitan readers is that the mixture of lineages in New Spain had collapsed traditional social binaries into a disorderly mass. Indeed, beginning with "Indians" and ending with Spaniards who have "degenerated from their obligations," the cacophonic list of casta names, only some of which Sigüenza translates for his Spanish audience, negates the two-republic model of colonial governance. And although the castas themselves receive Sigüenza's opprobrium he saves his severest words for the "Spanish" who he claims have avoided the "obligations" of their race.[133]

Throughout his letter, Sigüenza repeatedly represents plebeian politics as a heterogeneous mass dangerously poised on the edge of symbolic coherence. In Sigüenza's argument, the political reach of the riot thus goes beyond the momentary context of a grain shortage to touch upon the foundations of the viceregal order. Indeed, as the riot continues, plebeian subjects symbolically interrupt mercantile flows and challenge the ability of peninsular governance to contain dissent. According to Sigüenza, the most spectacular targets of crowd violence were objects of viceregal political power and Spanish luxury. While part of the crowd mocked the attributes of political power, burning the viceroy's palace and parading around the zócalo in his carriage, others destroyed stalls and crates in the marketplace, yelling "Eh Spanish rubbish, the fleet has come in! Come on you pansies, let's go to the crates to buy ribbons and wigs!" (¡Españoles de porquería, ya vino la flotta! ¡Andad, mariquitas, a los caxones a comprar sintas y cauelleras!).[134] By associating economic surplus and luxury with femininity, the crowd undermined gendered notions of economic right in much the same way that the politicized cries of indigenous women challenged the moral economy of patrimonialism. Balancing these acts of destruction, however, are slogans that projected the king as an imaginary source of justice, celebrations of the Holy Sacrament, praises of pulque, and other cries so insulting that Sigüenza declines to include them in the letter. For the metropolitan reader the horror of these scenes, including those recounting the ominous objects in the canal and the sweating and salivating dead woman, is that they suggest an alternative political economy within the viceregal polity. This was not simply a reversal of imperial law—while rejecting Spanish rule, the rioters apparently also rejected a return to an idealized preconquest purity; rather, the rioters appeared to invoke the past in order to find a place beyond the confines of present political language.[135]

If Sigüenza represents this threatening excess as a visible distortion of the social order, he presents himself as its unseen witness. In a well-known passage he recounts how, after the riot caught him unaware in his study, he descended to the street to enter its midst:

> In nothing of which I have told that happened that afternoon was I myself present because I was in my house buried in my books. And although I had heard from the street part of the noise, since because of the continual drunkenness of the Indians this irritation was common, I didn't even think to open the windows of my study to see what

was happening until my servant, arriving almost out of breath, called to me in an agitated voice: "Sir, riot!" I immediately opened the windows and seeing that an infinite number of people were running towards the plaza, I descended hurriedly and half-dressed into the midst of the cries: "Death to the viceroy and the magistrate who have hoarded our corn and are killing us of hunger!"

(En nada de quantto he dho que passó estta tarde me hallé presentte, porque me estaua en cassa sobre mis libros. Y aunque yo hauia oido en la calle parte del ruido, siendo hordinario los que por las continuas borracheras de los indios nos enfadan siempre, ni aun se me ofresio abrir las bidrieras de la benttana de mi estudio para ber lo que era hastta que, entrando un criado cassi ahogando, se me dixo a grandes Vosses; "¡Señor, tumultto!" Abrí las benttanas a ttoda prisa y, biendo que corría asia la plassa ynfinita gente a medio vestir y cassi corriendo, entre lo que yvan gritando: "¡Muera el virrey y el corregidor, que tienen atrauessado el maíz y nos matan de hambre!," me fui a ella.)[136]

Continuing his account, Sigüenza describes his reaction to the scene unfolding before him on the street:

I was stunned. It was such an extreme number of people, not only Indians but all [types of] castas, the cries and hollers were so rude, the rain of stones that fell on the palace so thick that the noise that was made on the doors and the windows exceeded that of more than a hundred drums of war being played at the same time; those who did not throw [stones], which were not many, waved their cloaks like banners and others threw their hats into the air and others created parodies; and to all the Indian women delivered stones with notable effort. And it was then only six thirty.

(me quedé atónito. Era tan estremo tantta la gentte, no solo de indios sino de todas casttas, tan desenttonados los grittos y el alarido, tan espesa la tempesttad de piedras que llouia sobre el palacio que exsedia el ruido que hacian en las puertaz y en las benttanas al de mas de cien caxaz de guerra que se tocasan juntas; de los que no tirauan, que no eran pocos, vnos tremolaban sus mantas como banderas y otros arrojauan al aire sus sombreros y burlaban otros; a ttodos les administraban piedras las indias con diligencia estraña. Y eran entonses las seis y media.)[137]

The scene encapsulates the awry perspective of a Creole scholar, a mixture of bookish distance and empirical proximity. His intention, clearly, is to pass on his own shock to his readers without providing moral closure to the scene. Indeed, by closing with the exact time he suggests that this is only the beginning of what will develop over the course of the night, thus leaving the narrative tinged with the horror of untold excess.

As Sigüenza descends into the streets, he continues to counterbalance the ineffectiveness of the usual symbols of authority with his own unseen perspective. From his ground-level view he reports that a representative of the church tried in vain to subdue the crowd: "thinking that the whole plebe would follow God their Father, [the priest] went bravely into the plaza; but, carried away with throwing stones, lighting fires and robbing the crates, they did not bend their knees nor adore him" (pensando seguiria a su Dios y Señor toda la pleue, se arrojó a la plasa pero empeñados en tirar piedras, en poner fuego y en rouar los cajones los que en ella estauan, ni le doblauan la rodilla ni le adorauan).[138] In contrast to the ineffectiveness of the priests, Sigüenza presents himself as heroically saving the archives, located in the burning viceregal palace:

> I will excuse myself from referring plainly at this point to the much (or little, as those enemies who are never absent would have it) that I did freely and spontaneously without reflecting on my state and without looking for a reward. With a bar and an axe I cut beams, pried open doors, and through my efforts the fire was put out not only in some rooms of the palace but in entire halls and in the best archives of the city. Enough about my role in these events.
>
> (escusare desde aqui para lo de adelante referirme nudamentte lo mucho (o nada, o lo que quisieron emulos que nunca falttan) que, sin haserme reflexa a mi estado, hisse esponttanea y graciossamentte, y sin mirar al premio quando ya con una varreta, ya con una acha cortando vigas, apalacando puerttas, por mi industria se le quitaron al fuego de entre las manos no sólo algunos quartos del Palacio sino tribunales enteros y de la ciudad su mejor archiuo. Vasta con estto lo que a mi toca.)[139]

As Kathleen Ross has argued, Sigüenza presents his rescue of the papers that documented the foundation of colonial Mexico as a heroic deed, perhaps in imitation of the conquerors themselves. Ross brings to bear on this interpretation another passage in which Sigüenza directly invokes Cortés as a model: "And exhorting one another to have courage, remembering that there was no other Cortés to subjugate them, they rushed into the plaza to accompany the others throwing stones" (Y exsortándose vnos a otros a tener valor, supuesto que ya no hauía otro Corttes que los sujetase, se arrojauan a la plassa a acompañar a los otros y a tirar piedras).[140]

Yet if Sigüenza saves the city archives in an attempt to provide this "other Cortés," it is perhaps because a return to historical foundations, not the glorious violence of the conquest, is the only means to contest the new figure of seventeenth-century insurrection. Indeed, the only figure in viceregal government that might have provided symbolic continuity with the Spanish conquest is conspicuously absent from Sigüenza's account. Throughout the riot, the viceroy remains hidden in a church outside the center of the city, an action that proved contentious in reports sent to Madrid after the riot. The governor's absence from the scene of the riot forecloses his ability to fulfill the somatic ideal of governance outlined earlier in Sigüenza's letter. Despite the argument of an anonymous chronicler of the riot that it has never been prudent for the head of the body politic to stick out when the body itself is rebelling,[141] the viceroy literally disappears inside the convent, where he can hear but not see the riot:

> at the news of the actions of the rebels and the confusion and uprising happening in the plaza, the honorable viceroy found himself in the convent of San Francisco. The first report that he heard attributed the events to youthful pranks but by the second it was clear that it was instead an enormous movement of all of Mexico, all conspiring to take the life of his excellency, as they yelled at the top of their lungs.
>
> (la notisia de la [sic] acometimiento que le hisieron los sediciossos y de la confusion y aluoroto que en la plaça auia halló al señor virrey en el conbentto de San Francisco. La vos primera que allí se oio atribuyó a trabesura de muchachos lo que hauia sido, y afirmó la segunda no ser sino mobimiento gigantte de todo México, conspirado sin exsepcion de personas para quitarle la vida a su excelencia, como lo desian a vosses.)[142]

Absent from the scene of events, the viceroy becomes defined as curiously effeminate and ineffectual. While the crowd wages an attack on the luxurious trappings of the viceregal elite, moreover, the viceroy's wife herself represents this very symbolic excess: Sigüenza reports that after first visiting the Virgin de Remedios, she went strolling in the San Cosme gardens to "enjoy the view" (diuertir la vista).[143]

It is clear from these scenes that the riot itself has exceeded the model of an organic polity idealized by Thomistic theopolitics. To offset the power of this disturbance, Sigüenza's subjective and disembodied perspective permits a ground-level view and insight into the rioters' actions. Yet although he claims an inside knowledge of the riot, Sigüenza erases any suggestion of a social relationship between himself and the casta subjects that surround him. Notably, after an initial interruption of his solitary studies by his servant, who relates to him the gravity of the situation on the city streets outside, Sigüenza holds no other dialogues as he reports on the riot's progress. Despite his recognition in trial records of a mulatto man named Antonio who helped save the city's archives,[144] Sigüenza represents his actions during the riot as an individual feat. The servant who warns of the plebeian rebellion and the mulatto who helped save the archives, perhaps the same man, disappear from his account altogether. These details are symbolic of the segregated order that Sigüenza will advocate as the solution to the plebeian disturbance. Rather than a reversal of the symbolic structures, the rioters in Sigüenza's account have perverted them through contamination. Sigüenza's solution to this erasure of boundaries is the purification of the city center as a bulwark against the incommensurate mixing of Christianity and idolatry, Spanish and Nahuatl, and indigenous and nonindigenous subjects in urban spaces.

To return the city to order, then, Sigüenza advocates the rationalization of public spaces. The canals should be cleansed and the residue that continually fell back into them cleared for good. The marketplace (Baratillo), he argues, was particularly susceptible to the rioters' actions since "the space in the plaza not filled with crates was occupied by Indian stalls formed of reeds and *petates*, which are mats, where they sold by day and closed up at night with the result that one of the most extensive and best plazas in the world appears a badly ordered village to some and to all a pigsty" (lo que quedaua en la plaça sin los cajones se ocupaua con puestos de indios, formados de carriso y pettates, que son estteras, donde vendian de dia y se recojian de noche, resulttando de ttodo ello el que una de las mas dilattadas y mejores plassas que tiene el mundo, algunos les paresiesse una mal fundada aldea, y saurda a ttodos).[145] Tellingly, these were the very areas in late seventeenth-century Mexico City that most permitted continuities in indigenous social practices and provided spaces of plebeian sociability in the present. Rhetorically, he also effects a cleansing by closing his account of the riot in a striking reversal of the noche triste of the Spanish conquest, the memory of which he claims had instigated the riot. While Cortés's soldiers died attempting to escape the city with pillaged gold, he asserts that those responsible for the riot escaped freely on the canals with their ransacked loot.[146] Once this pillaging had ended, however, the riot itself petered out.[147] In the void that followed, he appears to suggest, only the archive can return order to the ransacked city. It is through this active control, rather than burial, of the past that Sigüenza advocates building a Creole polity amid imperial ruins.

Sigüenza's letter was written several months after the riot, at which point the elite of Mexico City had begun to give symbolic closure to the unprecedented events. Indeed, the viceroy had already put into effect exemplary punishments. Sigüenza reports at the end of his letter that

> having found four Indians in the very barracks of the palace while it was being burned and, [these] having confessed without torture that they were accomplices in the riot and had been involved in the burning, on Wednesday the 11th they shot all of them except for one who had killed himself with poison the night before; they hung five or six, burned one and whipped many others over several days and I understand that they are now proceeding with others that are jailed.
>
> (hauiendose coxido quatro indios en los mismos quarteles de palacio al ponerles Fuego y, confessando sin tormento alguno hauer sido complises en el tumultto y coperado al insendio, menos a uno que con beneno la noche antes se matto a si mismo, el Miercoles onse por la mañana los arcabuscaron; ahorcaron a sinco o seiz, quemaron a uno y asotaron a muchos en diferentes dias, y jusgo que se ba prosediendo contra otros que se hallan presos.)[148]

Despite Sigüenza's assertion that women were the instigators of the riot, the trials and punishment focused almost exclusively on men and primarily on the supposed ringleader, a one-eyed crippled man named José de los Santos whom Sigüenza surprisingly does not include in his narrative.[149] These differences between the trial records and Sigüenza's version of the riot correspond to their distinct goals. While the trials were concerned with finding suitable culprits, Sigüenza's letter looks forward to a new administrative governance capable of responding to present social configurations rather than past ideals. In this sense, Sigüenza's letter shows that late seventeenth-century Creole politics emerged in dialectical concert with what he portrayed to be a politicized plebeian culture able to overturn the fragile imperial contract that held the viceroyalty together.

While it is difficult to know whether Sigüenza's letter is correct in assigning plebeian rioters this role, its perspective clearly resonated with governmental fears in the last years of Habsburg rule. When the Neapolitan Giovanni Gemelli Careri visited Mexico in 1697, for instance, he found a city in which public memory was seen as a threat to imperial governance: "I went in vain to Santiago de Tlatelolco to have the ancient Indian dress shown to me" (andai indarno in S. Iago de Taltelucco per farmi disegnare gli abiti antichi degl'Indiani), he writes, "since, after the tumult to which I have referred, the viceroy had ordered the ancient painting that was found there to be whitewashed so that there might be no register nor memory of their former liberty" (perche il V. Re dopo il tumulto mentovato avea fatta cancellare un'antica dipintura, che quivi si ritrovava: acciò non restasse vestigio, nè memoria dell'antica lor libertà).[150] Meanwhile, the viceregal palace had been rebuilt following a more militaristic model, "with two towers pointing toward the plaza, supplied with small bronze artillery pieces to be used in case of an uprising" (con due Torri verso la Piazza, fornite de piccioli [*sic*] pezzi di bronzo, per servirsene in occasion di tumulto).[151] Finally, Gemelli notes that the viceroy himself failed to appear as scheduled in the annual August 13 celebration of San Hipólito, in which Cortés's banner was paraded through the streets: "It was reported that his excellency the viceroy had stayed away out of fear, since he had fallen off of his horse in his first entrance" (Si disse, che il Signor Vicerè si era rimaso por timore, essendo caduto da cavallo nella sua prima entrata), he comments but then adds his own interpretation, "but perhaps the memory of the conquest was hard for him" (ma forse gli era dura la rimembranza di tal conquista).[152]

Gemelli's comments seem to support Sigüenza's contention that the conquest was a dangerous site of counterhistory that had permitted the unprecedented tumult in 1692. Given the public iconographic references to the conquest in viceregal culture it is not difficult to imagine that the conquest could become such a theme in Mexico City's complex political juncture at the end of the seventeenth century. But whether a plebeian version of the conquest served something akin to what Michel Foucault called a counterhistorical perspective, which rewrote colonial social categories in terms that reflected present injustice, is more difficult to ascertain. The history of plebeian politics in 1692, like most subaltern history, depends on a written record whose intent is to disarm it.[153] The inherent limitations in the archives of the riot mean that the most compelling evidence of a postconquest indigenous and plebeian politics is inextricably tied to the rhetorical figures of Creole governance. It is certainly possible that Sigüenza correctly sensed the volatility of history at the end of the seventeenth century, even if his motivation in representing this volatility was ultimately to better governmental control. But despite valiant efforts of social

historians, our reconstructions of the rioters' own beliefs and politics are hypothetical at best. What Sigüenza's complex letter does most clearly indicate is a shift in notions of Spanish imperial governance at the end of the seventeenth century. Creole ideas of community, so clearly represented in patriotic images and statements, were also tied to fears of alternative political bodies among plebeians and castas. Strikingly, both of these political shifts emerged most forcefully in the last years of the seventeenth century when the Habsburg regime, which had structured colonial governance for the first century and a half, was on the verge of collapse.

If the biombo of the Spanish conquest (see Figure 1) painted around the time of the riot represents notions of governance that preceded the riot,[154] one only has to compare it to Cristobal de Villalpando's representation of the zócalo (Figure 18) painted for the same viceroy, Conde de Galve, upon his return to Spain, to see the haunting effect of the riot as well as the attempt to build an alternative urban imaginary in its wake. While the viceregal palace remains a charred ruin in the background, a reminder of the riot's destruction, the zócalo is now populated. The subjects who congregate there, however, are not the vulgo of seventeenth-century street processions and festivities. Rather, they stand separated from one another, disaggregated and individualized, even while obviously convened by the activity of buying and selling in the marketplace. Both the painting and Sigüenza's letter seem to ask what kind of order could develop in the shadow of the crumbling façade of viceregal governance. Villalpando seems to present the moment as a turning point in which the market itself will become the center of a disaggregated polity, eclipsing the symbolic apparatus of the Habsburg state. By translating the riot's violence for a peninsular audience, by contrast, Sigüenza invoked a long-standing phantasmagoric specter of plebeian alliance. At the same time, he argued that only Creole insight could dispel this alliance by understanding its deeply perverse causes. In Sigüenza's version of governance, a polity of citizens would become the foundation for future viceregal politics. It was to this foundation that he turned in the final years of the seventeenth century.

Figure 18 (opposite page). The Mexico City zócalo showing the viceregal palace after it had been burned during the 1692 riot. Oil on canvas (ca. 1695) by Cristobal de Villalpando (1639–1714). Courtesy of Corsham Court, Wiltshire, UK / The Bridgeman Art Library.

CHAPTER 5

Creole Citizenship, Race, and the Modern World System

The final years of Habsburg rule in Spain coincided with the perception, both inside and outside the peninsula, that the empire was in steep decline.[1] Whether or not this perception was accurate, at the very least the rule of Carlos II, the "invalid king," greatly weakened centralized administration from Madrid. During this period, Spain also lost its grasp over commercial routes and failed to prevent lucrative trade in contraband within its empire. At the same time the Dutch surpassed much of the Iberian trade in Asia and, despite attempts to circumvent interviceregal trade, a steady flow of bullion and goods transversed the Pacific coast of the Americas. Meanwhile, throughout the seventeenth century pirate attacks continually menaced Spanish ports and galleon fleets in the Pacific, Caribbean, and Atlantic. The same years saw increased pressure from English and French on the frontiers of the Spanish Empire. In 1682 the Frenchman René-Robert Cavelier, Sieur de la Salle had begun exploring an area around the Mississippi River nominally held by the Spanish, and during the same period English pirates entered a deserted stretch of the Yucatan Peninsula, where they began logging and trading in contraband.[2] With the Spanish cession of Jamaica to England in 1670, the island became the departure point for illegal trade with the Spanish colonies as well as the center of the British foray into sugar production.[3] As its fiscal crisis deepened, the Spanish monarchy was unable to ward off these multiple attacks on territory it claimed as its own.

The Habsburg court confronted the decline of its empire with a contradictory combination of pragmatism and ideological defensiveness.

Under pressure from European competitors, the assorted imperial councils that governed the Spanish Empire conceded on specific points when necessary but also continued to insist on the foundational goals of a universal Christian monarchy and to engage in a vigorous critique of the geopolitical ascent of other European nations. While Spain continued to expand into indigenous territories throughout the seventeenth century, the vast borders of the empire precluded any centralized defense of these. Indeed, after centuries of Spanish presence, imperial territories were still defined more by occupation through evangelization, trade networks, and mining centers than by clearly demarcated borders. Under fiscal pressure at the end of the century, the Crown became increasingly pragmatic: at times and places of international encroachment or pirate attacks, it was roused to increase revenue for defensive fortification, but local governments were also expected to provide for their own defense. The problem of revenue created constant tensions between local town councils (*cabildos*) and viceregal administration and contributed to notable reverses in defense policy over the course of the century.[4]

The Spanish monarchy's fiscal troubles had a particularly acute effect on New Spain, a territory effectively exposed on both Pacific and Atlantic coasts and in the north where European rivals were encroaching on missionary outposts. The consternation this exposure caused for the viceregal elite in New Spain can be measured by the numerous entries in Antonio de Robles's seventeenth-century diary of events in Mexico City recounting pirate attacks on the coast and indigenous uprisings in the north.[5] Yet the expectation that local governments participate in their own defense also provided new opportunities for regional elites to take active roles in imperial politics. As a mathematician, historian, and propagandist, Sigüenza y Góngora became a favored confidant of the viceroy Conde de Galve and contributed his opinion on such defensive measures as the construction of San Juan de Ulúa, the fort in Veracruz, and the fortification of Pensacola Bay in Florida. It is no coincidence that during these same years Sigüenza saw a number of his works published.[6] In 1690, for instance, even as he prepared reports for the viceroy on French advances into the Spanish-held territories of Florida, Sigüenza's polemic with the Austrian Jesuit Eusebio Kino over the significance of the 1680 comet finally made it to print. In the same year he also published the *Infortunios de Alonso Ramírez* (Misfortunes of Alonso Ramírez), a firsthand account of a Creole commoner from Puerto Rico who, after having been captured by pirates while trading off the coast of the Philippines, traveled the globe with them before being released and returning triumphantly to Mexico City. Additionally, Sigüenza published two propagandistic warnings on the French menace in the Caribbean: a pamphlet titled *Armada de Barlovento* (Windward Fleet) recounting the ousting of the French from Santo Domingo and an expanded narrative of the same attack in a longer piece titled *Trofeo de la justicia* (Trophey of Justice). Finally, in 1693 he published *Mercurio volante* (Flying Mercury), a short account of the reconquest of New Mexico by the Spanish settlers after their 1680 expulsion from the territory by the Pueblo tribes.[7]

Of all of these texts, the *Infortunios* is literarily the most complex and the only one to have merited sustained critical attention. While most recent scholars agree that the subject of the account, Alonso Ramírez, refers to a historical figure, he does not appear in any other historical record of the period.[8] Sigüenza's modeling of the story has also lent an aura of fictional elaboration to the tale of a common Creole subject. Indeed, early literary scholarship on the *Infortunios* focused heavily on the question of genre. The first section, recounting Ramírez's departure from Puerto Rico and search for work on the mainland, generally follows the structure of the Spanish picaresque novel in which an abandoned youth lives by his wits while searching for a position in society.[9] The second two-thirds of the narrative is more complex: Ramírez heads to the Philippines, the colonial entrepôt between Asia and the Americas, where his ship is captured by pirates. After traveling the world aboard the pirate ship, Ramírez and his crew are released near the Yucatan coast. From there, he finally makes his way to Mexico City, where, received as a hero, he recounts his tale to Sigüenza. The diverse models for the second part of the narrative include Baroque travel writings, descriptions of French and English piracy, captivity narratives, and early chronicles of Spanish colonization.[10] Rather than following one prototype, the second two-thirds of the text weave together these diverse influences in a wide-ranging geographical and social commentary.[11]

Yet these models only partially explain the narrative. When it is read alongside other writings of Sigüenza's from the same period, it becomes clear that the story of Ramírez's world journey is an allegory for Creole citizenship in a postimperial world. The relationship between Ramírez, as protagonist and witness, and Sigüenza y Góngora, as amanuensis, is key to the construction of this allegory of citizenship, which must find a point of alliance between elite and common Creole subjects. For the most part disguised by Ramírez's firsthand narration, the relationship between the two Creoles becomes discernible only at the end of the narrative when Ramírez arrives at Sigüenza's doorstep. Addressing the viceroy, who has sent him to Sigüenza after having heard his tale "in summary," Ramírez asserts:

> You sent me (either out of affection for him or perhaps, because he was ill, so that he could forget his woes with the account that I could give of so many of my own) to visit Don Carlos de Sigüenza y Góngora, cosmographer, the king our lord's chair in mathematics in the Mexican Academy and first chaplain of the Hospital Real del Amor de Dios in Mexico City (these are titles that sound important but are worth very little, to whose exercise he is bound more by reputation than by personal advantage).
>
> (Mandóme (o por el afecto con que lo mira o quizá porque, estando enfermo, divirtiese sus males con la noticia que yo le daría de los muchos míos) fuese a visitar a don Carlos de Sigüenza y Góngora, cosmógrafo y catedrático de matemáticas del Rey Nuestro Señor en la Academia Mexicana y capellán mayor del Hospital Real del Amor de Dios de la ciudad de México (títulos son éstos que suenan mucho y que valen muy poco, y a cuyo ejercicio le empeña más la reputación que la conveniencia).)[12]

The parenthetical interjections, ostensibly in Ramírez's voice but quite clearly reflecting Sigüenza's point of view, disrupt what would otherwise represent customary relations of vassalage between Ramírez and the viceroy. The first parenthesis draws a parallel between Ramírez and Sigüenza, implying a sympathy between the two based on their common experiences of misfortune and suggesting the tale's value as an entertaining distraction from these. The second parenthesis, echoing the Creole scholar's often voiced complaints about his financial difficulties, makes clear that these woes cannot be solved by official forms of recognition alone.[13]

Although many critics have seen this closing episode as a form of "identification" between Sigüenza and his subject, it is also important to note the subtle critique of viceregal administration in the passage.[14] As John Blanco has recently pointed out, by stating that Sigüenza is bound more by "reputation than by personal advantage," the passage questions the structure of accommodation (*conveniencia*) on which early modern Spanish governance depended.[15] In its entries for *conveniencia*, the 1734 *Diccionario de Autoridades* gives as definitions both "utility, benefit, and advantage" (utilidad, beneficio y aprovechimiento) and "correlation and conformity between two distinct objects" (correlación y conformidad entre dos cosas distintas), adding "it also refers to accommodation in service, since when some servant seeks a master he often explains this as 'I seek *conveniencia*, I have found *conveniencia*'" (vale tambien comodidad para servir: pues cuando algun criado busca Amo: suele explicarse diciendo Busco conveniencia, ya he hallado conveniencia).[16] A lack of "conveniencia" thus threatens a breakdown in the system of favors, service, and social hierarchy that sustained viceregal order. In this sense, it is important to note that by emphasizing that the exercise of titles is carried out more for "reputation" than for economic gain, the passage suggests the compensatory creation of another social order. If the crisis in the imperial Atlantic system loosened individual subjects from the bounds of social hierarchies, these subjects could nonetheless be incorporated into a nascent polity composed of more horizontal social relations. Indeed, the passage goes on to relate that Ramírez is rewarded not only with the publication of his story but also with a position in the Armada de Barlovento, the very battalion charged with defending his birthplace in the Caribbean. The passage thus subtly rewrites the system of procurement central to the empire, the titles that do not "pay," with new forms of recognition tied to citizenship.[17]

Although scholars have often focused on the picaresque aspects of the *Infortunios*, this conclusion contradicts what José Antonio Maravall isolates as the characteristic trait of the Spanish *pícaro*: a lack of social attachment. For Maravall, the pícaro's ceaseless travel and constant violation of his natural link to a homeland or patria expresses an essential "alienation" (*desvinculación*). Expelled from a patria chica but marginal to a patria grande, the pícaro symbolizes the incomplete transition from feudal fiefdom to absolutist state.[18] Adapting Maravall's interpretation of the picaresque novel to the Spanish imperial frontier makes it easier to understand the relationship among the various genres that appear in Sigüenza's text. Although the journey is presented as a series of misfortunes, suggesting Ramírez's suffering and piety while captive of the Protestant pirates, the narrative also establishes a cosmopolitan figure who was able to travel the world and return to tell his tale. This cosmopolitanism contradicts the national closure of the Spanish picaresque genre, which, as Maravall notes, never took place in the Americas.[19] It also contributes to the imagination of a greater nation, beyond Ramírez's ties to his patria chica. The bond he establishes with Sigüenza overcomes the social breach that caused him to leave the Mexican territory in the first place and is a crucial element that ties the text's narrative closure to territorial enclosure. Although it is suggested that Sigüenza listens out of pity for Ramírez's suffering, the journey itself has also transformed the Creole commoner from a vassal into an autonomous subject who may be charged with enforcing territorial unity and control. Ramírez thus moves from social anomie and isolation on the embattled frontier of the viceroyalty to the defense of the same as part of an invigorated local citizenry.

In 1690 the Atlantic circuit that had defined Spanish imperial politics in the first century of colonization was rapidly being displaced by global mercantile relations. In this paradigmatic shift, the Spanish monarchy appeared increasingly impotent and imagining a patria on the viceregal frontier became a pressing need for an imperial defense led by citizen militias. At the same time, fissures in Spanish imperial authority and accommodation (*conveniencia*) called for new concepts of citizenry beyond vassalage. The *Infortunios* answers these needs by creating an allegory of Creole citizenship as an alternative to what the narrative represents as a new form of barbarism: the extrasovereign economic exchange structuring global commerce and piracy. Ramírez's world journey is the basis for this allegory. While his travels expose him to the violence of a world beyond sovereignty, the narrative uses the threat of this violence, epitomized by the pirates who capture Ramírez and his crew, to advocate a local citizenship defined by lineage and virtue. In this allegorical vision of a new global order, patrimonialism becomes the central value that distinguishes Spanish governance from that of a sovereignless marketplace. Faced with the lure of mercantile freedoms and the threat of mixed lineages, the *Infortunios* ironically protects the hierarchical values of Spanish imperialism in the new figure of an autonomous Creole citizenry.

CITIZENSHIP ON THE IMPERIAL FRONTIER

While drawing on conventional seventeenth-century narratives of captivity and piracy, the *Infortunios* adapts these to a world stage beyond the confessional lines that usually marked the genre. Pirate attacks had been a problem for the colonies ever since the galleons began shipping large cargoes of gold and silver back to Europe.[20] The pirates who led these attacks often became figures in imperial epics that represented them as Protestant heretics driven by greed and self-interest.[21] These narratives, moreover, often treated pirates as extensions of national interests, particularly of France and England, and for this reason symbolic of the violation of national trading rights in the mercantile system. Indeed, Spanish narratives often employed well-known pirates as foils, the ousting of whom cleared the way for providentialist interpretations of Spanish imperial history.[22] Yet this narrative figure of the pirate in Spanish colonial discourse belies the fact that pirates were themselves problematic national subjects who as often reflected the juridical and mercantile vicissitudes of early modern trade as they did state interests. Pirates were often "privateers" who not only created alliances among themselves and with other extranational subjects such as marooned slaves but on occasion were even known to attack their own countries' vessels.[23]

While most early accounts of piracy fell into a propagandistic framework, several notable examples created nuances that admitted these complexities of identity and nation on both sides. In early foundational epics such as Silvestre de Balboa's 1608 *Espejo de Paciencia* (Mirror of Patience), for instance, a pirate attack on Cuba becomes an excuse to recount the collective defense of the island by its inhabitants, including Afro-cubans, mestizos, and Creoles.[24] By contrast, in his 1692 letter to Admiral Pez, Sigüenza recounts a centralized response to multifaceted forces threatening New Spain. Rather than a defense by a unified local community, such as the one that defends Cuba in Balboa's short epic poem, Sigüenza depicts an extensive territory centrally administered by the viceroy.[25] Another of Sigüenza's writings of this period, the short imprint describing the French corsairs' attack on Hispaniola, begins by drawing a parallel between the Counter-Reformation wars waged by the "Catholic arms" (católicas armas) of Spain in Europe and New Spain's territorial defense: "The sparks of the bellicose fires that blaze across Europe have now reached America, but if Catholic arms are employed there as they have been here, the most Christian king of France will find that his violent plans shall result only in repentance and remorse" (Ya llegan hasta la América las centellas de los incendios marciales con que se abrasa Europa, pero si allá se desempeñan las católicas armas, como acá se ha hecho, sólo será el arrepentimiento y pesar lo que se inferirá de sus violentas resoluciones el cristianísimo rey de Francia).[26] Despite these official representations of attacks on the Americas as a continuation of wars waged in Europe, in a private report to the viceroy

Creole Citizenship, Race, and the Modern World System

Sigüenza indicates his awareness of Spain's precarious financial situation and suggests that the fortification of Pensacola Bay, the unsuccessful proposal that would occupy the final years of his life, could best be carried out by populating the area with subjects from other points of the viceroyalty.

The active creation of communities of citizens (*vecinos*) would become the essence of Sigüenza's vision of the territorial defense of New Spain. As opposed to the racially mixed community of Balboa's poem, however, in his report on Pensacola Bay Sigüenza suggests that the fortification of the Floridian coast should be carried out exclusively by Creole and Spanish immigrants:

> At the same time, or somewhat later, the principal settlement will be underway on the Almirante River and in order to begin to give form to this site, while waiting for families to come from Spain or the islands, it seems to me that the proposal should be publicly proclaimed in this city, in Puebla, and in Veracruz and others and that the first settlers should be promised wide tracts of land, exemption from taxes, and privileges of nobility. This, together with the fame that already circulates about those lands will induce many who, given some help, will go there to settle. With these provisions, in only a few months, with the help of the Indians who I presume will be very pleased and benefited, the Spanish will have cut wood, created plaster from oyster shells, sought stones and mud to bake bricks, and, having done all this, will be able to fortify the mouth of the river with these materials.
>
> (Al mismo tiempo, o poco después, se ha de comenzar la población principal en el Río del Almirante y para que, en el interín que viene de España o de islas algunas familias, se le dé a aquélla alguna forma, me parece se pregone en esta Ciudad, en la de la Puebla, Veracruz y otras la intenta, y se les prometa a los que primero la poblaran muchas tierras y exenciones de gabelas y privilegios de nobleza, lo cual y la fama que ya corre de aquellas tierras estimulará a muchos el que, ayudándolos con algo, se vayan a ella. Por este medio, en pocos meses y con ayuda de los indios que presupongo muy agradados y beneficiados, se habrán aplicado los españoles a cortar maderas, a hacer cal de concha de ostiones, a buscar piedras y barriales para cocer ladrillos y, conseguido esto, se puede pasar a fortificar, con estos materiales, la boca de la bahía.).[27]

Despite Sigüenza's assurances that the native Floridian inhabitants would welcome these migrants, his vision of communities on the embattled frontiers of the territory clearly presupposed a military component. Even as early as 1680, in his description of the festivities celebrating the inauguration of the Querétaro chapel to the Virgin of Guadalupe, *Glorias de Querétaro*, Sigüenza had been able to see in the procession of Otomís a potential army that would control the wild movements of the barbarous "Chichimecs."[28] In areas further north in which native communities actively resisted Spanish expansion, the image of the settler implied an even more vigorous defense of the territory.

Sigüenza's vision of defensive communities of citizens presupposed a sharp division between settlers of Spanish and non-Spanish descent. In 1693, *Mercurio volante*, recounting the reconquest of New Mexico twelve years after the Pueblo Revolt, he asserts that the colony is "ennobled" by the arrival of subjects from central Mexico.[29] In language echoing his description of the 1692 riot the year before,[30] the text goes on to represent the uprising as the result of the pernicious influence of uncolonized nomadic peoples on newly Christianized nations and the Pueblo tribes' "innate hatred" of "Spaniards":

> appealing to frivolous pretexts, perhaps emulating the idle life of their gentile neighbors or, most likely, out of the innate hatred they have for Spaniards (I would suppose that at first this would be among only a few), the Indians of all the villages (without exception), both young and old alike, began to conspire to rebel with the most deliberate secrecy ever known.
>
> (valiéndose los indios de todos sus pueblos (sin excepción) de pretextos frívolos, emulándoles quizás a sus vecinos gentiles de la vida ociosa o, lo más cierto, por el odio innato que a los españoles les tienen (presupongo que sería al principio entre algunos pocos), comenzaron con el más ponderable secreto que jamás ha habido a discurrir entre chicos y grandes a sublevarse.)[31]

Blaming the uprising on instigations by two Indian leaders, Antonio Catiti and "another Indian no less evil who was called Popé" (otro no menos malvado indio que se llamaba Popé),[32] Sigüenza proceeds to narrate how, under the pretext of attending Mass, the villagers' rebellion ended in the death of five hundred Spaniards, including twenty-one members of the clergy. The villagers also profaned the church, and destroyed anything associated with Spanish culture: "in their rage against the Spanish nation they even targeted wheat" (aun en el trigo en odio de la nación española se empleó su enojo).[33]

As a counterpoint to these figures of rebellious apostasy, Sigüenza attributes the eventual recuperation of the territory by the Spanish, twelve years later, to alliances with neighboring tribes. The physical description of Don Luis Tupatu, the Hispanicized leader of the neighboring town of San Juan, symbolizes the negotiated resolution to the revolt:

> He arrived mounted on a handsome steed, carrying a musket with a pouch of gunpowder and munition, a mother-of-pearl crown on his head and dressed in Spanish attire except for animal skins. At a distance of sixty steps from the general's tent he halted and the escort of two hundred Indians formed themselves into a squadron. Dismounting, he walked gravely toward [the tent] and, bowing three times, got down on one knee before Don Diego, who was outside, kissing his hand. All these gestures were met with an embrace in return and this first encounter was limited to mutual salutations. After having presented the general with seal, tapir, and bison skins and accepting in return a handsome steed, Don Luis, his countenance betraying his inner satisfaction, took his leave in order to return the following day for a longer meeting.
>
> (Venía montado en un hermoso caballo, traía escopeta con graniel de pólvora y munición, y en la frente una concha de nácar como corona, y vestido a la española, pero de gamuzas. A distancia de sesenta pasos de la tienda del general hizo alto, y se encuadronó la guardia de doscientos indios; y desmontado, se encaminó a ella con gravedad, y haciendo tres reverencias, hincó la rodilla a don Diego, que estaba fuera, y le besó la mano. Retornóle todo esto con un abrazo, y se redujo esta primera vista a las salutaciones comunes; y mostrando don Luis en el rostro su interior gusto después de haber regalado al general con pieles de lobos marinos, danta y cíbolas, y admitido en recompensa un hermoso caballo que recibió con estima, se despidió para volver el día siguiente con más espacio.)[34]

In Sigüenza's narration, the peaceful encounter between the Creole Don Diego de Vargas and the Indian noble Don Luis Tupatu leads to the nonviolent reconquest of New Mexico in which "without having used even one ounce of gunpowder or unsheathed a sword and (what is even more remarkable and impressive) without having cost the Royal Treasury even one *maravedí*, innumerable peoples were returned to the fold of the Catholic Church and an entire kingdom was restored to our king and lord Carlos II" (sin gastar una sola onza de pólvora o desenvainar una espada y (lo que es más digno de ponderación y estima) sin que le costase a la Real Hacienda ni un solo maravedí, se reunieron al gremio de la Iglesia Católica innumerables gentes y se le restituyó a la majestad de nuestro rey y señor Carlos Segundo un reino entero).[35] If Sigüenza represents the insurrection of the Pueblo tribes as the frontier indigenous nations' negation of Hispanic society, the description of Don Luis Tupatu is meant to reveal the inevitability of religious conversion and mercantilist transculturation. More important than the idea of political necessity—that only the Spanish Crown is fit to rule—is the cultural necessity that has been inscribed into Tupatu's body.[36]

The contrast between a Hispanicized society based on peaceful exchange and the barbarous resistance of nomadic tribes anticipates a distinction that would be crucial to the eighteenth-century genre of casta paintings (Figures 19 and 20). Painted either on separate panels or on one panel divided into a grid-like composition, the casta paintings share a basic compositional structure: each scene represents a mixed-race family composed of a man, a woman, and their offspring, either infants or young children, and labeled with the racial nomenclature used to classify the various permutations. Additionally, almost all of the casta series contain a final scene representing a family of nomadic Indians. These are generically labeled "barbarous Indians" (indios bárbaros), "heathen Indians" (indios gentiles), *apaches*, or a variation on the term the Mexica used to designate those tribes outside of their empire: *chichimecas* or *indios mecos*. The fact that this is the only family not of mixed race in this kind of painting suggests a striking equation between racial mixture, urbanity, and civilization (*policía*). Perhaps even more striking, given the ubiquity of this scene in casta paintings, is the absence of the other source of racial mixture in New Spain: enslaved Africans. Whereas indigenous nomads are represented to establish a contrast between the civilization of urban casta society and the barbarism of the frontier, the enslavement of Africans and Afro-Americans cannot enter representation without exposing the dependence of this civilization on enslavement.

If Sigüenza's 1693 *Mercurio volante* delineates a contrast between Hispanicized civilization and frontier nomadism, in his 1692 *Infortunios de Alonso Ramírez* it is the exclusion of African subjects from representation that underpins the emergence of Creole citizenship. Ramírez's body becomes an emblem of this emergence. While it is the basis for identification between himself and the casta crew while they are captive, as the narrative develops, his body gradually disappears from view. The bodies of his casta crew, by contrast, remain subject to violence, even enslavement. The distinction between the Creole Ramírez and those who may be enslaved establishes the basis for a paternalistic relationship of care between them. This relationship is sealed when Ramírez sells a slave whom he has acquired during

Creole Citizenship, Race, and the Modern World System 213

Figure 19. *Casta* painting with the Virgin of Guadalupe. Luis de Mena (eighteenth century). Courtesy of the Museo de America, Madrid, Spain / The Bridgeman Art Library.

his journeys in order to pay his crew for their services. The surprising appearance of a slave, of whom no mention has been made before the crew is freed by its captors, follows the representational logic of the casta paintings, which, despite large numbers of Africans in New Spain, did not include visibly enslaved subjects in their depictions. Likewise, in the *Infortunios*, slavery becomes the receding horizon of representation whose elimination signals the ideological rejection of the violent exchanges of a global market. In order to posit a

Figure 20. "Barbarous mecos Indians" ("Indios Mecos barbaros"). From casta paintings series (eighteenth century). Courtesy of the Museo de America, Madrid, Spain / The Bridgeman Art Library.

patrimonial economy of care as an alternative to this violence, the narrative distinguishes the fate of the casta crew from that of subjects on the frontiers of the world system: the impoverished inhabitants of Asian islands, the barbarous indigenous subjects that the crew encounters upon its arrival in the Yucatan, and African slaves. Finally, in an allegory that combines imperial defense with a racialized notion of citizenship, Ramírez himself attains both autonomy and privilege within a Novohispanic society defined by the patrimonialist idiom of the Spanish Empire.

ACCIDENTS AND IMPERIAL DECLINE

Throughout the narrative of the *Infortunios*, Ramírez's subjective voice constantly invokes a structural transformation that will conclude in a figure of Creole citizenship. Indeed, the opening lines of the narrative introduce the distinction between this conclusion and Ramírez's trials at the confines of the Spanish Empire:

> I would like the curious person who reads this to be entertained during a few hours with the account of what caused me mortal tribulations over many years. And although one often extracts maxims and aphorisms, which cultivate the reason of whoever encounters them, embedded in the pleasures of an entertaining narrative, this is not my purpose here. Rather, I intend to solicit sympathy which, although posterior to my travails, will at least make their memory tolerable, providing company for the pity I felt for myself in my suffering. Nonetheless, I am not so overwhelmed by my pain that I wish to merit the ugly epithet of pusillanimous. Thus, omitting details which in others who are less afflicted than I was might have given rise to complaint, I will state what first comes to mind as being the most noteworthy in the series of my experiences.
>
> (Quiero que se entretenga el curioso que esto leyere por algunas horas con las noticias de lo que a mí me causó tribulaciones de muerte por muchos años. Y aunque de sucesos que sólo subsistieron en la idea de quien lo finge se suelen deducir máximas y aforismos que, entre lo deleitable de la narración que entretiene, cultiven la razón de quien en ello se ocupa, no será esto lo que yo aquí intente, sino solicitar lástimas que, aunque posteriores a mis trabajos, harán por lo menos tolerable su memoria, trayéndolas a compañía de las que me tenía a mí mismo cuando me aquejaban. No por esto estoy tan de parte de mi dolor que quiera incurrir en la fea nota de pusilánime; y así, omitiendo menudencias que, a otros menos atribulados que yo lo estuve, pudieran dar asunto de muchas quejas, diré lo

primero que me ocurriere por ser en la serie de mis sucesos lo más notable.)³⁷

While many critics have interpreted Ramirez's stated desire to "entertain" as the will to transform real events into a fictional and imaginary work with no utility other than pleasure, it is perhaps better to understand this passage as establishing a constitutional division between what can and cannot be said about the travails of the journey.³⁸ The acknowledgment of the reception by a reader who has not experienced the "tribulations of death" as he has, and who might be in search of entertainment in the vicarious experience, effects an ontological split between a discursive *here* of the subject who speaks and what was experienced *there* in the flesh but cannot be communicated.

The narrative of trials that cannot be communicated ironically serves to fortify Ramírez's subjectivity by retaining a private experience outside the public account. These divisions are raised to an allegorical status when, immediately afterward, Ramírez notes that his birthplace is also a place "in between": "My name is Alonso Ramírez and my patria is the city of San Juan in Puerto Rico, the capital of the island that, under this name in our times and by that of Borriquen in its antiquity, divides the Gulf of Mexico from the Atlantic Ocean" (Es mi nombre Alonso Ramírez y mi patria la ciudad de San Juan de Puerto Rico, cabeza de la isla que, en los tiempo de ahora con este nombre y con el de Borriquen en la antigüedad, entre el Seno Mexicano y el mar Atlántico divide términos). Ramírez goes on to praise his birthplace as a paradisiacal stopping point for those who "journey anxiously to New Spain" (navegan sedientos a la Nueva España), defended against corsair attacks by fortresses and "the spirit that the character of that land passes on to her sons" (el espíritu que a sus hijos les reparte el genio de aquella tierra).³⁹ This ambivalence is quickly resolved as he admits that the landscape is now in ruin and decline:

> Its natives direct their honor and fidelity to this determination, without further motive, even though it is certain that the wealth that gave it its name has now been reduced to poverty because of the loss of the original inhabitants who worked its gold mines and because of the vehemence with which the tempestuous hurricanes have battered the cacao trees that provided for those who traded in them in place of gold and, consequently, [who] benefited the rest of the island's inhabitants.
>
> (Empeño es éste en que pone a sus naturales su pundonor y fidelidad, sin otro motivo, cuando es cierto que la riqueza que le dio nombre

por los veneros de oro que en ella se hallan, hoy por falta de sus originarios habitadores que los trabajen y por la vehemencia con que los huracanes procelosos rozaron los árboles de cacao que a falta de oro provisionaban de lo necesario a los que lo traficaban y, por el consiguiente, al resto de los isleños se transformó en pobreza.)[40]

In an inversion that borders on Baroque *desengaño*, the seventeenth-century rhetoric of moral disillusion, the paradisiacal descriptions that abounded in Spanish American literature of this time dissolve with the loss of the land's "natural" provisions: the gold that had fueled the original Spanish invasion, the Indian labor considered fruit of the conquest, and finally the cacao production ravaged by continual hurricanes. The dystopic rendition of a familiarly American trope of nature as paradise marks, then, an advanced stage of colonization when easy riches through indigenous labor, mining, and logging have been exhausted and the island has degenerated to a stopping point for those in search of wealth on the mainland.[41]

Indeed, as Immanuel Wallerstein notes, the seventeenth-century shift in production from the exploitation of nature to the cultivation of sugar led to massive emigration of lower-class Creoles to the mainland as the traditional employment in shipbuilding was replaced by slave labor in the plantation economy.[42] This frame is crucial to the changes that the *Infortunios* effects on the Spanish picaresque narrative, whose generic structure centers on a young male subject who has been abandoned by his family and is left to fend for himself in the city. By contrast, Ramírez knows and defends his parents as examples of virtue. His father, he says, was named Lucas de Villanueva and "although I do not know his birthplace, I do know, because several times he said so, that he was Andalusian" (aunque ignoro el lugar de su nacimiento, cónsteme, porque varias veces se le oía decir, que era andaluz). About his mother, "I know for a fact that she was born in the same city of Puerto Rico and that her name is Ana Ramírez, and that due to her Christianity I received in my childhood the only thing that the poor can give to their children, and that is guidance to incline them towards virtue" (sé muy bien haber nacido mi madre en la misma ciudad de Puerto Rico, y es su nombre Ana Ramírez, a cuya cristiandad le debí en mi niñez lo que los pobres sólo le pueden dar a sus hijos, que son consejos para inclinarlos a la virtud). Although the passage retains the taint of illegitimacy, in that Ramírez has taken his mother's name, he appears to have been recognized and aided by his father, who attempted to instill in him interest in his vocation as a shipbuilder. Indeed, it is Ramírez who breaks with his father when he decides against a future as a shipwright: "My father was a shipwright and he instilled in me (as soon as I was of age) the same vocation, but recognizing that the work was not continuous and fearing for this reason that I would not be able to live with the privations that, although still only a boy, had already affected me, I decided to steal my body from my own patria to search for better accommodations in those far away" (Era mi padre carpintero de ribera, e impúsome (en cuanto permitía la edad) al propio ejercicio; pero reconociendo no ser continua la fábrica y temiéndome no vivir siempre, por esta causa, con las incomodidades que, aunque muchacho, me hacían fuerza, determiné hurtarle el cuerpo a mi misma patria para buscar en las ajenas más conveniencia).[43]

It is out of fear of a future of poverty rather than abandonment by his parents, therefore, that Ramírez leaves his birthplace to search for a better situation. In contrast to the fidelity he has attributed to Puerto Rico's "sons," Ramírez represents his departure as "stealing" his body from his birthplace.[44] And rather than the notion of divine necessity that imbued seventeenth-century providentialist readings of the Spanish American landscape, Ramírez presents his fate as the confluence of self-interest and accidents. Taking advantage of a passing ship to make his escape, for instance, Ramírez remarks that the captain's name, "Cork" (Corcho), ironically signals his future prospects:

> For this, I took advantage of Captain Juan del Corcho's cargo ship which was departing from that port for Havana and on which they received me as a page, although I was less than thirteen years old in the year 1675. I didn't find the work to be difficult since I felt free from the chore of cutting wood but I confess that, perhaps in a premonition of what was to come, I doubted whether anything good would come from pinning my fate to a cork to begin my fortune. And who could deny that these doubts were well founded, since that beginning already anticipated the resulting events?
>
> (Valíme de la ocasión que me ofreció para esto una urqueta del capitán Juan del Corcho, que salía de aquel puerto para el de la Habana, en que, corriendo el año de 1675 y siendo menos de trece los de mi edad, me recibieron por paje. No me pareció trabajosa la ocupación, considerándome en libertad y sin la pensión de cortar madera; pero confieso que, tal vez presagiando lo porvenir, dudaba si podría prometerme algo que fuese bueno, habiéndome valido de un corcho para principiar mi fortuna. Mas ¿quién podrá negarme que dudé bien, advirtiendo consiguientes mis sucesos a aquel principio?)[45]

Although the narrative suggests that a postprovidential world provides subjects with new opportunities to decide their own fate, through the play on the name of the captain of the ship "Cork" as an ill-advised faith in light wood rather than the substance of his father's trade, Ramírez also notes that such a world is equally without guarantees.

This rupture of providence, already foretold by the ruined landscape of his homeland, becomes the frame for Ramírez's search for "freedom" (*libertad*) from manual labor on the mainland. Although the desire to escape from physical hardship has prompted his departure from Puerto Rico, it soon becomes clear that these hardships will continue in mainland New Spain. Ramírez describes his passage through the mountains of Veracruz, for instance, as full of physical discomforts.[46] And although upon arriving in Puebla and then in Mexico City he associates the grandeur of these cities with the possibility of riches free of labor, his hopes are dashed as he finds that he must continue to work as a carpenter in order to survive.[47] Finally, after hearing that a relative on his mother's side is an alderman in Oaxaca, he travels there in the hopes of receiving patronage but, upon being disabused of this idea, is forced to accept work as an assistant to a merchant who sells to indigenous communities in the region. This work, although above manual labor, continues to tax him physically in a dreary and treacherous landscape:

> The experience of the rough mountainous terrain . . . is no less than the repeated fear of falling because of the steep paths, the horrific depth of the canyons, the continual downpours, and the laborious bogs, to which could be added the extreme heat of the small valleys where there are many mosquitoes and everywhere the creatures that threaten all living things with their mortal poison.
>
> (Lo que se experimenta en la fragosidad de la sierra . . . no es otra cosa sino repetidos sustos de derrumbarse por lo acantilado de las veredas, profundidad horrorosa de las barrancas, aguas continuas, atolladeros penosos, a que se añaden en los pequeños calidísimos valles que allí se hacen muchos mosquitos y en cualquier parte sabandijas abominables a todo viviente por su mortal veneno.)[48]

Fittingly, it is another accident that propels Ramírez into the life of leisure (*descanso*) that he desires when the merchant suddenly dies and leaves him a small inheritance.[49]

From here the narrative appears to have turned toward a moral confirmation of the patrimonial system of accommodation as, after a stint in honest trade, Ramírez is able to become a citizen of Mexico City (*avecindarme*) through a propitious marriage to the niece of the deacon of the Metropolitan Church. The fragility of his situation, however, is made clear upon the death of his wife in childbirth. With this event, Ramírez realizes that his momentary incorporation into an adopted homeland is an illusion. Representing this crisis as a loss of self ("I was beside myself with her loss" [quedé casi sin ella]), he briefly returns to his former route as if to commence again ("and to make matters worse I returned to Puebla" [y para errarlo todo me volví a Puebla]), before making the surprising decision to "exile himself" to the Philippines: "Despairing that I would ever become someone and finding myself in the tribunal of my own conscience, not only accused but convicted of uselessness, I decided to subject myself to the sentence that they give in Mexico to those who are delinquents, which is to send them to the Philippines in exile" (Desesperé entonces de poder ser algo, y hallándome en el tribunal de mi propia conciencia, no sólo acusado sino convenido de inútil, quise darme por pena de este delito la que se da en México a los que son delincuentes, que es enviarlos desterrados a las Filipinas).[50] The moment of Ramírez's "self-exile" to the Philippines is a key transition in the narrative, reflecting the abandonment of both the picaresque frame and the Atlantic geography that dominates most texts of the Spanish Empire. But beyond that, Ramírez's act signals the crisis in the system of patrimonialism that structured the search for wealth through accommodation in the first part of his narrative. Indeed, by occupying the place of justice, either preemptively or in its absence, Ramírez calls attention to the distance between the viceroyalty and Spanish imperial law.

In substituting the vassal for the sovereign the narrative reads this distance as a crisis rather than a break: the Creole commoner, becoming both executioner and executed, preserves the law by internalizing it in the "tribunal of my own conscience." Thus, as the patrimonial system that linked the two sides of the Atlantic breaks down, sovereignty itself becomes the province of the individual. This has an ambiguous effect on the narrative as at the moment that Ramírez short-circuits sovereign decision and condemns himself to exile in the Philippines, he also achieves freedom from the broken system of procurement on which he has depended. In a reversal of what he has posed as the successful trajectory of his wife's uncle, who after living in the Philippines returned triumphantly to Mexico City ("renouncing the miter of the archbishop of Manila to die, like a Phoenix, in his homeland" [renunciando la mitra arzobispal de Manila por morir, como Fénix, en su patrio nido]),[51] Ramírez searches for a solution to the ruined anomie of the mainland at the very edge of the Spanish

Empire. From here, the second two-thirds of the narrative literally opens to a new horizon beyond the Atlantic system of vassalage that had framed his tale until then.

WORLD COMMERCE AND THE NEW BARBARISM

Strikingly, at the moment that Ramírez occupies the place of an absent sovereign power, his body vanishes. His journey by sea to the Philippines provides the narrative space for this transition. After confirming once more the degraded nature of the mainland in a description of the inhospitable conditions of Acapulco that "incite departure from the port" (estimula solicitar la salida del puerto),[52] Ramírez recounts the navigational details of the journey to the Philippines, complete with cartographic calculations.[53] This introspective space also permits a transition from the themes of guilt and accident that had dominated Ramírez's search for work on the mainland, a shift that he signals in a moment of self-reflection: "Disabused during the course of my travels of the idea that I would eventually overcome my position, upset that many with more humble beginnings bettered theirs, I banished all the ideas that had occupied my imagination for the past years" (Desengañado en el discurso de mi viaje de que jamás saldría de mi esfera con sentimiento de que muchos con menores fundamentos perfeccionasen las suyas, despedí cuantas ideas me embarazaron la imaginación por algunos años).[54] Upon his arrival in Manila, a port whose wondrous abundance provides a striking contrast to the degraded ports and unproductive cities of mainland New Spain, Ramírez sounds an optimistic note for the first time:

> The abundance of those islands, and especially that which is enjoyed in the city of Manila, is superlative. Because of the diligence with which the Chinese try to enrich themselves in their Parián, which is a place outside of the city walls where they settled with permission of the Spanish, one finds there anything one needs to be fed and dressed at a modest price. This, together with the beauty and fortifications of the city, accompanied by the delight of their river and orchards and everything else that makes the European colonies in the Orient famous, compels all inhabitants to live in pleasure.

> (Es la abundancia de aquellas islas, y con especialidad la que se goza en la ciudad de Manila, en extremo mucha. Hállase allí para el sustento y vestuario cuanto se quiere a moderado precio, debido a la solicitud con que por enriquecer los sangleyes lo comercian en su Parian, que es el lugar donde fuera de las murallas, con permiso de

los españoles, se avecindaron. Esto, y lo hermoso y fortalecido de la ciudad, coadyuvado con la amenidad de su río y huertas, y lo demás que la hace célebre entre las colonias que tienen los europeos en el Oriente, obliga a pasar gustosos a los que en ella viven.)[55]

Notably, Ramírez's optimism is related to an economy of abundance that had long since declined in New Spain. Whereas in his 1604 poem *Grandeza mexicana*, Bernardo de Balbuena found Mexico City to be the commercial center of the Spanish Empire, Ramírez's late seventeenth-century vision displaces this center to the Philippines and, with this geographical displacement, opens up the imperial imaginary to its Asian frontier. The Chinese neighborhood of the Parián, a border region of commerce outside Manila's city walls, represents this abundance as a new world of trade stretching west.

In what provides the most definitive turn in his narrative, it is into this world that Ramírez enters by becoming a merchant and traveling the area surrounding the Philippines. Trade not only provides Ramírez autonomy but also opens up a new geography beyond the Spanish Empire: "Through this means, I was able not only to trade in objects from which I profited and which promised sufficient gain for the future but also during my voyages to see diverse East Indian cities and ports" (Conseguí por este medio no sólo mercadear en cosas en que hallé ganancia y en que me prometía para lo venidero bastante logro sino el ver diversas ciudades y puertos de la India en diferentes viajes).[56] The map of these journeys, however, is an archeology of the changes in European possession over the course of the seventeenth century. The cities along Ramírez's route are a string of ruins, ciphers of the slow erosion of Iberian control that had resulted in Dutch possession of much of what used to be the key points of Portuguese commerce in Asia:

> I passed through Malacca, the key to all of India and its commerce because of its position in the strait of Singapore and to whose governor all who sail through it pay tribute. The Dutch are owners of this [city] and of many others, under whose yoke the hapless Catholics who have remained there suffer, not being permitted to practice the true religion even while the Moors and gentiles, [Dutch] subjects, are not prevented from practicing their sacrifices.
>
> (Estuve en Malaca, llave de toda la India y de sus comercios por el lugar que tiene en el estrecho de Singapur, y a cuyo gobernador pagan anclaje cuantos lo navegan. Son dueños de ella y de otras muchas los holandeses, debajo de cuyo yugo gimen los desvalidos católicos

que allí han quedado, a quienes no se permite el uso de la religión verdadera, no estorbándoles a los moros y gentiles, sus vasallos, sus sacrificios.)[57]

Despite Ramírez's condemnation of this "godless colonialism," the allure that this frontier holds for him is palpable in his description of Dutch-held Jakarta:

> I passed through Jakarta, the most celebrated city that the [Dutch] possess in Upper Java and where the governor and general captain of the Dutch States resides. Its walls, bulwarks and forts are admirable. The concourse that one sees there, of Malaysians, Makassarese, Siamese, Buginese, Chinese, Armenians, French, English, Danish, Portuguese, and Castilians is immeasurable. One finds in this emporium as many products as exist in Europe as well as those which Asia sends in return. They produce there, for whoever wishes to buy them, excellent arms. But by saying that the entire universe is found there in compendium, I have said it all.
>
> (Estuve en Batavia, ciudad celebérrima que poseen los mismos en la Java Mayor y adonde reside el gobernador y capitán general de los Estados de Holanda. Sus murallas, baluartes y fortalezas son admirables. El concurso que allí se ve de navíos de malayos, mascasares, siameses, bugises, chinos, armenios, franceses, ingleses, dinamarcos, portugueses y castellanos no tiene número. Hállanse en este emporio cuantos artefactos hay en la Europa y los que en retorno de ellos le envía la Asia. Fábricanse allí, para quien quisiere comprarlas, excelentes armas. Pero con decir estar allí compendiado todo el universo lo digo todo.)[58]

Indeed, it is this "concourse" of goods and people that provides for the reversal in Ramírez's fortunes from his beginnings in the economically depressed Caribbean. Motored by companies with no missionary pretensions, Dutch imperialism shifted European expansion from conversion to commerce and allowed for this release of goods onto the world market, essentially creating zones of free trade in the interstices of mercantilist control.[59]

While the aperture afforded by the seas beyond Spanish dominion provides Ramírez opportunities for autonomy, however, it also exposes him to new risks. As opposed to New Spain's northern frontier, in which the dominant problem remained conversion and its resistance, the commercial frontier of the *Infortunios* produces confused identities. A lone agent of the Spanish Empire, Ramírez is subject not only to trickery, such as the "fraud" (*supercherías*) of the Chinese merchants who surround Portuguese Macao,[60] but to even worse threats by contending interests. The circumstances leading up to his capture confirm the danger of working on the edge of the Spanish Empire. On a trip to Ilocos to secure arms for the *presidio* in Cavite by orders of the governor of the Philippines, Gabriel de Cuzalegui, Ramírez negligently goes unarmed, confident, it would seem, that the islands were under Spanish control. Ramírez's innocence is such that he even mistakes the pirate ship for a Spanish vessel and thus allows it to approach his own. The rapid change in his circumstances is marked by the pirates' peals of laughter upon finding the ship not only undefended but, ironically, transporting arms for the Spanish fort. Upon realizing that Ramírez is captain of the captured ship, the pirate captain promises to free him if he will tell them which of the islands would yield the most riches.[61] Ramírez responds with a dissimulation, as he will throughout his journey, by which he claims that as a Spaniard he is too cowardly to become a pirate. While the pirate captain thus offers Ramírez the opportunity to join their ranks, effectively becoming a free agent outside the laws of national sovereignty, loyalty to the Spanish Empire carries the price of continued captivity. Ramírez's dissimulated loyalty to Spain, evident to the reader but hidden from the pirates, thus permits him to continue on the pirate ship without accepting their offer to join them.

What is important about this exchange is that it introduces the idea that at the edge of empire identity is one of choice, albeit constrained by the threat of violence.[62] Immediately after his act of dissimulation, Ramírez recounts the first instance of bodily torture: "Setting the prows of their frigates (they carried mine in tow) toward Caponiz, they began with pistols and cutlasses in hand to interrogate me once again and even to torture me" (Puestas las proas de sus fragatas (llevaban la mía a remolque) para Caponiz, comenzaron con pistolas y alfanjes en las manos a examinarme de nuevo y aun a atormentarme).[63] It soon becomes clear, however, that the violence directed toward Ramírez is continually displaced onto the casta members of his crew. The first moment of violence directly represented in the narrative exemplifies this displacement. As Ramírez explains, they tied both him and another crewmate to the main mast and "as I did not respond to their questions about the places where they could find the silver and gold that they asked us about, taking hold of Francisco de la Cruz, a Chinese mestizo, my crewmate, they subjected him to such a cruel punishment with ropes that he was left faint and almost lifeless on the deck" (como no se les respondía a propósito acerca de los parajes donde podían hallar la plata y oro por que nos preguntaban, echando mano de Francisco de la Cruz, sangley mestizo, mi compañero, con cruelísimos tratos de cuerda que le dieron, quedó desmayado en el combés y casi sin vida). Thereafter the pirates throw Ramírez and his crew in the hold and from there "I heard screams and a gunshot" (percibí grandes voces y un trabucazo). Returning to the deck he sees copious blood and hears from the pirates "that they had killed a member of my crew and that the same would happen to me if I did not provide the answers they were seeking" (me dijeron ser de uno de los míos, a quien habían muerto y que lo mismo sería de mí si no respondía a propósito de lo que preguntaban).[64] To this Ramírez responds that they should do with him what they will because he had nothing more to add to his first answers. Attempting to learn whose blood had been shed, moreover, he notes that all of his crew was present and later finds out that it had been a dog that was killed.

Not only does Ramírez confirm that the pirates' threats are false but the scene also marks a difference between their treatment of him and that of his casta crew. Tied to the same mast as "Francisco de la Cruz, Chinese mestizo," Ramírez does not receive physical torture but experiences it vicariously through his crewmate whose body is left "almost lifeless" (casi sin vida). Indeed, the only time Ramírez himself becomes directly subject to violence is after one of his crew members betrays him by telling the pirate captain that the port to which Ramírez is leading them is not uninhabited, as the Creole has affirmed, but rather guarded by a Spanish *presidio*. Even then, the pirates commute their threats to a lighter sentence of "kicks and punches that they unloaded upon me and which left me incapable of movement for many days" (patadas y pescozones que descargaron en mí que me dejaron incapaz de movimiento por muchos días).[65] Thus, even while the pirates threaten violence against Ramírez, ostensibly to persuade him to abandon his loyalty to Spain, the actual infliction of violence draws a distinction between him and his casta crew. Ramírez's ambivalent identification with his crew is evident in his commentary that the original betrayal has come from an Amerindian crew member ("who as an Indian never could be counted on for anything good" [quien por indio jamás se podía prometer cosa que buena fuese]).[66] While the incident registers an exception to the supposition of loyalty among his crew, it also introduces for the first time the possibility of internal divisions based on race.

Ramírez's ambivalent position, identified with his crew members by nationality and the pirates by race, allows him to register the activities of the pirate ship without participating in them. The majority of these activities involve sacking cargo ships carrying merchandise between points in Asia and Europe, pursuits that Ramírez describes in terms reminiscent of the picaresque tradition ("it seemed to them that they were not alive if they did not steal" [pareciéndoles no vivían mientras no hurtaban]).[67] In contrast to national figures such as the pícaro or the bandit, however, the pirates also participate in what Ramírez represents as a barbarous form of trade with subjects on the frontiers of the world market. After the crew lands on a small island off the coast of Cambodia, for instance, Ramírez recounts that the inhabitants come out to greet the pirates and receive from them stolen clothes and other objects in exchange for "tar, grease, salted turtle meat, and other items" (brea, grasa y carne salada de tortuga y con otras cosas). Ramírez comments that, to his surprise, "the poor barbarians" (los pobres bárbaros) not only happily participate in this unequal exchange, but even sell their daughters and wives to the pirates:

> It must be the lack of shelter on that island or the extremity of their desire for what comes from other regions, for either their nakedness or curiosity forced them to commit the most shameful depravity that I've ever seen. Mothers brought their daughters and the men even brought their wives and, touting their beauty, they turned them over to the Englishmen for the miserable price of a blanket or an equivalent item.
>
> (Debe ser la falta que hay de abrigo en aquella isla o el deseo que tienen de lo que en otras partes se hace en extremo mucho, pues les forzaba la desnudez o la curiosidad a cometer la más desvergonzada vileza que jamás vi. Traían las madres a las hijas y los mismos maridos a sus mujeres, y se las entregaban con la recomendación de hermosas a los ingleses por el vilísimo precio de una manta o equivalente cosa.)[68]

Ramírez's representation of these subjects goes far beyond the childlike innocence of the Arawaks who give gold for the beads that Columbus brings with him from Europe, a scene constantly repeated in Spanish colonial texts that even appears in Sigüenza's description of Pensacola Bay from the same period.[69] As opposed to the innocent "confusion" of value by Amerindians, the subjects of the small island have already been transformed by contact with the world economy, their desire for goods driving them to what Ramírez represents as the unnatural act of selling family members to the pirates.

Ramírez's description of these commercial activities becomes the backbone of his representation of a world market outside of mercantilist control and law. The extent to which the pirates themselves are defined by their willingness to trade under these conditions may explain one of the stranger, and most commented on, episodes of the narrative. In this passage, Ramírez describes how, after having burned their villages and stolen what little they possessed, the pirates proceed to cannibalize the subjects of the island: "Among the spoils that came from the town . . . was a human arm of those who died in the blaze; from this each one [of the pirates] cut a small piece and, praising the flavor of such good meat, amid repeated cheers they finished it off" (Entre los despojos con que vinieron del pueblo . . . estaba un brazo humano de los que perecieron en el incendio; de éste cortó cada uno una pequeña presa, y alabando el gusto de tan linda carne, entre repetidas saludes le dieron fin). Ramírez reports that he is disgusted by such a "bestial" action and repeatedly refuses the pirate who incites him to take a bite ("I looked upon such a bestial action with horror and anguish" [Miraba yo con escándolo y congoja tan bestial acción]).[70] Ramírez's commentary echoes a long tradition in Spanish historiography of associating barbarism with cannibalism. While the trope of cannibalism in colonial texts conventionally expressed a fear of being devoured by the enemy and engulfed by savagery, however, in the *Infortunios* the severed and cannibalized arm recalls the breakdown of natural bonds in the previous episode of the pirates' barbaric commerce. Indeed, by cannibalizing the very barbarous subjects whom they have robbed and destroyed, the pirates give evidence that they likewise live outside of natural law.[71]

The parallel between severed body parts and unscrupulous trade on the world market is furthered by a final incident in this section of the narrative. Upon arriving in Siam, Ramírez recounts the case of a solitary and isolated Genovese ("I do not know under what circumstances he came to be there" [no sé las circunstancias con que vino allí]),[72] who, after becoming the chief lieutenant of the port, had cut off the hands of two Portuguese mariners who had happened to arrive there. Immediately following this anecdote, Ramírez describes his experience of a strange object he encountered in the port:

> I saw and touched with my own hands something like a tower or castle of pure gold, one yard high and decorated with diamonds and other precious stones, and equally curious, although not of such value, were many silver ornaments, a quantity of camphor, amber,

and musk, not to mention the rest of what there was on the ship for buying and selling in that kingdom.

(Vi y toqué con mis manos una como torre o castillo de vara en alto de puro oro, sembrada de diamantes y otras preciosas piedras, y aunque no de tanto valor, le igualaban en lo curioso muchas alhajas de plata, cantidad de canfora, ámbar y almizcle, sin el resto de lo que para comerciar y vender en aquel reino había en la embarcación.)[73]

Like the exotic items that cause Cambodians to sever filial bonds or the hands of the merchants cut off by the Genovese, the object Ramírez touches appears dislocated from any natural context. Massive, made of pure gold, and exorbitantly decorated with diamonds and precious stones, it cannot be classified. The juxtaposition of these anecdotes betrays their commonality: Ramírez represents the world of commerce in which the pirates operate as one of anarchic violence, beyond law and decorum. It is as if by touching the object Ramírez has reached the geographical heart of a world system governed only by value, a place that he understands to be at the antipodal extreme of the Christian values of the Spanish Empire.

DISSIMULATION, FREEDOM, AND SLAVERY

Until recently, scholarship on the *Infortunios* has not explicitly addressed the global dimension of the text. After initially focusing on the text's status as history or fiction, including debating whether it could be considered the first Spanish American novel, criticism has more recently turned to the relationship between Sigüenza y Góngora and Ramírez. These readings have tended to treat the world stage upon which much of the narrative takes place as an extension of the national territory in which the tale starts rather than as an integral element of the narrative telos. In reading Ramírez's world travels, nearly two-thirds of the text, critics have therefore focused heavily on the social relations among Ramírez, his crew, and the pirates, for the most part ignoring the geographical context of the journey. Although some readers have portrayed the relationships among Ramírez, the pirates, and the casta crew as identical to national or confessional interests, moreover, these readings do not account for the anomalous nature of these figures. In the first place, the pirates who capture Ramírez are renegades who attack English ships as well as foreign ones and who include among their crew such misfits as a lapsed Sevillan Catholic named Miguel. Secondly, Ramírez's identification with his crew, the majority of whom are castas who mix lineages from across the Spanish Empire, is decidedly ambivalent.[74] Although it has been tempting to see the ship as a reflection of the heterogeneity of Novohispanic society, therefore, it would be more accurate to say that it reflects the permeability of identities on the high seas. The question, indeed, becomes what law will govern relations between such a motley group of individuals outside the context of a sovereign territory.

As John Blanco has recently shown, it is this question that draws the *Infortunios* into the unlikely company of the early modern political theories of Hugo Grotius. As Blanco points out, Ramírez's global travels begin in the Pacific and pass through the very site of the event that spurred Hugo Grotius to write his 1609 manifesto *The Free Sea (Mare Liberum)*.[75] In his defense of the 1603 Dutch attack on a Portuguese trading ship in Indonesia, Grotius's treatise inaugurated a turn toward individual rights in European political theory by designating the ocean a space outside sovereign territory. In what Richard Tuck calls an "untheistic theory" Grotius argued that individual rights in areas outside sovereign bounds were based solely on occupation, use, and usufruct, a theoretical reversal that freed colonial interests from Thomistic-Aristotelian notions of divine authority.[76] As Blanco has suggested, Grotius's vision of a globe inhabited by individual sovereign agents, with the right to take and to punish, has strong resonances with Ramírez's description of commerce and piracy in the Asian Pacific. Yet while Ramírez conflates all the commerce he witnesses among the pirates with plunder, and in turn condemns these as contrary to natural law, criticism has long noted that he differentiates among the pirates and even comes to sympathize with two in particular.[77] It should also be remembered that Ramírez begins his world journey with a peculiar short-circuiting of sovereign law and thus, although he constantly invokes a Spanish identity, does not represent traditional Spanish vassalage. Indeed, Ramírez's assumption of the position of the sovereign is strangely similar to Grotius's vision of endowed individuals acting in nonsovereign spaces. Yet rather than initiating a regime of individual sovereign rights, Ramírez's self-exile points to an internalized law that, even in the absence of the sovereign, still holds jurisdiction over its subjects.

The narrative develops this curious positioning of Ramírez between piratical individualism and Spanish imperial law through his simultaneous dissimulated compliance with the pirates and rejection of their practices. As the ship passes through Africa and the Americas, geographies codified by Europeans as nonsovereign states of nature, this negotiation with the pirates become more tense, forcing a resolution of his two identities. Two incidents in particular frame the evolving terms of Ramírez's captivity. The first is an encounter with an English trading ship off the coast of Madagascar. The pirates' desire to take the ship and its contents is thwarted in the first instance by the realization that the ship is well armed. Intent upon their goal, the pirates attempt to trick the ship's captain into allowing them to board. To gain information, they send Ramírez and two of his crewmates to make contact with the English traders. Upon penalty of death, the pirates instruct the three captives to present themselves as "free, wage-earning seamen" (marineros voluntarios y que nos pagaban).[78] Although Ramírez appears to abide by this order, the other two crew members communicate with a Portuguese seaman aboard the English ship. For their actions, Ramírez's companions are whipped so hard by the pirates that they die.[79]

Although, as usual, Ramírez escapes the fate of his hapless crewmates, immediately following this event the pirates decide to abandon him and the "the few crewmates that remained" (pocos compañeros que habían quedado) on the island of Madagascar. This threat provokes a plea from Ramírez who directly compares the two possible fates:

> considering the barbarity of the black Moors who lived there, on my knees and kissing [the pirates'] feet in submission after reminding them of the extent that I had served them and offering to attend to them on their voyage as if I were their slave, I was able to convince them to take me with them. They proposed at that point, as they had at others, that if I were to vow to follow them always they would give me arms. I thanked them for the consideration and, reflecting upon the obligations with which I was born, I answered with feigned humility, presenting myself as a Spaniard and therefore a chicken and a coward and not worthy of joining their ranks, that I was so afraid of bullets that I preferred to serve them than to fight with others.
>
> (considerando la barbaridad de los negros moros que allí vivían, hincado de rodillas y besándoles los pies con gran rendimiento, después de reconvenirles con lo mucho que les había servido y ofreciéndome a asistirles en su viaje como si fuese esclavo, conseguí que me llevasen consigo. Propusiéronme entonces, como ya otras veces me lo habían dicho, el que jurase de acompañarlos siempre y me darían armas. Agradecíles la merced, y haciendo refleja a las obligaciones con que nací, les respondí con afectada humildad el que más me acomodaba a servirlos a ellos que a pelear con otros por ser grande el

temor que les tenía a las balas, tratándome de español cobarde y gallina y por eso indigno de estar en su compañía.)[80]

This moment marks a turning point in Ramírez's relations with the pirates. From the beginning of the narrative Ramírez had always refused to join the pirates' ranks, giving as an excuse the weakness of Spanish character. This ironic dissimulation had allowed him to avoid the fate of several members of his crew who had been tortured or killed, while at the same time drawing a sharp moral line between his values and those of the pirates. But the threat of this passage is of a different order than the physical violence that the pirates had meted out until then: Ramírez understands abandonment among the "black Moors" as equivalent to death and counters this with a new offer to serve the pirates "as if I were their slave."

Ramírez's contrast between the fates of abandonment on Madagascar, on the one hand, and enslavement to the pirates, on the other, draws a sharp distinction between voluntary enslavement, in this case within patrimonial norms and to Europeans, and abandonment among peoples whose reputed barbarism had become the principal justification for mercantile slavery.[81] The moral stakes of these two fates are more explicitly addressed the second time the pirates threaten to abandon Ramírez. Following his negotiation with the pirates, Ramírez's narrative skips over the description of the rest of Africa, mentioning only that they passed the Cape of Good Hope and skirted the coastline for a month and a half. From there, the ship turns toward the Americas and in twenty-five days reaches the coast of Brazil. At the mouth of the Amazon River, the pirates once again decide to leave Ramírez and his crew ashore. Upon this second threat of abandonment Ramírez acknowledges the sympathy he has received from two pirates, Nicpat and Dick. Indeed, the second time the pirates debate the fate of their captives, Nicpat interjects an impassioned plea for Ramírez's freedom:

> "It is enough," he said, "that we have degenerated from who we are, robbing the best of the Orient under impious circumstances. Is it possible that the innocent people from whom we took what they had earned by their own sweat and who lost their lives are not crying out to the heavens? What has this poor Spaniard done now to lose his? To have served us as a slave in gratitude for what we have done for him since we captured him. To leave him at this river where it appears there is nothing more than barbarous Indians is ingratitude. To slit his throat, as others say, is worse than impious and so that his

innocent blood does not cry out for the whole world to hear, I and those on my side will vouch for them."

(—Bástanos—decía éste—haber degenerado de quienes somos, robando lo mejor del Oriente con circunstancias impías. ¿Por ventura no están clamando al cielo tantos inocentes a quienes les llevamos lo que a costa de sudores poseían, a quienes les quitamos la vida? ¿Qué es lo que hizo este pobre español ahora para que la pierda? Habernos servido como un esclavo en agradecimiento de lo que con él se ha hecho desde que lo cogimos. Dejarlo en este río donde juzgo no hay otra cosa sino indios bárbaros es ingratitud. Degollarlo, como otros decís, es más que impiedad, y porque no dé voces que se oigan por todo el mundo su inocente sangre, yo soy, y los míos quien los patrocina.)[82]

As has often been noted, Ramírez takes this plea as evidence of Nicpat's hidden Catholicism, thus equating his distinguishing values with confessional differences.[83] But it should also be noted that Nicpat presents clemency as a choice between humanity and barbarism: Ramírez's preference for voluntary enslavement to Europeans, even if they are pirates, establishes a distinction between a shared expectation of civility among Europeans and the barbaric acts and threats that associate them with peoples outside of European values.

It is therefore not surprising that the pirates opt for the solution that agrees with what Nicpat has posed as proof of their humanity: Ramírez is left, along with the remaining crew, with a ship, a compass, food, and water, to find his way back to the Mexican mainland. Immediately following this unexpected turn of events Ramírez makes a remarkable speech in praise of freedom:

> I praise all those who, even risking death, seek liberty since it merits respect even among brute animals. This unexpected good news resulted in copious tears from me and my crewmates and I am sure that what we had previously left repressed and hidden in our sorrows now ran down our faces. As unexpected rejoicing often impedes speech, and since we felt that what was occurring was a dream, it took a moment to understand that we were free. Our first action was to lift our voices to the heavens exalting divine clemency as best we could and immediately afterward give thanks to the lodestar that had guided us amidst so many storms at sea. I believe that my freedom would have been impossible if I had not continuously turned my memory and affection to the Most Holy Mary of Guadalupe of Mexico, whom I will always proclaim and to whom I will live as a slave for what I owe to her.

> (Alabo a cuantos, aun con riesgo de la vida, solicitan la libertad, por ser ella la que merece, aun entre animales brutos, la estimación.

Sacónos a mí y a mis compañeros tan no esperada dicha copiosas lágrimas, y juzgo corrían gustosas por nuestros rostros por lo que antes les habíamos tenido reprimidas y ocultas en nuestras penas. Con un regocijo nunca esperado suele de ordinario embarazarse el discurso, y pareciéndonos sueño lo que pasaba, se necesitó de mucha refleja para creernos libres. Fue nuestra acción primera levantar las voces al cielo engrandeciendo a la divina misericordia como mejor pudimos, y con inmediación dimos las gracias a la que en el mar de tantas borrascas fue nuestra estrella. Creo hubiera sido imposible mi libertad si continuamente no hubiera ocupado la memoria y afectos en María Santísima de Guadalupe de México, de quien siempre protesto y viviré esclavo por lo que le debo.)[84]

Given the fact that he has just escaped enslavement to the pirates, Ramírez's declaration that he will live "as a slave" to the Virgin of Guadalupe is particularly striking. In the language of patrimonial devotion, Ramírez defines liberty as the freedom to choose voluntary enslavement to a devotional end. The period of the voyage that has opened with his occupation of the place of the sovereign in an act of individual autonomy ends, therefore, with a clear return to patrimonial values and a rejection of the pragmatic individualism that has defined the world beyond the Spanish Empire.

Remarkably, it is at this point in the narrative that race first explicitly enters Ramírez's negotiations with his crew. Immediately following their freedom, Ramírez identifies the crew members who remain. Of the twenty-five original members of the crew, he recounts that eight have escaped with him: "Juan de Casas, Spaniard, native of Puebla de los Angeles in New Spain; Juan de Pinto and Marcos de la Cruz, the former a Pangasinan Indian and the latter a Pampango Indian; Francisco de la Cruz and Antonio González, Chinese; Juan Díaz of Malabar; and my slave Pedro, a black from Mozambique" (Juan de Casas, español, natural de la Puebla de los Angeles en Nueva España; Juan Pinto y Marcos de la Cruz, indios pangasinán aquél y éste pampango; Francisco de la Cruz y Antonio González, sangleyes; Juan Díaz, de malabar, y Pedro, negro de Mozambique, esclavo mio).[85] This list, which imitates the juridical language of race that permeated much of Novohispanic society, emphasizes distinctions among the crew, despite their collective suffering.[86] Indeed, immediately afterward, in a retrospective reflection on the trials of captivity, Ramírez recounts the racial fissures between himself and his crew members. Following a description of the punishment of the only other Spanish subject on the ship, forced to drink the watered-down excrement of the pirate captain,[87] Ramírez explains that he had decided not to try to escape because he did not trust those among the crew who were not "Spanish:" "it could be that I did not trust them . . . because Juan de Casas was the only other Spaniard among them" (puede ser que no me fiara de ellos . . . por no haber otro español entre ellos sino Juan de Casas).[88] Although finally free, but drifting in an unknown region in the Caribbean with little to remind them of a land-bound hierarchical society, this memory of mistrust between Ramírez and his casta crew haunts their relations. Indeed, as they now had not even the hardship at the hands of the pirates to unite them, the crew's collective freedom may even have aggravated the underlying problem of individuation outside of sovereign bounds.

CREOLE PATRIMONIALISM AND A NEW PATRIA

Even at the moment of their euphoric freedom, then, the narrative signals the need for the crew members to form a collective identity or risk further disaggregation. Faced with an unknown seascape, however, they are unable to return to a known destination and its attendant social order: "Neither I nor my crew knew our whereabouts nor the destination of our voyage because we didn't understand the Dutch sea charts nor did we have a map that would help us in such a confused state, and for all of us this was the first time that we had been in that place" (No sabía yo ni mis compañeros el paraje en que nos hallábamos ni el término que tendría nuestro viaje, porque ni entendía el derrotero holandés ni teníamos carta que entre tantas confusiones nos sirviera de algo, y para todos era aquella la primera vez que allí nos veíamos).[89] Just as in their travels through Asia, the ship passes by Caribbean islands that have fallen to the French and English, confirming the loss of Spanish control over the region. Faced with this geographic uncertainty, and unable to retrace his steps to known territory, Ramírez charts a negative route away from the pirates, who had warned the crew that if they found them again they would kill them. Significantly, they cannot return to Ramírez's homeland, as he explains that "since I had left my patria at such a young age I never knew (nor worried about knowing afterward) which islands were nearby and what their names were" (habiendo salido de mi patria de tan poca edad, nunca supe (ni cuidé de ello después) qué islas son circunvecinas y cuáles sus nombres).[90] It is precisely the impossibility of an easy return home, both because of his lack of knowledge and the threat of renewed captivity, that forces Ramírez to negotiate a new relationship with his crew.

Once again, slavery provides the terms that will frame the negotiation between Ramírez and his crew members. Although they have assiduously avoided landing at islands under English control, when a boat from French-controlled Guadalupe comes out to greet them Ramírez recommends that they trust in Catholic piety and land. The crew, however, "forcefully opposed my suggestion, stating that because of their color and the fact that they were not Spaniards, they would be made slaves and that it would be preferable that I threw them in the sea with my own hands than that I left them in the hands of foreigners to suffer their cruelties" (Opusiéronse a este dictamen mío con grande esfuerzo, siendo el motivo el que a ellos, por su color y por no ser españoles, los harían esclavos y que les sería menos sensible el que yo con mis manos los echase al mar que ponerse en las de extranjeros para experimentar sus rigores).[91] Although the narrative has suggested that Ramírez and his casta crew suffered distinct types of torture at the hands of the pirates, this is the first time that skin color has been explicitly codified in relation to enslavement. It is precisely the threat of this exposure that prompts Ramírez for the first time to occupy the position of a paternal protector: "In order not to afflict them, feeling their troubles more than mine, I set sail all day toward the north and the next toward the north-northeast" (Por no contristarlos, sintiendo más sus desconsuelos que los míos, mareé la vuelta del Norte todo el día y el siguiente al Nornordeste).[92]

From this point on, the journey becomes a series of moments in which Ramirez's ability to save his casta crew members from fates associated with their skin color establishes new patrimonial bonds between them. After having given up the opportunity to land in Guadalupe, the crew faces dire conditions on board the ship and eventually swims to an unknown shore. Once on land, with many of the crew members near death, Ramírez explicitly assumes a paternal position toward them, offering to search for food and help:

> Embracing me, they begged with words of love and tenderness for me not to abandon them and, as it seemed physically impossible that even the strongest would live four days longer, and this being such a short period, I wished as father to all of them to give them

my blessing in their dying moments and then that they go on to receive what their unhappiness and calamity had denied them in such a strange land.

(Abrazándose de mí, me pedían con mil amores y ternuras que no les desamparase y que, pareciendo imposible en lo natural poder vivir el más robusto ni aun cuatro días, siendo la demora tan corta, quisiese, como padre que era de todos, darles mi bendición en sus postreras boqueadas y que después prosiguiese muy enhorabuena a buscar lo que a ellos les negaba su infelicidad y desventura en tan extraños climas.)[93]

In this section of the narrative, moreover, Ramírez himself repeatedly asks the Virgin of Guadalupe to "give succor to us as her sons" (nos socorriese como a hijos) and attributes the rain showers that save them from certain death as a miraculous intervention.[94] The language of patrimonialism, in which the captain is father to the crew and all are sons of the Virgin Mary, thus forcefully returns the narrative to a Thomistic political language that marked the national space of the mainland.

This newly codified paternalistic relationship between Ramírez and his crew takes place in a landscape described through a confusing mixture of tropes of primary and secondary conquest. Having found a deserted hut, Ramírez and his crew enter to rest, during which time he is plagued by "imaginations conjured by my distress, without doubt the worst of which was that I was on the coast of Florida in America and, as its inhabitants were most cruel, we were going to end up with our lives in their bloody hands" (imaginaciones que me ofreció el desconsuelo en esta ocasión fue la más molesta el que sin duda estaba en las costas de la Florida en la América y que, siendo cruelísimos en extremo sus habitadores, por último habíamos de reunir las vidas en sus sangrientas manos).[95] Even as he is engaged in this fantasy, Ramírez is interrupted by the shouts of his crew "that people were on the coast and that they were naked" (que descubría gente por la costa y que venía desnuda).[96] Ramírez's fear that these might be the "barbarous" Indians of Florida is soon put to rest, however, as the Indians greet the crew in Spanish and ask for mercy. Soon afterward they are joined by their "master" (amo) who informs the crew that in fact they have landed on the Yucatan Peninsula and that it was lucky that "his Indians didn't see me first from far off, since if they had taken us for pirates they would have fled to the bushes to take refuge in its thickets and we never would have gotten out of that savage and solitary place" (no me hubiesen visto sus indios primero y a largo trecho, porque si teniéndonos por piratas se retiraran al monte para guarecerse en su espesura, jamás saldríamos de aquel paraje inculto y solitario).[97]

As Kathleen Ross has argued, Ramírez's fears of a still untamed northern territory of Florida resonate with the chronicles of the conquest, albeit in a secondary "Creole" phase in which conquest will occur more by the pen than the sword.[98] Yet it is important to note that this secondary moment of Spanish colonization is also marked by a confusing social landscape in which identities cannot be quickly discerned. While the elements of a primary colonization continue to thrive—in passing Ramírez mentions that the crew and their Yucatan hosts capture a canoe of non-Christianized Indians and take them with them to the town to be baptized[99]—the geography in which they arrive is also a labyrinth of trade, piracy, and contraband in which subjects are as much individual agents as representatives of broader social categories. Within this context, initial impressions are often mistaken, and indeed the crew is repeatedly taken for the pirates who have been invading sections of the Yucatan coastland. Yet once the illusion of violent primary colonization has been dispelled, the landscape becomes a place of intellectual curiosity. This alienation of the landscape from the battles of the conquest accords with the new social relations that the narrative documents, not only those among individuals on the frontier, but also between author and reading public. In an antiquarian note, Ramírez remarks on ancient wells nearby and a striking "building" (edificio), apparently a shrine or temple: "I found out that not only this [building] but also others much larger that are found in parts of that province were built by people who arrived here many centuries before the Spanish conquered it" (supe el que no sólo éste sino otros que se hallan en partes de aquella provincia, y mucho mayores, fueron fábrica de gentes que muchos siglos antes que la conquistaran los españoles vinieron a ella).[100] This slightly jarring digression in the narrative, while clearly consistent with Sigüenza's antiquarian interests, also appeals to the geographically distant reader by evoking an archaic past that can be appropriated as a local marvel.

These new forms of collective identification attempt to overcome the vicissitudes of individuation that had marked the crew's journey with the pirates but still do not address the racial divisions previously introduced into the narrative. It is in this context that slavery once again appears in the narrative. As if it were a passing digression, Ramírez mentions an encounter with a swindler who attempts to confiscate Pedro, his Mozambican slave. Ramírez cites the words of a man who approaches him claiming to be an old friend: "Is it possible, my friend and dear compatriot, that I am seeing you with my own eyes? Oh, how many times have I drowned in tears remembering you? Who would have guessed that I would find you in such misery? Embrace me tightly, soul mate, and give thanks to God that I am here" (—¿Es posible, amigo y querido paisano mío, que os ven mis ojos? ¡Oh, cuántas veces se me han anegado en lágrimas al acordarme de vos! ¡Quién me dijera que os había de ver en tanta miseria! Abrazadme recio, mitad de mi alma, y dadle gracias a Dios de que esté yo aquí). When Ramírez replies that he does not know him at all, the man insists: "How is this? . . . When you didn't have a better friend in your youth" (—¿Cómo es eso? . . . —Cuando no tuvisteis en vuestros primeros años mayor amigo).[101] The man goes on to say that he wishes to save Ramírez from the rumors that claim that he is a pirate. In order to help him, he argues, he needs to take his slave, Pedro, to the local official who will be able to put a stop to the story. Recognizing this as an attempt to trick him out of his slave, Ramírez replies by accusing the man of swindling better than the "best corsairs": "I am not such a simpleton, I told him, that I do not recognize that you are a great swindler who could give lessons in robbing to the best corsairs. To whoever gives me three hundred pieces of eight, I will give my black and [may he] go with God" (No soy tan simple—le respondí—que no reconozca ser vuestra merced un grande embustero y que puede dar lecciones de robar a los mayores corsarios. A quien me regalaré con trescientos reales de a ocho que vale, le regalaré con mi negro, y vaya con Dios).[102]

Despite Ramírez's suggestion that this is merely an entertaining digression, the interjection of slavery once again into the narrative becomes an integral element in the narrative of Ramírez's return to Mexico City. While the swindler's attempt to trick him out of his slave is another example of the confusion of identities on the frontier, his suggestion that Ramírez's true identity depends on whether his slave is actually his or not is also notable since the origin of this slave has been omitted from the narrative. There is no way for the reader to know, in fact, whether Ramírez has purchased or kidnapped the slave on his journey through Africa. In this sense his possession of a slave does indeed, as the swindler suggests, pose questions about the extent to which he drew a moral line between his activities and those of the pirates while aboard. Despite this murky origin, it is clear that once they are on the Mexican mainland Ramírez's slave has become a symbol of patrimonial status and that his rightful ownership of Pedro could seal his transformation from a dispossessed commoner to a citizen. In further evidence of these connections, Ramírez recounts that after more difficulties in Mérida he decides to sell Pedro to pay for his journey back to Mexico City: "and with Pedro's declaration that he was my slave, I sold him for three hundred pesos with which I clothed [my crew] and, giving them a small stipend so that they could find their way, I allowed them (as they had promised to accompany me forever) to turn their prow in whatever direction their inclinations pointed" (y con declaración que hizo el negro Pedro de ser mi esclavo, lo vendí en trescientos pesos con que vestí a aquellos y, dándoles alguna ayuda de costa para que buscasen su vida, permití (porque se había juramentado de asistirme siempre) pusiesen la proa de su elección donde los llamase el genio).[103] The sale ingeniously closes several open-ended elements of the narrative. Not only has Pedro himself declared that he is indeed Ramírez's property, thus eliminating any confusion on this issue, but his sale also confirms the Creole's patrimonial obligations to his crew. Ironically, although this moment gives him both patrimonial status as a master and owner of labor, the sale terminates these relationships by making Pedro a slave to another and by freeing the casta crew members from their personal bonds to him. In effect, Ramírez becomes an authorized subject in the patrimonial culture of New Spain at the same time that he creates free agents who can now make their way in the same fragmented social landscape that marked the first section of the narrative.

While his crew thus returns to the landscape of social anomie that began his tale, Ramírez himself has been transformed. Indeed, immediately following the sale of Pedro, the narrative ends rather abruptly with Ramírez's arrival in Mexico City. Here, at last, he finds the acceptance he has sought throughout the narrative, as Sigüenza y Góngora, upon hearing his tale, arranges a post for him as a mariner in the Armada de Barlovento:

Feeling compassion for my travails, [Sigüenza] not only produced this account of them but obtained, with the intercession and requests that he made in my presence to his excellency the viceroy, a decree so that Don Sebastián de Guzmán y Córdoba, agent, overseer, and purveyor of the Royal Treasury, would come to my aid, as he did. [He gave] another [decree] that allowed me to pass my time in the Royal Armada de Barlovento until I found another position and instructed the governor of Yucatán to order the ministers in charge of the embargo or insurance to hand over to me or to my executor, with no questions or delays, all that was on the vessel or found on the shore.

(Compadecido de mis trabajos no sólo formó esta relación en que se contienen sino que me consiguió con la intercesión y súplicas que en mi presencia hizo al excelentísimo señor virrey, decreto para que don Sebastián de Guzmán y Córdoba, factor, veedor y proveedor de las cajas reales, me socorriese, como se hizo. Otro para que se me entretenga en la Real Armada de Barlovento hasta acomodarme, y mandamiento para que el gobernador de Yucatán haga que los ministros que corrieron con el embargo o seguro de lo que estaba en las playas y hallaron a bordo, a mí o a mi [p]odatorio sin réplica ni pretexto le entreguen todo.)[104]

Thus Sigüenza's intervention achieves two rewards for Ramírez. On the one hand, he is recognized in patrimonial terms as an owner and possessor of all that he has obtained during his journey and on the other, he is given a position in the Armada de Barlovento, the battalion whose feats defending the Caribbean Sigüenza describes in his *Trofeo de la justicia*, published the following year.

The ideological interplay between the *Infortunios* and its propagandistic counterpart, *Trofeo de la justicia*, may be seen by comparing their endings. In the latter, a short text recounting the Spanish victories against the French in the Caribbean, Sigüenza describes the ranks of the fleet as an organized hierarchy of Creole and casta soldiers.[105] He pointedly distinguishes this orderly racial picture from the tactics of the French, whom Sigüenza accuses of deliberately freeing the slaves on Hispaniola in order to incorporate them into their own army.[106] As if it were a miniature of the society idealized in the casta paintings, the army of castas displays a peaceful patrimonial order by excluding from their order slavery and indigenous nomadism. As an allegory for Novohispanic citizenship, by contrast, the *Infortunios* shows the scaffolding on which this vision is built. Rather than positing a polity of local citizens divorced from the Habsburg empire, it affirms the empire's patrimonial values by drawing a sharp distinction between national space and frontier barbarism, whether indigenous or commercial.

For this reason it is particularly significant that in the last lines of the *Infortunios* Ramírez has been both recognized as an autonomous subject and taken out of the system of economic exchange that might seal this autonomy:

> [Sigüenza y Góngora] helped me with my travel to the extent that he could and, arranging that I journey to Veracruz in the company of Don Juan Enríquez Barroto, artillery captain of the Royal Armada de Barlovento, an excellent youth who is very talented in hydrography, learned in the mathematical sciences and, for this reason, intimate friend and his guest on this occasion, covered my expenses.
>
> (Ayudóme para mi viático con lo que pudo, y disponiendo bajase a la Vera Cruz en compañía de don Juan Enríquez Barroto, capitán de la artillería de la Real Armada de Barlovento, mancebo excelentemente consumado en la hidrografía, docto en las ciencias matemáticas y, por eso, íntimo amigo y huésped suyo en esta ocasión, me excusó de gastos.)[107]

Thus, Ramírez becomes an ideal figure of the new Creole citizen, a free agent who nonetheless reproduces the patrimonial values that distinguished Habsburg imperialism. Without breaking with Spanish right, by the end of his journey Ramírez is thus able to shift the terms of imperial sovereignty from those of dependent vassals of a distant king to autonomous citizens of a local polity. Resisting the temptations of the high seas, witnessing the fate of Europeans and non-Europeans in the world economy, and finally returning to the safety of a patrimonial hierarchy defined by race and status, Ramírez and his world journey thus become an allegory for the closure of national space that Sigüenza y Góngora understood as the best way to defend Spain's overextended empire.

Although not the only possible reaction to the crisis of the Habsburg empire, the *Infortunios* was surely the most innovative attempt to rethink viceregal politics in a world that had moved beyond the original terms of Spanish imperial sovereignty. To the extent that the account reflected Sigüenza's hand, it also resonates with other projects that occupied the Creole scholar in the last decade of his life. While his writings documenting these projects have none of the narrative intricacy of the *Infortunios*, they show an acute

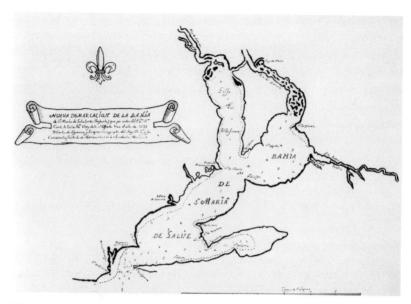

Figure 21. "New Demarcation of the Bay of Santa María de Galve" ("Nueva Demarcación de la Bahia de Santa María de Galve"). Sigüenza y Góngora's 1693 Map of Pensacola Bay, Florida. Courtesy of the State Archives of Florida.

awareness of the problems of imperial governance and propose, in different ways, the delineation of a Creole citizenry to combat these. Even in such technical documents as Sigüenza's intervention in the contentious debate over the design for the fort on San Juan de Ulúa, the island protecting Veracruz harbor, the Creole scholar remained aware of the social demands of imperial defense. In response to a critique by an understudy of the Austrian engineer who had built the fort, Sigüenza wrote a scathing rebuttal of the subaltern's attack. The letter is typical of Sigüenza's sarcastic responses to what he perceived as ignorance of mathematical truth, a tone that appeared in his debate with Eusebio Kino in his 1691 *Libra astronómica* as well as in a dispute over his own cartographic rendering of Pensacola Bay.[108] But it also shows a subtle political stance toward the defense of the viceroyalty, which, after all, was the main objective of the redesign of the fort. Noting that the assistant's critique was based on the assumption of a weakened or incompetent regiment at the fort, Sigüenza takes the opportunity to reflect on what he perceived as a decline in the quality of the viceregal militia: "if the persons employed in that garrison were well treated, better paid, and well stocked, [these forts] would not be manned by the boys and novices nor the forced recruits that are there today, but rather by the experienced and well disciplined persons that were there in the past" (contener [*sic*] bien tratada y mejor pagada a la gente de que se compone aquella guarnición; y lleno el número de su dotación, no habrá los muchachos y visoños ni forzados que oy tiene, sino gente experta y bien disciplinada como la huvo antes).[109]

Sigüenza's participation in the 1693 expedition to map Pensacola Bay (Figure 21) is marked by a similar focus on the social context of fortifying New Spain's northern frontier. Produced at the request of the viceroy, who needed accurate information on the bay in order to arm his petition to the Council on War in Madrid that the area be fortified, Sigüenza's maps have been hailed for their care and accuracy. Indeed, the maps undoubtedly exemplified the technical translation of nature into the language of mathematical relations for the pragmatic needs of imperial defense. Yet Sigüenza's accompanying report also imbues the disputed Floridian territory with a more symbolic meaning. The report details Sigüenza's reading of the landscape, including the reasons that he assigned place names from central Mexico to points along the bay, and advocates the immediate occupation of the area by citizens (*vecinos*) from the central areas of the viceroyalty.[110] This metascientific information provides a clue as to the conceptual framework for Sigüenza's other cartographic projects during this period and especially one of the most important and enigmatic of these: the first locally rendered general map of New Spain. Completed sometime between 1681 and 1689, the original map has now been lost and scholars have had to rely on copies such as the adaptation made by José Alzate y Ramírez, the eighteenth-century Mexican scientist and gazetteer (Figure 22).[111] Indeed, Alzate y Ramírez's praise of Sigüenza's cartographic acumen is at least partially responsible for the fame the map has subsequently held.[112]

However, despite several recent articles that reiterate Alzate's assessment of Sigüenza's cartographic abilities, there has been little speculation about why the Creole scholar would undertake a complete cartographic survey of New Spain or how his interest in this type of project may have differed from Spanish imperial

cartography. Works such as the *Mercurio volante* and the *Infortunios*, themselves deeply engaged with the geography of the nebulous frontiers of the Spanish Empire, suggest that Sigüenza's cartographic knowledge was related to a consciousness of Spain's global decline. The difference between Sigüenza's conceptual framework and others of the period may be seen by comparing his reports to Gemelli Careri's commentary on the hydrographic rendition of the valley of Mexico (Figure 23), included in the Neapolitan's account of his 1697 travels through New Spain. The map, declares Gemelli Careri, gives credence to the idea that the Mexicas were agents of the devil, since the layout of the lakes and waterways imitated Satan's physiognomy. Through complicated acrostics, he also argues that the names of the Mexica kings may be given values that add up to 666, thus proving the satanic origins of the geography and genealogy of central Mexico.[113] At first glance, Gemelli's desire to read the hydrographic map as a cipher for the demonic nature of Mexica leadership appears to accord methodologically with Sigüenza's interest in uncovering hermetic truths about the pre-Columbian past. Significantly, however, Sigüenza did not engage in this highly symbolic, Neoplatonic understanding of cartography. Following the same early seventeenth-century sources, Sigüenza drew a map very similar to the one reproduced in Gemelli's account (Figure 24). While, like his general map of New Spain, the original has now been lost, it is clear from the eighteenth-century reproductions that Sigüenza corrected and added to the early seventeenth-century prototype drawn by the engineer Adrian Boot and thus that his interest was the map's technical accuracy rather than symbolic visual meaning.[114] In this case, he eschewed the social and symbolic meanings of the waterways for geographically and mathematically grounded knowledge, in a clear example of the pragmatic bent of Novohispanic science.[115]

Yet even as he embraced mathematical truth as a proof-based grounds for assessing and representing nature, Sigüenza understood this truth in social terms. In Sigüenza's 1681 scientific

Figure 22 (opposite page). "New Geographical Map of Septentrional America." ("Nuevo Mapa Geographico de la America Septentrional") (1768). By José Antonio Alzate y Ramírez after a seventeenth-century map by Carlos de Sigüenza y Góngora. Courtesy of the Bancroft Library, University of California, University of California, Berkeley.

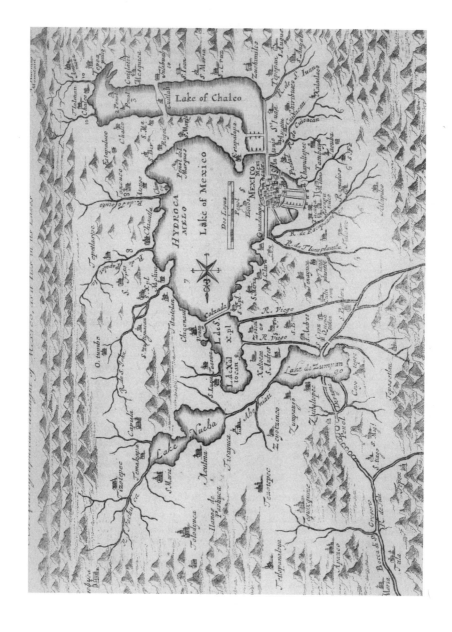

dispute with the Jesuit missionary Eusebio Kino, for instance, the Creole scholar implied that mathematics was a form of universal reason that could create the basis for a cosmopolitan scientific community well beyond New Spain.[116] He used his yearly astrological almanacs written at the same time, which he claimed to write only reluctantly out of obligation to his university post as professor of mathematics, to question astrology before a more popular audience. Like his ephemeral publication of the same period, the "Noticia cronologica de los reyes," Sigüenza's popular almanacs sought to extend his scholarly erudition to a larger community of common viceregal subjects by actively fighting against the astrological practices on which they were based.[117] For Sigüenza, then, mathematical truth was not divorced from the need to form and educate a local citizenry. His maps, moreover, were surely tied to the desire to expand this Creole citizenry to the furthest reaches of the viceroyalty. But before these citizens could be separated from their popular and symbolic notions of nature, geography, and history, they had to be recognized amid the increasingly complex ethnic and social mixtures of the viceregal population.

It is not surprising, then, that at the end of the seventeenth century Sigüenza would take such a strong interest in publishing the tale of a common Creole subject's journey to the borders of the Spanish Empire. It was through this tale of limits that he could best define New Spain, as a nation, a territory, and a people, in relation to an emerging geopolitical order. Sigüenza's vision of a local territory and citizenry was also heavily inflected by a concept of race drawn directly from the social and juridical structures of Spanish colonialism. Yet while Creoles could appropriate the language of race prevalent in Spanish imperial law and institutions, their relationship to those of non-European or mixed descent was neither pastoral nor genealogical. Since Creoles had no deep genealogical links to the territory that they called their homeland, their definition of a national community of citizens was necessarily based on moral distinctions. To the administrative logic of imperial governance, with its confused notions of race and vassalage, Creoles added historical necessity drawn from their local archive. These

Figure 23 (opposite page). "An Hydrographicall Draught of Mexico as It Lies in Its Lakes." From Giovanni Gemelli Careri, *A Collection of Voyages and Travels* (London, 1704). Courtesy of the John Carter Brown Library at Brown University.

projects were all closely linked to a cartographic vision of New Spain in which clearly delineated and fortified borders paralleled a moral defense of Spanish imperial ideology. Rather than disparate and disconnected, then, Sigüenza's scholarship during the final years of his life provided the piecemeal elements for addressing the political crisis of the period. At a time when the Spanish monarchy and its imperial vision appeared to falter, it was necessary to transform New Spain from a viceroyalty subordinated to a universal Christian monarchy to a national territory able to fend off global threats. The first step toward the actual occupation of this territory was the imagination of a known and unified polity whose patrimonial governance could best understand and respond to a world in which Spain was no longer the preeminent global power.

Figure 24 (opposite page). "Map of the Waters from a Circumference of 90 Leagues that Lead to Texcoco" ("Mapa de las Aguas que por el Circulo de 90 Leguas Vienen a la Tescuco") (1748). A copy of a seventeenth-century map by Carlos de Sigüenza y Góngora. Courtesy of the Bancroft Library, University of California, Berkeley.

Conclusion

The Afterlife of a Baroque Archive

In an obituary dated August 22, 1700, the Mexico City chronicler Antonio de Robles announced the death of his friend Carlos de Sigüenza y Góngora:

> the Licenciado Don Carlos de Sigüenza y Góngora has died; a lay priest, native of this city, great mathematician, [and] emeritus professor of the same discipline, he was in the Society of Jesus for seven years, leaving it in the year 1667. He printed several very erudite works, had acquired all the histories and reports of the Indies, [and] by royal decree and commission of the viceroy, Conde de Galve, went to the Bay of Santa María de Galve, alias Pensacola, to explore that region, after which he reported on the advantages of populating it. He was royal cosmographer, accountant for the Royal Mexican University, distinguished in all sciences, general examiner of the artillery, corrector for the Holy Office of the Inquisition of this New Spain, head chaplain of the Hospital of the Love of God. He was a distinguished philosopher, comparable to those celebrated by antiquity, a great poet.
>
> (murió el Lic. D. Carlos de Sigüenza y Góngora, presbítero, natural de esta ciudad, gran matemático, catedrático jubilado de esta facultad; había estado en la Compañía siete años, y se salió de ella el año de 1667; imprimió algunas obras muy eruditas; había adquirido todas las historias y noticias de Indias; fue por comisión del virrey, conde de Galve, por cédula real a la bahia de Santa María de Galve, alias Panzacola, a reconocer aquella tierra, de que informó cuanto convenía su población; fue cosmógrafo de S. M. contador de la real Universidad mexicana, insigne en todas ciencias, examinador general de artilleros, corrector del Santo Oficio de la Inquisición de esta Nueva España,

Conclusion 251

capellán mayor del hospital del Amor de Dios; fue insigne filósofo, que se pudo comparar a aquellos que celebra la antigüedad; grande poeta.)[1]

In an example of the symbiotic relationship among fields of knowledge during the seventeenth century, Robles presents Sigüenza's disparate pursuits as the product of a precocious and cultured intellect, lamenting that the viceroyalty had lost such a leading scholar. While in the following century local authors continued to praise Sigüenza for his eclecticism, however, they began distancing themselves from the rhetorical patina of much of his prose.[2] By the early twentieth century, historians and literary critics alike went even further, explicitly emphasizing Sigüenza's scientific and antiquarian pursuits over what they viewed as his Baroque excesses. At the same time, they began to promote Sigüenza as a very early patriot who wrote for the "love of his country" well before the advent of Mexican independence.[3]

Although there has recently been renewed interest in the rhetorical structure of Sigüenza's writings, studies continue to separate his style from the political context of late seventeenth-century New Spain.[4] While building on the literary methodology of these studies, this book has argued that Sigüenza's diverse works elucidate the interdependence of style, rhetoric, and political ideals in late seventeenth-century Mexico. It has proposed that what has often been interpreted as the emergence of a patriotic "consciousness" can better be understood as an "archive," which, in both a material and metaphorical sense, was formative for a specifically Creole authority. From Sigüenza's perspective, the art of gathering, combining, and relating disparate objects from an archaic past or a confused present, of comprehending and organizing the diverse population and territory of the Novohispanic present, or of establishing a politically endowed citizenry all demanded an understanding of local conditions. This notion of a local collection permeated all of his writings, regardless of their specific style or topic. Although even at the end of his life the completion and coherence of his archive was more a desire situated in the imaginary sphere of his writings than a material and institutional reality, these writings also delineate the political force that he attributed to his archive. It is clear that through his collection Sigüenza hoped to respond to the urgent need to establish points of stability and transition during the final years of Habsburg rule. The recovery of a unified past, the formation of a local community of citizens defined by lineage and virtue, and the closure of national borders were all linked to the creation of a strong Creole authority that he believed could provide such stability.

The idea that Sigüenza's true scholarly interests diverged from the rhetoric and poetics of his writings has often led to his portrayal as a critical savant out of place in an era still dominated by Neo-scholastic reason and weighty prose. To support this argument scholars have often turned to a citation from Sigüenza's 1684 *Parayso occidental* in which he warns against the excesses of Gongorism through the striking metaphor of a woman's corpse:

> To write of a dead woman that "instead of displaying a wan sadness or wilted perfection she blushed with red hues, or a complexion of crimson roses, which embellished, more than can be justly praised, the sweet countenance of the rigid corpse," and attempt with all this circumlocution to say that she preserved the same complexion after death as she did in life, what other end would the author serve than to condemn his book (and all the more so when it is composed only of such phrases) never to be read? And not wishing such a fate for my own, since I like to have said about it what is said about others, I assure you that you will find "horizons," "stars," and "colures" in the authors that write about the spheres; "chrysolites," "topaz," and "carbuncles" in the lapidaries; "ambers" and "musks" in the perfume makers; "jasmines," "carnations," and "sunflowers" in the gardens, and all this with much more in those that presume to imitate Fray Hortenso Paravicino and D. Luis de Góngora. In any case, as this is not the manner of everyday conversation, which should be the style used in writing histories, I adamantly affirm that one will not find such a catalogue in the present work, because I know that this is the reef upon which many run aground.
>
> (Escrivir de una difunta el que en vez de mostrar palidas tristezas o marchitas perfecciones se sonroseaba de rojas colores, o colorido de rosas carmesies, las quales alindaban, mas de lo que puede encarecerse, la cara apacible de la difunta yerta, y servir todo este circumloquio para decir el que conservaba despues de muerta los mismos colores que quando viva, que otra cosa es sino condenar un Autor su libro (y más formandose todo el de semejantes periodos) a que jamás se lea; y no quieriendo tan mal a este mio, que guste ver por el que de otros dizen, aseguro que se hallaran los orizontes, las estrellas y los coluros en los Autores que escriven de esfera; en los Lapidarios los chrysolitos, los topacios, y los carbunclos: los ambares, y almizcles en los Guanteros: los jazmines, los claveles, y mirasoles en los jardines, y todo esto con mucho mas en los que se presuman imitadores de Fray Hortenso Paravicino y D. Luis de Góngora, y como quiera que no es esto lo que se gasta en las comunes platicas, debiendo ser el estilo que entonces se usa el que se debe seguir

quando se escriven historias, desde luego afirmo el que no se hallará el cathologo de essas cosas en la presente, porque sé que es este el escollo en que peligran muchos.)[5]

While the passage is certainly a critique of what had become over the course of the seventeenth century an institutional rhetorical style, the terms in which Sigüenza poses this critique suggest that his true concern was finding a public for his works. In Sigüenza's example, the description of a dead woman strikingly equates Gongoresque poetics with death, in this case the death of the book whose rhetorical excess guarantees that it will never be read. While the passage he cites affirms that the corpse retains a lifelike beauty, therefore, Sigüenza reads its rhetorical artifice as a figurative embalming. Histories, as he declares in another section of the prologue, should enliven artifacts by "mak[ing] the past present as it once was" (hacer presente lo pasado como fue entonces).[6] In this case, his own unadorned history of the Royal Convent of Jesús María in Mexico City, written in the language of everyday speech, will stay alive precisely by guaranteeing a readership beyond the court and the university.

Rather than simply a question of style, Sigüenza's critique of Gongorism relates to a more general concern about the circulation and reception of his works. Thus, he did not reject all forms of Gongoresque metaphor, allusion, and the excessive citations common to much writing of the period, but rather employed these rhetorical forms selectively to provide access to hermetic truths not readily available to common insight. This truth, however, then had to be translated for a nonerudite audience for whom recondite Gongoresque language would have proven to be an obstacle to comprehension. The role of the Creole savant, as Sigüenza saw it, was to mediate between the complex and arcane language of erudite scholarship and a public that could be guided by the principles found therein.[7] For this reason, in the latter part of his life Sigüenza appeared increasingly aware of the need to establish an audience for works "whose composition" (cuya composición), as he asserts in another section of the prologue to the 1684 *Parayso occidental*, "has been inspired by the great love that I have for my *patria*" (me ha estimulado el sumo amor que a mi patria tengo). Bitterly he notes that these works "will probably die with me (for I will never have the resources to print them due to my great poverty)" (probablemente morirán conmigo (pues jamás tendré con qué poder imprimirlo por mi gran pobreza)).[8] Sigüenza, who worked outside the various institutional and corporate bodies that supported most scholarship of the period, appears to have been especially interested in directing his knowledge toward a greater political community that would receive and use it. It is this preoccupation with collecting and transmitting local truths for a common good that links his writings to the context of a greater crisis in authority during the period. The archive became the medium for supplementing traditional forms of authority with an archaic local law.

Sigüenza's will, signed only weeks before his death at the age of fifty-five, contains the most poignant attempt to prevent the dispersal of this fledgling archive. In this lengthy document, Sigüenza draws a sharp line between the transitory fate of his individual patrimony and the need to preserve his extensive collection for posterity. As Robles reports in his obituary, Sigüenza had spent his last days in pain, afflicted by stones in his kidneys or bladder. Since the doctors treating him had been unable to specify the source of his affliction, Sigüenza had requested that his corpse be surgically examined by trained physicians in the hope that "through their experience other patients will benefit" (con su experiencia aprovechar a otros enfermos).[9] In his will Sigüenza indeed does make this request and adds, with characteristic irony, "I ask for the love of God that this be done for the public good, and I order my heir in no way to obstruct this, for it matters little what is done to a body that in two days time will be decaying and putrid" (pido por amor de Dios que assí sea para bien público, y mando a mi heredero que de ninguna manera lo estorve pues Ymporta poco, que se haga esto con un Cuerpo que dentro de dos días ha de estar corrompido y hediondo).[10] The rest of the document reflects a similar desire to dispense his material possessions, which he asks be distributed to his large network of family and friends, used to pay off debts, and donated as alms for nuns and frontier missions.[11]

By contrast, Sigüenza takes pains to protect what he appears to have considered his true legacy: his extensive library and antiquarian collection. Throughout his will, Sigüenza emphasizes the difficulties involved in amassing his archive and specifies the steps that should be taken to preserve it after his death. His books he describes as

> pertaining to matters of the Indies, both the general and particular histories of the provinces, conquests and spiritual gains achieved, as well as the moral, medical, and natural histories, along with the lives of illustrious men that have flourished here, whose collection has cost me great pains and care, and a considerable sum of money, it not being easy to find another such library in all of the Indies

Conclusion

(libros pertenecientes a cosas de Yndias assi de historias generales y particulares de sus Provincias, Conquistas y fructo Spiritual que se he hecho en ellas, como de cosas morales, naturales, medicinales de ellas, y de Vidas de Varones Ynsignes que en ellas han florecido cuya Collección me ha costado sumo desvelo y cuidado, y suma muy considerable de dinero, no siendo fácil conseguir otro pedaso de librería de esta lignea en todas las Yndias)[12]

and asks that they be placed with others of their kind. His manuscripts, "some of them in Castilian and some in the Mexican language . . . because they are irreplaceable and deal with very extraordinary matters should be held in high regard and as a great treasure, for which reason I am obliged to request that they be kept separately in a safe place" (parte de ellos en Castellano y parte en lengua Mexicana . . . por ser Unicos y de matheria singularíssimas deven Estimarse y guardarse como un thesoro grande, motivo que me obliga a que solicite se conserven separadamente en parte tan segura).[13] Finally, he notes that "with great effort and diligence, as well as a considerable cost to my estate, I have acquired different books or original maps of the ancient Indians, called in the time of their heathendom *texamatl* or *amoxtle*" (con mayor desbelo y solicitud y gasto muy conciderable de mi hazienda he Conseguido diferentes libros, o Mapas originales de los Antiguos Yndios Mexicanos que ellos en su Gentilidad llamavan texamatl o Amoxtle).[14] He asks that these be placed, together with what he claims was an antediluvian elephant tooth, in "an elegant box of cedar from Havana with a key, spending whatever is necessary from my estate" (un Cajón de Cedro de la havana muy curioso con su llave gastando en ello de mi hacienda quanto fuere necesario).[15]

While there is perhaps no clearer indication of the transcendental value that Sigüenza attributed to his archive than these instructions, his will also underlines the distinct problem of keeping the collection intact in the absence of its originator. After detailing these steps to safeguard individual items, Sigüenza bequeathed the entire contents of his archive to the library of the Jesuit college of San Pedro y San Pablo. As he goes on to explain, this decision differed from his original intention to have the collection sent to European libraries after his death:

although my inclination was always to send some to the Vatican library, where one has been held for many years now with great admiration, others to the Escorial and the remaining to the library of the Great Duke of Florence, who expressed his interest through the very excellent Sir Duke of Jovenazzo, I believe it is more advantageous that treasures so worthy of esteem and veneration due to their antiquity and provenance be held at the aforementioned library of the College of San Pedro y San Pablo.

(aunque mi animo fue siempre remitir algunos de ellos a la librería Baticana donde se conserve Uno, muchos años a, con grande aprecio, otros al Escurial y los restantes a la Biblioteca del Gran Duque de Florencia, quien por mano del Excelentísimo Señor Duque de Jobenazzo me lo havía insinuado, tengo por mas conveniente que alhajas tan dignas de aprecio y beneración por su antigüedad, y ser originales se conservan en dicha librería del Collegio Maximo de Señor San Pedro y San Pablo.)[16]

Although it appears that Sigüenza did send other items to the Duke of Florence's library, including a portrait of a heroic Moctezuma (Figure 25),[17] his decision to retain other "treasures so worthy of esteem and veneration" in a local context tells much about how he conceived of his collection. While the works would surely have received attention as individual curiosities in Europe, for Sigüenza they were only fully intelligible when brought together in their place of origin. The power of the archive lay not in the magnificence of the individual items per se, but rather in their consignment to a locale where they might empower magistrates to link past, present, and future in one law.

Sigüenza's choice of the Jesuit library to house his collection is likewise significant. Not only did the Creole scholar often express gratitude to the order in which he had been educated as a youth,[18] but the Jesuits' training in such diverse foundations as mathematical reason and Neoplatonic hermeticism had greatly influenced his own interpretive approach. At the end of the seventeenth century, moreover, when a series of crises sabotaged centralized governance in New Spain, it could be that Sigüenza thought that the Jesuits provided a more permanent safeguard for the collection than did the viceregal state or even the university. It is ironic, then, that the decision to donate his archive to the Jesuit library resulted in the loss and dispersal of his collection. The dismemberment of Sigüenza's collection began soon after his death when his nephew and designated heir distributed some of his manuscripts to friends. Other items seem to have been lost or pilfered from the Jesuit library over the course of the following century since the eighteenth-century Mexican archivist Eguiara y Eguren already had to speculate as to what his predecessor had possessed.[19] With the expulsion of the Jesuits from New Spain in 1767 and the dismantling of their extensive educational network the loss became irreparable. Although the Italian collector Lorenzo Boturini Benaduci seems to have salvaged several items before the expulsion, the greater part of Sigüenza's collection disappeared at that time, only to reemerge much later as individual pieces in private and public collections. Much of what Sigüenza is assumed to have held is now known only through inventories made by those who saw the collection before its rapid dismemberment in the eighteenth century.[20]

Yet even as his collection was dispersed over the course of the eighteenth century, Sigüenza's name became synonymous with the will to collect for a public good. The first to comment on the dispersal of the collection was Sigüenza's nephew and the executor of his will, Gabriel López de Sigüenza, in his posthumous edition of Sigüenza's youthful poem written to celebrate Saint Francis Xavier, *Oriental planeta evangelico* (Eastern Evangelical Planet) (1700).[21] In a letter to the prominent Creole Antonio de Aunzibay written only two months after Sigüenza's death, López de Sigüenza depicts his uncle as a scholar who sought to print his works "for the common good" (la utilidad común).[22] He then repeats Sigüenza's own complaint that many of his manuscripts remained unpublished during his lifetime, noting that several sponsors had not followed through on their promises to subsidize publication. His uncle, he asserted, had left many other manuscripts at his death, including various titles that had not been included in Agustín Vetancurt's list in the *Teatro mexicano* (1698). Finally, after remembering his uncle's heroic efforts to salvage books and documents from the burning viceregal palace during the 1692 riot, López de Sigüenza remarks that several of these had already left his possession: "I have some of the papers that he had taken from these books for "The History [of Mexico]" in my possession, others he or I have given away, and many books were stolen from me upon his death, among other things" (los cuales papeles que para la Historia tenía sacados de dichos libros algunos tengo en mi poder, otros dió, y dí yo, y con bastantes libros me hurtaron en su muerte, y otras cosas).[23] The inheritance transferred to the Jesuit college of San Pedro y San Pablo, he claims, was 470 books, including 28 volumes of manuscripts "both his own works and those of others, all originals" (así de cosas suyas como de otros, todos originales).[24]

While López de Sigüenza took pains to inscribe his uncle's work within an overall narrative of piety, as his publication of Sigüenza's poem dedicated to Francis Xavier attests, in the next century Sigüenza

Figure 25. Portrait of Moctezuma commissioned by Sigüenza y Góngora to be sent to Cosimo de Medici III. Attributed to Antonio Rodríguez (ca. 1680–91). Courtesy of the Palazzo Pitti, Florence, Italy / The Bridgeman Art Library.

was increasingly remembered as a more systematic scientist and antiquarian. In the prologues to his *Bibliotheca mexicana*, for instance, Eguiara y Eguren called Sigüenza "D. Carolus de Sigüenza et Gongora, Natione Mexicanus et Patria, si quis illus, benemeritus de ipsa" and described him foremost as an enlightened scholar of American antiquities:

> Moreover, devoted to the study of the antiquities of America, once he had obtained with the greatest diligence the records of the ancient Indians, he studied them, and with the most rigorous criticism and assiduous readings of their histories, he investigated them, and submitted them to calm judgment and translated them into various and many books, in which he brought hidden and concealed things into the midday light. In order to compose these [works] he had learned the Mexican language and the science needed by a most ingenious Oedipus, that is, to know thoroughly the hieroglyphs, characters, and images which the inhabitants of North America used as letters in order to convey their things and record the most famous of them from their first steps in this region.
>
> (Porro Americae cruendis antiquitatibus deditus, priscorum monumenta Indorum diligentissime conquisita, evolvit, et qua erat justissima Critica, Historiarumque accurata et multa lectione, revocavit ad trutinam atque in Libros a se conditos varios multosque traduxit, quibus abdita et offusa caligine in Solem tradidit et meridiem. His conficiendis Idioma imbiberat Mexicanum, et qua OEdipo eget ingenisissimo, Scientiam penitissime calluit Hieroglyphicorum, Characterum, et Imaginum, queis Septentrionalis Americae incolae litterarum vice utebantur, resque ab usque ipsarum prima in hunc Orbem trajectione celebriores memoriae prodiderant.)[25]

It is clear from Eguiara y Eguren's characterization that the eighteenth-century Creole scholar had already moved past the idea of hermetic truth that marked Sigüenza's own interpretive framework. Instead, he portrays Sigüenza as a translator of universally valid knowledge in a more enlightened vein. Indeed, as other scholars and travelers came into fleeting contact with inventories of Sigüenza's collection, the Creole savant became known above all as the collector of a unique archive that was quickly being dispersed by misuse, theft, and, most disastrously, sale after the expulsion of the Jesuits from Mexico in 1767.[26]

With the definitive loss of his original artifacts, indeed, Sigüenza has been monumentalized as a prescient scholar who understood the needs of a nation before it existed. In one of the most detailed attempts to trace the course of Sigüenza's collection as it was broken up, moved, and sold during the eighteenth and nineteenth centuries, the historian Elías Trabulse has lamented the loss of the collection as a sign of a problem endemic to Mexico:

> Any scholar of the history of Mexican culture knows that one of the greatest problems he or she will face is the loss of all manner of manuscripts written by many of this nation's scholars, who sometimes spent the greater part of their lives composing these works. In order to appreciate the magnitude of the loss, it suffices to peruse the old bibliographic compilations that have become their sole register. This is without a doubt one of the most deplorable facts of our history.
>
> (Cualquier investigador de la historia de la cultura mexicana sabe que uno de los mayores problemas al que debe hacer frente es el de la pérdida de las obras manuscritas de todo género, producidos por muchos sabios de esta tierra que a veces consumieron en esos trabajos buena parte de sus esfuerzos de sus vidas. Basta recorrer las antiguas compilaciones bibliográficas que los registran para lamentar la magnitud de lo que se ha perdido. Sin exagerar, éste es sin duda uno de los hechos más deplorables de nuestra historia.)[27]

A resounding call for the preservation of local patrimony, Trabulse's remarks nonetheless run the risk of lifing Sigüenza out of his context and thus divorcing the stylistic elements of his manuscripts from the purpose of his collection. While unified around a regional patrimony, Sigüenza's collection was both more fragmented and sparser than his reputation suggests. His own work accounted for this fragmentation not by denying it or filling in its missing pieces but by searching for unity in a lost archaic past accessible only through the hermetic interpretation. The purpose of his archive was not completion but composition—the very act of bringing together objects in one conceptual framework.

It is this strangely disjointed and nostalgic composition that must be analyzed to understand the transition from imperial sovereignty to a local polity in New Spain. The archive was an attempt to move beyond the history of a clearly violent past by bringing indigenous and Creole documents into one overarching genealogy. And while Sigüenza was perhaps unique in his dogged pursuit of this goal, he should not be considered a prescient or pre-Enlightenment scholar working beyond his time. His works, indeed, were intricately connected to the rhetoric and politics of late seventeenth-century New Spain. They responded, above all, to the fear that alternative collections,

Conclusion

orderings, and interpretations would undermine Spanish governance of New Spain. While Sigüenza looked to protect the Spanish monarch against these threats, his unique combination of local history, religious devotion, and science did not require the intervention of the king. The concept of a local citizen, defined by lineage and virtue, was crucial to Sigüenza's notion of governance by patrimonial privilege rather than sovereign decision. Perhaps the strongest figures that haunt the edges of Sigüenza's writings, then, are those of sovereignless political figures such as the mob that sacked Mexico City in 1692 or the pirates unfettered by mercantilist policies. Through his archive, Sigüenza sought to create a bulwark against such figures by directing interpretation toward the patrimonial values that he believed would best order Novohispanic society.

By relating Sigüenza's works to their historical context, this study has eschewed the attempt to place his writings in a teleological march toward Spanish American independence from Spain. Yet neither has it embraced José Lezama Lima's characterization of Sigüenza as the prototype of Baroque erudition, at least in the terms that Lezama defined this quality. Instead, it has argued that Sigüenza y Góngora's writings can perhaps best be understood as part of the "high Baroque" in Spanish America: a coalescence of style, epistemology, and politics that combined hermeticism and scientific critique. This unique hermeneutics, which also marked other writers of the period, continued well into the eighteenth century when it engaged with the political and economic transition to Bourbon rule in Spain and Spanish America.[28] While just one participant in this transition, Sigüenza y Góngora provided the most innovative and complete reflections of its tendencies. Yet despite Sigüenza's attempts to intervene actively in the politics of the period, his works tell us more about the possibilities and limits of political ideals among the Novohispanic elite at the end of the seventeenth century than about their actual accomplishments. Indeed, if placed in this historical context, what has often been glossed as Sigüenza's propensity to Baroque contradiction appears instead to be a more subtle adjustment of political theology, metaphysics, and historiography to an era in which Spain could no longer justify its vast empire through the epic goals of universal Christianity.

While none of Sigüenza's diverse works are theories of statecraft, they are all complex documents of the transition from the ideals of Spanish imperialism to Creole notions of sovereignty. By analyzing one moment in this transition, moreover, we can avoid the temptation to construct teleological histories. The figures of Creole sovereignty were subject to historical contingency, reversals, and constant pressures from alternative notions of justice and governance. That we are dependent on texts such as Sigüenza's to understand the transition from imperial to local sovereignty should not hinder our attempt to read these against the grain. Produced in a period still dominated by the figure of a distant sovereign, Sigüenza's writings were aimed at consolidating a cultural and ethnic privilege for the small Creole elite of New Spain. By insisting on the privileged position of the regional savant, indeed, Sigüenza's works established a division between erudite and popular knowledge that marked the many subsequent reimaginations of Mexican and Spanish American polities. But Sigüenza's works also document the everyday forms of memory and politics that countered this vision and prevented its implementation. Further studies of the crucial period of the late seventeenth century, outside the language of continuity and stagnation, will surely show that the crisis engendered innovations from Creoles and non-Creoles alike that prevented any realization of absolute sovereignty. By directly engaging two contradictory forces, one tending toward order by transcendental laws and the other toward immanent critique, Sigüenza y Góngora attempted to foreclose the many other political possibilities of the last days of the Habsburg monarchy. Rather than a detriment to analysis, the constitutional fragmentation and loss that marked his archive is the best evidence of the embattled foundations of the new polities by which Novohispanic Creoles hoped to inherit the privileges of empire.

NOTES

I have retained the spelling and punctuation of all non-modernized original sources. All translations, unless otherwise noted, are mine.

INTRODUCTION

1. López de Gómara opens his 1552 *Historia general de las indias* by dedicating the work to Carlos V with a hyperbolic providentialism: "The greatest event, after the creation of the world, excepting the incarnation and death of the one who created it, is the discovery of the Indies" (La mayor cosa después de la creación del mundo, sacando la encarnación y muerte del que lo crió, es el descubrimiento de Indias). Francisco López de Gómara, *Historia de la conquista de México* (Mexico: Porrúa, 1988), 3. He goes on to narrate Cortés's victory over the Mexica in an equally providentialist vein.

2. Jaime Cuadriello, "El origen del reino y la configuración de su empresa: Episodios y alegorías de triunfo y fundación," in *Los pinceles de la historia: El origen del reino de la Nueva España, 1680–1750*, ed. Jaime Soler Frost (Mexico: Museo Nacional de Arte, 1999), 67.

3. On Cortés's representation of Moctezuma's capitulation as a *translatio imperii*, see Anthony Pagden, *Lords of All the World: Ideologies of Empire in Spain, Britain and France, c. 1500–c. 1800* (New Haven, Conn.: Yale University Press, 1995), 32.

4. According to Richard Kagan, Boot took the map with him to the Netherlands when he returned in 1634. From there, it ended up in the hands of Willem Johannes Blaeu, the well-known Amsterdam mapmaker. Richard Kagan, *Urban Images of the Hispanic World, 1493–1793* (New Haven, Conn.: Yale University Press, 2000), 152–53.

5. Cuadriello, "El origen del reino," 69. For an excellent reading of the relationship between the screen's "panoramic vision" and viceregal authority, see Michael Schreffler, *The Art of Allegiance: Visual Culture and Imperial Power in Baroque New Spain* (University Park: Pennsylvania State University Press, 2007), 25–30.

6. Cuadriello, "El origen del reino," 67; Schreffler, *The Art of Allegiance*, 30.

7. For Moorish motifs in Spain, see Barbara Fuchs, *Exotic Nation: Maurophilia and the Early Modern Construction of Spain* (Philadelphia: University of Pennsylvania Press, 2009), 51–59.

8. In fact, the biombo aestheticizes the problem of history in a way that suggests a paradoxical transcendence rather than historical transformation. For a reading of the Spanish *comedia* as performing a similar ideological function, see Anthony J. Cascardi, *Ideologies of History in the Spanish Golden Age* (University Park: Pennsylvania State University Press, 1997), 3–8, 17–46.

9. Cuadriello, "El origen del reino," 69.

10. Throughout this study I will use the term "Creole" to refer to colonial subjects of Spanish descent who identify with an American rather than European homeland. For the most part, these subjects were born in the Americas or moved there at a young age. Because I am interested in how subjects self-identified, rather than their birthplaces, I will not make the distinction between Creoles and *radicados*, Spaniards who lived in the Americas and came to identify with Creoles. For this distinction, see Stephanie Merrim, *The Spectacular City, Mexico, and Colonial Hispanic Literary Culture* (Austin: University of Texas Press, 2010), 4.

11. See José Rabasa, "Pre-Columbian Pasts and Indian Presents in Mexican History," in *Colonialism Past and Present*, ed. Alvaro Félix Bolaños and Gustavo Verdesio (Albany: State University of New York Press, 2002), 52.

12. D. A. Brading gives an excellent summary of the major authors of both the mendicant and indigenous historiographical traditions. D. A. Brading, *The First America: The Spanish Monarchy, Creole Patriots, and the Liberal State, 1492–1867* (Cambridge: Cambridge University Press, 1991). See also Jorge Cañizares-Esguerra, *How to Write the History of the New World: Histories, Epistemologies, and Identities in the Eighteenth-Century Atlantic World* (Stanford, Calif.: Stanford University Press, 2001); and see Rolena Adorno's various articles on the subject of mestizo and indigenous historians: Rolena Adorno, "Arms, Letters and the Native Historian in Early Colonial Mexico," in *1492–1992: Re/Discovering Colonial Writing*, ed. René Jara and Nicholas Spadaccini (Minneapolis: Prisma Institute, 1992); "The Indigenous Ethnographer: The 'Indio Ladino' as Historian and Cultural Mediation," in *Implicit Understandings: Observing, Reporting and Reflecting on the Encounters between Europeans and Other Peoples in the Early Modern Era*, ed. Stuart B. Schwartz (Cambridge: Cambridge University Press, 1994); *The Polemics of Possession in Spanish American Narrative* (New Haven, Conn.: Yale University Press, 2007), 139–46.

13. For Creole politics as an "identity," see particularly Anthony Pagden, "Identity Formation in Spanish America," in *Colonial Identity in the Atlantic World: 1500–1800*, ed. Nicholas Canny and Anthony Pagden (Princeton, N.J.: Princeton University Press, 1987). Brading prefers the term "consciousness" in *The First America*. Writings in Spanish also tend to favor the term "consciousness." See, for instance, Mabel Moraña, "Barroco y conciencia criolla en Hispanoamerica," *Revista de Crítica Literaria Latinoamericana* 28, no. 2 (1988); Antonio Lorente Medina, *La prosa de Sigüenza y Góngora y la formación de la conciencia criolla mexicana* (Mexico: Fondo de Cultura Económica, 1996); Solange Alberro, "La emergencia de la conciencia criolla: El caso novohispano," in *Agencias criollas: La ambigüedad "colonial" en las*

letras hispanoamericanas, ed. José Antonio Mazzotti (Pittsburgh: Instituto Internacional de Literatura Latinoamericana, 2000). In their introduction to a recent anthology on Creole writings in the Americas, Ralph Bauer and José Antonio Mazzotti employ "identity," "subjectivity," and "consciousness" interchangeably. See Ralph Bauer and José Antonio Mazzotti, introduction to *Creole Subjects in the Colonial Americas*, ed. Ralph Bauer and José Antonio Mazzotti (Chapel Hill: University of North Carolina Press, 2009).

14. J. H. Elliott cites 1563 as the first time the term "Creole" was used for American-born Spaniards. J. H. Elliott, *Empires of the Atlantic World: Britain and Spain in America, 1492–1830* (New Haven, Conn.: Yale University Press, 2006), 234. In his earlier work, José Juan Arrom declares that the term was first used in Juan López de Velasco's 1571 *Geografía de las Indias*. José Arrom, *Certidumbre de América: Estudios de letras, folklore y cultura* (Madrid: Gredos, 1971), 12. Bauer and Mazzotti have clarified that the *Geografía* contained the first appearance of the term in *print*. See Bauer and Mazzotti, introduction, 3–4.

15. The transmission of the term in the seventeenth-century Iberian world has been confusing. Arrom declares that "we received it, as a loan-word, from the Portuguese *crioulo*." Arrom, *Certidumbre de América*, 14–15. However, Antônio Houaiss finds that the term *crioulo* itself "must have been disseminated through the Spanish *criollo*." Antônio Houaiss and Mauro de Salles Villar, *Diccionário Houiass da Língua Portuguesa* (Rio de Janeiro: Editorial Objetiva, 2001), 871. According to both, the Spanish term ultimately derived from a phonological interpretation among African slaves of the Portuguese term *criadouro*.

16. María Elena Martínez, *Genealogical Fictions: Limpieza de Sangre, Religion, and Gender in Colonial Mexico* (Stanford, Calif.: Stanford University Press, 2008), 141.

17. The racial inflections of the prerepublican term "nation" explain Sigüenza y Góngora's use of the term "Creole nation" (*nación criolla*) to describe a Creole citizenry in his *Theatro de virtudes políticas* (1680). Carlos de Sigüenza y Gongora, *Theatro de virtudes politicas, que constituyen à un principe* (Mexico: Viuda de Bernardo Calderón, 1680), 17. In fact, *nación* could mean both territory and ethnicity. Covarrubias's 1611 *Tesoro de la lengua castellana o española* limits "nation" (*nación*) to "kingdom or extended province, such as the Spanish nation" (reyno o provincia estendida, como la nación española) for instance. Sebastián de Covarrubias, *Tesoro de la lengua castellana o española* (1611; reprint, Barcelona: S. A. Horta, 1943), 823. But by 1734, the *Diccionario de autoridades* had defined *nación* as "the collection of inhabitants of a province, country, or kingdom" (la colección de habitadores en alguna provincia, pais, o reino). *Diccionario de la lengua castellana* (Madrid, 1734), 644, http://buscon.rae.es/ntlle/SrvltGUIMenuNtlle?cmd=Lema&sec=1.0.0.0.0. See also Martínez, *Genealogical Fictions*, 153.

18. The bibliographies on these themes are immense. For recent work, see D. A. Brading, *Mexican Phoenix: Our Lady of Guadalupe: Image and Tradition across Five Centuries* (Cambridge: Cambridge University Press,

2001); Cañizares-Esguerra, *How to Write the History of the New World*; Ramón Mujica Pinilla, *Rosa limensis: Mística, política e iconografía en torno a la patrona de América* (Lima: Fondo de Cultura Económica, 2001); Jorge Cañizares-Esguerra, *Puritan Conquistadors: Iberianizing the Atlantic, 1550–1700* (Stanford, Calif.: Stanford University Press, 2006).

19. Perhaps the most forceful proponent of this view is Brading, who, in his monumental survey of its development in Spanish America, ascribes seventeenth-century Creole patriotism to a continuation of the problems between the Spanish Crown and the sixteenth-century encomenderos. See Brading, *The First America*, 2. See also Bernard Lavallé, *Las promesas ambiguas: Ensayos sobre el criollismo colonial en los Andes* (Lima: Instituto Riva-Agüero, 1993), for a similar interpretation of Creoles in Peru.

20. Martínez, *Genealogical Fictions*, 125. Martínez provides one of the most nuanced versions of this idea of Creole ambivalence: "The ubiquity of purity requirements, their centrality to the crown's creation of secular and religious hierarchies, and the archival practices that they set in motion produced a particularly strong preoccupation with bloodlines among the descendants of Spaniards, which in turn made their patriotic and 'nativeness' discourses profoundly ambivalent with regard to issues of race. . . . The concept was woven so tightly into the fabric of colonial relations that criollo elites apparently could not bring themselves to question its primacy." Martínez, *Genealogical Fictions*, 199.

21. Martínez argues that the use of the term "kingdom" (reino) in seventeenth-century Creole texts indicates a desire for inclusion in the greater Spanish monarchy. Martínez, *Genealogical Fictions*, 196. My own readings of Creole texts have found patria and *nación,* both of which implied an exclusive local citizenship based on birthright or self-identification, to have been more commonly used terms.

22. Both Pagden and Brading locate the origins of this argument in a series of early seventeenth-century tracts in which Creoles claimed that birthplace should determine rights to holding administrative offices. Brading, *The First America*, 2, 293–301; Pagden, "Identity Formation in Spanish America," 60–61.

23. José Antonio Mazzotti, for instance, relates the "ambiguity" of Creole discourse to a subjective position poised between Europeans and indigenous Americans. See José Antonio Mazzotti, ed., *Agencias criollas: La ambigüedad "colonial" en las letras hispanoamericanas* (Pittsburgh: Instituto Internacional de Literatura Latinoamericana, 2000), 20. Mabel Moraña has recently associated the Baroque with a "hybrid identity" Mabel Moraña, "Baroque/Neobaroque/Ultrabaroque: Disruptive Readings of Modernity," in *Hispanic Baroques: Reading Cultures in Context*, ed. Nicholas Spadaccini and Luis Martín-Estudillo (Nashville: Vanderbilt University Press, 2005), 246. Kathleen Ross notes an "oscillating pattern that constitutes a criollo historiography written from an American perspective, but still fundamentally identified with Spain." Kathleen Ross, *The Baroque Narrative of Carlos de Sigüenza y Góngora: A New World Paradise* (Cambridge: Cambridge University Press, 1993), 47. Stephanie Merrim argues that Creoles had

a "janus-faced, unstable identity and loyalties." Merrim, *The Spectacular City*, 5.

24. The criticism on Góngora is extensive. Dámaso Alonso still provides the best introduction in *Góngora y el "Polifemo"* (Madrid: Gredos, 1961). See also Andrée Collard, *Nueva poesia: Conceptismo, culteranismo en la crítica española* (Madrid: Castalia, 1971); on Gongorism in Spanish America, see John Beverley, *Essays on the Literary Baroque in Spain and Spanish America* (Woodbridge, England: Tamesis, 2008), 72–84. Merrim gives an excellent summary of the paradox of the institutionalization of Gongorism in the Americas. Merrim, *The Spectacular City*, 202–4.

25. Octavio Paz, *Sor Juana Inés de la Cruz o las trampas de la fe*, 3rd ed. (Mexico: Fondo de Cultura Económica, 1983), 86.

26. By focusing on the term *vecino* rather than *ciudadano*, Tamar Herzog and María Elena Martínez have been able to find the complex links between racial and state discourses that defined citizenship in local and national communities and have thus avoided the static quality of the term "identity." As Herzog writes, "We need to abandon the quest for 'identity' and examine instead processes of 'identification,' that is, the processes through which people claimed to be or were identified as members of the community." Tamar Herzog, *Defining Nations: Immigrants and Citizens in Early Modern Spain and Spanish America* (New Haven, Conn.: Yale University Press, 2003), 6. Martínez in particular has stressed the relationship in Creole discourse among identity, citizenship, and purity of blood. Martínez, *Genealogical Fictions*, 190–98.

27. Pagden, *Lords of All the World*, 80–86, 101.

28. The following statement by D. A. Brading, for instance, appears to assume that patriotic sentiment in Spanish America was a natural passion repressed by censorship: "In an epoch when the Catholic monarchy exercised a rigorous censorship and attracted a quasi-religious veneration, patriotic sentiment could only find expression in historical myths and symbols." Brading, *The First America*, 4.

29. Maurizio Viroli, *For Love of Country: An Essay on Patriotism and Nationalism* (Oxford: Oxford University Press, 1995), 24–25.

30. Ibid., 41.

31. Viroli contemplates this idea when he asserts that patriotism is "eminently rhetorical; it aims at resuscitating, strengthening, and directing the passions of a particular people with a specific cultural and historical identity rather than attaining the reasoned approval of impersonal rational agents." Ibid., 8.

32. Anthony Pagden provides a useful discussion of the politics of native nobility, who were protected under Spanish law, as applied to the Creoles. Pagden, "Identity Formation in Spanish America," 68. More recently, scholars have begun to examine the close relationship between the indigenous nobility and Creole elite in colonial Mexico. See Martínez, *Genealogical Fictions*, 197–98; Peter Villella, "The True Heirs to Anáhuac: Native Nobles, Creole Patriots, and the 'Natural Lords' of Colonial Mexico" (Ph.D. diss., University of California, Los Angeles, 2009).

33. Martínez, *Genealogical Fictions*, 198.

34. "'Traditions' which appear or claim to be old are often quite recent in origin and sometimes invented." Eric Hobsbawm, "Introduction: Inventing Traditions," in *The Invention of Tradition*, ed. Eric Hobsbawm and Terence Ranger (Cambridge: Cambridge University Press, 1992), 1.

35. Kenneth Mills, *Idolatry and Its Enemies: Colonial Andean Religion and Extirpation, 1640–1750* (Princeton, N.J.: Princeton University Press, 1997), 47.

36. *Diccionario de la lengua castellana*, (Madrid, 1739), 314.

37. This is the meaning that Francisco de Florencia gives the term in the title of his 1685 account of the miraculous discovery of the statue of the Virgin of Remedios: *The Miraculous Invention of a Treasure Hidden in a Field* [*La milagrosa invención de un tesoro escondido en un campo*].

38. Ullrich Langer, "Invention," in *The Cambridge History of Literary Criticism*, ed. Glyn P. Norton (Cambridge: Cambridge University Press, 1999), 140.

39. Ibid., 144.

40. Baltasar Gracián, *Agudeza y arte de ingenio* (Mexico: UNAM, 1996), 33. For a recent discussion of theories of wit in the seventeenth century, see Christopher Johnson, *Hyperboles: The Rhetoric of Excess in Baroque Literature and Thought* (Cambridge, Mass.: Harvard University Press, 2010), 95–125.

41. This view is one of the central tenets of what has been termed the Latin American "Neobaroque." While its earliest expression may be found in the work of the midcentury Cuban authors Alejo Carpentier and José Lezama Lima, the idea that the strength of the Iberian American Baroque derived from its ability to mix Western and non-Western forms continues to be a powerful one. See, for instance, two recent influential studies: Roberto González Echevarría, *Celestina's Brood: Continuities of the Baroque in Spanish and Latin American Literature* (Durham, N.C.: Duke University Press, 1993), 150–69; Lois Parkinson Zamora, *The Inordinate Eye: New World Baroque and Latin American Fiction* (Chicago: University of Chicago Press, 2006), xiii–xxiii.

42. For a clear discussion of Creoles' divided stance toward an indigenous past and present, see Pagden, "Identity Formation in Spanish America," 65–70.

43. See Susan Buck-Morss on the relationship between these two concepts in Benjamin's work. Susan Buck-Morss, *The Dialectics of Seeing: Walter Benjamin and the Arcades Project* (Cambridge, Mass.: Massachusetts Institute of Technology Press, 1989), 170.

44. On the particularly Franciscan form of sixteenth-century evangelical utopianism, see John Leddy Phelan, *The Millenial Kingdom of the Franciscans in the New World* (Berkeley: University of California Press, 1970); Georges Baudot, *Utopia and History in Mexico: The First Chroniclers of Mexican Civilization (1520–1569)*, trans. Bernard R. Ortiz de Montellano and Thelma Ortiz de Montellano (Niwot: University Press of Colorado,

1995). On the pessimism of the following century, see Pagden, *Lords of All the World*, 48–52.

45. Pagden, *Lords of All the World*, 31.

46. See Chapter 1.

47. Jacques Derrida, *Archive Fever: A Freudian Impression*, trans. Eric Prenowitz (Chicago: University of Chicago Press, 1996), 1–3.

48. Martínez, *Genealogical Fictions*, 198.

49. Don Cameron Allen, *Mysteriously Meant: The Rediscovery of Pagan Symbolism and Allegorical Interpretation in the Renaissance* (Baltimore: Johns Hopkins University Press, 1970), 112–33. Many studies have underlined the importance of Neoplatonic hermeticism for late seventeenth-century Spanish American authors. See especially Octavio Paz's reflections on Sor Juana's Neoplatonism and José Pascual Buxó's study of the influence of emblematics on the literature of New Spain. Paz, *Sor Juana Inés de la Cruz o las trampas de la fe*; José Pascual Buxó, *El resplandor intelectual de las imágenes: Estudios de emblemática y literatura novohispana* (Mexico: Oak Editorial, 2001); José Pascual Buxó, "El resplandor intelectual de las imágenes: Jeroglífica y emblemática," in *Juegos de ingenio y agudeza: La pintura emblemática de la Nueva España*, ed. Ana Laura Cue (Mexico: Museo Nacional de Arte, 1994).

50. Laura Benítez Grobet's early work argued that Sigüenza's writings reflected a Creole "nationalism." Laura Benítez Grobet, "El nacionalismo en Carlos de Sigüenza y Góngora," *Estudios de Historia Novohispana* 8 (1985); Laura Benítez Grobet, *La idea de historia en Carlos de Sigüenza y Góngora* (Mexico: UNAM, 1982). More recently, historians have favored the term "patriotism" as a more accurate reflection of prerepublican political ideals. Pagden in particular has assigned Sigüenza a leading role in the early Creole political imaginary. Pagden, "Identity Formation in Spanish America," 71–75; Anthony Pagden, *Spanish Imperialism and the Political Imagination: Studies in European and Spanish-American Social and Political Theory, 1513–1830* (New Haven, Conn.: Yale University Press, 1990), 91–97. Brading places Sigüenza in a long trajectory of Creole ideas. Brading, *The First America*, 363–72. The most recent book-length studies on Sigüenza by Antonio Lorente Medina and Alicia Mayer draw on fundamental biographical information to place Sigüenza in his period. Both interpret Sigüenza as fervently religious and providentialist. Lorente Medina, *La prosa de Sigüenza y Góngora*; Alicia Mayer, *Dos americanos, dos pensamientos* (Mexico: UNAM, 1998); Alicia Mayer, "El guadalupanismo en Carlos de Sigüenza y Góngora," in *Carlos de Sigüenza y Góngora: Homenaje 1700–2000*, ed. Alicia Mayer, 2nd vol. (Mexico: UNAM, 2000).

51. Elliott, *Empires of the Atlantic World*, 227.

52. Although the subject is beyond the scope of this study, it is probable that regional variations in Creole patriotism across Spanish America, with some areas showing more autonomy among the elite than others, may be mapped fruitfully onto the greater geopolitical conditions of the Spanish Empire during the seventeenth century.

53. See Chapter 2.

54. For a survey of mendicant and Creole interests in indigenous manuscripts, see Cañizares-Esguerra, *How to Write the History of the New World*, 60–129.

55. Pilar Gonzalbo Aizpuru, *Historia de la educación en la epoca colonial: La educación de los criollos y la vida urbana* (Mexico: El Colegio de México, 1990), 159–95.

56. Irving Leonard, *Baroque Times in Old Mexico* (Ann Arbor: University of Michigan Press, 1959), 157–71.

57. Antonio de Robles's diary of events in Mexico City between the years 1665 and 1703 gives a clear portrait of the regular news from Spain, the northern frontiers, the Caribbean, and other points of Spain's vast empire. Antonio de Robles, *Diario de sucesos notables (1665–1703)*, 2nd ed., 3 vols. (Mexico: Porrúa, 1972).

58. María Elena Martínez notes that the seventeenth-century "Novohispanic aristocracy" was centered in the cities of Mexico City, Morelia, and Puebla and was "highly endogamous." Martínez, *Genealogical Fictions*, 190–91.

59. As Kathleen Ross has pointed out, as contemporaneous authors Sor Juana and Sigüenza are often compared, almost always to the detriment of the latter. Ross, *The Baroque Narrative*, 41.

60. Francisco Pérez Salazar, *Biografía de D. Carlos de Sigüenza y Góngora* (Mexico: Antigua Imprenta de Murguia, 1928), 9–10.

61. Edmundo O'Gorman, "Datos sobre Don Carlos de Sigüenza y Góngora," *Boletín del Archivo General de la Nación* 15, no. 4 (1944); Ernest J. Burrus, "Sigüenza y Góngora's Efforts for Readmission into the Jesuit Order," *Hispanic American Historical Review* 33 (1953). Burrus's article includes documents that clarify the dates of Sigüenza's several petitions for readmission to the order. He also declares that after finishing the novitiate at Tepotzotlán, Sigüenza studied philosophy at the Jesuit Colegio de San Pedro y San Pablo in Mexico City "and would have returned here for theology had he not been dismissed from the Order" (391, n. 6). The expulsion, he notes, was effected in Mexico City and not in Puebla, where Sigüenza was teaching while finishing his studies for the priesthood.

62. Víctor Navarro Brotóns, "La *Libra astronómica y filosófica* de Sigüenza y Góngora: La polémica sobre el cometa de 1680," in *Carlos de Sigüenza y Góngora: Homenaje 1700–2000*, ed. Alicia Mayer, 2 vols. (Mexico: UNAM, 2000), 1: 178.

63. Irving Leonard, "Sigüenza y Góngora and the Chaplaincy of the Hospital del Amor de Dios," *Hispanic American Historical Review* 39, no. 4 (1959); José Miguel Quintana, *La astrología en la Nueva España en el Siglo XVII (de Enrico Martínez a Sigüenza y Góngora)* (Mexico: Bibliófilos mexicanos, 1969), 278–79.

64. Elías Trabulse, "La obra científica de Don Carlos de Sigüenza y Góngora (1667–1700)," in *Carlos de Sigüenza y Góngora, Homenaje 1700–2000*, ed. Alícia Mayer, 2 vols. (Mexico: UNAM, 2000), 1: 101–4.

65. For Sigüenza's cartography, see Mitchell Codding, "Perfecting the Geography of New Spain: Alzate and the Cartographic Legacy of Sigüenza

y Góngora," *Colonial Latin American Review* 3, no. 1–2 (1994); Miguel A. Sánchez Lamego, *El primer mapa general de México elaborado por un mexicano* (Mexico: Instituto panamericano de geografía e historia, 1955); Elías Trabulse, "La obra cartográfica de Don Carlos de Sigüenza y Góngora," *Caravelle* 76–77 (2001).

66. For Sigüenza's ill-fated trip to Pensacola, see the documents edited and introduced by Irving Leonard. Irving Leonard, *Spanish Approach to Pensacola, 1689–1693* (Albuquerque, N. Mex.: Quivira Society, 1939).

67. On Kircher, see Paula Findlen's several essays, chapters, and recent edited collection. Paula Findlen, *Possessing Nature: Museums, Collecting, and Scientific Culture in Early Modern Italy* (Berkeley: University of California Press, 1994); Paula Findlen, "Scientific Spectacle in Baroque Rome: Athanasius Kircher and the Roman College Museum," in *Jesuit Science and the Republic of Letters*, ed. Mordechai Feingold (Cambridge, Mass.: Massachusetts Institute of Technology Press, 2003), 225–84; Paula Findlen, "A Jesuit's Books in the New World: Athanasius Kircher and His American Readers," in *Athanasius Kircher: The Last Man Who Knew Everything*, ed. Paula Findlen (New York: Routledge, 2004), 329–64.

68. As his friend and sponsor Sebastián de Guzmán y Córdova declared in his dedicatory remarks to Sigüenza y Góngora's *Libra astronómica*, "I don't know whether he is quicker to imagine and formulate a book or to forget it and move on. At best, he dedicates it to a desk drawer, a fate that he feels is reward enough for his work. Any paper of his that achieves this fate should be considered lucky indeed, since others, after they have been polished, are either taken from atop the table by curious persons or die in the hands of he to whom they owe their life" (No sé si es más veloz en idear y formar un libro, que en olvidarlo. Encomiéndalo cuando mucho a la gaveta de un escritorio, y éste le parece bastante premio de su trabajo. Dichoso puede llamarse el papel suyo que esto consigue, porque otros, después de perfectos, o de sobra la mesa se los llevaron curiosos, murieron rotos en las manos a que debían el ser). Carlos de Sigüenza y Góngora, *Libra astronómica y filosófica*, 2nd ed. (Mexico: UNAM, 1984), 14. In his history of the Convento de Jesús María in Mexico City, *Parayso occidental* (1684), Sigüenza himself writes: "If there were someone in New Spain who would cover the printing costs (just as the Royal Convent of Jesús María has now done), there is no doubt that I would have brought to light different works, whose composition has been stimulated by the great love I have for my patria" (si hubiera quien costeara en la Nueva España las impresiones (como lo ha hecho ahora el Convento Real de Jesús María), no hay duda sino que sacara yo a luz diferentes obras, a cuya composición me ha estimulado el sumo amor que a mi patria tengo). Carlos de Sigüenza y Góngora, *Parayso occidental, plantado y cultivado por la liberal benéfica mano* (1684; reprint, Mexico: UNAM/Condumex, 1995), 48.

69. Juan José de Eguiara y Eguren, *Biblioteca mexicana*, trans. Benjamín Fernández Valenzuela (Mexico: UNAM, 1986), 720; Irving A. Leonard, *Don Carlos de Sigüenza y Góngora: A Mexican Savant of the Seventeenth Century* (Berkeley: University of California Press, 1929), 21–22.

70. Ernest J. Burrus, "Clavigero and the Lost Sigüenza Manuscripts," *Estudios de Cultura Nahuatl* 1 (1959): 60.

71. See Chapter 3, notes 25 and 26 below.

72. Elías Trabulse, *Los manuscritos perdidos de Sigüenza y Góngora* (Mexico: Colegio de México, 1988), 11–12.

73. José Lezama Lima, *La expresión americana y otros ensayos* (Montevideo: ARCA, 1969), 84.

74. The fundamental biographies of Sigüenza y Góngora continue to be Leonard, *Don Carlos de Sigüenza y Góngora*; Pérez Salazar, *Biografía de D. Carlos de Sigüenza y Góngora*; José Rojas Garcidueñas, *Don Carlos de Sigüenza y Góngora: Erudito barroco* (Mexico: Ediciones Xóchitl, 1945). Other important sources on Sigüenza's life, aside from those cited above, are the introduction by Jaime Delgado, "Estudio preliminar," to Carlos de Sigüenza y Góngora, *Piedad heroyca de Don Fernando Cortés* (Madrid: José Porrúa Turranzas, 1960); Lorente Medina, *La prosa de Sigüenza y Góngora*; Mayer, *Dos americanos*.

75. Kathleen Ross, "*Alboroto y motín de Mexico:* Una noche triste criolla," *Hispanic Review* 56, no. 2 (Spring 1988); Ross, *The Baroque Narrative*, 40; Kathleen Ross, "Cuestiones de género en *Infortunios de Alonso Ramírez*," *Revista Iberoamericana* 61, no. 172–73 (1995).

76. "For it is ultimately a patrimony that Sigüenza sets out to create." Ross, *The Baroque Narrative*, 149.

77. Sigüenza y Gongora, *Theatro de virtudes*, 7–8.

78. Carlos de Sigüenza y Góngora, "Testamento de Don Carlos de Sigüenza y Góngora," in *Biografía de Don Carlos de Sigüenza y Góngora, seguida de varios documentos inéditos*, ed. Francisco Pérez Salazar (Mexico: Robredo, 1928), 169.

79. Fernando Alva de Ixtlilxochitl, *Obras históricas*, 2 vols. (Mexico: UNAM, 1975), 1: 41.

80. "Instrumentos manuscriptos," Agustín Vetancurt, *Teatro mexicano: Descripción breve de los sucesos ejemplares históricos y religiosos del nuevo mundo de las indias* (Mexico: Doña María de Benavides Viuda de Juan Ribera, 1698; reprint, Mexico: Porrúa, 1982), n.p.

81. See Chapter 2 and Jacques Lafaye, *Quetzalcóatl and Guadalupe: The Formation of Mexican National Consciousness*, trans. by Benjamin Keen (Chicago: University of Chicago Press, 1976), 187–89.

82. Giovanni Francesco Gemelli Careri, *Giro del mondo del Dottor D. Gio. Francesco Gemelli Careri*, 6 vols. (Venice: Sebastiano Coleti, 1728), vol. 6; Sigüenza y Góngora, *Libra astronómica y filosófica*, 181. See also Anna More, "Cosmopolitanism and Scientific Reason in New Spain: Sigüenza y Góngora and the Dispute over the 1680 Comet," in *Science in the Spanish and Portuguese Empires, 1500–1800*, ed. Daniela Bleichmar et al. (Stanford, Calif.: Stanford University Press, 2009).

83. Carlos de Sigüenza y Góngora, "Contestación a Don Andrés de Arriola," in *Biografía de Don Carlos de Sigüenza y Góngora, seguida de varios documentos inéditos*, ed. Francisco Pérez Salazar (Mexico: Robredo, 1928), 142.

84. See, for instance, Brading's comments that "such a maze of conflicting opinions more served to magnify Sigüenza's erudition than to expose his own sentiments." Brading, *The First America*, 363.

85. For collecting in Europe, see Horst Bredekamp, *The Lure of Antiquity and the Cult of the Machine: The Kunstkammer and the Evolution of Nature, Art and Technology*, trans. Allison Brown (Princeton, N.J.: Markus Wiener, 1995), 11–62; Findlen, *Possessing Nature*, 48–150.

86. For Kircher's museum, see Findlen, *Possessing Nature*, 78–96; "Scientific Spectacle in Baroque Rome."

87. Ralph Bauer, *The Cultural Geography of Colonial American Literature* (Cambridge: Cambridge University Press, 2003), 4.

88. For ambivalence as a condition of colonialism, see Bhabha's well-known essay on colonial mimesis: Homi K. Bhabha, *The Location of Culture* (London: Routledge, 1994), 85–92.

89. A number of key books have steadily revised the picture of political stasis in the seventeenth century by investigating the racial undercurrents, indigenous rebellions, and tensions between Creoles and viceregal administrators in the seventeenth century. See Alejandro Cañeque, *The King's Living Image: The Culture and Politics of Viceregal Power in Colonial Mexico* (New York: Routledge, 2004); R. Douglas Cope, *The Limits of Racial Domination: Plebeian Society in Colonial Mexico City, 1660–1720* (Madison: University of Wisconsin Press, 1994); J. I. Israel, *Race, Class and Politics in Colonial Mexico, 1610–1670* (Oxford: Oxford University Press, 1975); Martínez, *Genealogical Fictions*.

90. Recently, studies have begun to blur the sharp distinction made between seventeenth-century Baroque scholasticism and eighteenth-century enlightened critique. See Ruth Hill, *Sceptres and Sciences in the Spains* (Liverpool: Liverpool University Press, 2000); Jesús Pérez Magellón, *Construyendo la modernidad: La cultura española en el tiempo de los novatores [1675–1725]* (Madrid: Consejo Superior de Investigaciones Científicas, 2002); Jeremy Robbins, "The Arts of Perception," *Bulletin of Spanish Studies* 82, no. 8 (2005).

CHAPTER 1

1. Juan Solórzano Pereyra, *Política indiana*, 3 vols. (Madrid: Biblioteca Castro, 1996), 1: 608.

2. Ibid., 1: 609.

3. Ibid., 1: 612.

4. For the politics and institutionalization of the two-republic model, see María Elena Martínez, *Genealogical Fictions: Limpieza de Sangre, Religion, and Gender in Colonial Mexico* (Stanford, Calif.: Stanford University Press, 2008), 99–103.

5. For a succinct summary of this demographic decline and recovery, see R. Douglas Cope, *The Limits of Racial Domination: Plebeian Society in Colonial Mexico City, 1660–1720* (Madison: University of Wisconsin Press, 1994), 12–14.

6. Patricia Seed notes that toward the end of the sixteenth century the Crown attempted to require blacks and mulattoes to pay tribute, an obligation previously limited to indigenous subjects, but was unable to do so given the social disarticulation of black communities. Patricia Seed, *American Pentimento: The Invention of Indians and the Pursuit of Riches* (Minneapolis: University of Minnesota Press, 2001), 80–81. Other restrictions included prohibitions on carrying arms, sumptuary laws, and limits on casta mobility. Cope, *The Limits of Racial Domination*, 17. Restrictions on mestizos not only limited their access to privileges of the *república de españoles* but also to those of the *república de indios*. Martínez, *Genealogical Fictions*, 148.

7. See María Elena Martínez's extensive documentation of the transfer of the notion of blood purity from the peninsular to the American context. Martínez, *Genealogical Fictions*, 173–226.

8. According to Woodrow Borah, Solórzano was the first to apply the category of "miserable" persons, a juridical concept of medieval origin, to indigenous subjects. Woodrow Borah, *Justice by Insurance: The General Indian Court of Colonial Mexico and the Legal Aides of the Half-Real* (Berkeley: University of California Press, 1983), 80–83. See also Alejandro Cañeque, *The King's Living Image: The Culture and Politics of Viceregal Power in Colonial Mexico* (New York: Routledge, 2004), 186–92; J. H. Elliott, *Empires of the Atlantic World: Britain and Spain in America, 1492–1830* (New Haven, Conn.: Yale University Press, 2006), 77.

9. Solórzano Pereyra, *Política indiana*, 1: 575.

10. Martínez associates the term *calidad* with the eighteenth-century inscription of social categories in a lexicon of blood. Martínez, *Genealogical Fictions*, 247–48, 262.

11. The logic of the two-republic model dictated Solórzano's exclusive focus on the mixture of Spanish and non-Spanish lineage. He does not consider, for instance, the mixture of indigenous and African lineage. For the exclusion of subjects of African descent from the notion of purity of blood, see Martínez, *Genealogical Fictions*, 169–70.

12. Cope, *The Limits of Racial Domination*, 14–15.

13. Solórzano Pereyra, *Política indiana*, 1: 612.

14. Ibid., 1: 612–3.

15. Ibid., 1: 615.

16. See the scathing indictment of the mines in José de Acosta's influential 1590 *Historia natural*. Joseph de Acosta, *Historia natural y moral de las Indias*, 2nd ed. (Mexico: Fondo de Cultura Económica, 1962), 154–55.

17. Carlos II's 1697 decree that declared indigenous *caciques* and their descendants to be of pure blood was the culmination of the divergence between a discourse of indigenous "misery" and "nobility." See Martínez, *Genealogical Fictions*, 205–10.

18. See Richard Tuck, *Natural Rights Theories: Their Origin and Development* (Cambridge: Cambridge University Press, 1979), 45–50.

19. Anthony Pagden, *Lords of All the World: Ideologies of Empire in Spain, Britain and France, c. 1500–c.1800* (New Haven, Conn.: Yale University Press, 1995), 43.

20. Anthony Pagden, *Spanish Imperialism and the Political Imagination: Studies in European and Spanish-American Social and Political Theory 1513–1830* (New Haven, Conn.: Yale University Press, 1990), 13–15.

21. Hernán Cortés, *Cartas de relación* (Madrid: Castalia, 1993), 161.

22. Anthony Pagden, introduction to *Letters from Mexico*, by Hernán Cortés, trans. Anthony Pagden (New Haven, Conn.: Yale University Press, 2001), lxviii. See also Elliott, *Empires of the Atlantic World*, 5.

23. Elliott, *Empires of the Atlantic World*, 119; Pagden, *Spanish Imperialism and the Political Imagination*, 3.

24. Elliott, *Empires of the Atlantic World*, 119–22.

25. J. H. Elliott, *Imperial Spain, 1469–1716* (London: Penguin, 1963), 174; Elliott, *Empires of the Atlantic World*, 122–27.

26. See J. H. Elliott, "Spain and America in the Sixteenth and Seventeenth Centuries," in *The Cambridge History of Latin America*, ed. Leslie Bethell (Cambridge: Cambridge University Press, 1984), 302–3.

27. Although, as has often been noted, the term "colonial" was never used to describe the Spanish American viceroyalties, neither did they enjoy the rights of peninsular kingdoms. See Anthony Pagden, "Identity Formation in Spanish America," in *Colonial Identity in the Atlantic World: 1500–1800*, ed. Nicholas Canny and Anthony Pagden (Princeton, N.J.: Princeton University Press, 1987), 63–64. See also Elliott, *Empires of the Atlantic World*, 129.

28. Elliott, *Empires of the Atlantic World*, 129–30; Henry Kamen, *Empire: How Spain Became a World Power, 1492–1763* (New York: Harper Collins, 2003), 142.

29. Pagden, *Lords of All the World*, 47.

30. Rolena Adorno, *The Polemics of Possession in Spanish American Narrative* (New Haven, Conn.: Yale University Press, 2007), 109.

31. Taken up by the impassioned Dominican missionary Bartolomé de las Casas, the question of the "correct form of converting" the indigenous peoples of the Americas overrode the previous reliance on the papal donation or the argument that Amerindians were naturally subordinate to Europeans. As Las Casas was to write starkly in his final publication, *De Regia Potestate* (1554): "the only title that Your Majesty has is this: that all, or the greater part of, the Indians wish voluntarily to be your vassals and hold it an honour to be so." Cited in Pagden, *Spanish Imperialism and the Political Imagination*, 32.

32. Adorno, *The Polemics of Possession*, 100; Charles Gibson, *The Aztecs under Spanish Rule* (Stanford, Calif.: Stanford University Press, 1964), 58–59.

33. Las Casas's defense of indigenous subjects has received extensive attention. For an introduction, see Lewis Hanke, *The Spanish Struggle for Justice in the Conquest of America* (Boston: Little, Brown, 1965); more recently, see Adorno, *The Polemics of Possession*, 60–124.

34. Elliott, *Empires of the Atlantic World*, 132–33.

35. For summaries of this debate, see Adorno, *The Polemics of Possession*, 99–124; Anthony Pagden, *The Fall of Natural Man: The American*

Indian and the Origins of Comparative Ethnology (Cambridge: Cambridge University Press, 1982), 109–45.

36. Gibson notes the continuity between Aztec and Spanish practices of tribute. Gibson, *The Aztecs under Spanish Rule*, 194–219. By contrast, Seed argues that tribute derived from "social humiliation" practices in Islamic warfare. Seed, *American Pentimento*, 77–81. Both agree that tribute established a permanent relationship of social and economic hierarchy between Spanish and indigenous subjects.

37. Elliott notes that Crown policy was caught between the "twin imperatives of its thirst for precious metals and its obligations towards its new Indian vassals." Elliott, *Empires of the Atlantic World*, 130. Even Vitoria admitted that voluntary submission of indigenous subjects would have negative consequences for the Crown "exchequer." Francisco de Vitoria, *Political Writings*, trans. Jeremy Lawrance (Cambridge: Cambridge University Press, 1991), 291.

38. For the seventeenth-century crisis, see Kamen, *Empire*, 177–81, 400–406, 416–34, 436. Kamen's earlier work on late seventeenth-century Spain noted that the distress of the Spanish court at the end of the century led to the strengthening of regional oligarchies. Henry Kamen, *Spain in the Later Seventeenth Century, 1665–1700* (London: Longman, 1980), 159–61.

39. J. H. Elliott, *Spain and Its World, 1500–1700* (New Haven, Conn.: Yale University Press, 1989), 241–61.

40. While Kamen disputes the term "decline," saying "Spain was no worse off in 1700 than it had been in 1600 or in 1500; in fact, its economy and population were now in better shape than ever," this does not contradict Elliott's argument that the Spanish court was consumed by the *perception* of decline. Kamen, *Empire*, 443. Cf. Elliott, *Spain and Its World*, 241–61.

41. Elliott, *Empires of the Atlantic World*, 220.

42. While in Spain the transition to Bourbon rule occurred only after the War of Succession, J. H. Elliott notes that the French monarchs were received by the Creole elite with relative calm, another sign of the gulf between Spanish and Spanish American interests and concerns. Ibid., 229.

43. Solórzano complains particularly about Hugo Grotius's 1609 *The Free Sea* (*Mare Liberum*), which argued against Spanish sovereignty in Asia in favor of the rights of the Dutch to trade there. Solórzano Pereyra, *Política indiana*, 1: 115. For Grotius's use of Vitoria, see David Armitage, introduction to *The Free Sea*, by Hugo Grotius (Indianapolis: Liberty Fund, 2004), xv. For a brief summary of the fate of Las Casas's *Brevíssima* in the seventeenth century, see Adorno, *The Polemics of Possession*, 78–79.

44. Pagden, *Spanish Imperialism and the Political Imagination*, 34–35.

45. Solórzano Pereyra, *Política indiana*, 1: 143.

46. Ibid., 1: 111. All ellipses in Spanish quotations indicate omissions from the original complete quotation.

47. Ibid., 1: 117.

48. Pagden, *Lords of All the World*, 110–11.

49. Solórzano Pereyra, *Política indiana*, 1: 5.

50. Ibid.

51. Ibid., 1: 6.

52. Ibid., 1: 5.

53. "Prudence" and "constancy" were two of the most touted values for governance in the literature of the Spanish state. As Pagden notes, while Machiavelli had already referred to prudence as a value for governance, it received renewed attention from the late sixteenth-century Tacitists and Neostoics such as Justus Lipsius. Pagden, *Spanish Imperialism and the Political Imagination*, 46. For a definition of *constancy* in Lipsius, see Gerhard Oestreich, *Neostoicism and the Early Modern State* (Cambridge: Cambridge University Press, 1982), 19. In Spain, Saavedra Fajardo coupled Neostoic prudence with constancy as the primary supports for the monarchy in times of turmoil. See the introduction to Diego Saavedra Fajardo, *Empresas políticas* (Madrid: Cátedra, 1999), 76–88.

54. For a summary of the *Recopilación*, including the involvement of Solórzano and León Pinelo, see D. A. Brading, *The First America: The Spanish Monarchy, Creole Patriots, and the Liberal State, 1492–1867* (Cambridge: Cambridge University Press, 1991), 212–27. See also Elliott, *Empires of the Atlantic World*, 128.

55. For example, the *Recopilación*'s book 6, dedicated to laws pertaining to Indian subjects, begins with the 1580 law that stated: "It is our wish to entrust to the viceroys, the presidents, and the audiencias the responsibility to look after them and to give appropriate orders so that they may be protected, favored, and released from burdens, since we wish that they survive and live free of worries and vexations, let this be understood, taking into account the laws in this *Recopilation*, that favor, protect, and defend them from all abuses and which protect and create the appropriate protection, punishing with particular and rigorous example those that transgress them. And we demand and entrust the ecclesiastical prelates, as the true spiritual fathers of this new Christianity, to look after this and that all conserve them in their privileges, prerogatives, and that they have their protection" (Es nuestra voluntad encargar a los Virreyes, Presidentes, y Audiencias el cuidado de mirar por ellos, y dar las ordenes convenientes, para que sean amparados, favorecidos, y sobrellevados, por lo que deseamos, que padecen, y vivan sin molestia, ni vejacion, quedando esto de una vez assentado, y teniendo muy presentes las leyes de esta Recopilacion, que les favorecen, amparan, y defienden de qualesquier agravios, y que les guardan, y hagan guardar muy puntualmente, castigando con particular y rigurosa demostracion a los transgressores. Y rogamos y encargamos a los Prelados Eclesiasticos, que por su parte lo procuren como verdaderos padres espirituales de esta nueva Christiandad, y todos los conserven en sus privilegios, y prerrogativas, y tengan en su proteccion). *Recopilación de leyes de los reynos de las Indias* (Madrid: Julian de Paredes, 1681), book 6, tit. 1, law 1.

56. Elliott, "Spain and America in the Sixteenth and Seventeenth Centuries," 334–38; Elliott, *Empires of the Atlantic World*, 224.

57. Elliott, *Empires of the Atlantic World*, 175–76.

58. J. I. Israel, *Race, Class and Politics in Colonial Mexico, 1610–1670* (Oxford: Oxford University Press, 1975), 94–102. Alejandro Cañeque has

recently argued that Israel overemphasizes the ability of the Mexico City cabildo to represent Creole interests and asserts that the cabildo was more an administrative than a political force. Cañeque, *The King's Living Image*, 65–73. Elliott gives an example of a cabildo in the capital of a province in New Granada in which the local oligarchy was forced to negotiate with the governor even for municipal levies. Elliott, *Empires of the Atlantic World*, 145.

59. Elliott, *Empires of the Atlantic World*, 201. For a study of the alternativa in Peru, see Bernard Lavallé, *Las promesas ambiguas: Ensayos sobre el criollismo colonial en los Andes* (Lima: Instituto Riva-Agüero, 1993), 157–72; Antonine Tibesar, "The *Alternativa:* A Study in Spanish-Creole Relations in Seventeenth-Century Peru," *The Americas* 11, no. 3 (1955). Israel discusses the alternativa in Mexico in Israel, *Race, Class and Politics*, 102–8.

60. Tensions around the enforcement of the alternativa among the Franciscans in Lima in 1676 eventually ended in bloodshed. Tibesar, "The *Alternativa*," 260–74. Elliott lists the sale of high office, especially in Peru, and the corruption of treasury officials as two factors that led to de facto Creole political autonomy in the viceroyalties. Elliott, *Empires of the Atlantic World*, 228–29. Cañeque has argued that the relative peace between the Mexico City cabildo and the viceroys in the last third of the seventeenth century may be because the Crown's problems relieved fiscal pressures on the cabildo. Cañeque, *The King's Living Image*, 77.

61. Tibesar's detailed account of letters sent to Rome and Madrid shows that peninsular clerics implicitly questioned Creole loyalty. Tibesar, "The *Alternativa*," 248–49.

62. Brading, *The First America*, 215–16.

63. Solórzano Pereyra, *Política indiana*, 1: 609.

64. Ibid., 1: 611.

65. Ibid., 2: 1629.

66. Ibid., 2: 1635–36.

67. Brading has most forcefully stated the viewpoint that Solórzano defended Creoles. Brading, *The First America*, 227. See also Pagden, "Identity Formation in Spanish America," 64. However, Elliott notes a distinction between the rigid centralization of the *Recopilación*, for which Solórzano was largely responsible, and the flexibility of actual Creole politics by the end of the seventeenth century. Elliott, *Empires of the Atlantic World*, 229.

68. As Sabine MacCormack writes, in seventeenth-century Peru *patria* referred primarily to one's birthplace. Sabine MacCormack, *On the Wings of Time: Rome, the Incas, Spain and Peru* (Princeton, N.J.: Princeton University Press, 2007), 106.

69. Ernst K. Kantorowicz, *The King's Two Bodies: A Study in Mediaeval Political Theology* (Princeton, N.J.: Princeton University Press, 1957), 246–47; José Antonio Maravall, *Estado moderno y mentalidad social (Siglos XV a XVII)*, 2 vols. (Madrid: Revista de Occidente, 1972), 1: 458.

70. Maravall, *Estado moderno y mentalidad social*, 479, 487.

71. Maravall notes the metaphor of the celestial patria. Ibid., 458. In his well-known study, Kantorowicz argues by the time humanism invested

the term with more republican values, patria had already "taken shape and had been ethicized by both theology and jurisprudence." Kantorowicz, *The King's Two Bodies*, 249.

72. Maravall asserts that the expansion of the term patria in the sixteenth century was closely linked to the militarization of the state and the subsequent integration of transregional subjects into its defense. Maravall, *Estado moderno y mentalidad social*, 496–97.

73. See introduction, note 17, above.

74. Jeremy Adelman, *Sovereignty and Revolution in the Iberian Atlantic* (Princeton, N.J.: Princeton University Press, 2006), 8–9.

75. Benedict Anderson, *Imagined Communities: Reflections on the Origin and Spread of Nationalism*, 2nd ed. (London: Verso, 1991), 6–7.

76. Partha Chatterjee, *The Nation and Its Fragments: Colonial and Postcolonial Histories* (Princeton, N.J.: Princeton University Press, 1993), 6. Emphasis mine.

77. Pagden, *Lords of All the World*, 31. Solórzano's statement is representative of this position: "since there was no other way, nor has there been another found by now, to reduce them, they can justly be discovered and dominated because in order to make them Christians it was first necessary to make them men and to oblige and teach them in order to consider and treat them as such" (como no se halló, ni hoy se halla, otro modo de reducirlos, pudieron con justicia ser develados y dominados porque para hacerlos cristianos era primero necesario hacerlos hombres y obligarlos y enseñarlos a que se tuviesen y tratasen por tales y como tales). Solórzano Pereyra, *Política indiana*, 1: 118.

78. As María Elena Martínez succinctly puts it: "During [the Spanish Empire's] first two centuries, its main ideological contradiction stemmed from, on the one hand, universalist Christian doctrines that touted the redemptive powers of baptism and the equality of all members of the church and, on the other, the construction of different categories of Christians." Martínez, *Genealogical Fictions*, 15–16.

79. Sepúlveda writes of indigenous subjects: "Thus with the passage of time, when they have become more human and when our rule has confirmed in them good customs and the Christian religion, they may be treated with greater freedom and liberty." Cited in Pagden, *The Fall of Natural Man*, 116. For changes in the seventeenth century, see Martínez, *Genealogical Fictions*, 143–99.

80. See Chapter 4.

81. See Adorno on the paternalism inherent in Vitoria and Sepúlveda. Adorno, *The Polemics of Possession*, 118–19.

82. Max Weber, *Economy and Society: An Outline of Interpretive Sociology*, trans. Ephraim Fischoff, et al., 2 vols. (Berkeley: University of California Press, 1978), 1: 227.

83. Ibid.

84. Cited in Roberto González Echevarría, *Myth and Archive: A Theory of Latin American Narrative* (Durham, N.C.: Duke University Press, 1998), 53. Alejandro Cañeque cites an earlier publication by John Leddy Phelan in which the historian had already noted that "[t]he Spanish bureaucracy

contained both patrimonial and legal features in a bewildering combination." Cañeque, *The King's Living Image*, 340.

85. One version of this legal precept may be found in the *Recopilación*, book 2, tit. 1, law 22. See also Elliott, *Empires of the Atlantic World*, 131–32.

86. Other forms of colonial authority are treated, respectively, in Cope, *The Limits of Racial Domination*; Charles Gibson, "The Aztec Aristocracy in Colonial Mexico," *Comparative Studies in Society and History* 2, no. 2 (1960); Stuart Schwartz, *Sugar Plantations in the Formation of Brazilian Society: Bahia, 1550–1835* (Cambridge: Cambridge University Press, 1985).

87. For this reason, Morse concludes that the three centuries of Spanish vicergal governance were "dominantly Thomistic, with recessive Machiavellian characteristics." Richard M. Morse, "Toward a Theory of Spanish American Government," *Journal of the History of Ideas* 15, no. 1 (1954): 75.

88. Solórzano Pereyra, *Política indiana*, 2: 1635–36.

89. Weber, *Economy and Society*, 1: 227.

90. Pagden, *Spanish Imperialism and the Political Imagination*, 91.

91. For the idea of the seventeenth-century American landscape as a new paradise, see Jorge Cañizares-Esguerra, *Puritan Conquistadors: Iberianizing the Atlantic, 1550–1700* (Stanford, Calif.: Stanford University Press, 2006), 178–214; Jacques Lafaye, *Quetzalcóatl and Guadalupe: The Formation of Mexican National Consciousness*, trans. Benjamin Keen (Chicago: University of Chicago Press, 1976), 51–76. For Creole antiquarianism, see Pagden's succinct summary in Pagden, "Identity Formation in Spanish America," 70–80; and see Cañizares-Esguerra's more extensive treatment in Jorge Cañizares-Esguerra, *How to Write the History of the New World: Histories, Epistemologies, and Identities in the Eighteenth-Century Atlantic World* (Stanford, Calif.: Stanford University Press, 2001), 204–65.

92. Jacques Derrida, *Archive Fever: A Freudian Impression*, trans. Eric Prenowitz (Chicago: University of Chicago Press, 1996), 1.

93. Ibid., 3.

94. Ibid., 2–3, 7.

95. The contrary interpretations of the archive in Latin American literary history probably derive from a gap in Foucault's definition of the archive as a "system of enunciability." In *The Archaeology of Knowledge*, Foucault defined an "archive" as a discursive rather than material structure that limits the permutations of "statements" at any given moment. But in anticipation of his later espousal of a genealogical method in history, he also stressed the need to elucidate the breaks, discontinuities, and chance events that condition the emergence of a statement as an event of a discursive formation. See Michel Foucault, *The Archaeology of Knowledge*, trans. A. M. Sheridan Smith (New York: Pantheon Books, 1972), 129–31.

96. González Echevarría, *Myth and Archive*, 33.

97. More precisely, "I interrogate how the very idea of a rupture, or foundational moment, is a necessary fiction within the process of the *criollo* subject's unfolding." Antony Higgins, *Constructing the Criollo Archive* (West Lafayette, Ind.: Purdue University Press, 2000), 10.

98. Ibid., 8.

99. The recent bibliography on European cabinets of curiosity is extensive. For an introduction, see Horst Bredekamp, *The Lure of Antiquity and the Cult of the Machine: The Kunstkammer and the Evolution of Nature, Art and Technology*, trans. Allison Brown (Princeton, N.J.: Markus Wiener, 1995); Paula Findlen, *Possessing Nature: Museums, Collecting, and Scientific Culture in Early Modern Italy* (Berkeley: University of California Press, 1994); Paula Findlen, "Scientific Spectacle in Baroque Rome: Athanasius Kircher and the Roman College Museum," in *Jesuit Science and the Republic of Letters*, ed. Mordechai Feingold (Cambridge, Mass.: Massachusetts Institute of Technology Press, 2003), 225–84.

100. For the inclusion of American objects in European cabinets of curiosity, see Anthony Alan Shelton, "Cabinets of Transgression: Renaissance Collections and the Incorporation of the New World," in *The Cultures of Collecting*, ed. John Elsner and Roger Cardinal (Cambridge, Mass.: Harvard University Press, 1994).

101. Both Bredekamp and Findlen relate the cabinets of curiosity to scientific empiricism and the development of taxonomies. Bredekamp, *The Lure of Antiquity and the Cult of the Machine*, 11–36; Findlen, *Possessing Nature*, especially 194–240; Findlen, "Scientific Spectacle in Baroque Rome: Athanasius Kircher and the Roman College Museum."

102. Diana Taylor, *The Archive and the Repertoire: Performing Cultural Memory in the Americas* (Durham, N.C.: Duke University Press, 2003), 18.

103. Ibid., 44.

104. The Jesuit method of inner prayer set forth in the *Spiritual Exercises* is only one example of the way in which the body became the locus of belief as a directed and disciplined passion during the seventeenth century. The elaborate processions and rituals of Iberian public culture likewise rested on the assumption that the aesthetic and theatrical coordination of bodies was necessary for transcendental unity. For the relationship between the *Spiritual Exercises* and popular culture in seventeenth-century Mexico, see Pilar Gonzalbo Aizpuru, *La educación popular de los Jesuitas* (Mexico: Universidad Iberoamericana, 1989), 57–62.

105. For Oaxaca, see Serge Gruzinski, *The Conquest of Mexico: The Incorporation of Indian Societies into the Western World, 16th–18th Centuries*, trans. Eileen Corrigan (Cambridge: Polity, 1993), 146–83. For Peru, see Kenneth Mills, *Idolatry and Its Enemies: Colonial Andean Religion and Extirpation, 1640–1750* (Princeton, N.J.: Princeton University Press, 1997), 47.

106. See Chapter 4.

107. All of Baroque art, Maravall writes, entailed the "submission of the individual to the confines of the social order." José Antonio Maravall, *Culture of the Baroque: Analysis of a Historical Structure*, trans. Terry Cochran (Minneapolis: University of Minnesota Press, 1986), 35.

108. Maravall's conclusions have been extended to the Spanish viceroyalties to interpret the spectacular and ostentatious displays of public processions, sermons, and court theater as the rhetorical arm of the Spanish colonial state. See, for instance, Linda Curcio-Nagy, *The Great Festivals of*

Colonial Mexico City: Performing Power and Identity (Albuquerque: University of New Mexico Press, 2004), 19–22; Alejandra Osorio, "The King in Lima: Simulacra, Ritual, and Rule in Seventeenth-Century Peru," *Hispanic American Historical Review* 84, no. 3 (2004): 474; Dalmacio Rodríguez Hernández, *Texto y fiesta en la literatura novohispana* (Mexico: UNAM, 1998), 121–36.

109. José Lezama Lima, *La expresión americana y otros ensayos* (Montevideo: ARCA, 1969), 80. For two recent versions of the Spanish American Baroque that follow Lezama Lima closely, see Roberto González Echevarría, *Celestina's Brood: Continuities of the Baroque in Spanish and Latin American Literature* (Durham, N.C.: Duke University Press, 1993); Lois Parkinson Zamora, *The Inordinate Eye: New World Baroque and Latin American Fiction* (Chicago: University of Chicago Press, 2006).

110. Historians have particularly critiqued Maravall's model of the Spanish state and its imperial extension. See, for instance, J. H. Elliott, "Concerto Barroco," *New York Review of Books* 34, no. 6 (1987); Cañeque, *The King's Living Image*, 4, 258. John Beverley has provided one of the most elaborate critiques of Maravall's notion of state power. John Beverley, "Going Baroque?" *boundary 2* 15, no. 3 (1988): 35, 38. Elsewhere he asserts: "the paradox of Spanish Baroque writing, both in the metropolis and the colonies, is that it was, like postmodernism today, at once a technique of power of a dominant class in a period of reaction and a figuration of the consciousness of the limits of that power." John Beverley, *Against Literature* (Minneapolis: University of Minnesota Press, 1993), 60, 64. In their introduction to a recent anthology of criticism on the Hispanic Baroque, Nicholas Spadaccini and Luis Martín-Estudillo interpret the Baroque as a play of "freedom and containment." Although their emphasis on "freedom" corrects Maravall's argument that the Baroque was an aesthetic of state domination, they do not question the unitary aspect of his notion of the "state." Nicholas Spadaccini and Luis Martín-Estudillo, eds., *Hispanic Baroques: Reading Cultures in Context* (Nashville: Vanderbilt University Press, 2005), xiv–xv.

111. Mabel Moraña, for instance, employs Deleuze's metaphor to analyze the Mexico City riot of 1692. Mabel Moraña, "El 'Tumulto de Indios' de 1692," in *Agencias criollas: La ambigüedad "colonial" en las letras hispanoamericanas*, ed. José Antonio Mazzotti (Pittsburgh: Instituto Internacional de Literatura Iberoamericana, 2000), 162. William Egginton has questioned the applicability of the "fold" as a metaphor to peninsular Baroque texts. William Egginton, "Corporeal Image and the New World Baroque," *South Atlantic Quarterly* 106, no. 1 (2007): 109, 123–24; William Egginton, "Of Baroque Holes and Baroque Folds," in *Hispanic Baroques: Reading Cultures in Context*, ed. Nicholas Spadaccini and Luis Martín-Estudillo (Nashville: Vanderbilt University Press, 2005), 55 and 69.

112. Again, John Beverley has been a notable exception. In his 1988 review, he writes, "still the greatest single work on Baroque representation is Benjamin's *The Origins of German Tragic Drama*." Beverley,

"Going Baroque?" 29. See also Anthony J. Cascardi, "Allegories of Power in Calderón," in *Ideologies of History in the Spanish Golden Age* (University Park: Pennsylvania State University Press, 1997). Lois Parkinson Zamora and Stephanie Merrim also include brief discussions of Benjamin's account of allegory in their recent work. Parkinson Zamora, *The Inordinate Eye*, 271–76. Stephanie Merrim, *The Spectacular City, Mexico, and Colonial Hispanic Literary Culture* (Austin: University of Texas Press, 2010), 159.

113. Walter Benjamin, *The Origins of German Tragic Drama*, trans. John Osborne (London: New Left Books, 1977), 178.

114. Beatrice Hanssen, *Walter Benjamin's Other History: Of Stones, Animals, Human Beings, and Angels* (Berkeley: University of California Press, 1998), 67.

115. "The sovereign is the representative of history. He holds the course of history in his hand like a sceptre." Benjamin, *The Origins of German Tragic Drama*, 65.

116. Ibid., 71.

117. Ibid., 81.

118. Ibid., 73–75, 88–89, 95–97.

119. Hanssen, *Walter Benjamin's Other History*, 60, 64.

120. For the symbolics of state rituals, see Cañeque, *The King's Living Image*, 26–46, 124–37; Osorio, "The King in Lima."

121. See Chapter 4 for examples in documents following the 1692 riot in Mexico City.

122. María Elena Martínez has noted that the accusations of idolatry in Mexico came in waves and were invariably intended to uphold Spanish sovereignty. Martínez, *Genealogical Fictions*, 213–14. Likewise, pulque became the perennial target of clerical complaints and generated numerous petitions and tracts. See William B. Taylor, *Drinking, Homicide, and Rebellion in Colonial Mexican Villages* (Stanford, Calif.: Stanford University Press, 1979), 40–43.

123. New Spain provided the clearest case of antiquarianism. Both Anthony Pagden and David Brading comment that in Peru, where the Inca nobility remained a political force well into the eighteenth century, Creoles were less likely to turn to the indigenous past in their elaborations of a regional identity. See Pagden, "Identity Formation in Spanish America," 66–67; Brading, *The First America*, 342.

124. Cañizares-Esguerra, *How to Write the History of the New World*, 320–21.

125. Ibid., 321.

126. Ibid., 344.

127. For the use of *exempla* in Baroque theology, see Stephen Gilman, "An Introduction to the Ideology of the Baroque in Spain," *Symposium* 1, no. 1 (1946): 86–88. Antonio de la Calancha, *Crónica moralizada*, 6 vols. (Lima: Universidad Nacional Mayor de San Marcos, 1981), is an ecclesiastical history based almost exclusively on examples of clerics in the field. For the breakdown of the epic in the Spanish Baroque, see John Beverley, *Essays*

on the Literary Baroque in Spain and Spanish America (Woodbridge, England: Tamesis, 2008), 30–35.

128. Antonio de Solís, *Historia de la conquista de México, población y progresos de la América septentrional, conocida por el nombre de Nueva España*, 2nd ed. (1704; reprint, Mexico: Porrúa, 1988), 5–6. See also Anna More, "Soberanía y violencia en las representaciones barrocas de la conquista mexicana," in *Estudios coloniales latinoamericanos en el siglo XXI: Nuevos itinerarios*, ed. Stephanie Kirk (Pittsburgh: Instituto Internacional de Literatura Iberoamericana, 2011), 231–58.

129. Benjamin, *The Origins of German Tragic Drama*, 166.

130. See, for example, Maureen Ahern, "Visual and Verbal Sites: The Construction of Jesuit Martyrdom in Northwest New Spain in Andres Pérez de Ribas' *Historia de los triumphos de nuestra Santa Fee* (1645)," *Colonial Latin American Review* 8, no. 1 (1999); Leonardo García Pabón, "Sleeping with Corpses, Eating Hearts and Walking Skulls: Criollo's [sic] Subjectivity in Antonio de la Calancha and Bartolomé Arzans de Orsúa y Vela," in *Hispanic Baroques: Reading Cultures in Context*, ed. Nicholas Spadaccini and Luis Martín-Estudillo (Nashville: Vanderbilt University Press, 2005).

131. Gruzinski, *The Conquest of Mexico*, 15.

132. See Cañizares-Esguerra, *Puritan Conquistadors*, 35–177.

133. For the relationship between local saints and landscape, see William B. Taylor, "The Virgin of Guadalupe in New Spain: An Inquiry into the Social History of Marian Devotion," *American Ethnologist* 14, no. 1 (1987); Kenneth Mills, "The Naturalization of Andean Christianities," in *The Cambridge History of Christianity*, ed. R. Po Chia Hsia (Cambridge: Cambridge University Press, 2007).

134. Benjamin, *The Origins of German Tragic Drama*, 235.

135. Hanssen, *Walter Benjamin's Other History*, 59.

136. The theme of the ruin appears in the second and third generation after the conquest. Perhaps the most poignant example is to be found in the Inca Garcilaso de la Vega's meditation on the ruins of the Inca fortress Saqsawaman. For a reading of the passage, see José Antonio Mazzotti, "The Lightning Bolt Yields to the Rainbow: Indigenous History and Colonial Semiosis in the *Royal Commentaries* of the Inca Garcilaso," *MLQ* 57, no. 2 (1996): 201–8.

137. For early archaeology in New Spain, see Ignacio Bernal, *A History of Mexican Archaeology* (London: Thames and Hudson, 1980), 49–66. Athanasius Kircher's Neoplatonic Egyptology was a decisive influence in the reconsideration of Amerindian ruins. For Kircher's interest in Egypt, see Findlen, "Scientific Spectacle in Baroque Rome," 235–39.

138. This gap has often been commented, but remains little explored. See, for instance, Cañizares-Esguerra, *How to Write the History of the New World*, 201.

CHAPTER 2

1. The compendium registers fifty poets but Sigüenza declares that the competitions attracted over five hundred entries. Carlos de Sigüenza y Góngora, *Triunfo parténico* (Mexico: Ediciones Xóchitl, 1945), 139. Manuel Toussaint, the first to take an active interest in the *Triunfo*, called it "the most valuable document for the History of Mexican Literature during the seventeenth century" and published the first list of its poets. Manuel Toussaint, *Compendio bibliográfico del Triunfo parténico de Don Carlos de Sigüenza y Góngora* (Mexico: Imprenta Universitaria, 1941), 5, 45–46.

2. José Rojas Garcidueñas, "Prólogo," in *Triunfo parténico*, by Carlos de Sigüenza y Góngora (Mexico: Ediciones Xochitl, 1945), 12–13. See also José Quiñones Melgoza, "Don Carlos de Sigüenza y Góngora: Su *Triunfo parténico*," in *Carlos de Sigüenza y Góngora, Homenaje 1700–2000*, ed. Alicia Mayer, 2 vols. (Mexico: UNAM, 2000), 1: 86–89.

3. Irving Leonard, "Some Gongora Centones in Mexico," *Hispania* 12, no. 6 (1929): 567, 565. For a summary of the critical reception of the *Triunfo parténico*, see José Pascual Buxó, *El resplandor intelectual de las imágenes: Estudios de emblemática y literatura novohispana* (Mexico: Oak Editorial, 2001), 213–19.

4. Buxó, who has perhaps done more to document and revive the history of Gongorism in New Spain than any other scholar, describes the "aesthetic-ideological paradigms" of the *Triunfo parthénico* in order to restore its horizon of reception. Buxó, *El resplandor intelectual de las imágenes*, 219, 229. Even so, the critique of Sigüenza's style continues to be voiced even among scholars dedicated to Góngora's poetics. Of the *Triunfo parthénico*, Antonio Carreira has recently written: "it would be difficult to find examples of a more lumbering prose to describe something that, with much benevolence, we could call ephemeral art" (dificilmente se encontrarán ejemplos de prosa más pesada para describir algo que, con mucha benevolencia, podríamos denominar arte efímero). Antonio Carreira, "Pros y contras de la influencia gongorina en el *Triunfo parténico* (1683) de Sigüenza y Góngora," in *Homenaje a Henri Guerreiro: La hagiografía entre la historia y literatura en España de la edad media y del siglo de oro*, ed. Marc Vitse (Madrid: Iberoamericana; Frankfurt am Main: Vervuert, 2005), 348.

5. Toussaint, *Compendio bibliográfico del Triunfo parténico de Don Carlos de Sigüenza y Góngora*, 46.

6. Sigüenza y Góngora, *Triunfo parténico*, 37.

7. Ibid., 44.

8. Miguel Leon-Portilla, "Introducción," in *México en 1554: Tres diálogos latinos de Francisco Cervantes de Salazar* (Mexico: UNAM, 2001), vii–xiii. For the history of the foundation of the University of Mexico, see Pilar Gonzalbo Aizpuru, *Historia de la educación en la época colonial: La educación de los criollos y la vida urbana* (Mexico: El Colegio de México, 1990), 57–70.

9. Francisco Cervantes de Salazar, *Life in the Imperial and Loyal City of Mexico in New Spain*, trans. Minnie Lee Barrett Shepard (Austin: University of Texas Press, 1953), 26; Sigüenza y Góngora, *Triunfo parténico*, 38.

10. Cervantes de Salazar, *Life in the Imperial and Loyal City of Mexico in New Spain*, 36; Sigüenza y Góngora, *Triunfo parténico*, 38.

11. Bernardo de Balbuena, *Grandeza mexicana* (Mexico: UNAM, 1992), 36–37; Sigüenza y Góngora, *Triunfo parténico*, 39.

12. Sigüenza y Góngora, *Triunfo parténico*, 39.

13. Ibid., 40.

14. Ibid., 41.

15. Mandated by Felipe IV in 1639, the constitutions had been written by the powerful bishop of Puebla and later viceroy Juan de Palafox y Mendoza in 1645, approved by Madrid in 1649, but adopted officially in New Spain only in 1668. See Gonzalbo Aizpuru, *Historia de la educación en la época colonial*, 89–93.

16. Sigüenza y Góngora, *Triunfo parténico*, 43.

17. Ibid., 44.

18. Ibid., 40.

19. Ibid., 44.

20. Ibid., 46.

21. The clearest example of a spatial metaphor for the coalescence of a local elite is found in Ángel Rama's 1984 *La ciudad letrada*. Rama suggests that the written word served a double purpose in the Americas: both a mark of internal distinction and a structure of European imitation. Unlike studies of an emergent Creole identity, Rama's notion of a lettered city does not make a strong distinction between the Creole elite and Spanish imperial administration. The central metaphor in Rama's study is that of the "lettered city," the educated elite whose disproportionate political power rested on access to the written word. In the Americas, the metaphorical lettered city was built as a "fortress" that sought to shut out an ignorant and barbarous population that surrounded it. See Ángel Rama, *La ciudad letrada* (Hanover, N.H.: Ediciones del Norte, 1984), 24–25. See also Merrim's useful discussion of the critique of Rama. Stephanie Merrim, *The Spectacular City, Mexico, and Colonial Hispanic Literary Culture* (Austin: University of Texas Press, 2010), 115–17.

22. In his approval of the *Triunfo parthénico*, Francisco de Florencia calls the university a "literary republic." Sigüenza, for his part, calls it a "storehouse of erudition, treasury of letters, emporium of knowledge and endless fountain from which the erudite imbibe the most sweet nector of the sciences" (depósito de erudición, erario de las letras, emporio de la sabiduría y fuente inagotable donde beben los eruditos el néctar suavísimo de las ciencias). Sigüenza y Góngora, *Triunfo parténico*, 18, 39.

23. Sigüenza y Góngora, *Triunfo parténico*, 101.

24. Ibid., 33.

25. Ibid., 81–82.

26. Ibid., 87.

27. Ibid., 99–100.

28. For the trope of *horror vacui*, see David Castillo, "Horror (Vacui): The Baroque Condition," in *Hispanic Baroques: Reading Cultures in Context*, ed. Nicholas Spadaccini and Luis Martín-Estudillo (Nashville: Vanderbilt University Press, 2005), 87–88.

29. For an excellent analysis of Balbuena's poetics, see Ángel Rama, "Fundación del manierismo hispanoamericano por Bernardo de Balbuena," *University of Dayton Review* 16, no. 2 (1983). See also Merrim, *The Spectacular City*, 114–15.

30. John Beverley, *Essays on the Literary Baroque in Spain and Spanish America* (Woodbridge, England: Tamesis, 2008), 81.

31. Octavio Paz, *Sor Juana Inés de la Cruz o las trampas de la fe*, 3rd ed. (Mexico: Fondo de Cultura Económica, 1983), 73.

32. Balbuena, *Grandeza mexicana*, 83.

33. Sigüenza y Góngora, *Triunfo parténico*, 273.

34. Beverley, *Essays on the Literary Baroque in Spain and Spanish America*, 143.

35. Balbuena, *Grandeza mexicana*, 40.

36. Ibid., 49.

37. Cañizares-Esguerra extensively documents these two metaphors in seventeenth-century Spanish American writings. Jorge Cañizares-Esguerra, *Puritan Conquistadors: Iberianizing the Atlantic, 1550–1700* (Stanford, Calif.: Stanford University Press, 2006), 195–97.

38. Walter Benjamin, *The Origins of German Tragic Drama*, trans. John Osborne (London: New Left Books, 1977), 92. John Beverley, one of the few critics to have engaged Benjamin's theory of the Baroque for colonial Spanish America, interprets Balbuena's pastoral motif as the nostalgia for a bucolic past rather than a consciously artificial renewal. Beverley, *Essays on the Literary Baroque in Spain and Spanish America*, 143.

39. In his dedication of his 1684 history of a Mexican convent, *Parayso occidental*, Sigüenza y Góngora uses the idea of paradise metaphorically to describe the transformation of the pre-Colombian houses that held vestal virgins into convents in which nuns are symbolically wed to Christ. Carlos de Sigüenza y Góngora, *Parayso occidental, plantado y cultivado por la liberal benefica mano* (1684; reprint, Mexico: UNAM/Condumex, 1995), n.p.

40. For Rama, see note 21, above.

41. For Juan Eusebio Nieremberg, see the excellent recent essays by Domingo Ledezma, "Una legitimación imaginativa del nuevo mundo: *La Historia Naturae, Maxime Peregrine* del Jesuita Juan Eusebio Nieremberg," in *El saber de los Jesuitas, historias naturales y el nuevo mundo*, ed. Luis Millones Figueroa and Domingo Ledezma (Madrid: Iberoamericana; Frankfurt am Main: Vervuert, 2005); Juan Pimentel, "Baroque Natures: Juan E. Nieremberg, American Wonders, and Preterimperial Natural Science," in *Science in the Spanish and Portuguese Empires, 1500–1800*, ed. Daniela Bleichmar et al. (Stanford, Calif.: Stanford University Press, 2009).

42. Pimentel, "Baroque Natures," 109.

43. Ibid., 102, 110.
44. Ibid., 102.
45. Cañizares-Esguerra, *Puritan Conquistadors*, 126–27, 36–38.
46. Agustín Vetancurt, "Tratado de la ciudad de mexico, y las grandezas que la ilustran despues de que la fundaron españoles," in *Teatro mexicano: Descripción breve de los sucessos ejemplares históricos y religiosos del nuevo mundo de las indias* (Mexico: Doña María de Benavides Viuda de Juan Ribera, 1698; reprint, Mexico: Porrúa, 1982), 2.
47. Ibid.
48. Ibid., 3.
49. Cañizares-Esguerra, *Puritan Conquistadors*, 157.
50. Manuel de Nóbrega, *Cartas do Brasil e Mais Escritos* (Coimbra: Universidade de Coimbra, 1955), 66.
51. Jacques Lafaye, *Quetzalcóatl and Guadalupe: The Formation of Mexican National Consciousness*, trans. Benjamin Keen (Chicago: University of Chicago Press, 1977), 152, 169–72.
52. Ibid., 182.
53. Juan Solórzano Pereyra, *Política indiana*, 3 vols. (1648; reprint, Madrid: Biblioteca Castro, 1996), 1: 95.
54. Antonio de la Calancha, *Crónica moralizada*, 6 vols. (Lima: Universidad Nacional Mayor de San Marcos, 1981), 710.
55. Lafaye, *Quetzalcóatl and Guadalupe*, 183.
56. Calancha, *Crónica moralizada*, 714.
57. Ibid., 755.
58. Ibid., 770–71.
59. Ibid., 743.
60. Ibid., 744.
61. Calancha tells of one stone in which St. Thomas's footprint had remained despite the fact that it had been excavated and removed from its original site; other stones were themselves responsible for miracles, especially miraculous cures through healing waters that ran beneath them. Ibid., 750.
62. Simão de Vasconcellos, *Crónica da Companhia de Jesus*, 2 vols. (Petrópolis: Editora Vozes; Brasília: Instituto Nacional do Livro, Ministério da Educação e Cultura, 1977), 2: 128.
63. Ibid., 128–29.
64. Jorge Cañizares-Esguerra, *How to Write the History of the New World: Histories, Epistemologies, and Identities in the Eighteenth-Century Atlantic World* (Stanford, Calif.: Stanford University Press, 2001), 64.
65. Arnaldo Momigliano, *The Classical Foundations of Modern Historiography* (Berkeley: University of California Press, 1990), 58.
66. Ibid., 56–57.
67. According to Bacon, antiquarianism was history that was *tamquam imperfecte mista* as it had been carried out by the diligence of "industrious persons" who "by an exact and scrupulous diligence and observation, out of monuments, names, words, proverbs, traditions, private records and evidences, fragments of stories, passages of books that concern not story, and

the like, do save and recover [history] somewhat from the deluge of time." Francis Bacon, *Francis Bacon: The Major Works* (Oxford: Oxford University Press, 1996), 179. See also Momigliano, *The Classical Foundations of Modern Historiography*, 71.

68. Manuel Duarte, "El apóstol Santo Tomás en el Nuevo Mundo," in *Biblioteca mexicana del siglo XVIII*, ed. Nicolás León, *Boletín del Instituto Bibliográfico Mexicano*, no. 7 (Mexico: La viuda de Francisco Díaz León, 1906), 472.

69. The matter is considered carefully in Lafaye, *Quetzalcóatl and Guadalupe*, 187–89.

70. The argument was originally Luis Becerra Tanco's. Duarte, "El apóstol Santo Tomás en el Nuevo Mundo," 454, 517.

71. Ibid., 392.

72. Lafaye, *Quetzalcóatl and Guadalupe*, 160–61.

73. Duarte, "El apóstol Santo Tomás en el Nuevo Mundo," 397.

74. Ibid.

75. Ibid., 513.

76. Ibid., 516.

77. Mariano Veytia, *Historia antigua de México* (Mexico: Editorial Leyenda, 1944), 123–24. In his introduction to Duarte's manuscript, Ramírez in turn scoffed at Echeverría y Veytia, saying "And Veytia passed on this explanation, [even] improving upon it by adding the Flood, the Tower of Babel, etc.!" (¡Y Veytia dió pasaporte a la explicación mejorándola hasta agregarle el diluvio, la torre de Babel, &a!). Duarte, "El apóstol Santo Tomás en el Nuevo Mundo," 367. See also Cañizares-Esguerra, *How to Write the History of the New World*, 221.

78. Benjamin, *The Origins of German Tragic Drama*, 166.

79. Solórzano Pereyra, *Política indiana*, 1:534.

80. Borah cites medieval precedent in the *Leyes del Estilo* and *Siete Partidas* for the category of "miserable" persons but says these "undoubtedly merely codified what was already common practice and widely accepted in the religious and ethical thought of the period." Woodrow Borah, *Justice by Insurance: The General Indian Court of Colonial Mexico and the Legal Aides of the Half-Real* (Berkeley: University of California Press, 1983), 13. See also Chapter 1, note 8, above.

81. Lafaye does say that the importance of the myth of St. Thomas "was that it abolished the break with the American past that the Conquest represented and thereby endowed America with a spiritual status (and consequently a juridical and political status) that put her on a footing of equality with the tutelary power, Spain." Lafaye, *Quetzalcóatl and Guadalupe*, 191.

82. Miguel Sanchez, "Imagen de la Virgen María Madre de Dios de Guadalupe," in *Testimonios históricos guadalupanos*, ed. Ernesto de la Torre Villar and Ramiro Navarro de Anda (Mexico: Fondo de Cultura Económica, 1982), 179–80.

83. Ibid., 181–85.

84. Ibid., 186–90.

85. William A. Christian, *Apparitions in Late Medieval and Renaissance Spain* (Princeton, N.J.: Princeton University Press, 1981), 8.

86. Stafford Poole, *Our Lady of Guadalupe: The Origins and Sources of a Mexican National Symbol, 1531–1797* (Tucson: University of Arizona Press, 1995), 28–29. See also Serge Gruzinski, *Images at War: Mexico from Columbus to Blade Runner (1492–2019)*, trans. Heather McLean (Durham, N.C.: Duke University Press, 2001), 130.

87. For example, Poole, *Our Lady of Guadalupe*, 106.

88. Sanchez, "Imagen de la Virgen María Madre de Dios de Guadalupe," 198.

89. Ibid.

90. Ibid., 157.

91. Ibid., 167, 169.

92. On Juan Diego's "imagination," see ibid., 181. For a comparison between the Extremaduran and Mexican Guadalupan narratives, see Lafaye, *Quetzalcóatl and Guadalupe*, 294–97.

93. Sanchez, "Imagen de la Virgen María Madre de Dios de Guadalupe," 179.

94. Ibid., 158.

95. Ibid., 159.

96. D. A. Brading, *Mexican Phoenix: Our Lady of Guadalupe: Image and Tradition across Five Centuries* (Cambridge: Cambridge University Press, 2001), 96.

97. For the history of this publication, see the introduction to Luis Laso de la Vega, *The Story of Guadalupe: Luis Laso de la Vega's Hui Tlamahuiçoltica of 1649* (Stanford, Calif.: Stanford University Press/UCLA Latin American Center Publications, 1998), 1–47.

98. Poole, *Our Lady of Guadalupe*, 108.

99. For a summary of the testimonies, see Brading, *Mexican Phoenix*, 77–81; Poole, *Our Lady of Guadalupe*, 128–43. Brading argues that nonindigenous subjects were interviewed to compensate for indigenous testimony. Brading, *Mexican Phoenix*, 79.

100. Luis Becerra Tanco, "Origen milagroso del santuario de Nuestra Señora de Guadalupe," in *Testimonios históricos guadalupanos*, ed. Ernesto de la Torre Villar and Ramiro Navarro de Anda (Mexico: Fondo de Cultura Económica, 1982), 311.

101. Ibid.

102. Ibid.

103. Ibid., 323.

104. Ibid., 324.

105. Ibid., 331.

106. Duarte, "El apóstol Santo Tomás en el Nuevo Mundo," 517.

107. Becerra Tanco, "Origen milagroso del santuario de Nuestra Señora de Guadalupe," 330.

108. The Virgin, he notes, spoke to Juan Diego in his own language and Juan Diego did not understand Bishop Zumárraga's questions in Castilian. Ibid., 313, 316. Poole comments that Becerra follows closely Lasso de la Vega's version of the narrative. Poole, *Our Lady of Guadalupe*, 145.

Notes to Chapter 2

109. See Gruzinski, *Images at War*, 141.

110. Francisco de la Maza, *El guadalupanismo mexicano* (Mexico: Fondo de Cultura Económica, 1981), 54.

111. Brading, *Mexican Phoenix*, 68; Poole, *Our Lady of Guadalupe*, 97; William B. Taylor, "Mexico's Virgin of Guadalupe in the Seventeenth Century: Hagiography and Beyond," in *Colonial Saints: Discovering the Holy in the Americas, 1500–1800*, ed. Allan Greer and Jodi Bilinkoff (New York: Routledge, 2003), 287–88.

112. Jeanette Favrot Peterson, "Creating the Virgin of Guadalupe: The Cloth, the Artist, and Sources in Sixteenth-Century New Spain," *The Americas* 61, no. 4 (2005): 584–85; Poole, *Our Lady of Guadalupe*, 58–64.

113. William B. Taylor, "The Virgin of Guadalupe in New Spain: An Inquiry into the Social History of Marian Devotion," *American Ethnologist* 14, no. 1 (1987): 15.

114. Jeanette Favrot Peterson, "Canonizing a Cult: A Wonder-Working Guadalupe in the Seventeenth Century," in *Religion in New Spain*, ed. Susan Schroeder and Stafford Poole (Albuquerque: University of New Mexico Press, 2007), 125.

115. See, for example, the description of the tilma in Sanchez, "Imagen de la Virgen María Madre de Dios de Guadalupe," 187.

116. Francisco de Florencia, *La estrella de el norte de México* (Mexico: Antonio Velazquez, a costa del dicho D. Juan Leonardo, 1741), 149–51; Poole, *Our Lady of Guadalupe*, 142.

117. Peterson, "Creating the Virgin of Guadalupe," 590–94.

118. Ibid., 585–90.

119. Sigüenza y Góngora, *Triunfo parténico*, 121.

120. Sanchez, "Imagen de la Virgen María Madre de Dios de Guadalupe," 158.

121. See Poole, *Our Lady of Guadalupe*, 29.

122. Alicia Mayer's work is an exception. See Alicia Mayer, *Dos americanos, dos pensamientos* (Mexico: UNAM, 1998); Alicia Mayer, "El guadalupanismo en Carlos de Sigüenza y Góngora," in *Carlos de Sigüenza y Góngora: Homenaje 1700–2000*, ed. Alicia Mayer, 1st vol. (Mexico: UNAM, 2000).

123. Carlos de Sigüenza y Góngora, "Primavera indiana," in *Testimonios históricos guadalupanos*, ed. Ernesto de la Torre Villar and Ramiro Navarro de Anda (Mexico: Fondo de Cultura Ecónomica, 1982), 348.

124. Ibid.
125. Ibid.
126. Ibid.
127. Ibid.
128. Ibid.

129. Jaime Delgado, "Estudio preliminar," in *Piedad heroyca de Don Fernando Cortés*, by Carlos de Sigüenza y Góngora (Madrid: José Porrúa Turranzas, 1940), xciv.

130. Carlos de Sigüenza y Góngora, *Piedad heroyca de Don Fernando Cortés* (Madrid: José Porrúa Turranzas, 1940), 65.

131. Carlos de Sigüenza y Góngora, *Glorias de Querétaro* (Querétaro: Ediciones Cimatario, 1945), 2.
132. Ibid., 4.
133. Ibid., 1.
134. Ibid., 3.
135. Ibid., 34–35.
136. On the panegyric nature of Sigüenza's description of the Querétaro procession, see Merrim, *The Spectacular City*, 173–75.
137. Sigüenza y Góngora, *Glorias de Querétaro* , 50.
138. Ibid.,
139. Ibid., 51.
140. Ibid.
141. Ibid., 51–52.
142. Ibid., 54.
143. Ibid., 54–55.
144. Ibid., 55.
145. For the Spanish justification of tribute, see Patricia Seed, *American Pentimento: The Invention of Indians and the Pursuit of Riches* (Minneapolis: University of Minnesota Press, 2001), 73–83.
146. Sigüenza y Góngora, *Glorias de Querétaro*, 55.
147. Ibid., 75.
148. Gruzinski, *Images at War*, 137.
149. Florencia, *La estrella de el norte de México*, 46.
150. Ibid., 29.
151. Ibid., 39.
152. Ibid., 108.
153. Ibid., 101.
154. Ibid., 222.
155. Ibid., 186.
156. Ibid., 154.
157. Ibid., 118. A hotly debated subject, this assertion in Florencia's work appears to have the purpose of promoting the idea of Juan Diego's innocent piety. See Poole, *Our Lady of Guadalupe*, 29, 125, 149, 159.
158. Carlos de Sigüenza y Góngora, "Aprobación," in Florencia, *La estrella de el norte*, n.p.
159. Florencia, *La estrella de el norte de México*, 83.
160. Sigüenza y Góngora, *Piedad heroyca de Fernando Cortés*, 65.
161. Ibid.,
162. Alicia Mayer, "Presentación," in *Carlos de Sigüenza y Góngora, Homenaje 1700–2000*, ed. Alicia Mayer, 2 vols. (Mexico: UNAM, 2000), 1: 19. One of the most contradictory sources of evidence for Sigüenza's authorship is the citation in third person of the "second Góngora" as the author of the *Primavera indiana*. Carlos de Sigüenza y Góngora, "Anotaciones críticas sobre el primer apóstol de Nueva España y sobre la imagen de Guadalupe de México," in *Carlos de Sigüenza y Góngora: Homenaje 1700–2000*, ed. Alicia Mayer, 2 vols. (Mexico: UNAM, 2000), 1: 307.
163. Sigüenza y Góngora, "Anotaciones críticas," 364.

164. Ibid., 298.
165. Ibid., 299.
166. See Chapter 3.
167. Sigüenza y Góngora, "Anotaciones críticas," 302.
168. Ibid., 308.
169. Ibid., 304.
170. Ibid., 339.
171. Ibid., 373.
172. Ibid., 374–75.
173. Ibid., 375.
174. Ibid., 377.
175. Juan de Palafox y Mendoza, *Manual de estados y profesiones / De la naturaleza del indio* (Mexico: UNAM/Porrúa, 1986), 47–48.
176. Florencia, *La estrella de el norte de México*, 3.
177. Ibid., 168.
178. Ibid., 160. Florencia gives Zumárraga the title of "archbishop," but this is anachronistic. The miracle was said to occur in 1531 and Zumárraga was made archbishop in 1548.

CHAPTER 3

1. The literature on festivals in the Spanish Habsburg world is extensive. For a representative sample, see José Antonio Maravall, "Teatro, fiesta e ideología en el barroco," in *Teatro y literatura en la sociedad barroca*, ed. Francisco Abad (Barcelona: Editorial Crítica, 1990); Alejandro Cañeque, *The King's Living Image: The Culture and Politics of Viceregal Power in Colonial Mexico* (New York: Routledge, 2004); Linda Curcio-Nagy, *The Great Festivals of Colonial Mexico City: Performing Power and Identity* (Albuquerque: University of New Mexico Press, 2004); Carolyn Dean, *Inka Bodies and the Body of Christ: Corpus Christi in Colonial Cuzco, Peru* (Durham, N.C.: Duke University Press, 1999); Nancy Fee, "La Entrada Angelopolitana: Ritual and Myth in the Viceregal Entry in Puebla de Los Angeles," *The Americas* 52, no. 3 (1996); Pilar Gonzalbo Aizpuru, "Las fiestas novohispanas: Espectáculo y ejemplo," *Mexican Studies/Estudios Mexicanos* 9, no. 1 (1993); Alejandra Osorio, "The King in Lima: Simulacra, Ritual, and Rule in Seventeenth-Century Peru," *Hispanic American Historical Review* 84, no. 3 (2004).
2. Linda Curcio-Nagy, "Giants and Gypsies: Corpus Christi in Colonial Mexico City," in *Rituals of Rule, Rituals of Resistance*, ed. William H. Beezley, Cheryl English Martin, and William E. French (Wilmington, Del.: Scholarly Resources, 1994), 1.
3. Gonzalbo Aizpuru, "Las fiestas novohispanas," 30.
4. Maravall, "Teatro, fiesta e ideología," 178.
5. Ibid., 188.
6. Ibid., 180.
7. The strongest versions of these two critiques are to be found respectively in J. H. Elliott's review of the English translation of Maravall's 1974 *Cultura del barroco* and John Beverley's response to Elliott. J. H. Elliott,

"Concerto Barroco," *New York Review of Books* 34, no. 6 (1987); John Beverley, "Going Baroque?" *boundary 2* 15, no. 3 (1988). See also the Introduction, note 110, above.

8. Roy Strong, *Art and Power: Renaissance Festivals, 1450–1650* (Berkeley: University of California Press, 1984), 22–41.

9. For the early rediscovery and adaptation of Roman triumph by Petrarch, see ibid., 44–50.

10. Studies of viceregal triumphal arches may be found in Ignacio Osorio, *Conquistar el eco: la paradoja de la conciencia criolla* (Mexico: UNAM, 1989), 173–88; José Pascual Buxó, "El resplandor intelectual de las imágenes: Jeroglífica y emblemática," in *Juegos de ingenio y agudeza: La pintura emblemática de la Nueva España*, ed. Ana Laura Cue (Mexico: Museo Nacional de Arte, 1994); José Pascual Buxó, "Función política de los emblemas en el *Neptuno alegórico* de Sor Juana Inés de la Cruz," in *Sor Juana Inés de la Cruz y sus contemporáneos*, ed. Margo Glantz (Mexico: Facultad de Filosofía y Letras, UNAM, and Centro de Estudios de Historia de México, Condumex, 1998). See Nancy Fee for a detailed description of the arches erected for seventeenth-century viceregal entrances into Puebla. Fee, "La *Entrada Angelopolitana*," 293–300.

11. For the political language of descriptions of triumphal arches, see Cañeque, *The King's Living Image*, 26–28; Dalmacio Rodríguez Hernández, "Los arcos triunfales en la época de Carlos II: Una aproximación desde la retórica," in *Teatro y poder en la época de Carlos II: Fiestas en torno a reyes y virreyes*, ed. Judith Farré Vidal (Madrid: Iberoamericana; Frankfurt am Main: Vervuert, 2007).

12. The most complete handbook on emblems remains Mario Praz, *Studies in Seventeenth-Century Imagery*, 2nd ed. (Rome: Edizioni de Storia e Letteratura, 1975). On the interest in Egyptian hieroglyphs in the Renaissance, see Don Cameron Allen, *Mysteriously Meant: The Rediscovery of Pagan Symbolism and Allegorical Interpretation in the Renaissance* (Baltimore: Johns Hopkins University Press, 1970); Jean Seznec, *The Survival of the Pagan Gods: The Mythological Tradition and Its Place in Renaissance Humanism and Art*, trans. Barbara F. Sessions (Princeton, N.J.: Princeton University Press, 1953).

13. Recent studies have shown the influence of emblematics on nearly all areas of elite cultural life in New Spain. See especially Buxó, "El resplandor intelectual de las imágenes"; Buxó, *El resplandor intelectual de las imágenes: Estudios de emblemática y literatura novohispana* (Mexico: Oak Editorial, 2001). It is likely that this influence was directly nurtured by the Jesuits, who printed an edition of Alciato's *Emblemata* in Mexico in 1577 as part of their pedagogical program. Pilar Gonzalbo Aizpuru, "La influencia de la Compañía de Jesus en la sociedad novohispana del siglo XVI," *Historia Mexicana* 32, no. 2 (1982): 268–69.

14. As José Pascual Buxó notes, this meaning was never fully explicit in the iconic-literary pairing and could be left unexplained, especially in the case of the more conventional iconographic symbols. More commonly,

however, the emblem had to be explained in a third component of the text, the epigram or *explicatio*. Buxó, *El resplandor intelectual de las imágenes*, 51.

15. See Cañeque, *The King's Living Image*, 26–36, for examples from seventeenth-century New Spain.

16. Sor Juana Inés de la Cruz, "Neptuno alegórico, oceáno de colores, simulacro político," in *Obras completas de Sor Juana Inés de la Cruz*, ed. Alberto Salceda, 4 vols. (Mexico: Fondo de Cultura Económica, 1957), 4: 377.

17. Carlos de Sigüenza y Góngora, *Theatro de virtudes politicas, que constituyen à un principe* (Mexico: Viuda de Bernardo Calderón, 1680), 9.

18. See numerous examples in Solange Alberro, *El águila y la cruz: Orígenes religiosos de la conciencia criolla, México, siglos XVI–XVII* (Mexico: El Colegio de México, Fedeicomiso Historia de las Américas, and Fondo de Cultura Económica, 1999), 70–114.

19. Solange Alberro, "Imagen y fiesta barroca: Nueva España, siglos XVI–XVII," in *Barrocos y modernos: Nuevos caminos en la investigación del barroco iberoamericano*, ed. Petra Schumm (Madrid: Iberoamericana; Frankfurt am Main: Vervuert, 1998), 42.

20. Dalmacio Rodríguez Hernández, *Texto y fiesta en la literatura novohispana* (Mexico: UNAM, 1998), 250.

21. Sigüenza y Góngora, *Theatro de virtudes*, 5.

22. Antonio Lorente Medina, *La prosa de Sigüenza y Góngora y la formación de la conciencia criolla mexicana* (Mexico: Fondo de Cultura Económica, 1996), 37; Anthony Pagden, *Spanish Imperialism and the Political Imagination: Studies in European and Spanish-American Social and Political Theory, 1513–1830* (New Haven, Conn.: Yale University Press, 1990), 96.

23. The style of *Theatro de virtudes* is particularly remarkable given Sigüenza's own condemnation of Gongoresque prose in the prologue to his *Parayso occidental*, published only four years later in 1684. Carlos de Sigüenza y Góngora, "Prólogo al lector," in *Parayso occidental, plantado y cultivado por la liberal benefica mano* (1684; reprint, Mexico: UNAM/Condumex, 1995). See also the Conclusion, below.

24. Much has been written on the polemics surrounding Góngora's "difficult" style. For a recent summary and reconsideration of the debate in terms of theological principles, see Christopher Johnson, "De Doctrina Gongorina: Góngora's Defence of Obscurity," *Bulletin of Hispanic Studies* 77 (2000).

25. D. A. Brading, *The First America: The Spanish Monarchy, Creole Patriots, and the Liberal State 1492–1867* (Cambridge: Cambridge University Press, 1991), 363.

26. Pagden, *Spanish Imperialism and the Political Imagination*, 93.

27. Serge Gruzinski, *Images at War: Mexico from Columbus to Blade Runner (1492–2019)*, trans. Heather McLean (Durham, N.C.: Duke University Press, 2001), 150.

28. Roberto González Echevarría, *Celestina's Brood: Continuities of the Baroque in Spanish and Latin American Literature* (Durham, N.C.: Duke University Press, 1993), 146.

29. Sigüenza y Góngora, *Theatro de virtudes*, 8.
30. Ibid.
31. Ibid., 7.
32. "*Ei qui symbolum aliquod commode volet effingere, spectanda haec primum proponuntur, ut iusta sit animi, et corporis analogia (per animum, sententiam uno, altero, vel certe paucis comprehensum verbis intelligo: nomine corporis symbolum ipsum designari placet.*" Ibid., 33–34. This definition may be found, for example, in Juan de Horozco Covarrubias's 1591 treatise on emblems. Cited in Buxó, *El resplandor intelectual de las imágenes*, 25.
33. Sigüenza y Góngora, *Theatro de virtudes*, n.p.
34. Ibid., 83.
35. Like Christ, the king was a *persona mixta* who combined two natures, secular and divine. The difference between Christ and monarch, according to Kantorowicz, is that while Christ is dual by nature, the king "*becomes a twin personality through his anointment and consecration.*" Ernst K. Kantorowicz, *The King's Two Bodies: A Study in Mediaeval Political Theology* (Princeton, N.J.: Princeton University Press, 1957), 49.
36. J. H. Elliott, *Spain and Its World, 1500–1700* (New Haven, Conn.: Yale University Press, 1989), 167.
37. Ibid., 167–70.
38. Dian Fox, *Kings in Calderón: A Study in Characterization and Political Theory* (London: Tamesis, 1986), 3.
39. J. H. Elliott, *Imperial Spain, 1469–1716* (London: Penguin, 1963), 170, 176–77.
40. Ibid., 176.
41. Ibid., 175.
42. J. H. Elliott, *Empires of the Atlantic World: Britain and Spain in America, 1492–1830* (New Haven, Conn.: Yale University Press, 2006), 122–28, 138.
43. Diego de Saavedra Fajardo, *Idea de un príncipe político-cristiano representada en cien empresas* (Murcia: Academia Alfonso X el Sabio, 1985), 221.
44. On the importance of constancy in early modern Neostoicism, see Gerhard Oestreich, *Neostoicism and the Early Modern State* (Cambridge: Cambridge University Press, 1982), 13–19. For Neostoicism in seventeenth-century Spain, especially in the work of Saavedra Fajardo, see Jeremy Robbins, "The Arts of Perception," *Bulletin of Spanish Studies* 82, no. 8 (2005): 39–63.
45. Cañeque, *The King's Living Image*, 28–29.
46. Cruz, "Neptuno alegórico," 355–56.
47. Sigüenza y Góngora, *Theatro de virtudes*, 5–6.
48. Ibid., 6.
49. Ibid. Citing Ovid, he argues that the obscurity of "fables" always hid pagan divinities.
50. Ibid., 83–84.
51. For this reason, even before emblems became commonplace adornments for arches, the fascination of Maximilian I of Austria with the newly

published interpretations of Egyptian hieroglyphs prompted Albrecht Durer to use them to decorate the massive triumphal arch he designed for the emperor. Erwin Panofsky, *The Life and Art of Albrecht Dürer*, 4th ed. (Princeton, N.J.: Princeton University Press, 1955), 176–79.

52. Alberro, *El águila y la cruz*, 83.
53. Ibid., 85.
54. Seznec, *The Survival of the Pagan Gods*, 278.
55. Walter Benjamin, *The Origins of German Tragic Drama*, trans. John Osborne (London: New Left Books, 1977), 220–34.
56. Sigüenza y Góngora, *Theatro de virtudes*, 27.
57. Ibid., 26.
58. Ibid., 25.
59. Ibid., 39.
60. Seznec, *The Survival of the Pagan Gods*, 11–13.
61. Sigüenza y Góngora, *Theatro de virtudes*, 37.
62. Ibid.
63. Ibid., 38.
64. Ibid.
65. Ibid.
66. Ibid.
67. Juan de Torquemada, *Monarquía indiana*, 3rd ed., 7 vols. (Mexico: UNAM, 1975–1983), 3: 114.
68. Sigüenza y Góngora, *Theatro de virtudes*, 38.
69. Ibid., 40–41.
70. Torquemada, *Monarquía indiana*, 3: 112.
71. Gruzinski, *Images at War*, 115.
72. This combination of the figure of Huitzilopochtli, traditionally demonized, with a historical allegory based on the glyph of his name mixes two divergent traditions in the European representation of the god. According to Elizabeth Boone, European iconography represented Huitzilopochtli either as a classical god or as the devil. In each, the symbolic attributes of the glyphic representation remain opaque. Although the shield and spear give the dignity of a herald to the classical figure, Huitzilopochtli is blindfolded to signify the error of pagan religion. Elizabeth Boone, *Incarnations of the Aztec Supernatural: The Image of Huitzilopochtli in Mexico and Europe* (Philadelphia: American Philosophical Society, 1989), 57–83.
73. Ibid., 25–29.
74. Benjamin, *The Origins of German Tragic Drama*, 92–95.
75. Sigüenza y Góngora, *Theatro de virtudes*, 81.
76. Ibid., 29.
77. Ibid., 84.
78. Ibid., 82.
79. At least once, Sigüenza assigns an "ardent spirit" to the Mexica emperors independent of the viceroy: "This very beautiful machine of colors was animated, for the reasons that I laid out in the Prelude 2, with the ardent spirit of the Mexican emperors" (Animóse esta hermossisima maquina de

colores, por las razones que dexo escritas en el Preludio 2. con el ardiente espiritu de los Mexicanos Emperadores). Ibid., 25.

80. Ibid., 32.

81. Ibid., 30.

82. Justino Cortés Castellanos, *El catecismo en pictogramas de Fray Pedro de Gante* (Madrid: Fundación Universitaria Española, 1987), 453–54.

83. Brading, *The First America*, 363.

84. Sigüenza y Góngora, *Theatro de virtudes*, 1–2.

85. "Lo curioso es que, al mencionar a 'las invasiones sangrientas' de los europeos, no reparase—o fingiese no reparar—en el ejemplo que tenía a la vista: la conquista de México por los españoles. En la actitud de Sigüenza aparece otra vez la contradicción que minaba el sueño criollo y que acabó por desgarrarlo." Octavio Paz, *Sor Juana Inés de la Cruz o las trampas de la fe*, 3rd ed. (Mexico: Fondo de Cultura Económica, 1983), 208.

86. David Lupher argues that Solórzano Pereyra was the most influential jurist to institute the distinction, following Augustine, between Roman and Christian empires. David A. Lupher, *Romans in the New World: Classical Models in Sixteenth-Century Spanish America* (Ann Arbor: University of Michigan Press, 2003), 186–88.

87. Sigüenza y Góngora, *Theatro de virtudes*, 2–3.

88. Ibid., 3.

89. Ibid.

90. Ibid., 4.

91. Ibid.

92. For this understanding of violence, see Gordon Teskey, *Allegory and Violence* (Ithaca, N.Y.: Cornell University Press, 1996), 9.

93. Sigüenza y Góngora, *Theatro de virtudes*, 2.

94. Angus Fletcher, *Allegory: The Theory of a Symbolic Mode* (Ithaca, N.Y.: Cornell University Press, 1964), 2 n. 1.

95. Sigüenza y Góngora, *Theatro de virtudes*, 24.

96. Ibid., 15.

97. See Chapter 2.

98. Sigüenza y Góngora, *Theatro de virtudes*, 15.

99. For the juridical term "misery" as applied to indigenous subjects, see Chapter 1, above.

100. Sigüenza y Góngora, *Theatro de virtudes*, 16.

101. Ibid., 17.

102. Ibid.

103. See Chapter 2.

104. Carlos de Sigüenza y Góngora, *Glorias de Querétaro* (Querétaro: Ediciones Cimatario, 1945), 55.

105. Sigüenza y Góngora, *Theatro de virtudes*, 20.

106. Ibid., 1.

107. María Castañeda de la Paz, *Pintura de la peregrinación de los Culhuaque-Mexitin (El Mapa de Sigüenza)* (Mexico: Conaculta-INAH, 2006), 14–16.

108. Van Doesburg, "Review: Castañeda de la Paz, María: Pintura de la peregrinación de los Culhuaque-Mexitin (El Mapa de Sigüenza)," *Anuario*

de Estudios Americanos 65, no. 2 (2008): 317; Castañeda de la Paz, *Pintura de la peregrinación*, 62.

109. Castañeda de la Paz, *Pintura de la peregrinación*, 15.

110. Ibid., 44.

111. Giovanni Francesco Gemelli Careri, *Giro del mondo del Dottor D. Gio. Francesco Gemelli Careri*, 6 vols. (Venice: Sebastiano Coleti, 1728), 6: 44.

112. Sigüenza y Góngora, *Theatro de virtudes*, 18.

113. Carlos de Sigüenza y Góngora, *Noticia chronológica de los reyes, emperadores, governadores, presidentes, y vir-reyes, que desde su primera fundacion hasta el tiempo presupone han governado esta nobilissima imperial ciudad de Mexico* (1681?), n.p.

114. The 1647 edict prohibiting judiciary astrology in New Spain, for instance, cites the dangers of astrology for "rustic and ignorant men" (hombres rústicos e ignorantes). José Miguel Quintana, *La astrología en la Nueva España en el siglo XVII (de Enrico Martínez a Sigüenza y Góngora)* (Mexico: Bibliofilos mexicanos, 1969), 101.

115. Jacques Lafaye, *Quetzalcóatl and Guadalupe: The Formation of Mexican National Consciousness*, trans. Benjamin Keen (Chicago: University of Chicago Press, 1976), 65–66.

116. Gemelli Careri, *Giro del mondo*, 44–45.

117. See Chapter 2, note 67, above.

118. Edmundo O'Gorman's edition of Ixtlilxochitl's historical works contains the relevant documents for these events, which he summarizes as a chronology in his introduction. Fernando Alva de Ixtlilxochitl, *Obras históricas*, 2 vols. (Mexico: UNAM, 1975), 1: 17–42.

119. Ibid., 2: 354–69.

120. Ibid., 1: 40–42.

121. Ibid., 1: 168.

122. Sigüenza y Góngora, *Parayso occidental, plantado y cultivado por la liberal benefica mano*, 2.

CHAPTER 4

1. R. Douglas Cope, *The Limits of Racial Domination: Plebeian Society in Colonial Mexico City, 1660–1720* (Madison: University of Wisconsin Press, 1994), 17.

2. Ibid., 125; J. I. Israel, *Race, Class and Politics in Colonial Mexico, 1610–1670* (Oxford: Oxford University Press, 1975), 160. William Taylor's work remains the best source on seventeenth-century rural rebellions. William B. Taylor, *Drinking, Homicide, and Rebellion in Colonial Mexican Villages* (Stanford, Calif.: Stanford University Press, 1979), 113–51.

3. Cope, *The Limits of Racial Domination*, 17–18. Thirty-five Africans and mulattoes were hanged after the alleged conspiracy. For a summary of the events, see María Elena Martínez, "The Black Blood of New Spain: Limpieza de Sangre, Racial Violence, and Gendered Power in Early Colonial Mexico," *William and Mary Quarterly* (2004).

4. Israel ventures the suggestion that Palafox's political downfall might have been linked to that of the Duke of Olivares, with whom he was aligned. Israel, *Race, Class and Politics in Colonial Mexico*, 199–216, 244.

5. The system of checks and balances, crucial to Spanish imperial governance, created constant tension among ecclesiastical and state administrators and between the viceroy and the local governance. See ibid. For a critique of Israel's sharp divisions between Creoles and peninsulars, see Alejandro Cañeque, *The King's Living Image: The Culture and Politics of Viceregal Power in Colonial Mexico* (New York: Routledge, 2004), 65.

6. Israel, *Race, Class and Politics in Colonial Mexico, 1610–1670*, 142–52.

7. The main sources for the riot are Carlos de Sigüenza y Góngora's 1692 letter and the letters and records of the trial that are found in the Archivo General de Indias (AGI), Patronato 226, n.1. Irving Leonard's early edition of Sigüenza's letter remains the most accurate. Carlos de Sigüenza y Góngora, *Alboroto y motín de México del 8 de junio de 1692*, ed. Irving Leonard (Mexico: Talleres Gráficos del Museo Nacional de Arqueología, Historia y Etnografía, 1932). This edition also includes letters from officials and trial records. Another anonymous source may be found as "Tumulto acaecido en la ciudad de México el año de 1692," in *Tumultos y rebeliones acaecidos en México*, ed. Génaro García, *Documentos inéditos o muy raros para la historia de México* (Mexico: Centro de Estudios Históricos de Agrarismo en México, 1981).

8. Leonard reproduces one of these letters in Sigüenza y Góngora, *Alboroto y motín*, 131–38. See also Cope, *The Limits of Racial Domination*, 132–33.

9. For this argument, see Iván Escamilla González, "El siglo de oro vindicado: Carlos de Sigüenza y Góngora, el Conde de Galve y el tumulto de 1692," in *Carlos de Sigüenza y Góngora: Homenaje 1700–2000*, ed. Alicia Mayer, 2 vols. (Mexico: UNAM, 2002), 2: 189–90.

10. Cope, *The Limits of Racial Domination*, 147.

11. Natalia Silva Prada, *La política de una rebelión: Los indígenas frente al tumulto de 1692 en la ciudad de México* (Mexico: El Colegio de México, 2007), especially 441, 511.

12. As Max Weber writes, in a patrimonial system resistance "is directed against the master or his servant personally, the accusation being that he failed to observe the traditional limits of his power." Max Weber, *Economy and Society: An Outline of Interpretive Sociology*, trans. Ephraim Fischoff et al., 2 vols. (Berkeley: University of California Press, 1978), 1: 227.

13. Sigüenza y Góngora, *Alboroto y motín*, 79.

14. Irving A. Leonard, *Don Carlos de Sigüenza y Góngora: A Mexican Savant of the Seventeenth Century* (Berkeley: University of California Press, 1929), 111. More recently, D. A. Brading has asserted that the letter was a "concise, unvarnished narrative of the great riot of 1692 in Mexico City." D. A. Brading, *Mexican Phoenix: Our Lady of Guadalupe: Image and Tradition across Five Centuries* (Cambridge: Cambridge University Press, 2001), 131.

15. Kathleen Ross, "*Alboroto y motín de México:* Una noche triste criolla," *Hispanic Review* 56, no. 2 (Spring 1988).

16. As José Rabasa has written, "the task of subaltern studies, however, would consist of recuperating the strategies of mobilization, the interracial allegiances, the role of women, the anticolonial positionings, and the tactics of rumor that remain sedimented in Sigüenza's text. But in doing this sort of reading we should remain careful not to forget that we are dealing with an ideological elaboration and therefore should avoid claiming access to reality itself. For we witness Sigüenza's phantasms, not the uprising itself. It is not a love of Indian things that Sigüenza loses in the rebellion of 1692. We should trace instead his fear of insurgency by people of color (along with marginal Spaniards) and racial hatred." José Rabasa, "Pre-Columbian Pasts and Indian Presents in Mexican History," in *Colonialism Past and Present*, ed. Alvaro Félix Bolaños and Gustavo Verdesio (Albany: State University of New York Press, 2002), 65. In her reading of the letter, Mabel Moraña writes that the "ideology of racism appears as a cultural construct of variable importance and value according to the historical junctures and sectoral alliances that were necessary in each case in order to solidify an ascendant Creole power during a protonational stage" (ideología del racismo aparece como un constructo cultural de importancia y valores variables, según las coyunturas históricas y las alianzas sectoriales que fueran necesarias en cada caso, para la solidificación de un poder criollo ascendente en las etapas protonacionales). Mabel Moraña, "El 'Tumulto de Indios' de 1692," in *Agencias criollas: La ambigüedad "colonial" en las letras hispanoamericanas*, ed. José Antonio Mazzotti (Pittsburgh: Instituto Internacional de Literatura Iberoamericana, 2000), 172.

17. Gilles Deleuze, *The Fold: Leibniz and the Baroque*, trans. Tom Conley (Minneapolis: University of Minnesota Press, 1993), 19–20.

18. Etienne Balibar and Immanuel Wallerstein, *Race, Nation, Class: Ambiguous Identities*, trans. Chris Turner (London: Verso, 1991), 19.

19. Ibid., 54–55.

20. Ibid., 50.

21. See Michel Foucault, *"Society Must Be Defended:" Lectures at the Collège de France, 1975–76*, trans. David Macey (New York: Picador, 2003), particularly 66–78, 87–88, 103.

22. Ross, "*Alboroto y motín de México:* Una noche triste criolla," 185; Rabasa, "Pre-Columbian Pasts and Indian Presents in Mexican History," 64.

23. Foucault defines counterhistory as a discourse that "demands rights that have not been recognized, or in other words, to declare war by rights declaring rights." Foucault, *"Society Must Be Defended,"* 73.

24. The requests and responses are reproduced in Edmundo O'Gorman, "Sobre los inconvenientes de vivir los indios en el centro de la ciudad," *Boletín del Archivo General de la Nación* 9, no. 1–34 (1938): 9–10.

25. For the politics surrounding the *traza* from the sixteenth century until the end of the seventeenth century, see Charles Gibson, *The Aztecs under Spanish Rule* (Stanford, Calif.: Stanford University Press, 1964), 370–77.

26. O'Gorman, "Sobre los inconvenientes de vivir los indios en el centro de la ciudad," 2–3.

27. See *Recopilación de leyes de los reynos de las Indias*, book 6, tit. 1, law 19.

28. O'Gorman, "Sobre los inconvenientes de vivir los indios en el centro de la ciudad," 3–4.

29. Ibid., 3.
30. Ibid., 13.
31. Ibid., 23–24.
32. Ibid., 20.
33. Ibid., 4, 14.
34. Ibid., 13.
35. Ibid., 12.
36. Ibid., 18.
37. Ibid., 13.
38. Ibid., 20.

39. For Foucault, pastoral care is the pastor's individual knowledge of each congregant through techniques of "examination, confession, guidance, and obedience." Michel Foucault, "'Omnes et Singulatim': Toward a Critique of Political Reason," in *Power*, ed. James D. Faubion, trans. Robert Hurley, vol. 3 of *Essential Works of Foucault, 1954–1984*, 3 vols. (New York: New Press, 2000), 310.

40. O'Gorman, "Sobre los inconvenientes de vivir los indios en el centro de la ciudad," 3.

41. Ibid., 18.
42. Ibid., 3.
43. Ibid., 19.
44. Ibid., 11.
45. Ibid., 29.
46. Ibid., 6.
47. Ibid.
48. Ibid., 7.

49. Anthony Pagden, *The Fall of Natural Man: The American Indian and the Origins of Comparative Ethnology* (Cambridge: Cambridge University Press, 1982), 116.

50. Sigüenza thus advocates something closer to what Foucault calls the "art of government." See Michel Foucault, "Governmentality," in *Power*, ed. James D. Faubion, trans. Robert Hurley, vol. 3 of *Essential Works of Foucault, 1954–1984*, 3 vols. (New York: New Press, 2000). Foucault notes that the Franciscan friars were an especially important source of the pastoral mode of governance in early modern Europe. Foucault, "'Omnes et Singulatim,'" 313.

51. O'Gorman, "Sobre los inconvenientes de vivir los indios en el centro de la ciudad," 7.

52. For a succinct summary of the use of the term *reducción* in Spanish colonization, see William F. Hanks, *Converting Words: Maya in the Age of the Cross* (Berkeley: University of California Press, 2010), 2–4.

Notes to Chapter 4

53. Sigüenza y Góngora, *Alboroto y motín*, 82. The admiral never seems to have taken up this suggestion and, indeed, quite possibly never even saw the letter, dated August 30. By October 1692 he had already returned to New Spain. See Leonard's "advertencia preliminar" in Sigüenza y Góngora, *Alboroto y motín*, 13.

54. Other letters are dated from between June 30 and August 23. Leonard includes various letters, including one written by Sigüenza's brother Francisco and the two written by the viceroy Conde de Galve, in the appendix to his edition of Sigüenza's letter. Sigüenza y Góngora, *Alboroto y motín*. Others may be found in AGI, Patronato 226, n. 1.

55. Sigüenza y Góngora, *Alboroto y motín*, 25.

56. Ibid., 26.

57. Juan de Borja, *Empresas morales* (Madrid: Fundación Universitaria Española, 1981), 92. Stephanie Merrim has recently suggested that the inspiration for this passage came from a poem of Sor Juana's, Soneto 152. Stephanie Merrim, *The Spectacular City, Mexico, and Colonial Hispanic Literary Culture* (Austin: University of Texas Press, 2010), 238.

58. Deleuze, *The Fold*, 21. For Renaissance perspectivism, see the classic study by Erwin Panofsky, *Perspective as Symbolic Form*, trans. Christopher S. Wood (New York: Zone Books, 1997), 67–72.

59. Sigüenza y Góngora, *Alboroto y motín*, 27.

60. Ibid.

61. Ibid., 29. For Sigüenza's involvement in the engineering of the San Juan de Ulúa fort, see Chapter 5.

62. Mumford asserts that the Baroque city became conceived increasingly as a fortress even as its ideal function was to facilitate internal movement with avenues and wheeled transport. Lewis Mumford, *The City in History: Its Origins, Its Transformations, and Its Prospects* (New York: Harcourt, Brace & World, 1961), 360.

63. Sigüenza y Góngora, *Alboroto y motín*, 30.

64. Ibid., 36–37.

65. Ibid., 34.

66. Ibid., 35.

67. Ibid., 36.

68. Ibid., 47.

69. Ibid.

70. Cope, *The Limits of Racial Domination*, 130–31.

71. Sigüenza y Góngora, *Alboroto y motín*, 44.

72. Ibid.

73. Ibid., 45.

74. Ibid., 53.

75. Ibid., 38.

76. Ibid., 41.

77. Ibid., 55–56.

78. For this reading, see Rabasa, "Pre-Columbian Pasts and Indian Presents in Mexican History," 71. See also Ross's interpretation of the objects as

a medium for Sigüenza to identify with the Spanish officials. Ross, "*Alboroto y Motín de México:* Una noche triste criolla," 184.

79. The Mexican extirpator Hernando Ruiz de Alarcón used the term in the title of his early seventeenth-century treatise on idolatry. Hernando Ruiz de Alarcón, *Tratado de las supersticiones y costumbres gentílicas que hoy viven entre los indios naturales desta Nueva España* (Mexico: SEP, 1988).

80. During the early seventeenth-century campaigns in Oaxaca, inquisitors found signs of idolatry in ancestor bundles (*bultos*). Serge Gruzinski, *The Conquest of Mexico: The Incorporation of Indian Societies into the Western World, 16th–18th Centuries*, trans. Eileen Corrigan (Cambridge: Polity, 1993), 175. For a description of the ancestor bundles, see Elizabeth Boone, *Incarnations of the Aztec Supernatural: The Image of Huitzilopochtli in Mexico and Europe* (Philadelphia: American Philosophical Society, 1989), 25–28. As objects of Spanish inquisitorial suspicion, bundles were remarkably similar to the *huacas* targeted by the Peruvian extirpation campaigns and included in the 1609 *auto-da-fe* in Lima. Kenneth Mills, *Idolatry and Its Enemies: Colonial Andean Religion and Extirpation, 1640–1750* (Princeton, N.J.: Princeton UP, 1997), 30.

81. Agustín Vetancurt, *Teatro mexicano: Descripción breve de los sucesos ejemplares históricos y religiosos del nuevo mundo de las Indias* (Mexico: Doña María de Benavides Viuda de Juan Ribera, 1698; reprint, Mexico: Porrúa, 1982), 143. Solís argues, by contrast, that those who were tempted by the gold were trapped in the city. Antonio de Solís, *Historia de la conquista de México, población y progresos de la América septentrional, conocida por el nombre de Nueva España*, 2nd ed. (1704; reprint, Mexico: Porrúa, 1988), 430.

82. Susan Buck-Morss, *The Dialectics of Seeing: Walter Benjamin and the Arcades Project* (Cambridge, Mass.: Massachusetts Institute of Technology Press, 1989), 218–20.

83. Michael Taussig, *Mimesis and Alterity: A Particular History of the Senses* (New York: Routledge, 1993), 39–40.

84. Ibid., 253–55.

85. For a graphic description of the sanitary conditions of Mexico City during this period, see Cope, *The Limits of Racial Domination*, 27–48.

86. Sigüenza y Góngora, *Alboroto y motín*, 56.

87. Ibid.

88. Rabasa has remarked on Sigüenza's combination of historical and ethnographic evidence in light of a more general expropriation of indigenous history in New Spain. See Rabasa, "Pre-Columbian Pasts and Indian Presents in Mexican History," 52–53.

89. For Pietz, the discourse of the fetish "always posits this double consciousness of absorbed credulity and degraded or distanced incredulity. The site of this latter disillusioned judgement by its very nature seems to represent a power of the ultimate degradation and, by implication, of the radical creation of value." William Pietz, "The Problem of the Fetish, I," *Res* 9 (Spring 1985): 14.

90. Whereas before the conquest pulque had been limited to elites and was regulated by rituals, the dissolution of the indigenous elite had relaxed

these restrictions. Seventeenth-century colonial administrators and priests considered pulque drinking to be both a continuation of perverse habits and a sign of the degeneration of indigenous culture after the conquest. Taylor, *Drinking, Homicide, and Rebellion*, 43.

91. Vetancurt, *Teatro mexicano*, 96.
92. Ibid., 95.
93. For a summary of the colonial politics of pulque, see Juan Pedro Viqueira Albán, *Propriety and Permissiveness in Bourbon Mexico*, trans. Sonia Lipsett-Rivera and Sergio Rivera Ayala (Lanham, Md.: SR Books, 1999), 129–52.
94. Vetancurt, *Teatro mexicano*, 98.
95. "Informe que la real universidad y claustro pleno de ella de la ciudad de Mexico de esta Nueva España haze al excellentissimo Señor Virrey de ella en conformidad de orden de Su Excelencia de 3 de julio de este año 1692," fol. 10r.
96. *Oxford English Dictionary*, s.v. monopoly, http://www.oed.com/ (accessed December 19, 2011).
97. Sigüenza y Góngora, *Alboroto y motín*, 55.
98. Ibid.
99. *Oxford English Dictionary*, s.v. evidence, http://www.oed.com/ (accessed December 19, 2011).
100. Silva Prada has recently argued that the "Mouse" (Ratton) was an Indian named Felipe de la Cruz. Based on evidence from another colonial riot not long afterward, Silva Prada suggests that this nickname might have derived from Felipe's astronomically determined animal spirit (*nagual*), noting that "mouse" was also a term used by the Mexica for wartime spies. Silva Prada, *La política de una rebellion*, 269–72.
101. Sigüenza y Góngora, *Alboroto y motín*, 79–80.
102. Carlos de Sigüenza y Góngora, *Parayso occidental, plantado y cultivado por la liberal benefica mano* (Mexico: UNAM/Condumex, 1995), n.p.
103. Sigüenza y Góngora, *Alboroto y motín*, 80.
104. Ibid.
105. Taylor, *Drinking, Homicide, and Rebellion*, 110.
106. E. P. Thompson, *Customs in Common: Studies in Traditional Popular Culture* (New York: New York University Press, 1993), 233–38. In his study of gender and popular culture in eighteenth-century Mexico, for instance, Steve Stern concludes that women's participation in political disturbances was an "ad hoc politics associated with emergencies" that occurred to correct an imbalance or abuse of power within a shared notion of reciprocal obligation. Steve J. Stern, *The Secret History of Gender: Women, Men and Power in Late Colonial Mexico* (Chapel Hill: University of North Carolina Press, 1995), 204. See also Cope, *The Limits of Racial Domination*, 157.
107. Silva Prada, *La política de una rebelión*, 483–86.
108. Taylor, *Drinking, Homicide, and Rebellion*, 53.
109. Ibid.
110. "Informe que la real universidad," fol. 10v.

111. Vetancurt, *Teatro mexicano*, 96.
112. Sigüenza y Góngora, *Alboroto y motín*, 54.
113. Ibid.
114. Ibid., 60.
115. Ibid., 54. According to Cope, the archbishop also asserted that nearly forty thousand people in the city were eating tortillas who had never done so before. Cope, *The Limits of Racial Domination*, 129.
116. Sigüenza y Góngora, *Alboroto y motín*, 55.
117. Ibid.
118. "Tumulto acaecido en la ciudad de México el año de 1692," 237–38.
119. Sigüenza y Góngora, *Alboroto y motín*, 58.
120. Ibid., 59.
121. Ibid., 61.
122. Ibid., 62.
123. Interestingly, in the other anonymous account of the riot the "honest man" in Sigüenza's account appears as a priest whose own authority is sufficient to confirm the veracity of his statement. "Tumulto acaecido en la ciudad de México el año de 1692," 238.
124. The paradox of this response is similar to one in a parable told by Toni Morrison and analyzed by Judith Butler. In Morrison's parable two boys confront a blind woman. Holding out their hands to the woman, the boys say to her, "we have a bird in our hands. Is it dead or alive?" The woman answers them, "I do not know that. But I do know one thing: it's in your hands." As Morrison reads the parable, the bird in the boys' hands is language. Thus, as Butler argues, the woman deflects the violence of the boys' speech by returning to them the responsibility to care for language or to kill it. Judith Butler, *Excitable Speech: A Politics of the Performative* (New York: Routledge, 1997), 10.
125. Cope, *The Limits of Racial Domination*, 18.
126. Perhaps the most iconic image of America as a woman is Jan van der Straet's late sixteenth-century image of Amerigo Vespucci being greeted by a scantily clad woman reclining in a hammock. For a reading of this image, see José Rabasa, *Inventing America: Spanish Historiography and the Formation of Eurocentrism* (Norman: University of Oklahoma Press, 1993), 23–38.
127. Cope, *The Limits of Racial Domination*, 96.
128. As Butler suggests in another context, there are paradoxical speech acts that address forms of social death. In fact, it is the very denial of the terms of life and death that allows these speech acts to constitute politics by positing another form of living. Judith Butler, *Antigone's Claim: Kinship between Life and Death* (New York: Columbia University Press, 2000), 54–55.
129. While Sigüenza does not refer explicitly to the tradition of voluntarism in Spanish imperial right, as he does in his *Theatro de virtudes* (1680), the idea was implicit in his accusation that indigenous subjects were "insolent" and "ungrateful," common topoi in elite reactions to popular disturbances. Carlos de Sigüenza y Góngora, *Theatro de virtudes politicas, que constituyen à un principe* (Mexico: Viuda de Bernardo Calderón, 1680). See Cope, *The Limits of Racial Domination*, 160.

130. Sigüenza y Góngora, *Alboroto y motín*, 65.

131. See Julia Kristeva: "We may call it a border; abjection is above all ambiguity. Because, while releasing a hold, it does not radically cut off the subject from what threatens it—on the contrary, abjection acknowledges it to be in perpetual danger." Julia Kristeva, *Powers of Horror: An Essay on Abjection*, trans. Leon Roudiez (New York: Columbia University Press, 1982), 9.

132. Sigüenza y Góngora, *Alboroto y motín*, 51.

133. Rabasa, "Pre-Columbian Pasts and Indian Presents in Mexican History," 66.

134. Sigüenza y Góngora, *Alboroto y motín*, 72.

135. In this, the 1692 rioters can be distinguished from those of the conspiracy of 1612 in which Africans and mulattoes had supposedly conspired to return to African kingship. Martínez, "The Black Blood of New Spain," pars. 4–5.

136. Sigüenza y Góngora, *Alboroto y motín*, 64–65.

137. Ibid., 65.

138. Ibid., 71.

139. Ibid., 74–75.

140. Ibid., 65. Ross, "*Alboroto y motín de México*: Una noche triste criolla," 185–87.

141. "Tumulto acaecido en la ciudad de México el año de 1692," 242.

142. Sigüenza y Góngora, *Alboroto y motín*, 75.

143. Ibid., 61.

144. Ibid., 120.

145. Ibid., 67.

146. Ibid., 73.

147. Ibid., 77.

148. Ibid., 80.

149. As Cope notes, this unhappy subject appeared in the records simultaneously at various points in the city and was almost surely framed as a ringleader of the riot. Cope also notes the difference between Sigüenza's focus on women and the paucity of women in the trial records but gives little explanation beyond the suggestion that men were apt to consider women passive subjects. Cope, *The Limits of Racial Domination*, 140–41.

150. Giovanni Francesco Gemelli Careri, *Giro del mondo del Dottor D. Gio. Francesco Gemelli Careri*, 6 vols. (Venice: Sebastiano Coleti, 1728), 6: 104.

151. Ibid., 6: 101.

152. Ibid., 6: 114.

153. José Rabasa's reading of Sigüenza's letter analyzes it as an example of what Ranajit Guha calls the "prose of counter-insurgency." Rabasa, "Pre-Columbian Pasts and Indian Presents in Mexican History," 65. See also Ranajit Guha, "The Prose of Counter-Insurgency," in *Selected Subaltern Studies*, ed. Ranajit Guha and Gayatri Chakravorty Spivak (New York: Oxford University Press, 1988).

154. See the Introduction, above, for a reading of the biombo.

CHAPTER 5

1. While referring to the early seventeenth century, what J. H. Elliott calls the "self-perception of decline" in the Spanish Habsburg court applies equally to the end of the century. J. H. Elliott, *Spain and Its World, 1500–1700* (New Haven, Conn.: Yale University Press, 1989), 241–61. For changes in European geopolitics during this period, see J. H. Elliott, *Empires of the Atlantic World: Britain and Spain in America, 1492–1830* (New Haven, Conn.: Yale University Press, 2006), 219–29; Henry Kamen, *Empire: How Spain Became a World Power, 1492–1763* (New York: Harper Collins, 2003), 419–37.

2. David J. Weber, *The Spanish Frontier in North America* (New Haven, Conn.: Yale University Press, 1992), 148–52.

3. Immanuel Wallerstein, *Mercantilism and the Consolidation of the European World-Economy, 1600–1750*, vol. 2 of *The Modern World System*, 3 vols. (New York: Academic Press, 1980), 156–67. See also Richard S. Dunn, *Sugar and Slaves: The Rise of the Planter Class in the English West Indies, 1624–1713* (Chapel Hill: University of North Carolina Press, 1972).

4. For a summary of the use of Spanish and civilian militias in New Spain, see Ben Vinson III, *Bearing Arms for His Majesty: The Free-Colored Militia in Colonial Mexico* (Stanford, Calif.: Stanford University Press, 2001), 8–13. For the defense of the northern frontier, see Elliott, *Empires of the Atlantic World*, 269–72. For the use of regional taxes to pay for the Armada de Barlovento, the royal navy fleet in charge of defending the circum-Caribbean, see Bibiano Torres Ramírez, *La Armada de Barlovento* (Seville: Escuela de Estudios Hispano-Americanos, 1982), 96–97.

5. Antonio Robles, *Diario de Sucesos Notables (1665–1703)*, 2nd ed., 3 vols. (Mexico: Porrúa, 1972), 2: 104, 121, 143–44, 186–87.

6. Iván Escamilla González, "El siglo de oro vindicado: Carlos de Sigüenza y Góngora, el Conde de Galve y el tumulto de 1692," in *Carlos de Sigüenza y Góngora: Homenaje 1700–2000*, ed. Alicia Mayer, 2 vols. (Mexico: UNAM, 2002), 2: 187.

7. The most accessible editions of these works are Carlos de Sigüenza y Góngora, *Libra astronómica y filosófica*, 2nd ed. (Mexico: UNAM, 1984); Carlos de Sigüenza y Góngora, "Infortunios de Alonso Ramírez," in *Seis Obras*, ed. William G. Bryant (Caracas: Ayacucho, 1984); Carlos de Sigüenza y Góngora, "Mercurio volante," in *Seis Obras*, ed. William G. Bryant (Caracas: Ayacucho, 1984); Carlos de Sigüenza y Góngora, "Relación de lo sucedido a la Armada de Barlovento," in *Relaciones históricas*, ed. Manuel Romero de Terreros (Mexico: UNAM, 1940); Carlos de Sigüenza y Góngora, "Trofeo de la justicia española en el castigo de la alevosía francesa," in *Seis obras*, ed. William G. Bryant (Caracas: Ayacucho, 1984).

8. For questions of the narrative's historicity, see J. S. Cummins, "Infortunios de Alonso Ramírez: 'A Just History of Fact'?" *Bulletin of Hispanic Studies* 41, no. 3 (1984).

9. Although many readers have commented on the picaresque structure of the *Infortunios*, the most detailed studies are found in Julie Greer Johnson,

"Picaresque Elements in Carlos Sigüenza y Góngora's *Los Infortunios de Alonso Ramírez*," *Hispania* 64, no. 1 (1981); Aníbal González, "*Los Infortunios de Alonso Ramírez*: Picaresca e historia," *Hispanic Review* 51, no. 2 (1983); Kimberle S. López, "Identity and Alterity in the Emergence of a Creole Discourse: Sigüenza y Góngora's Infortunios de Alonso Ramírez," *Colonial Latin American Review* 5, no. 2 (1996).

10. Kathleen Ross mentions many of these generic influences in "Cuestiones de género en *Infortunios de Alonso Ramírez*," *Revista Iberoamericana* 61, no. 172–73 (1995): 592. Nina Gerrassi-Navarro places the text in the literature of piracy and notes the possible influence of José de Acosta's *The Pilgrimage of Bartolomé Lorenzo* (*Peregrinación de Bartolomé Lorenzo*), a late sixteenth-century narrative that was published in Alonso de Andrade's 1666 compendium of Jesuit lives. Nina Gerrassi-Navarro, *Pirate Novels: Fictions of Nation Building in Spanish America* (Durham, N.C.: Duke University Press, 1999), 62–66. On piracy and the *Infortunios*, see also Ralph Bauer, *The Cultural Geography of Colonial American Literature* (Cambridge: Cambridge University Press, 2003), 175–76. For a comparison to William Dampier's *A New Voyage around the World* (1697), see César Buscaglia-Salgado, *Undoing Empire: Race and Nation in the Mulatto Caribbean* (Minneapolis: University of Minnesota Press, 2003), 132–33.

11. The full title of the text suggests the relative importance of the motifs of Ramírez's captivity and world journey for the narrative: *The misfortunes that Alonso Ramírez, native of the city of San Juan of Puerto Rico, underwent both while in the power of the English Pirates who captured him in the Philippine Islands and while sailing alone, and without direction, until he landed on the coast of the Yucatan: achieving in this way a journey around the World. Described by D. Carlos de Sigüenza y Góngora, Cosmographer, and Professor of Mathematics of the King Our Lord in the Mexican Academy* (*Infortunios que Alonso Ramírez natural de la ciudad de S. Juan de Puerto Rico padeció, assi en poder de ingleses piratas que lo apresaron en las Islas Philipinas como navegando por si solo, y sin derrota, hasta varar en la Costa de Iucatan: Consiguiendo por este medio dar vuelta al Mundo. Descrivelos D. Carlos de Sigüenza y Góngora Cosmographo, y Cathedratico de Mathematicas, del Rey N. Señor en la Academia Mexicana*). Sigüenza y Góngora, "Infortunios de Alonso Ramírez," 3.

12. Ibid., 38.

13. In the *Libra Astrónomica*, published the following year, Sigüenza invokes his titles, not with irony, but as a means to legitimize his studies in the context of his "literary duel" with the Austrian Jesuit Eusebio Kino. Sigüenza y Góngora, *Libra astronómica y filosófica*, 6.

14. The literature that reads the *Infortunios* as an example of Creole assertion has looked most carefully at the relationship between Sigüenza and Ramírez. See, especially, López, "Identity and Alterity in the Emergence of a Creole Discourse"; Mabel Moraña, "Mascara autobiográfica y conciencia criolla en *Infortunios de Alonso Ramírez*, de Carlos de Sigüenza y Góngora," in *Viaje al silencio: Exploraciones del discurso barroco* (Mexico: UNAM, 1998); Carmen de Mora, *Escritura e identidades criollas*:

Modalidades discursivas en la prosa hispanoamericana del siglo XVII (Amsterdam: Rodopi, 2001). See also Bauer, *The Cultural Geography of Colonial American Literature*, 158–59. Recently, in an innovative approach to the same question, Yolanda Martínez San-Miguel has read the silences in the *Infortunios* as a reflection of Ramírez's authorship of the text. Yolanda Martínez-San Miguel, *From Lack to Excess: "Minor" Readings of Latin American Colonial Discourse* (Lewisburg, Pa.: Bucknell University Press, 2008), 145–64.

15. John D. Blanco, "Subjects of Baroque Economy: Creole and Pirate Epistemologies of Mercantilism in the Seventeenth-Century Spanish and Dutch East Indies," *Encounters* 1, no. 1 (2009): 33.

16. *Diccionario de la lengua castellana*, (Madrid, 1729), 575–76.

17. Ralph Bauer reads the *Infortunios* as replacing the system of procurement with the nascent "literary marketplace" of New Spain. To this, one could add the interest and obligations of territorial defense that are suggested by Ramírez's incorporation into the Armada de Barlovento. See Bauer, *The Cultural Geography of Colonial American Literature*, 177–78.

18. Indeed, Maravall links the pícaro's double alienation from both the patria chica and patria grande to a critique of the developing absolutist state in Spain. José Antonio Maravall, *La literatura picaresca desde la historia social (Siglos XVI y XVII)* (Madrid: Taurus, 1986), 48, 260–61.

19. Ibid., 266.
20. Gerassi-Navarro, *Pirate Novels*, 19–22.
21. Ibid., 51–52.
22. Ibid., 17.
23. Ibid., 18.
24. Ibid., 54–55.
25. See Chapter 4.
26. Sigüenza y Góngora, "Trofeo de la justicia española," 51.
27. Carlos de Sigüenza y Góngora, "Carta de 4 de Junio de 1693," in *Documentos inéditos de Don Carlos de Sigüenza y Góngora*, ed. Irving Leonard (Mexico: Centro Bibliográfico Juan José de Eguiara y Eguren, 1963), 99–100.
28. See Chapter 1.
29. Carlos de Sigüenza y Góngora, "Mercurio volante," in *Seis obras*, ed. William G. Bryant (Caracas: Ayacucho, 1984), 146.
30. See Chapter 4.
31. Sigüenza y Góngora, "Mercurio volante," 146.
32. Ibid., 147.
33. Ibid.
34. Ibid., 152.
35. Ibid., 160.
36. It is notable, in this sense, that Sigüenza ends his account with the rescue of sixty-four *genízaro* and mestizo children and the baptism of over two hundred infants. Ibid., 160. As opposed to histories of the Spanish conquest, in which baptism was a foundational moment for colonial society, here Sigüenza represents the children as a part of colonial society that has

been held in "captivity" during Pueblo rule. They, along with the infants, must be brought back into the fold, once again leaving resistant Indians outside.

37. Sigüenza y Góngora, "Infortunios de Alonso Ramírez," 7.

38. For a distinct reading of this "silence," see Martínez-San Miguel, *From Lack to Excess*, 151.

39. Sigüenza y Góngora, "Infortunios de Alonso Ramírez," 7.

40. Ibid., 7–8.

41. For an economic reading of paradise as a Baroque motif, see John Beverley, *Una modernidad obsoleta: Estudios sobre el barroco* (Los Teques: Fondo Editorial ALEM, 1997), 77–94. The representation of a ruined nature in the *Infortunios* parallels shifts in the Caribbean economy.

42. Wallerstein, *Mercantilism*, 161. See also Buscaglia-Salgado, *Undoing Empire*, 128–29.

43. Sigüenza y Góngora, "Infortunios de Alonso Ramírez," 8. In a creative reading of this section of the narrative, César Buscaglia-Salgado argues that Ramírez is fatherless and that even the name Lucas de Villanueva is a playful reference to the marginal fortune seekers who arrived in the Caribbean. Buscaglia-Salgado, *Undoing Empire*, 148.

44. Ramírez's disassociation from his homeland is strikingly different from that of the generic pícaro, however, for whom "stealing" (*hurtar*) becomes a metaphor for this individualism, even a parody of the bond to the homeland. In Mateo de Alemán's picaresque novels on the life of Guzmán de Alfarache, for instance, pícaros are those for whom "the whole world is their common patria, and for whom wherever they find something to steal they will call home" (todo el mundo es patria común, y donde hallan qué hurtar de allí son originarios). Cited in Maravall, *La literatura picaresca*, 262.

45. Sigüenza y Góngora, "Infortunios de Alonso Ramírez," 8.

46. Ibid.

47. Ibid., 9.

48. Ibid.

49. Ibid.

50. Ibid., 10.

51. Ibid.

52. Ibid.

53. Some have found this section to represent the irruption of Sigüenza's voice into the narrative. For a summary of the literature that supports this idea, see Alvaro Félix Bolaños, "Sobre 'relaciones' e identidades en crisis: El 'otro' lado del ex-cautivo Alonso Ramírez," *Revista de Crítica Literaria Latinoamericana* 42, no. 2 (1995): 137.

54. Sigüenza y Góngora, "Infortunios de Alonso Ramírez," 12.

55. Ibid.

56. Ibid.

57. Ibid.

58. Ibid.

59. Wallerstein, *Mercantilism*, 51.

60. Sigüenza y Góngora, "Infortunios de Alonso Ramírez," 12–13.

61. Ibid., 14.

62. For divergent readings on the question of whether or not Ramírez actually remained loyal to Spain during his period of captivity, see Martínez-San Miguel, *From Lack to Excess*, 154.

63. Sigüenza y Góngora, "Infortunios de Alonso Ramírez," 14–15.

64. Ibid., 15.

65. Ibid.

66. Ibid.

67. Ibid.

68. Ibid.

69. Among Sigüenza's recommendations for the settlement of Pensacola Bay is that the Spanish take with them objects of little value to trade with the Indians of Florida in order to "pacify" them. Sigüenza y Góngora, "Carta de 4 de Junio de 1693," 98.

70. Sigüenza y Góngora, "Infortunios de Alonso Ramírez," 16.

71. For the cultural meanings of cannibalism in early colonial texts, see Peter Hulme, *Colonial Encounters: Europe and the Native Caribbean, 1492–1797* (London: Methuen, 1986), 13–43; Neil Whitehead, "Hans Staden and the Cultural Politics of Cannibalism," *Hispanic American Historical Review* 80, no. 4 (2001): 733.

72. Sigüenza y Góngora, "Infortunios de Alonso Ramírez," 17.

73. Ibid.

74. Both Mabel Moraña and Yolanda Martínez San-Miguel, for instance, have noted the anxiety that the Sevillian renegade, Miguel, causes for Ramírez. Moraña, "Mascara autobiográfica," 223–24; Martínez-San Miguel, *From Lack to Excess*, 159–60.

75. Blanco, "Subjects of Baroque Economy," 41.

76. Richard Tuck, *Natural Rights Theories: Their Origin and Development* (Cambridge: Cambridge University Press, 1979), 60.

77. See, for instance, Bauer, *The Cultural Geography of Colonial American Literature*, 174.

78. Sigüenza y Góngora, "Infortunios de Alonso Ramírez," 19.

79. Ibid., 20.

80. Ibid.

81. See Robin Blackburn, *The Making of New World Slavery: From the Baroque to the Modern, 1492–1800*, 2nd ed. (London: Verso, 2010), 177–80, for a summary of early modern debates about voluntary slavery and captivity justified by war.

82. Sigüenza y Góngora, "Infortunios de Alonso Ramírez," 21.

83. Ibid., 20. See Bauer, *The Cultural Geography of Colonial American Literature*, 174.

84. Sigüenza y Góngora, "Infortunios de Alonso Ramírez," 21–22.

85. Ibid., 22.

86. See Ross, "Cuestiones de Género en *Infortunios de Alonso Ramírez*," 596–97, in which she argues that the scene evokes a "multiracial society." Buscaglia-Salgado also discusses the racial implications of the crew, finding in the list a fear of "disorder." Buscaglia-Salgado, *Undoing Empire*, 165–66.

87. Sigüenza y Góngora, "Infortunios de Alonso Ramírez," 23.
88. Ibid.
89. Ibid., 25.
90. Ibid., 26.
91. Ibid.
92. Ibid.
93. Ibid., 31.
94. Ibid., 29.
95. Ibid., 32.
96. Ibid.
97. Ibid.
98. Ross, "Cuestiones de Género en *Infortunios de Alonso Ramírez*," 600–601.
99. Sigüenza y Góngora, "Infortunios de Alonso Ramírez," 34.
100. Ibid., 33.
101. Ibid., 36.
102. Ibid.
103. Ibid., 37.
104. Ibid., 38.
105. Sigüenza y Góngora, "Trofeo de la justicia española," 60.
106. Ibid., 77.
107. Sigüenza y Góngora, "Infortunios de Alonso Ramírez," 38.
108. I have analyzed the rhetoric of Sigüenza's 1691 *Libra astronómica* in Anna More, "Cosmopolitanism and Scientific Reason in New Spain: Sigüenza y Góngora and the Dispute over the 1680 Comet," in *Science in the Spanish and Portuguese Empires, 1500–1800*, ed. Daniela Bleichmar et al. (Stanford, Calif.: Stanford University Press, 2009). Sigüenza's response to an attack on the accuracy of his maps of Pensacola Bay is found in Francisco Pérez Salazar, *Biografía de D. Carlos de Sigüenza y Góngora* (Mexico: Antigua Imprenta de Murguia, 1928), 119–60.
109. Irving Leonard, "Informe de Don Carlos de Sigüenza y Góngora sobre el castillo de San Juan de Ulúa (1695)," *Revista de Historia de América* 45 (1958): 141.
110. See Carlos de Sigüenza y Góngora, "Descripción que de la Bahía de Santa María de Galve (Antes Panzacola)," in *Documentos inéditos de Don Carlos de Sigüenza y Góngora*, ed. Irving Leonard (Mexico: Centro Bibliográfico Juan José de Eguiara y Eguren, 1963), 72; Sigüenza y Góngora, "Carta de 4 de Junio de 1693," 100.
111. Mitchell Codding, "Perfecting the Geography of New Spain: Alzate and the Cartographic Legacy of Sigüenza y Góngora," *Colonial Latin American Review* 3, no. 1–2 (1994): 188–201; Elías Trabulse, "La obra cartográfica de Don Carlos de Sigüenza y Góngora," *Caravelle* 76–77 (2001): 269–70.
112. José Alzate y Ramírez, *Gacetas de literatura de México*, 4 vols. (Puebla: Manuel Buen Abad, 1831), 4: 124–26.
113. Giovanni Francesco Gemelli Careri, *Giro del mondo del Dottor D. Gio. Francesco Gemelli Careri*, 6 vols. (Venice: Sebastiano Coleti, 1728), 6: 34–35.

114. Codding, "Perfecting the Geography of New Spain," 210–11.

115. In fact, Sigüenza most likely reworked Boot's earlier map around 1691, as part of his contribution to the project to drain Lake Texcoco. Irving A. Leonard, *Don Carlos de Sigüenza y Góngora: A Mexican Savant of the Seventeenth Century* (Berkeley: University of California Press, 1929), 85.

116. See More, "Cosmopolitanism and Scientific Reason in New Spain."

117. See particularly the almanac for 1694. José Miguel Quintana, *La astrología en la Nueva España en el siglo XVII (de Enrico Martínez a Sigüenza y Góngora)* (Mexico: Bibliófilos mexicanos, 1969), 242. See also Anna More, "Thinking with the Inquisition: Heretical Science and Popular Knowledge in Seventeenth-Century Mexico," *Romanic Review*, forthcoming.

CONCLUSION

1. Antonio Robles, *Diario de sucesos notables (1665–1703)*, 2nd ed., 3 vols. (Mexico: Porrúa, 1972), 3: 106–7.

2. The Jesuits Lorenzo Boturini Benaduci and Francisco Clavijero both commented on Sigüenza's collection, as did José Eguiara y Eguren, cited below. See Ernest J. Burrus, "Clavigero and the Lost Sigüenza Manuscripts," *Estudios de Cultura Nahuatl* 1 (1959): 64–68.

3. Of Sigüenza's main twentieth-century biographers, cited in the Introduction, note 74, above, Irving Leonard was most strident in his rejection of Baroque poetics. Pérez Salazar and Rojas Garcidueñas both emphasized Sigüenza's patriotism.

4. Recent full-length studies of Sigüenza's works have all justified Sigüenza's style as a reflection either of his erudite religiosity or his Creole identity. For examples of the former, see Alicia Mayer, *Dos americanos, dos pensamientos* (Mexico: UNAM, 1998); Antonio Lorente Medina, *La prosa de Sigüenza y Góngora y la formación de la conciencia criolla mexicana* (Mexico: Fondo de Cultura Económica, 1996). For an example of the latter, see Kathleen Ross, *The Baroque Narrative of Carlos de Sigüenza y Góngora: A New World Paradise* (Cambridge: Cambridge University Press, 1993).

5. Carlos de Sigüenza y Góngora, *Parayso occidental, plantado y cultivado por la liberal benefica mano* (1684; reprint, Mexico: UNAM/Condumex, 1995), n.p.

6. Ibid.

7. See Christopher Johnson for an argument that the Augustinian play between obscurity as a means to allegorical truths and clarity for communicating these to a greater public underlay seventeenth-century debates on Gongoresque poetics. Christopher Johnson, "De Doctrina Gongorina: Góngora's Defence of Obscurity," *Bulletin of Hispanic Studies* 77 (2000): 24.

8. Sigüenza y Góngora, *Parayso occidental, plantado y cultivado por la liberal benefica mano*, n.p.

9. Robles, *Diario de sucesos notables (1665–1703)*, 107.

10. Carlos de Sigüenza y Góngora, "Testamento de Don Carlos de Sigüenza y Góngora," in *Biografía de Don Carlos de Sigüenza y Góngora*,

seguida de varios documentos inéditos, ed. Francisco Pérez Salazar (Mexico: Robredo, 1928), 190.

11. Ibid., 162–68.
12. Ibid., 169–70.
13. Ibid., 170.
14. Ibid.
15. Ibid., 171.
16. Ibid.
17. Jaime Cuadriello, "Moctezuma through the Centuries," in *Race and Classification: The Case of Mexican America*, ed. Ilona Katzew and Susan Deans Smith (Stanford, Calif.: Stanford University Press, 2009), 133.
18. For Sigüenza's strongest expression of devotion to the Jesuits, see Carlos de Sigüenza y Góngora, *Libra astronómica y filosófica*, 2nd ed. (Mexico: UNAM, 1984), 1. See also Anna More, "Cosmopolitanism and Scientific Reason in New Spain: Sigüenza y Góngora and the Dispute over the 1680 Comet," in *Science in the Spanish and Portuguese Empires, 1500–1800*, ed. Daniela Bleichmar et al. (Stanford, Calif.: Stanford University Press, 2009), 125–26.
19. Juan José de Eguiara y Eguren, *Historia de sabios novohispanos* (Mexico: UNAM, 1998), 142.
20. Burrus, "Clavigero and the Lost Sigüenza Manuscripts," 64–72.
21. This had remained unedited, he asserted, because Sigüenza himself had believed that it contained astronomical errors. Carlos de Sigüenza y Góngora, *Oriental planeta evangélico* (Madrid: Iberoamericana; Frankfurt am Main: Vervuert, 2008), 81.
22. Ibid., 82.
23. Ibid., 84.
24. Ibid., 85.
25. Cited in Antony Higgins, *Constructing the Criollo Archive* (West Lafayette, Ind.: Purdue University Press, 2000), 100–101.
26. Aside from the scholars listed in note 2 above, Alexander von Humboldt also commented on Sigüenza's science, a knowledge of which he came to through the work of José Antonio Alzate. See Alexander von Humboldt, *Political Essay on the Kingdom of New Spain*, trans. John Black, 2 vols. (London: Longman, 1811), 1: xcvi.
27. Elías Trabulse, *Los manuscritos perdidos de Sigüenza y Góngora* (Mexico: Colegio de Mexico, 1988), 27.
28. See the introduction, note 90 above, for studies that have worked against the rigid division between studies of seventeenth- and eighteenth-century writings in Spain and Spanish America.

BIBLIOGRAPHY

Acosta, Joseph de. *Historia natural y moral de las Indias*. 2nd ed. Mexico: Fondo de Cultura Económica, 1962.

Adelman, Jeremy. *Sovereignty and Revolution in the Iberian Atlantic*. Princeton, N.J.: Princeton University Press, 2006.

Adorno, Rolena. "Arms, Letters and the Native Historian in Early Colonial Mexico." In *1492–1992: Re/Discovering Colonial Writing*, edited by René Jara and Nicholas Spadaccini, 201–24. Minneapolis: Prisma Institute, 1992.

———. "The Indigenous Ethnographer: The 'Indio Ladino' as Historian and Cultural Mediation." In *Implicit Understandings: Observing, Reporting and Reflecting on the Encounters between Europeans and Other Peoples in the Early Modern Era*, edited by Stuart B. Schwartz, 378–402. Cambridge: Cambridge University Press, 1994.

———. *The Polemics of Possession in Spanish American Narrative*. New Haven, Conn.: Yale University Press, 2007.

Ahern, Maureen. "Visual and Verbal Sites: The Construction of Jesuit Martyrdom in Northwest New Spain in Andres Pérez de Ribas' *Historia de los triumphos de nuestra Santa Fee* (1645)." *Colonial Latin American Review* 8, no. 1 (1999): 7–33.

Alberro, Solange. *El águila y la cruz: Orígenes religiosos de la conciencia criolla, México, siglos XVI–XVII*. Mexico: El Colegio de México, Fedeicomiso Historia de las Américas, and Fondo de Cultura Económica, 1999.

———. "Imagen y fiesta barroca: Nueva España, siglos XVI–XVII." In *Barrocos y modernos: Nuevos caminos en la investigación del barroco iberoamericano*, edited by Petra Schumm, 33–48. Madrid: Iberoamericana; Frankfurt am Main: Vervuert, 1998.

———. "La emergencia de la conciencia criolla: El caso novohispano." In *Agencias criollas: La ambigüedad "colonial" en las letras hispanoamer-

icanas, edited by José Antonio Mazzotti, 55–71. Pittsburgh: Instituto Internacional de Literatura Latinoamericana, 2000.

Allen, Don Cameron. *Mysteriously Meant: The Rediscovery of Pagan Symbolism and Allegorical Interpretation in the Renaissance*. Baltimore: Johns Hopkins University Press, 1970.

Alonso, Damaso. *Góngora y el "Polifemo."* Madrid: Gredos, 1961.

Alzate y Ramírez, José. *Gacetas de literatura de México*. 4 vols. Puebla: Manuel Buen Abad, 1831. Vol. 4.

Anderson, Benedict. *Imagined Communities: Reflections on the Origin and Spread of Nationalism*. 2nd ed. London: Verso, 1991.

Archivo General de Indias, Seville. Patronato 226, no. 1.

Armitage, David. Introduction to *The Free Sea*, by Hugo Grotius. Indianapolis: Liberty Fund, 2004.

Arrom, José. *Certidumbre de América: Estudios de letras, folklore y cultura*. Madrid: Gredos, 1971.

Bacon, Francis. *Francis Bacon: The Major Works*. Oxford: Oxford University Press, 1996.

Balbuena, Bernardo de. *Grandeza mexicana*. Mexico: UNAM, 1992.

Balibar, Etienne, and Immanuel Wallerstein. *Race, Nation, Class: Ambiguous Identities*. Translated by Chris Turner. London: Verso, 1991.

Baudot, Georges. *Utopia and History in Mexico: The First Chroniclers of Mexican Civilization (1520–1569)*. Translated by Bernard R. Ortiz de Montellano and Thelma Ortiz de Montellano. Niwot: University Press of Colorado, 1995.

Bauer, Ralph. *The Cultural Geography of Colonial American Literature*. Cambridge: Cambridge University Press, 2003.

Bauer, Ralph, and José Antonio Mazzotti. Introduction to *Creole Subjects in the Colonial Americas*, edited by Ralph Bauer and José Antonio Mazzotti, 1–57. Chapel Hill: University of North Carolina Press, 2009.

Becerra Tanco, Luis. "Origen milagroso del santuario de Nuestra Señora de Guadalupe." In *Testimonios históricos guadalupanos*, edited by Ernesto de la Torre Villar and Ramiro Navarro de Anda, 309–33. Mexico: Fondo de Cultura Económica, 1982.

Benítez Grobet, Laura. "El nacionalismo en Carlos de Sigüenza y Góngora." *Estudios de Historia Novohispana* 8 (1985): 203–23.

———. *La idea de historia en Carlos de Sigüenza y Góngora*. Mexico: UNAM, 1982.

Benjamin, Walter. *The Origins of German Tragic Drama*. Translated by John Osborne. London: New Left Books, 1977.

Bernal, Ignacio. *A History of Mexican Archaeology.* London: Thames and Hudson, 1980.

Beverley, John. *Against Literature.* Minneapolis: University of Minnesota Press, 1993.

———. *Essays on the Literary Baroque in Spain and Spanish America.* Woodbridge, England: Tamesis, 2008.

———. "Going Baroque?" *boundary 2* 15, no. 3 (1988): 27–39.

———. *Una modernidad obsoleta: Estudios sobre el barroco.* Los Teques: Fondo Editorial ALEM, 1997.

Bhabha, Homi K. *The Location of Culture.* London: Routledge, 1994.

Blackburn, Robin. *The Making of New World Slavery: From the Baroque to the Modern, 1492–1800.* 2nd ed. London: Verso, 2010.

Blanco, John D. "Subjects of Baroque Economy: Creole and Pirate Epistemologies of Mercantilism in the Seventeenth-Century Spanish and Dutch East Indies." *Encounters* 1, no. 1 (2009): 27–61.

Bolaños, Alvaro Félix. "Sobre 'relaciones' e identidades en crisis: El 'Otro' lado del ex-cautivo Alonso Ramírez." *Revista de Crítica Literaria Latinoamericana* 42, no. 2 (1995): 131–60.

Boone, Elizabeth. *Incarnations of the Aztec Supernatural: The Image of Huitzilopochtli in Mexico and Europe.* Philadelphia: American Philosophical Society, 1989.

Borah, Woodrow. *Justice by Insurance: The General Indian Court of Colonial Mexico and the Legal Aides of the Half-Real.* Berkeley: University of California Press, 1983.

Borja, Juan de. *Empresas morales.* Madrid: Fundación Universitaria Española, 1981.

Brading, D. A. *The First America: The Spanish Monarchy, Creole Patriots, and the Liberal State, 1492–1867.* Cambridge: Cambridge University Press, 1991.

———. *Mexican Phoenix: Our Lady of Guadalupe: Image and Tradition across Five Centuries.* Cambridge: Cambridge University Press, 2001.

Bredekamp, Horst. *The Lure of Antiquity and the Cult of the Machine: The Kunstkammer and the Evolution of Nature, Art and Technology.* Translated by Allison Brown. Princeton, N.J.: Markus Wiener, 1995.

Buck-Morss, Susan. *The Dialectics of Seeing: Walter Benjamin and the Arcades Project.* Cambridge, Mass.: Massachusetts Institute of Technology Press, 1989.

Burrus, Ernest J. "Clavigero and the Lost Sigüenza Manuscripts." *Estudios de Cultura Nahuatl* 1 (1959): 59–90.

———. "Sigüenza y Góngora's Efforts for Readmission into the Jesuit Order." *Hispanic American Historical Review* 33 (1953): 387–91.

Buscaglia-Salgado, César. *Undoing Empire: Race and Nation in the Mulatto Caribbean*. Minneapolis: University of Minnesota Press, 2003.

Butler, Judith. *Antigone's Claim: Kinship between Life and Death*. New York: Columbia University Press, 2000.

———. *Excitable Speech: A Politics of the Performative*. New York: Routledge, 1997.

Buxó, José Pascual. *El resplandor intelectual de las imágenes: Estudios de emblemática y literatura novohispana*. Mexico: Oak Editorial, 2001.

———. "El resplandor intelectual de las imágenes: Jeroglífica y emblemática." In *Juegos de ingenio y agudeza: La pintura emblemática de la Nueva España*, edited by Ana Laura Cue, 30–54. Mexico: Museo Nacional de Arte, 1994.

———. "Función política de los emblemas en el *Neptuno Alegórico* de Sor Juana Inés de la Cruz." In *Sor Juana Inés de la Cruz y sus contemporáneos*, edited by Margo Glantz, 245–55. Mexico: Facultad de Filosofía y Letras, UNAM, and Centro de Estudios de Historia de México, Condumex, 1998.

Calancha, Antonio. *Crónica moralizada*. 6 vols. Lima: Universidad Nacional Mayor de San Marcos, 1981.

Cañeque, Alejandro. *The King's Living Image: The Culture and Politics of Viceregal Power in Colonial Mexico*. New York: Routledge, 2004.

Cañizares-Esguerra, Jorge. *How to Write the History of the New World: Histories, Epistemologies, and Identities in the Eighteenth-Century Atlantic World*. Stanford, Calif.: Stanford University Press, 2001.

———. *Puritan Conquistadors: Iberianizing the Atlantic, 1550–1700*. Stanford, Calif.: Stanford University Press, 2006.

Carreira, Antonio. "Pros y contras de la influencia gongorina en el *Triunfo parténico* (1683) de Sigüenza y Góngora." In *Homenaje a Henri Guerreiro: La hagiografía entre la historia y literatura en España de la edad media y del siglo de oro*, edited by Marc Vitse, 347–64. Madrid: Iberoamericana; Frankfurt am Main: Vervuert, 2005.

Cascardi, Anthony J. *Ideologies of History in the Spanish Golden Age*. University Park: Pennsylvania State University Press, 1997.

Castañeda de la Paz, María. *Pintura de la peregrinación de los Culhuaque-Mexitin (El Mapa de Sigüenza)*. Mexico: Conaculta-INAH, 2006.

Castillo, David. "Horror (Vacui): The Baroque Condition." In *Hispanic Baroques: Reading Cultures in Context*, edited by Nicholas Spadaccini and Luis Martín-Estudillo, 87–104. Nashville: Vanderbilt University Press, 2005.

Cervantes de Salazar, Francisco. *Life in the Imperial and Loyal City of Mexico in New Spain*. Translated by Minnie Lee Barrett Shepard. Austin: University of Texas Press, 1953.

Chatterjee, Partha. *The Nation and Its Fragments: Colonial and Postcolonial Histories*. Princeton, N.J.: Princeton University Press, 1993.

Christian, William A. *Apparitions in Late Medieval and Renaissance Spain*. Princeton, N.J.: Princeton University Press, 1981.

Codding, Mitchell. "Perfecting the Geography of New Spain: Alzate and the Cartographic Legacy of Sigüenza y Góngora." *Colonial Latin American Review* 3, no. 1–2 (1994): 185–219.

Collard, Andrée. *Nueva poesia: Conceptismo, culteranismo en la crítica española*. Madrid: Castalia, 1971.

Cope, R. Douglas. *The Limits of Racial Domination: Plebeian Society in Colonial Mexico City, 1660–1720*. Madison: University of Wisconsin Press, 1994.

Cortés, Hernán. *Cartas de relación*. Madrid: Castalia, 1993.

Cortés Castellanos, Justino. *El catecismo en pictogramas de Fray Pedro de Gante*. Madrid: Fundación Universitaria Española, 1987.

Covarrubias, Sebastián de. *Tesoro de la lengua castellana o española*. 1611. Reprint, Barcelona: S. A. Horta, 1943.

Cruz, Sor Juana Inés de la. "Neptuno alegórico, océano de colores, simulacro político." In vol. 4 of *Obras completas de Sor Juana Inés de la Cruz*, edited by Alberto Salceda, 355–411. 4 vols. Mexico: Fondo de Cultura Económica, 1957.

Cuadriello, Jaime. "El origen del reino y la configuración de su empresa: Episodios y alegorías de triunfo y fundación." In *Los pinceles de la historia: El origen del reino de la Nueva España, 1680–1750*, edited by Jaime Soler Frost, 50–107. Mexico: Museo Nacional de Arte, 1999.

———. "Moctezuma through the Centuries." In *Race and Classification: The Case of Mexican America*, edited by Ilona Katzew and Susan Deans Smith, 119–50. Stanford, Calif.: Stanford University Press, 2009.

Cummins, J. S. "Infortunios de Alonso Ramírez: 'A Just History of Fact'?" *Bulletin of Hispanic Studies* 41, no. 3 (1984): 295–303.

Curcio-Nagy, Linda. "Giants and Gypsies: Corpus Christi in Colonial Mexico City." In *Rituals of Rule, Rituals of Resistance*, edited by William H. Beezley, Cheryl English Martin, and William E. French, 1–26. Wilmington, Del.: Scholarly Resources, 1994.

———. *The Great Festivals of Colonial Mexico City: Performing Power and Identity*. Albuquerque: University of New Mexico Press, 2004.

Dean, Carolyn. *Inka Bodies and the Body of Christ: Corpus Christi in Colonial Cuzco, Peru*. Durham, N.C.: Duke University Press, 1999.

Deleuze, Gilles. *The Fold: Leibniz and the Baroque*. Translated by Tom Conley. Minneapolis: University of Minnesota Press, 1993.

Delgado, Jaime. "Estudio preliminar." In *Piedad heroyca de Don Fernando Cortés*, by Carlos de Sigüenza y Góngora, xi–cviii. Madrid: José Porrúa Turranzas, 1940.

Derrida, Jacques. *Archive Fever: A Freudian Impression*. Translated by Eric Prenowitz. Chicago: University of Chicago Press, 1996.

Diccionario de la lengua castellana. Madrid, 1729. http://buscon.rae.es/ntlle/SrvltGUILoginNtlle (accessed December 19, 2011).

Diccionario de la lengua castellana. Madrid, 1734. http://buscon.rae.es/ntlle/SrvltGUILoginNtlle (accessed December 19, 2011).

Diccionario de la lengua castellana. Madrid, 1739. http://buscon.rae.es/ntlle/SrvltGUILoginNtlle (accessed December 19, 2011).

Doesburg, Van. "Review: Castañeda de la Paz, María: Pintura de la peregrinación de los Culhuaque-Mexitin (El Mapa de Sigüenza)." *Anuario de Estudios Americanos* 65, no. 2 (2008): 315–23.

Duarte, Manuel. "El apóstol Santo Tomás en el Nuevo Mundo." In *Biblioteca mexicana del siglo XVIII*, edited by Nicolás León, 353–532. *Boletín del Instituto Bibliográfico Mexicano*, 7. Mexico: La viuda de Francisco Díaz León, 1906.

Dunn, Richard S. *Sugar and Slaves: The Rise of the Planter Class in the English West Indies, 1624–1713*. Chapel Hill: University of North Carolina Press, 1972.

Egginton, William. "Corporeal Image and the New World Baroque." *South Atlantic Quarterly* 106, no. 1 (2007): 107–27.

———. "Of Baroque Holes and Baroque Folds." In *Hispanic Baroques: Reading Cultures in Context*, edited by Nicholas Spadaccini and Luis Martín-Estudillo, 55–69. Nashville: Vanderbilt University Press, 2005.

Eguiara y Eguren, Juan José de. *Biblioteca mexicana*. Translated by Benjamín Fernández Valenzuela. Mexico: UNAM, 1986.

———. *Historia de sabios novohispanos*. Mexico: UNAM, 1998.

Elliott, J. H. "Concerto Barroco." *New York Review of Books* 34, no. 6 (1987).

———. *Empires of the Atlantic World: Britain and Spain in America, 1492–1830*. New Haven, Conn.: Yale University Press, 2006.

———. *Imperial Spain, 1469–1716*. London: Penguin, 1963.

———. "Spain and America in the Sixteenth and Seventeenth Centuries." In

The Cambridge History of Latin America, edited by Leslie Bethell, 287–339. Cambridge: Cambridge University Press, 1984.

———. *Spain and Its World, 1500–1700*. New Haven, Conn.: Yale University Press, 1989.

Escamilla González, Iván. "El siglo de oro vindicado: Carlos de Sigüenza y Góngora, el Conde de Galve y el tumulto de 1692." In *Carlos de Sigüenza y Góngora: Homenaje 1700–2000*, edited by Alicia Mayer, 2: 179–204. 2 vols. Mexico: UNAM, 2002.

Fee, Nancy. "*La Entrada Angelopolitana:* Ritual and Myth in the Viceregal Entry in Puebla de Los Angeles." *The Americas* 52, no. 3 (1996): 283–320.

Findlen, Paula. "A Jesuit's Books in the New World: Athanasius Kircher and His American Readers." In *Athanasius Kircher: The Last Man Who Knew Everything*, edited by Paula Findlen, 329–64. New York: Routledge, 2004.

———, ed. *Athanasius Kircher: The Last Man Who Knew Everything*. New York: Routledge, 2004.

———. *Possessing Nature: Museums, Collecting, and Scientific Culture in Early Modern Italy*. Berkeley: University of California Press, 1994.

———. "Scientific Spectacle in Baroque Rome: Athanasius Kircher and the Roman College Museum." In *Jesuit Science and the Republic of Letters*, edited by Mordechai Feingold, 225–84. Cambridge, Mass.: Massachusetts Institute of Technology Press, 2003.

Fletcher, Angus. *Allegory: The Theory of a Symbolic Mode*. Ithaca, N.Y.: Cornell University Press, 1964.

Florencia, Francisco de. *La estrella de el norte de México*. Mexico: Antonio Velazquez, a costa del dicho D. Juan Leonardo, 1741.

Foucault, Michel. *The Archaeology of Knowledge*. Translated by A. M. Sheridan Smith. New York: Pantheon Books, 1972.

———. "Governmentality." In *Power*, edited by James D. Faubion, translated by Robert Hurley, 201–22. Vol. 3 of *Essential Works of Foucault, 1954–1984*. 3 vols. New York: New Press, 2000.

———. "'Omnes et Singulatim': Toward a Critique of Political Reason." In *Power*, edited by James D. Faubion, translated by Robert Hurley, 298–325. Vol. 3 of *Essential Works of Foucault, 1954–1984*. 3 vols. New York: New Press, 2000.

———. "Society Must Be Defended:" Lectures at the Collège de France, 1975–76*. Translated by David Macey. New York: Picador, 2003.

Fox, Dian. *Kings in Calderón: A Study in Characterization and Political Theory*. London: Tamesis, 1986.

Fuchs, Barbara. *Exotic Nation: Maurophilia and the Early Modern Construction of Spain*. Philadelphia: University of Pennsylvania Press, 2009.

García Pabón, Leonardo. "Sleeping with Corpses, Eating Hearts and Walking Skulls: *Criollo's* [sic] Subjectivity in Antonio de la Calancha and Bartolomé Arzans de Orsúa y Vela." In *Hispanic Baroques: Reading Cultures in Context*, edited by Nicholas Spadaccini and Luis Martín-Estudillo, 222–38. Nashville: Vanderbilt University Press, 2005.

Gemelli Careri, Giovanni Francesco. *A Collection of Voyages and Travels*. London: Awnsham and John Churchill, 1704.

———. *Giro del mondo del Dottor D. Gio. Francesco Gemelli Careri*. 6 vols. Venice: Sebastiano Coleti, 1728. Vol. 6.

Gerassi-Navarro, Nina. *Pirate Novels: Fictions of Nation Building in Spanish America*. Durham, N.C.: Duke University Press, 1999.

Gibson, Charles. "The Aztec Aristocracy in Colonial Mexico." *Comparative Studies in Society and History* 2, no. 2 (1960): 169–96.

———. *The Aztecs under Spanish Rule*. Stanford, Calif.: Stanford University Press, 1964.

Gilman, Stephen. "An Introduction to the Ideology of the Baroque in Spain." *Symposium* 1, no. 1 (1946): 82–107.

Gonzalbo Aizpuru, Pilar. *Historia de la educación en la epoca colonial: La educación de los criollos y la vida urbana*. Mexico: El Colegio de México, 1990.

———. *La educación popular de los Jesuitas*. Mexico: Universidad Iberoamericana, 1989.

———. "La influencia de la Compañía de Jesus en la sociedad novohispana del siglo XVI." *Historia Mexicana* 32, no. 2 (1982): 262–81.

———. "Las fiestas novohispanas: Espectáculo y ejemplo." *Mexican Studies/Estudios Mexicanos* 9, no. 1 (1993): 19–45.

González, Aníbal. "*Los Infortunios de Alonso Ramírez*: Picaresca e historia." *Hispanic Review* 51, no. 2 (1983): 189–204.

González Echevarría, Roberto. *Celestina's Brood: Continuities of the Baroque in Spanish and Latin American Literature*. Durham, N.C.: Duke University Press, 1993.

———. *Myth and Archive: A Theory of Latin American Narrative*. Durham, N.C.: Duke University Press, 1998.

Gracián, Baltasar. *Agudeza y arte de ingenio*. Mexico: UNAM, 1996.

Greer Johnson, Julie. "Picaresque Elements in Carlos Sigüenza y Góngora's *Los Infortunios de Alonso Ramírez*." *Hispania* 64, no. 1 (1981): 60–67.

Gruzinski, Serge. *The Conquest of Mexico: The Incorporation of Indian Societies into the Western World, 16th–18th Centuries*. Translated by Eileen Corrigan. Cambridge: Polity, 1993.

———. *Images at War: Mexico from Columbus to Blade Runner (1492–*

Bibliography

2019). Translated by Heather Maclean. Durham, N.C.: Duke University Press, 2001.

Guha, Ranajit. "The Prose of Counter-Insurgency." In *Selected Subaltern Studies*, edited by Ranajit Guha and Gayatri Chakravorty Spivak, 45–86. New York: Oxford University Press, 1988.

Hanke, Lewis. *The Spanish Struggle for Justice in the Conquest of America*. Boston: Little, Brown, 1965.

Hanks, William F. *Converting Words: Maya in the Age of the Cross*. Berkeley: University of California Press, 2010.

Hanssen, Beatrice. *Walter Benjamin's Other History: Of Stones, Animals, Human Beings, and Angels*. Berkeley: University of California Press, 1998.

Herzog, Tamar. *Defining Nations: Immigrants and Citizens in Early Modern Spain and Spanish America*. New Haven, Conn.: Yale University Press, 2003.

Higgins, Antony. *Constructing the Criollo Archive*. West Lafayette, Ind.: Purdue University Press, 2000.

Hill, Ruth. *Sceptres and Sciences in the Spains*. Liverpool: Liverpool University Press, 2000.

Hobsbawm, Eric. "Introduction: Inventing Traditions." In *The Invention of Tradition*, edited by Eric Hobsbawm and Terence Ranger, 1–14. Cambridge: Cambridge University Press, 1992.

Houaiss, Antônio, and Mauro de Salles Villar. *Diccionário Houiass da Língua Portuguesa*. Rio de Janeiro: Editorial Objetiva, 2001.

Hulme, Peter. *Colonial Encounters: Europe and the Native Caribbean, 1492–1797*. London: Methuen, 1986.

Humboldt, Alexander von. *Political Essay on the Kingdom of New Spain*. Translated by John Black. 2 vols. London: Longman, 1811. Vol. 1.

"Informe que la real universidad y claustro pleno de ella de la ciudad de Mexico de esta Nueva España haze al Excellentissimo Señor Virrey de ella en conformidad de orden de su Excelencia de 3 de julio de este año 1692." Ms. B692-M611i. John Carter Brown Library.

Israel, J. I. *Race, Class and Politics in Colonial Mexico, 1610–1670*. Oxford: Oxford University Press, 1975.

Ixtlilxochitl, Fernando Alva de. *Obras históricas*. 2 vols. Mexico: UNAM, 1975.

Johnson, Christopher. "De Doctrina Gongorina: Góngora's Defence of Obscurity." *Bulletin of Hispanic Studies* 77 (2000): 21–46.

———. *Hyperboles: The Rhetoric of Excess in Baroque Literature and Thought*. Cambridge, Mass.: Harvard University Press, 2010.

Kagan, Richard. *Urban Images of the Hispanic World, 1493–1793.* New Haven, Conn.: Yale University Press, 2000.

Kamen, Henry. *Empire: How Spain Became a World Power, 1492–1763.* New York: Harper Collins, 2003.

———. *Spain in the Later Seventeenth Century, 1665–1700.* London: Longman, 1980.

Kantorowicz, Ernst K. *The King's Two Bodies: A Study in Mediaeval Political Theology.* Princeton, N.J.: Princeton University Press, 1957.

Kristeva, Julia. *Powers of Horror: An Essay on Abjection.* Translated by Leon Roudiez. New York: Columbia University Press, 1982.

Lafaye, Jacques. *Quetzalcóatl and Guadalupe: The Formation of Mexican National Consciousness.* Translated by Benjamin Keen. Chicago: University of Chicago Press, 1976.

Langer, Ullrich. "Invention." In *The Cambridge History of Literary Criticism,* edited by Glyn P. Norton, 136–44. Cambridge: Cambridge University Press, 1999.

Laso de la Vega, Luis. *The Story of Guadalupe: Luis Laso de la Vega's Hui Tlamahuiçoltica of 1649.* Stanford, Calif.: Stanford University Press/ UCLA Latin American Center Publications, 1998.

Lavallé, Bernard. *Las promesas ambiguas: Ensayos sobre el criollismo colonial en los Andes.* Lima: Instituto Riva-Agüero, 1993.

Ledezma, Domingo. "Una legitimación imaginativa del nuevo mundo: *La Historia Naturae, Maxime Peregrine* del jesuita Juan Eusebio Nieremberg." In *El saber de los Jesuitas, historias naturales y el nuevo mundo,* edited by Luis Millones Figueroa and Domingo Ledezma, 53–77. Madrid: Iberoamericana; Frankfurt am Main: Vervuert, 2005.

Leonard, Irving. *Baroque Times in Old Mexico.* Ann Arbor: University of Michigan Press, 1959.

———. *Don Carlos de Sigüenza y Góngora: A Mexican Savant of the Seventeenth Century.* Berkeley: University of California Press, 1929.

———. "Informe de Don Carlos de Sigüenza y Góngora sobre el castillo de San Juan de Ulúa (1695)." *Revista de Historia de América* 45 (1958): 130–43.

———. "Sigüenza y Góngora and the Chaplaincy of the Hospital del Amor de Dios." *Hispanic American Historical Review* 39, no. 4 (1959): 580–87.

———. "Some Gongora Centones in Mexico." *Hispania* 12, no. 6 (1929): 563–72.

———. *Spanish Approach to Pensacola, 1689–1693.* Albuquerque, N. Mex.: Quivira Society, 1939.

Leon-Portilla, Miguel. Introducción to *México en 1554: Tres diálogos lati-*

nos de Francisco Cervantes de Salazar, by Francisco Cervantes de Salazar, xvii–xxvi. Mexico: UNAM, 2001.

Lezama Lima, José. *La expresión americana y otros ensayos*. Montevideo: ARCA, 1969.

López, Kimberle S. "Identity and Alterity in the Emergence of a Creole Discourse: Sigüenza y Góngora's Infortunios de Alonso Ramírez." *Colonial Latin American Review* 5, no. 2 (1996): 253–76.

López de Gómara, Francisco. *Historia de la conquista de México*. Mexico: Porrúa, 1988.

Lorente Medina, Antonio. *La prosa de Sigüenza y Góngora y la formación de la conciencia criolla mexicana*. Mexico: Fondo de Cultura Económica, 1996.

Lupher, David A. *Romans in the New World: Classical Models in Sixteenth-Century Spanish America*. Ann Arbor: University of Michigan Press, 2003.

MacCormack, Sabine. *On the Wings of Time: Rome, the Incas, Spain and Peru*. Princeton, N.J.: Princeton University Press, 2007.

Maravall, José Antonio. *Culture of the Baroque: Analysis of a Historical Structure*. Translated by Terry Cochran. Minneapolis: University of Minnesota Press, 1986.

———. *Estado moderno y mentalidad social (siglos XV a XVII)*. 2 vols. Madrid: Revista de Occidente, 1972. Vol. 1.

———. *La literatura picaresca desde la historia social (siglos XVI y XVII)*. Madrid: Taurus, 1986.

———. "Teatro, fiesta e ideología en el barroco." In *Teatro y literatura en la sociedad barroca*, edited by Francisco Abad, 159–88. Barcelona: Editorial Crítica, 1990.

Martínez, María Elena. "The Black Blood of New Spain: Limpieza de Sangre, Racial Violence, and Gendered Power in Early Colonial Mexico." *William and Mary Quarterly*, 55 pars, 2004. http://userpages.umbc.edu/~kars/history%20200/martinez.htm (accessed December 19, 2011).

———. *Genealogical Fictions: Limpieza de Sangre, Religion, and Gender in Colonial Mexico*. Stanford, Calif.: Stanford University Press, 2008.

Martínez-San Miguel, Yolanda. *From Lack to Excess: "Minor" Readings of Latin American Colonial Discourse*. Lewisburg, Pa.: Bucknell University Press, 2008.

Mayer, Alicia. *Dos americanos, dos pensamientos*. Mexico: UNAM, 1998.

———. "El guadalupanismo en Carlos de Sigüenza y Góngora." In *Carlos de Sigüenza y Góngora: Homenaje 1700–2000*, edited by Alicia Mayer, 1: 243–72. 2 vols. Mexico: UNAM, 2000.

———. "Presentación," in *Carlos de Sigüenza y Góngora, Homenaje 1700–2000*, edited by Alicia Mayer, 1: 7–20. 2 vols. Mexico: UNAM, 2000.

Maza, Francisco de la. *El guadalupanismo mexicano*. Mexico: Fondo de Cultura Económica, 1981.

Mazzotti, José Antonio, ed. *Agencias criollas: La ambigüedad "colonial" en las letras hispanoamericanas*. Pittsburgh: Instituto Internacional de Literatura Iberoamericana, 2000.

———. "The Lightning Bolt Yields to the Rainbow: Indigenous History and Colonial Semiosis in the *Royal Commentaries* of the Inca Garcilaso." *MLQ* 57, no. 2 (1996): 197–211.

Merrim, Stephanie. *The Spectacular City, Mexico, and Colonial Hispanic Literary Culture*. Austin: University of Texas Press, 2010.

Mills, Kenneth. *Idolatry and Its Enemies: Colonial Andean Religion and Extirpation, 1640–1750*. Princeton, N.J.: Princeton University Press, 1997.

———. "The Naturalization of Andean Christianities." In *The Cambridge History of Christianity*, edited by R. Po Chia Hsia, 504–35. Cambridge: Cambridge University Press, 2007.

Momigliano, Arnaldo. *The Classical Foundations of Modern Historiography*. Berkeley: University of California Press, 1990.

Mora, Carmen de. *Escritura e identidades criollas: Modalidades discursivas en la prosa hispanoamericana del siglo XVII*. Amsterdam: Rodopi, 2001.

Moraña, Mabel. "Baroque/Neobaroque/Ultrabaroque: Disruptive Readings of Modernity." In *Hispanic Baroques: Reading Cultures in Context*, edited by Nicholas Spadaccini and Luis Martín-Estudillo, 241–74. Nashville: Vanderbilt University Press, 2005.

———. "Barroco y conciencia criolla en Hispanoamerica." *Revista de Crítica Literaria Latinoamericana* 28, no. 2 (1988): 229–45.

———. "El 'Tumulto de Indios' de 1692." In *Agencias criollas: La ambigüedad "colonial" en las letras hispanoamericanas*, edited by José Antonio Mazzotti, 161–75. Pittsburgh: Instituto Internacional de Literatura Iberoamericana, 2000.

———. "Máscara autobiográfica y conciencia criolla en *Infortunios de Alonso Ramírez*, de Carlos de Sigüenza y Góngora." In *Viaje al silencio: Exploraciones del discurso barroco*, 217–30. México: UNAM, 1998.

More, Anna. "Cosmopolitanism and Scientific Reason in New Spain: Sigüenza y Góngora and the Dispute over the 1680 Comet." In *Science in the Spanish and Portuguese Empires, 1500–1800*, edited by Daniela Bleichmar, Paula De Vos, Kristin Huffine, and Kevin Sheehan, 115–31. Stanford, Calif.: Stanford University Press, 2009.

———. "Soberanía y violencia en las representaciones barrocas de la conquista mexicana." In *Estudios coloniales latinoamericanos en el siglo XXI: Nuevos itinerarios*, edited by Stephanie Kirk, 231–58. Pittsburgh: Instituto Internacional de Literatura Iberoamericana, 2011.

———. "Thinking with the Inquisition: Heretical Science and Popular Knowledge in Seventeenth-Century Mexico." *Romanic Review*, forthcoming.

Morse, Richard M. "Toward a Theory of Spanish American Government." *Journal of the History of Ideas* 15, no. 1 (1954): 71–93.

Mujica Pinilla, Ramón. *Rosa limensis: Mística, política e iconografía en torno a la patrona de América*. Lima: Fondo de Cultura Económica, 2001.

Mumford, Lewis. *The City in History: Its Origins, Its Transformations, and Its Prospects*. New York: Harcourt, Brace & World, 1961.

Navarro Brotóns, Víctor. "*La libra astronómica y filosófica* de Sigüenza y Góngora: La polémica sobre el cometa de 1680." In *Carlos de Sigüenza y Góngora: Homenaje 1700–2000*, edited by Alicia Mayer, 1: 145–85. 2 vols. Mexico: UNAM, 2000.

Nóbrega, Manuel de. *Cartas do Brasil e Mais Escritos*. Coimbra: Universidade de Coimbra, 1955.

Oestreich, Gerhard. *Neostoicism and the Early Modern State*. Cambridge: Cambridge University Press, 1982.

O'Gorman, Edmundo. "Datos sobre Don Carlos de Sigüenza y Góngora." *Boletín del Archivo General de la Nación* 15, no. 4 (1944): 600–12.

———. "Sobre los inconvenientes de vivir los indios en el centro de la ciudad." *Boletín del Archivo General de la Nación* 9 (1938): 1–34.

Osorio, Alejandra. "The King in Lima: Simulacra, Ritual, and Rule in Seventeenth-Century Peru." *Hispanic American Historical Review* 84, no. 3 (2004): 447–74.

Osorio, Ignacio. *Conquistar el eco: La paradoja de la conciencia criolla*. Mexico: UNAM, 1989.

Pagden, Anthony. *The Fall of Natural Man: The American Indian and the Origins of Comparative Ethnology*. Cambridge: Cambridge University Press, 1982.

———. "Identity Formation in Spanish America." In *Colonial Identity in the Atlantic World: 1500–1800*, edited by Nicholas Canny and Anthony Pagden, 51–93. Princeton, N.J.: Princeton University Press, 1987.

———. Introduction to *Letters from Mexico*, by Hernán Cortés. Translated by Anthony Pagden, xxxix–lxx. New Haven, Conn.: Yale University Press, 2001.

———. *Lords of All the World: Ideologies of Empire in Spain, Britain and France, c. 1500–c.1800*. New Haven, Conn.: Yale University Press, 1995.

———. *Spanish Imperialism and the Political Imagination: Studies in European and Spanish-American Social and Political Theory, 1513–1830.* New Haven, Conn.: Yale University Press, 1990.

Palafox y Mendoza, Juan de. *Manual de estados y profesiones / De la naturaleza del indio.* Mexico: UNAM/Porrúa, 1986.

Panofsky, Erwin. *The Life and Art of Albrecht Dürer.* 4th ed. Princeton, N.J.: Princeton University Press, 1955.

———. *Perspective as Symbolic Form.* Translated by Christopher S. Wood. New York: Zone Books, 1997.

Parkinson Zamora, Lois. *The Inordinate Eye: New World Baroque and Latin American Fiction.* Chicago: University of Chicago Press, 2006.

Paz, Octavio. *Sor Juana Inés de la Cruz o las trampas de la fe.* 3rd ed. Mexico: Fondo de Cultura Económica, 1983.

Pérez Magellón, Jesús. *Construyendo la modernidad: La cultura española en el tiempo de los novatores [1675–1725].* Madrid: Consejo Superior de Investigaciones Científicas, 2002.

Pérez Salazar, Francisco. *Biografía de D. Carlos de Sigüenza y Góngora.* Mexico: Antigua Imprenta de Murguia, 1928.

Peterson, Jeanette Favrot. "Canonizing a Cult: A Wonder-Working Guadalupe in the Seventeenth Century." In *Religion in New Spain,* edited by Susan Schroeder and Stafford Poole, 125–56. Albuquerque: University of New Mexico Press, 2007.

———. "Creating the Virgin of Guadalupe: The Cloth, the Artist, and Sources in Sixteenth-Century New Spain." *The Americas* 61, no. 4 (2005): 571–609.

Phelan, John Leddy. *The Millenial Kingdom of the Franciscans in the New World.* Berkeley: University of California Press, 1970.

Pietz, William. "The Problem of the Fetish, I." *Res* 9 (Spring 1985): 5–17.

Pimentel, Juan. "Baroque Natures: Juan E. Nieremberg, American Wonders, and Preterimperial Natural Science." In *Science in the Spanish and Portuguese Empires, 1500–1800,* edited by Daniela Bleichmar, Paula De Vos, Kristin Huffine, and Kevin Sheehan, 93–111. Stanford, Calif.: Stanford University Press, 2009.

Poole, Stafford. *Our Lady of Guadalupe: The Origins and Sources of a Mexican National Symbol, 1531–1797.* Tucson: University of Arizona Press, 1995.

Praz, Mario. *Studies in Seventeenth-Century Imagery.* 2nd ed. Rome: Edizioni de Storia e Letteratura, 1975.

Quiñones Melgoza, José. "Don Carlos de Sigüenza y Góngora: Su *Triunfo parténico.*" In *Carlos de Sigüenza y Góngora, Homenaje 1700–2000,* edited by Alicia Mayer, 1: 79–92. 2 vols. Mexico: UNAM, 2000.

Quintana, José Miguel. *La astrología en la Nueva España en el siglo XVII (de Enrico Martínez a Sigüenza y Góngora)*. Mexico: Bibliófilos mexicanos, 1969.

Rabasa, José. *Inventing America: Spanish Historiography and the Formation of Eurocentrism*. Norman: University of Oklahoma Press, 1993.

———. "Pre-Columbian Pasts and Indian Presents in Mexican History." In *Colonialism Past and Present*, edited by Alvaro Félix Bolaños and Gustavo Verdesio, 51–78. Albany: State University of New York Press, 2002.

Rama, Ángel. "Fundación del manierismo hispanoamericano por Bernardo de Balbuena." *University of Dayton Review* 16, no. 2 (1983): 13–21.

———. *La ciudad letrada*. Hanover, N.H.: Ediciones del Norte, 1984.

Recopilación de leyes de los reynos de las Indias. Madrid: Julian de Paredes, 1681. http://fondosdigitales.us.es/fondos/libros/752/14/recopilacion-de-leyes-de-los-reynos-de-las-indias/ (accessed December 19, 2011).

Robbins, Jeremy. "The Arts of Perception." *Bulletin of Spanish Studies* 82, no. 8 (2005): 1–289.

Robles, Antonio de. *Diario de sucesos notables (1665–1703)*. 2nd ed. 3 vols. Mexico: Porrúa, 1972.

Rodríguez Hernández, Dalmacio. "Los arcos triunfales en la época de Carlos II: Una aproximación desde la retórica." In *Teatro y poder en la época de Carlos II: Fiestas en torno a reyes y virreyes*, edited by Judith Farré Vidal, 267–86. Madrid: Iberoamericana; Frankfurt am Main: Vervuert, 2007.

———. *Texto y fiesta en la literatura novohispana*. Mexico: UNAM, 1998.

Rojas Garcidueñas, José. *Don Carlos de Sigüenza y Góngora: Erudito barroco*. Mexico: Ediciones Xóchitl, 1945.

———. "Prólogo." In *Triunfo parténico*, by Carlos de Sigüenza y Góngora, 9–15. Mexico: Ediciones Xochitl, 1945.

Ross, Kathleen. "*Alboroto y motín de México*: Una noche triste criolla." *Hispanic Review* 56, no. 2 (Spring 1988): 181–90.

———. *The Baroque Narrative of Carlos de Sigüenza y Góngora: A New World Paradise*. Cambridge: Cambridge University Press, 1993.

———. "Cuestiones de género en *Infortunios de Alonso Ramírez*." *Revista Iberoamericana* 61, no. 172–73 (1995): 591–603.

Ruiz de Alarcón, Hernando. *Tratado de las supersticiones y costumbres gentílicas que hoy viven entre los indios naturales desta Nueva España*. Mexico: SEP, 1988.

Saavedra Fajardo, Diego. *Empresas políticas*. Madrid: Cátedra, 1999.

———. *Idea de un príncipe político-cristiano representada en cien empresas*. Murcia: Academia Alfonso X el Sabio, 1985.

Sanchez, Miguel. "Imagen de la Virgen María Madre de Dios de Guadalupe." In *Testimonios históricos guadalupanos*, edited by Ernesto de la Torre Villar and Ramiro Navarro de Anda, 152–281. Mexico: Fondo de Cultura Económica, 1982.

Sánchez Lamego, Miguel A. *El primer mapa general de México elaborado por un mexicano*. Mexico: Instituto Panamericano de Geografía e Historia, 1955.

Schreffler, Michael. *The Art of Allegiance: Visual Culture and Imperial Power in Baroque New Spain*. University Park: Pennsylvania State University Press, 2007.

Schwartz, Stuart. *Sugar Plantations in the Formation of Brazilian Society: Bahia, 1550–1835*. Cambridge: Cambridge University Press, 1985.

Seed, Patricia. *American Pentimento: The Invention of Indians and the Pursuit of Riches*. Minneapolis: University of Minnesota Press, 2001.

Seznec, Jean. *The Survival of the Pagan Gods: The Mythological Tradition and Its Place in Renaissance Humanism and Art*. Translated by Barbara F. Sessions. Princeton, N.J.: Princeton University Press, 1953.

Shelton, Anthony Alan. "Cabinets of Transgression: Renaissance Collections and the Incorporation of the New World." In *The Cultures of Collecting*, edited by John Elsner and Roger Cardinal, 177–203. Cambridge, Mass.: Harvard University Press, 1994.

Sigüenza y Góngora, Carlos de. *Alboroto y motín de México del 8 de junio de 1692*. Edited by Irving Leonard. Mexico: Talleres Gráficos del Museo Nacional de Arqueología, Historia y Etnografía, 1932.

———. "Anotaciones críticas sobre el primer apóstol de Nueva España y sobre la imagen de Guadalupe de México." In *Carlos de Sigüenza y Góngora: Homenaje 1700–2000*, edited by Alicia Mayer, 1: 297–377. 2 vols. Mexico: UNAM, 2000.

———. "Carta de 4 de Junio de 1693." In *Documentos inéditos de Don Carlos de Sigüenza y Góngora*, edited by Irving Leonard, 98–100. Mexico: Centro Bibliográfico Juan José de Eguiara y Eguren, 1963.

———. "Contestación a Don Andrés de Arriola." In *Biografía de Don Carlos de Sigüenza y Góngora, seguida de varios documentos inéditos*, edited by Francisco Pérez Salazar, 119–60. Mexico: Robredo, 1928.

———. "Descripción que de la Bahía de Santa María de Galve (Antes Panzacola)." In *Documentos inéditos de Don Carlos de Sigüenza y Góngora*, edited by Irving Leonard, 63–92. Mexico: Centro Bibliográfico Juan José de Eguiara y Eguren, 1963.

———. *Glorias de Querétaro*. Querétaro: Ediciones Cimatario, 1945.

———. "Infortunios de Alonso Ramírez." In *Seis Obras*, edited by William G. Bryant, 3–47. Caracas: Ayacucho, 1984.

———. *Libra astronómica y filosófica*. 2nd ed. Mexico: UNAM, 1984.

———. "Mercurio volante." In *Seis Obras*, edited by William G. Bryant, 143–63. Caracas: Ayacucho, 1984.

———. *Noticia chronológica de los reyes, emperadores, governadores, presidentes, y vir-reyes, que desde su primera fundacion hasta el tiempo presupone han governado esta nobilissima imperial ciudad de Mexico*. n.p., [1681?].

———. *Oriental planeta evangélico*. Madrid: Iberoamericana; Frankfurt am Main: Vervuert, 2008.

———. *Parayso occidental, plantado y cultivado por la liberal benefica mano*, 1684. Reprint. Mexico: UNAM/Condumex, 1995.

———. *Piedad heroyca de Don Fernando Cortés*. Madrid: José Porrúa, 1960.

———. "Primavera indiana." In *Testimonios históricos guadalupanos*, edited by Ernesto de la Torre Villar and Ramiro Navarro de Anda, 334–58. Mexico: Fondo de Cultura Ecónomica, 1982.

———. "Relación de lo sucedido a la Armada de Barlovento." In *Relaciones históricas*, edited by Manuel Romero de Terreros, 75–89. Mexico: UNAM, 1940.

———. "Testamento de Don Carlos de Sigüenza y Góngora." In *Biografía de Don Carlos de Sigüenza y Góngora, seguida de varios documentos inéditos*, edited by Francisco Pérez Salazar, 161–94. Mexico: Robredo, 1928.

———. *Theatro de virtudes politicas, que constituyen à un principe*. Mexico: Viuda de Bernardo Calderón, 1680.

———. *Triunfo parténico*. Mexico: Ediciones Xóchitl, 1945

———. "Trofeo de la justicia española en el castigo de la alevosía francesa." In *Seis Obras*, edited by William G. Bryant, 51–92. Caracas: Ayacucho, 1984.

Silva Prada, Natalia. *La política de una rebelión: Los indígenas frente al tumulto de 1692 en la ciudad de México*. Mexico: El Colegio de México, 2007.

Solís, Antonio de. *Historia de la conquista de México, población y progresos de la América septentrional, conocida por el nombre de Nueva España*. 1704. 2nd ed. Reprint, Mexico: Porrúa, 1988.

Solórzano Pereyra, Juan. *Política indiana*. 3 vols. Madrid: Biblioteca Castro, 1996.

Spadaccini, Nicholas, and Luis Martín-Estudillo, eds. *Hispanic Baroques: Reading Cultures in Context*. Nashville: Vanderbilt University Press, 2005.

Stern, Steve J. *The Secret History of Gender: Women, Men and Power in*

Late Colonial Mexico. Chapel Hill: University of North Carolina Press, 1995.

Strong, Roy. *Art and Power: Renaissance Festivals, 1450–1650*. Berkeley: University of California Press, 1984.

Taussig, Michael. *Mimesis and Alterity: A Particular History of the Senses*. New York: Routledge, 1993.

Taylor, Diana. *The Archive and the Repertoire: Performing Cultural Memory in the Americas*. Durham, N.C.: Duke University Press, 2003.

Taylor, William B. *Drinking, Homicide, and Rebellion in Colonial Mexican Villages*. Stanford, Calif.: Stanford University Press, 1979.

———. "Mexico's Virgin of Guadalupe in the Seventeenth Century: Hagiography and Beyond." In *Colonial Saints: Discovering the Holy in the Americas, 1500–1800*, edited by Allan Greer and Jodi Bilinkoff, 277–98. New York: Routledge, 2003.

———. "The Virgin of Guadalupe in New Spain: An Inquiry into the Social History of Marian Devotion." *American Ethnologist* 14, no. 1 (1987): 9–33.

Teskey, Gordon. *Allegory and Violence*. Ithaca, N.Y.: Cornell University Press, 1996.

Thompson, E. P. *Customs in Common: Studies in Traditional Popular Culture*. New York: New York University Press, 1993.

Tibesar, Antonine. "The *Alternativa*: A Study in Spanish-Creole Relations in Seventeenth-Century Peru." *The Americas* 11, no. 3 (1955): 229–83.

Torquemada, Juan de. *Monarquía indiana*. 3rd ed. 7 vols. Mexico: UNAM, 1975–1983. Vol. 3.

Torres Ramírez, Bibiano. *La Armada de Barlovento*. Seville: Escuela de Estudios Hispano-Americanos, 1982.

Toussaint, Manuel. *Compendio bibliográfico del Triunfo parténico de Don Carlos de Sigüenza y Góngora*. Mexico: Imprenta Universitaria, 1941.

Trabulse, Elías. "La obra cartográfica de Don Carlos de Sigüenza y Góngora." *Caravelle* 76–77 (2001): 265–75.

———. "La obra científica de Don Carlos de Sigüenza y Góngora (1667–1700)." In *Carlos de Sigüenza y Góngora, Homenaje 1700–2000*, edited by Alícia Mayer, 1: 93–123. 2 vols. Mexico: UNAM, 2000.

———. *Los manuscritos perdidos de Sigüenza y Góngora*. Mexico: Colegio de Mexico, 1988.

Tuck, Richard. *Natural Rights Theories: Their Origin and Development*. Cambridge: Cambridge University Press, 1979.

"Tumulto acaecido en la ciudad de México el año de 1692." In *Tumultos y rebeliones acaecidos en México*, edited by Génaro García, 230–55. Docu-

Bibliography

mentos inéditos o muy raros para la historia de México. Mexico: Centro de Estudios Históricos de Agrarismo en México, 1981.

Vasconcellos, Simão de. *Crónica da Companhia de Jesus*. 2 vols. Petrópolis: Editora Vozes; Brasília: Instituto Nacional do Livro, Ministério da Educação e Cultura, 1977.

Vetancurt, Agustín. *Teatro mexicano: Descripción breve de los sucesos ejemplares históricos y religiosos del nuevo mundo de las indias*. Mexico: Doña María de Benavides Viuda de Juan Ribera, 1698. Reprint, Mexico: Porrúa, 1982.

Veytia, Mariano. *Historia antigua de México*. Mexico: Editorial Leyenda, 1944.

Villella, Peter. "The True Heirs to Anáhuac: Native Nobles, Creole Patriots, and the 'Natural Lords' of Colonial Mexico." Ph.D. diss., University of California, Los Angeles, 2009.

Vinson III, Ben. *Bearing Arms for His Majesty: The Free-Colored Militia in Colonial Mexico*. Stanford, Calif.: Stanford University Press, 2001.

Viqueira Albán, Juan Pedro. *Propriety and Permissiveness in Bourbon Mexico*. Translated by Sonia Lipsett-Rivera and Sergio Rivera Ayala. Lanham, Md.: SR Books, 1999.

Viroli, Maurizio. *For Love of Country: An Essay on Patriotism and Nationalism*. Oxford: Oxford University Press, 1995.

Vitoria, Francisco de. *Political Writings*. Translated by Jeremy Lawrance. Cambridge: Cambridge University Press, 1991.

Wallerstein, Immanuel. *Mercantilism and the Consolidation of the European World-Economy, 1600–1750*. Vol. 2 of *The Modern World System*. 3 vols. New York: Academic Press, 1980.

Weber, David J. *The Spanish Frontier in North America*. New Haven, Conn.: Yale University Press, 1992.

Weber, Max. *Economy and Society: An Outline of Interpretive Sociology*. Translated by Ephraim Fischoff, Hans Gerth, A. M. Henderson, Ferdinand Kolegar, C. Wright Mills, Talcott Parsons, Max Rheinstein, Guenther Roth, Edward Shils, and Claus Wittich. 2 vols. Berkeley: University of California Press, 1978. Vol. 1.

Whitehead, Neil. "Hans Staden and the Cultural Politics of Cannibalism." *Hispanic American Historical Review* 80, no. 4 (2001): 721–51.

INDEX

Acapulco, 221
Acosta, José de, 71, 72, 127, 274n16, 309n10
Africa, 229–31, 239
Africans, 8, 158, 212–13, 229–31, 265n15; 1612 rebellion, 158, 299n3, 307n135. *See also* slavery
Aguiar y Seijas, Francisco de, 171
Alberro, Solange, 123
allegory: archives and, 14; Benjamin, Walter, on, 13–14, 51, 54, 55, 80, 124, 132; Creole, 14–15, 52, 54–56, 80, 120–21, 132–33, 137, 145; counterallegory, 191; hermeneutics and, 7, 15–16, 52, 55, 76, 79, 85, 90, 178; hybridity and, 54, 55; of Mexica migration, 126, 132–33, 137, 143–44; of Mexico City, 190; pre-Columbian past and, 76, 79–80, 81, 114, 122; redemption and, 52–56, 80, 115, 137, 144; Renaissance, 123–24; ruins and, 55–56; violence of, 139–40; Virgin of Guadalupe and, 81, 84–85, 91–92, 93, 101, 107. *See also* emblems
Alzate y Ramírez, José, 243, 245 fig. 22, 315n26
The Ambassadors, 162, 162 fig. 17
Amerindians. *See* indigenous peoples
Anderson, Benedict, 42–43
antiquarianism: Bacon, Francis, on, 76, 155, 288–89n67; Creole, 8, 14–15, 45, 52, 55–56, 76–80, 92, 94, 107–9, 147–57, 237, 280n91; Momigliano, Arnaldo, on, 76; in New Spain, 76–80, 283n123; nineteenth-century, 76; Sigüenza y Góngora and, 19, 23, 53, 98–99, 130, 147–57, 251, 259. *See also* artifacts; pre-Columbian past

Aquinas, Thomas, Saint. *See* Thomism
archives, 14–15, 45–49; and allegory, 14; colonial, 45, 46–49, 163, 167–69, 195; Creole, 53, 55–56, 60–62, 107, 154–55, 157, 197–98, 251, 253–54, 257; and cultural autonomy, 61–62; embodied memory as, 48–49; European, 24, 47, 73, 151–52, 155; indigenous, 72–73, 75, 77–80, 87–88, 199; loss of, 60–62, 70–80, 89, 259–60; nomological structure of, 14–15, 45–46, 55–56; and orality, 48, 69, 71, 72–73, 75, 87, 92; and patrimonialism, 45–46; politics of, 6–8, 46, 77, 251; pre-Columbian past and, 7, 13–14, 15, 56, 66, 69, 79–80, 89, 107, 108–9, 199, 237, 260; and subaltern history, 199; *Triunfo parthénico* as, 61; and Virgin of Guadalupe, 86, 87–89, 92–93, 84, 102–3, 105–6. *See also under* Sigüenza y Góngora
Armada de Barlovento, 172, 204, 206, 239–41, 308n4, 310n17
artifacts, 13, 15, 76, 77, 79–80, 98–99, 281n100; *bultos* (bundles), 132, 177, 179, 304n80; hybrid, 54, 55, 56, 108–9, 113, 191–92; indigenous, 13–14, 52, 56, 71–72, 81, 100–101; profane, 51–52, 54; in Riot of 1692, 176–84, 303–4n78; Virgin of Guadalupe and, 84, 90–91
Asia, 5, 18, 64–65, 215, 221–28; commerce in, 221–23; Dutch dominance in, 202, 222–23, 229, 276n43. *See also* Philippines
astrology, 18, 154, 246, 299n114
Aztec. *See* Mexica
Aztlan, 125, 128, 133, 147, 147 fig. 13

337

Balbuena, Bernardo de, 59–60, 65–66, 67, 68, 222, 287n29, 287n38
Balibar, Etienne, 163, 181
barbarism, 97, 172, 236; associated with Americas, 58–59, 61, 113; frontier and, 14, 69, 212, 241; memory and, 61–62; pirates as, 227, 232; wilderness as, 66, 69. *See also* Chichimecs
Baroque, 13–14, 50; as anti-historical, 52–53; citation in, 22, 24, 28, 114, 137, 141–42, 253; Creole, 9–10, 26–27, 50, 52–58, 80; and excess, 9, 110, 193, 194, 196, 251; and freedom, 50, 207, 282n110; Hispanic, 58, 111, 282n110; and hybridity, 13–15, 49–50, 63–65; and the Jesuits, 24, 49, 123, 171, 294n13; Latin American, 13, 49, 50, 268n41; Neoscholasticism and, 252; as perspective, 162, 162 fig. 17, 170–72, 180–81; poetry, 57–58; and secularization, 7, 14–15, 51–52, 54, 55–56, 67, 123–24; Sigüenza y Góngora as, 19, 251; space and, 62, 64, 132, 172, 286n21, 287n28; time and, 53, 62, 64, 67, 132; wit, 12–13, 132. *See also* Benjamin, Walter; festivals; Gongorism; Neoplatonism
Bauer, Ralph, 310n17
Becerra Tanco, Luis, 87–89; Nahuatl, ability in, 88–89; on Saint Thomas the Apostle, 89–90, 107–8, 149–50, 289n70; on the Virgin of Guadalupe, 87–89, 94, 102–3, 290n110
Benjamin, Walter, 50–52, 80, 282–83n112; on allegory, 13–14, 51, 54, 55, 80, 124, 132; on dialectical images, 177, 268n43; on the pastoral, 66–67, 287n38; on ruins, 27
Beverley, John, 65; on Benjamin, 282–83n112, 287n38; on Maravall, 282n110
biombo (folding screen), 1, 2–3 fig. 1, 5–6, 201, 263n5, 264n8
Blanco, John, 205, 229
Borja, Juan de, 171
Boturini Benaduci, Lorenzo de, 257, 314n2
Brading, David, 86, 114, 137, 283n123, 290n99; on Creole patriotism, 266n19, 266n22, 267n28; on Sigüenza y Góngora, 273n84, 300n14

Burrus, Ernst, 19
Butler, Judith, 306n124, 306n128

cabildos (town councils), 39, 111–12, 113, 203, 277–78n58, 278n60
Calancha, Antonio de la, 54, 69–74, 70 fig. 3, 74 fig. 4, 75, 77, 128, 145
calendrics, 89, 107, 147, 153, 155; Calendar Wheel, 149–50, 150 fig. 15. *See also* chronology
canals, 4, 172, 175–76, 177, 197. *See also* desagüe
Cañizares-Esguerra, Jorge, 52–53, 66, 68, 69, 76, 284n138
cannibalism, 227
Caribbean, 202, 206, 234–35, 311n41; commerce in, 18, 217; English and French in, 36, 202, 204, 235, 240–41; Spanish settlement in, 33, 217. *See also* Armada de Barlovento; Puerto Rico
cartography, 221, 243–45; Dutch, 4, 263n4; hydrography, 19, 245, 246 fig. 23, 248 fig. 24; of Sigüenza y Góngora, 19, 167, 242 fig. 21, 245 fig. 22, 248 fig. 24, 243–49
Casas, Bartolomé de las, 7, 35, 36, 71, 275n31, 276n43
Cascardi, Anthony J., 264n8
Castañeda de la Paz, María, 147
Cervantes de Salazar, Francisco, 59, 60, 61–62
Chapultepec, 4, 147
Chatterjee, Partha, 42–43, 44
Chichimecs, 97, 99–100, 145, 210, 212, 214 fig. 20; Mexicas as, 126
chronology, 1–6, 15, 26, 53, 59, 85, 152 fig. 16, 153–54; and Mexica maps, 147
citizenship, 115–16, 168, 209, 243, 267n26; Creole, 7, 9, 11, 44, 56, 123, 152, 157, 164, 168–69, 247–49; in the *Infortunios*, 204–7, 241; militias and, 25, 206, 209, 240; patriotism and, 22, 24, 140; race and, 7, 16, 26–27, 41, 43, 168, 267n26; Republican 11, 43; vassalage and, 43, 164, 205
codices, 14, 17, 77, 79–80, 132, 154, 156, 179–80; Calendar Wheel, 149–50, 150 fig. 15; Codex Ixtlilxochitl, 130, 131 fig. 10; Mapa de Sigüenza, 146 fig. 13, 148 fig. 14, 147–50; Tovar, Juan de, 130 fig. 9
collecting. *See* archives
commerce: in Asia, 221–23; Galleon trade, 18, 207; global, 65, 155,

207, 213, 226, 227–8. *See also* mercantilism; Mexico City: marketplace

Conquest, Spanish: Creoles on, 20, 54, 237, 204; of Incas, 32; justice of, 7, 191; *noche triste* (sad night), 1, 177, 197; of Querétaro, 96, 99–100; reconquest of Spain and, 6, 32; represented, 1–6, 106–7, 108, 133, 138; in the Riot of 1692, 163, 167, 197, 198–99; Solís, Antonio de, on, 54, 304n81; as *translatio imperii*, 4, 33, 263n3; Virgin of Guadalupe allegory for, 84, 93–94

Cope, Douglas, 160, 174, 307n149

Cortés, Hernán, 1, 32–33, 156, 167, 177, 199, 263n1; invoked in the Riot of 1692, 195, 197

counterhistory, 163–64, 199, 260–61, 301n23. *See also* historiography

Counter-Reformation, 48–49, 53–54, 208

Creoles: as administrators, 40, 43, 162, 167–69, 266n22; and *alternativa* policy, 39, 278n60; authority of, 13, 15, 56, 147, 252; commoners 159, 165, 192, 204–5, 217–18, 247; cosmopolitanism of, 27, 150–51, 206–7; education of, 17; *encomenderos* and, 16, 266n19; erudition of, 40, 59–62, 63, 68, 247, 262; etymology of term, 8, 264n10; in festivals, 111–13; Habsburg decline and, 6, 11, 17, 39; as "hybrids," 9–10, 266n20, 266–67n23; identity of, 8–10, 264–65nn13–15; as "imagined community," 42–43; on indigenous commoners, 56, 157, 225; and indigenous languages (*see under* Nahuatl); on indigenous nobility, 98–99, 103, 155, 161; local knowledge and, 7, 13, 15, 65–66, 115, 117, 147, 152, 178–81, 201, 256; *nación* (nation), term for, 8, 41, 265n17, 266n21; nobility of, 267n32, 270n58, politics of, 9–10, 15–16, 25–26, 114–15, 198, 201; pre-Columbian past and, 13, 55–56, 66–67, 70–80, 81, 98–99, 100, 117, 124, 147–57; prejudice against, 40, 71–72, 278n61; race and, 12, 40, 68, 161, 163–64, 224–26, 301n16; regionalism of, 17, 39, 41, 46; *reino* (kingdom), term for, 266n21; Solórzano Pereyra on, 29, 40–41; sovereignty and, 16, 25, 169, 201, 220–21, 243–45, 247–49, 261–62; Spanish empire and, 119, 225, 240–41, 249; Virgin of Guadalupe and, 81, 91–92, 103. *See also under* allegory; archives; antiquarianism; citizenship; historiography; patriotism

death, symbolics of, 54, 188–91, 253
Deleuze, Gilles, 50, 162, 171, 282n111
demons, 54, 71, 122, 124–25, 244; agency of, 128; on frontier, 69; Huitzilopochtli and, 129–30, 180, 297n72; indigenous objects and, 55, 56; in landscape, 66, 67, 68, 245. *See also* idolatry
Derrida, Jacques, 14–15, 45–46, 47
desagüe, 5, 19, 113, 178
Díaz del Castillo, Bernal, 102, 106, 127, 128, 167
drinking, 52, 304–5n90. *See also pulque*
Duarte, Manuel de, 23, 76–80, 78 fig. 5, 89, 154, 289n77
Durán, Diego de, 77, 79

Echeverría y Veytia, Mariano Fernández de, 79, 289n77
Eguiara y Eguren, Juan José de, 19, 47, 53, 256, 259, 314n2
Egypt, 13, 107, 121; associated with pre-Columbian peoples, 125, 143, 151–52, 284n137. *See also* hieroglyphs
Elliott, J. H., 117–18, 120, 121; on the Bourbon succession, 276n42; on the term "Creole," 265n14; on imperial motives, 276n37; on Maravall, 282n110, 293n7, 308n1; on Spanish decline, 276n40; on vicregal politics, 277–78n58, 278n60, 278n67
emblems, 57, 119–22, 123–25, 171, 269n49, 294–95nn13–14, 296n32, 296–97n51; as hieroglyphs, 22, 112, 116, 121; as historiography, 121, 145–46; of Huitzilopochtli, 126–29, 130, 132; iconography of, 22, 112, 114, 116, 123, 125, 132, 147; of Mexica monarchs, 125, 133; of Spanish monarchs, 116, 119–20; theories of, 116–17, 121, 122–23, 124–25, 132, 136, 140–41, 145; triumphal arches and, 111, 112–13, 116–17, 132, 134, 139
encomenderos 34–35, 99, 158; as origin of Creole patriotism, 16, 266n19
engineering, 4, 140, 176, 178

eschatology, 15, 51, 53, 54–56; posteschatology, 56
evangelization, 14, 54–55, 237; administration, opposed to 43, 54; as bucolic activity, 69, 70 fig. 3; on frontier, 18, 30, 54, 254, 310–11n36; governance and, 14, 43, 54; hybrid objects and, 56, 80, 164–69; as justification for Spanish sovereignty, 34–35, 37 (*see also* voluntarism under Sovereignty, Spanish imperial); language and, 99; pastoral care and, 45, 166–68, 302n39, 302n50; pre-evangelization (*see* Thomas the Apostle, Saint); resistence to, 74; Virgin of Guadalupe and, 81, 92. *See also* Franciscans; mendicants; indigenous peoples: as neophytes

Farnesio, Alejandro, 116, 124
festivals, 48, 110, 173; confraternities in, 96, 110; Creole participation in, 111–13; of the Immaculate Conception, 57–65; indigenous participation in, 96–100, 113; in Querétaro, 94–101; *relaciones* (accounts) of, 94, 110–11; of San Hipólito, 199; viceregal entances, 111–13
Florencia, Francisco de, 90, 94, 107–8; *Estrella de el norte*, 101–5
Florida, 18, 209, 236, 243. *See also* Pensacola Bay
Foucault, Michel: on archives, 46–47, 280n95; on the art of government, 302n50; on counterhistory, 199, 301n23; on pastoral care, 163, 302n39
Fox, Dian, 118
Franciscans, 14, 18, 123; Colegio de Santa Cruz of Tlatelolco, 91, 94; Immaculate Conception and, 60; millenarianism of, 268n44; as source for Guadalupan image, 91
freedom, 219, 231–33; Baroque and, 50, 207, 282n110; indigenous 165, 199, 279n79; patria as source of, 11
frontier, 69, 94, 226, 270n57; barbarism of, 14, 69, 212, 241; defense of, 172, 202–3, 207, 208–9, 210–12, 229–30, 243, 249; French exploration of, 202; Louisiana, 18, 202; New Mexico, 172, 204, 210–11; Northern New Spain, 14, 18, 27, 172, 223, 243; Querétaro as, 94, 96–97; Yucatan as, 172, 236–39. *See also* Florida; Spanish empire: geopolitics of

García, Gregorio de, 71, 127
Garcilaso de la Vega, el Inca, 47, 284n136
Gemelli Careri, Giovanni, 23, 131 fig. 10, 147–50, 149 fig. 14, 150 fig. 15, 154–55, 198–201, 245, 247 fig. 23
glyphs, 17, 76–79, 107, 151–52; compared to hieroglyphs, 107, 125; for Huitzilopochtli, 130; name glyphs, 125, 128, 147–49; Spanish suspicions of, 199. *See also* codices
Góngora, Bartolomé de, 127
Gongorism, 9, 57–58, 63; Becerra Tanco opposed to, 88; compared to a corpse, 252–53; maligned, 58; Sánchez, Miguel imitation of, 84, 86; Sigüenza y Góngora, imitation of, 19, 63, 65, 93, 114–15, 285n4; Sigüenza y Góngora, rejection of, 57, 252–53
González Echevarría, Roberto, 46–47, 115
governance: Creole, 43, 162, 167–69, 175–76, 197–98, 201; ecclesiastical, 161, 164–69; evangelization and, 14, 43, 54; history and, 117, 168–69, 197–98; patrimonialism and, 205–6, 207, 219; *reducción* (reduction) as, 169, 279n77; theories of, 113–14, 138; viceregal, 5, 7–8, 161, 162, 164–69, 173–74, 198, 201. *See also* Spanish empire
Gracián, Balthasar, 12–13
Grotius, Hugo, 229, 276n43
Gruzinski, Serge, 54, 115, 129, 130

Habsburg monarchy: Carlos Baltasar, prince, 18, 119; Carlos II, 38, 113, 173, 202; Carlos V, emperor, 33, 34, 97, 118; decline of, 17, 36, 38–39, 49, 201, 202–3; Felipe II, 118; Felipe III, 60; Felipe IV, 11, 39
Hanssen, Beatrice, 55–56
Hernández, Francisco, 67, 68
Herrera, Antonio de, 79, 127, 167
Herzog, Tamar, 267n26
hieroglyphs: emblems as, 22, 112, 116, 121; and Mesoamerican glyphs, 107, 125
Higgins, Antony, 46–47, 280n97
historiography: Creole, 6–7, 11, 45, 52–58, 121–23, 163–64, 167–69; emblems as, 121, 145–46; indigenous, 7, 17, 89, 157;

mendicant, 7, 17; Neoplatonic, 7, 54; racism and, 163; redemption through, 54–56, 115; Spanish, 1, 53–54, 71, 208, 263n1, 304n81; subaltern studies and, 199. *See also* chronology; counterhistory; pre-Columbian past
Hobsbawm, Eric, 12, 268n34
Huitzilin (humming bird), 127, 128–29, 132, 144, 147; as Christian symbol, 136–37
Huitzilopochtli, 106, 125–32, 130 fig. 9, 142, 180, 297n72; glyph for, 130; as historical figure, 125–26, 128, 143; and Huitziton, 127, 128–29; and Mars, 128; in Mexica migration, 147; Spanish mispronunciation of, 127–28
hybridity, 14, 15, 56, 95, 191, 197, 296n35; allegory and, 54, 55; artifacts and, 54, 55, 56, 108–9, 113, 191–92; Baroque as, 13–15, 49–50, 63–65; Creoles as, 9–10, 266n20, 266–67n23; as "mimetic excess," 177–78, 179, 191, 192
hydrography. *See under* cartography

idolatry, 15, 48, 54, 74, 176–78, 179–81, 283n122, 304n79. *See also* demons; pre-Columbian past
Immaculate Conception, 57–59, 60–63; Virgin of Guadalupe and, 91–92
India, 69, 72, 74, 77, 78 fig. 5
indigenous peoples: as apostates, 27, 43, 80, 211; archives of, 72–73, 75, 77–80, 87–88, 199; as barbarous, 97, 99–100, 113, 145, 210, 212, 214 fig. 20; as commoners, 15, 56, 65, 67, 88; demographic decline of, 12, 16, 30, 35, 54; denigrated, 65, 67; on frontier, 97, 99–100, 209–10, 226, 237; historiography of, 7, 17, 89, 157; labor of, 34, 65; and loss of memory, 143; as neophytes, 27, 31, 35, 52, 80–81, 108 (*see also* Juan Diego); nobility, 12, 15–16, 88, 97–99, 103, 155–57, 183–84, 211–12, 274n17; as "miserable" persons, 31, 80, 107–8, 143, 289n80; *policía* (civilization) and, 35, 43, 212; popular culture and, 166–67; reliability of, 71–73, 75, 76, 77, 81, 88–89; Riot of 1692, participation in, 160, 184–91; segregation and, 164–69; theory of origins, 142. *See also*

pre-Columbian past; glyphs; idolatry; Nahuatl; *quipus*
Ixtlilxochitl family, 154–57; collection of, 23, 154–57; Fernando Alva de, 7, 23, 105, 107, 108, 154, 155–56; Juan Alva de, 23, 154, 156; Sigüenza y Góngora and, 23, 130, 154–57

Jesuits, 17, 48, 123, 259, 281n104; Baroque and, 24, 49, 123, 171, 294n13; Colegio imperial, 67; Colegio de San Pedro y San Pablo, 255; Collegio Romano 19, 24; and education, 17; Sigüenza y Góngora and, 18, 24, 255–57, 270n61
Juana Inés de la Cruz, Sor, 10, 18, 303n57; *Neptuno alegórico*, 113, 116, 121, 140, 141; patronage and, 18, 113; poem in *Triunfo parthénico*, 58
Juan Diego, 81–84, 91, 92, 93, 103, 104, 107–8; Cuauhtitlan, birthplace of, 87

Kantorowicz, Ernst, 118, 121, 278–79n71, 296n35
Kircher, Athanasius, 19, 23, 26–27; as collector, 24, 151–52; Egyptology of, 125, 143, 151–52, 284n137; on emblems, 124; on glyphs, 125, 143, 151
Kristeva, Julia, 307n131

Lafaye, Jacques, 72, 77, 81, 154, 289n81, 290n92
landscape: conquest and, 34, 191; Creoles and, 8, 11, 54, 66–69, 94, 209, 216–17; cultivation, theme of, 8, 66–69, 95–96; decline, as symbol of, 216–17, 221; demons in, 66, 67, 68, 245; Neoplatonism and, 54, 67; Saint Thomas' steps marked on, 70–74, 288n61; in Virgin of Guadalupe narrative, 81, 93, 105–6; as wilderness, 68–69. *See also* paradise, theme of
language: Greek, 73, 77; Hebrew, 73, 138; Latin, 73, 133. *See also* Nahuatl
law: anarchy and, 172, 228; archaic 14–15, 49, 55–56, 76, 79–80, 108, 112; imperial, 10–11, 37–38, 220, 229–30, 279–80n84; internalized, 220, 229; international, 229, 276n43; natural, 34, 227, 229; New Laws of 1542, 35; *obedezco pero no*

law (continued)
cumplo, 44; patrimonialism and, 45, 49, 207; *pulque* and, 181–82; race and, 29–31, 274n6; Roman, 101; *Siete Partidas,* 31, 289n80; two-republic system, 30–31, 42–43, 157, 192, 274n6, 274n11; of viceroyalties, 33, 119. *See also* archives: nomological structure of; *Recopilación de leyes de los reinos de las Indias*
Leonard, Irving, 19, 20, 58, 93, 160, 314n3
Lezama Lima, José, 20, 50, 261, 268n41
Lipsius, Justus, 58–59, 277n53
López de Gómara, Francisco, 1, 58, 263n1
Low Countries, 36; in Asia, 202, 222–23, 229, 276n43; Flemish source for Guadalupan image, 91; Holland, 4, 18, 235, 245. *See also* cartography: Dutch

Maravall, José Antonio: on Baroque, 50, 111, 281n107, 281–82n108, 282n110, 293–94n7; on patriotism, 279n72; on picaresque, 206, 310n18
Martínez, Enrico, 127
Martínez, María Elena, 266nn20–21, 267n26, 270n58, 274n10, 279n78, 283n122
Martínez-San Miguel, Yolanda, 309–10n14, 311n38, 312n62, 312n74
Maza, Francisco de la, 90
mendicants: and the *alternativa,* 39; Augustinians, 69; Dominicans 14, 73; historiography of, 7, 17. *See also* evangelization; Franciscans
Mendieta, Jerónimo de, 94, 105
mercantilism, 24, 193, 207, 208
Merrim, Stephanie, 264n10, 266–67nn23–24, 286n21, 303n57
Mexica, 97–99; conquest of, 32; migration of, 125–26, 128–29, 132–33. *See also* Moctezuma; monarchy, Mexica
Mexico City, 110–13, 133, 197–201, 203; archives of, 163, 167–69, 195; marketplace, 159, 193, 197, 201, 201 fig. 18; as paradise, 66, 68; rebuilt after the conquest, 4, 65, 167; segregation of, 164–69, 197; Virgin of Guadalupe and, 91. *See also* canals; *desagüe*
Militia, 97, 203, 243; citizenship and, 25, 206, 209, 240; race and, 207–9, 240, 308n4

Mills, Kenneth, 53
Moctezuma, 107; in conquest, 1; in festival, 114; portrait of, 256, 258 fig. 25
monarchy, 51, 118, 121, 296n35; natural body of, 140; Texcocan, 97–99, 130 fig. 10, 145, 154
monarchy, Mexica, 113, 116–17, 121, 133, 135–36; Cuauhtemoc, 133. *See also* Moctezuma
monarchy, Spanish, 8, 34, 52, 111, 116, 118–21; representation of, 118–21, 120 fig. 8; Spanish empire as, 118. *See also* Habsburgs
Moraña, Mabel, 161, 266n23, 282n111, 301n16, 312n74
Morse, Richard, 44, 208n87
Mumford, Lewis, 172, 303n62
mythology, classical, 112–13, 115, 121, 123–24, 128; as "fables," 121–22, 136, 139, 141

Nahuatl, 94, 128; and archaic law, 79; Creole ability in, 40, 77–79, 99, 88, 89, 99, 132, 191; Creole admiration of, 77–79, 99; in Riot of 1692, 159, 191
Neoplatonism, 7, 10, 13, 15, 269n49; archaic law and, 108, 112; landscape and, 54, 67
Neostoicism, 51, 61, 120, 133, 277n53, 296n44. *See also* Lipsius, Justus
Neptune, 113; as progenitor of Amerindians, 141–44, 150
New Spain, 5–7, 17–18, 25–26, 53, 54, 59, 61–62, 76–80, 117, 152–53, 158, 159–60, 172, 245, 251, 260–62; antiquarianism in, 76–80, 283n123 (*see also* Sigüenza y Góngora: as antiquarian); general map of, 244 fig. 22, 243; geopolitics of, 18, 203, 207–8, 209, 219, 222–23; print culture in, 17, 271n68. *See also* University of Mexico, Royal
Nieremberg, Juan Eusebio, 67–68
Nóbrega, Manuel de, 69, 72

Otomís, 96, 99, 145, 210
Ovalle, Alonso de, 75, 77

paganism. *See* idolatry; mythology, classical; pre-Columbian past
Pagden, Anthony: on Creoles, 45, 264n13, 266n22, 267n32, 283n123; on political theory, 277n53; on Sigüenza y Góngora, 114, 269n50; on Spanish empire, 275n27

Palafox, Juan de, Archbishop, 107–8, 158, 286n15, 300n4
paradise, theme of, 6, 8, 66–69, 217; climate and, 68; as divine, 66, 68; Querétaro as, 92, 94–95; Virgin of Guadalupe and, 85, 92, 105. *See also* Sigüenza y Góngora: *Parayso occidental*
patrimonialism, 219, 231, 300n12; antipatrimonialism, 190–91; and archive, 8, 46; Creole, 49, 214–15, 235–36, 239–40, 241, 262; defined, 44–45; and governance, 205–6, 207, 219; and popular culture, 160. *See also* Spanish empire: paternalism of
patriotism, 7, 11, 41, 115–17, 121, 267n31; Ciceronian, 11, 22, 41; and citizenship, 22, 24, 140; Creole, 8–9, 11, 26–28, 41–42, 115–17, 121, 145, 207, 251, 267n28; Horatian, 41; in New Spain, 17; *patria*, term used, 8, 22, 41, 115–17, 278n68, 279n72; of Sigüenza y Góngora, 18, 20–22, 23–24, 251, 256, 269n50
Paz, Octavio, 10, 65, 138, 269n49, 298n85
Pensacola Bay, 19, 160, 203, 209, 226, 242 fig. 21, 242–43, 312n69, 313n108
Pérez de Salazar, Francisco, 20
Peru, 40, 128, 185, 266n19, 278nn59–60, 278n68; antiquarianism, lack of, 283n123; conquest of, 33; extirpation campaigns in, 48, 54; Thomas the Apostle, Saint in, 72–74, 304n80
Peterson, Jeanette, 91
Pez, Andrés de, Admiral, 160, 169–70, 208, 209, 303n53
Philippines, 76, 77, 79, 204, 221–22, 224; and global trade, 221–22; as place of exile, 220;
picaresque, 204, 206–7, 226, 310n18, 311n44
Pietz, William, 180, 304n89
Pimentel, Juan, 67–68
pirate novels, 207–8, 209
pirates, 6, 202, 207–8, 224–26, 228–35
plagues: *chiahuixtle*, 173–74, 175, 181; *cocoliztli*, 83
Poole, Stafford, 84
popular culture, 48, 52, 111, 262; as hybrid, 55–56; as non-erudite, 63, 121, 174, 180; *poliplebio*, term for, 183; political consciousness of, 184–93, 261; *pulque* and, 181–83; racial mixture and, 164–69, 181, 192, 197; in Riot of 1692, 159, 160, 173–74, 191–95, 197, 198, 199; sociability of, 181–82, 197; as subaltern, 199; *vulgo*, term for, 63, 121, 140, 173–4, 175, 201. *See also* counterhistory; public sphere: popular
pre-Columbian past: allegory and, 76, 79–80, 81, 114, 122; as archive, 7, 13–14, 15, 56, 66, 69, 79–80, 89, 107, 108–9, 237, 260; Creoles and, 13, 55–56, 66–67, 70–80, 81, 98–99, 100, 117, 124, 147–57; pre-evangelization in (*see* Thomas the Apostle, Saint); politics of, 8, 56, 80, 81, 107; representation of, 65, 67, 98–99, 115; and Riot of 1692, 179–81; as ruins, 4, 56, 199, 237, 284n136; Sigüenza y Góngora on, 122–32, 147, 183–84, 296n49; Spanish attitude towards, 77, 127, 154. *See also* codices; idolatry
providentialism: Creole, 143–44, 184, 269n50; crisis of, 5, 7, 11, 67, 218–20; in Spanish historiography, 1, 53–54, 71, 208, 263n1; and Virgin of Guadalupe, 85, 92
public sphere: erudite, 170, 174, 185–86, 203, 237, 246–7, 253–4, 257, 310n17; history and, 153–54, 157; popular, 182, 198–99
Puebla, 18, 219, 220, 270n58
Puente, Antonio de la, 143
Puerto Rico, 203, 204, 216–19
pulque, 176, 304–5n90; antipulque treatises, 185–86; idolatry and, 183–84; in the Riot of 1692, 176–77, 178, 181–84, 187–88, 193; women and, 185–86
Purchas, Samuel, 151–52

Querétaro, 94–101, 144–45, 210
Quetzalcoatl, 77, 79
quipus (Andean knotted cords), 72–3; as archives, 73

Rabasa, José, 161, 301n16, 304n88, 307n153
race: *castas* (mixed-race), 30–32, 96–97, 157, 192, 196, 201, 208, 212, 224–26, 233–34; casta paintings, 212, 213–14 figs. 19–20; 240; Creoles and, 12, 40, 68, 161, 163–64, 224–26, 301n16; degeneration and, 8, 40, 192; history and, 163; in the

race (continued)
  Infortunios, 224–26, 228–29, 235;
    law and, 29–31, 274n6; mestizos,
    29–30, 159–60, 166–67, 181,
    192, 208, 224, 274n6, 310n36;
    militia and, 207–9, 240, 308n4;
    mulattoes, 31–32, 96, 158, 166,
    167, 181, 190, 197, 274n6, 299n3,
    307n135; purity of blood and, 7,
    30, 31, 163, 274n11, 274n17; in
    Riot of 1692, 159–60, 164, 166,
    179, 184, 187–94; segregation and,
    96, 164–69, 197; virtue, related to,
    7, 32, 41, 44, 207, 217, 251
racism: Creole, 161, 176–77, 179, 233–
    34, 301n16; history and, 163, 181
Rama, Ángel, 67, 286n21
rebellions, 168; 1624, against viceroy,
    158; 1612, Afro-Mexican, 158,
    299n3, 307n135; fears of, 158;
    indigenous, 160, 172; Pueblo revolt,
    New Mexico, 210–12; women,
    participation in, 185, 186–91. *See
    also* Riot of 1692
*Recopilación de leyes de los reinos de
    las Indias,* 10–11, 38, 45, 164,
    277n55, 278n67
Riot of 1692, 159–201; artifacts
    in canals, 176–84, 303–4n78;
    counterhistory and, 163; food
    shortage and, 173–74, 186–88;
    governance and, 178–79, 193,
    195–96; marketplace and, 193,
    197; popular culture and, 179–81;
    pre-Columbian past and, 179–81;
    race and, 159–60, 164, 166, 179,
    184, 187–94; rioters' cries during,
    185, 193, 194, 195; rumors and,
    186; trial records, 160; viceregal
    palace burned, 195, 201 fig. 18,
    201; women and, 160, 186–91,
    305n106, 307n149
Ripa, Cesare, 112
Robles, Antonio de, 203, 250–51, 254
Rose of Lima, Saint, 8
Ross, Kathleen, 20, 161, 195, 237,
    266n23, 270n59, 303–4n78
ruins: indigenous, 4, 56, 199, 284n136;
    allegory as, 55–56; in Yucatan, 237

Saavedra Fajardo, Diego de, 119–20,
    120 fig. 8, 277n53
Sepúlveda, Ginés de, 35, 44, 169,
    279n29, 279n81
Seznec, Jean, 123, 126–27
Sigüenza y Góngora, Carlos de, 16,
    18–26, 53; "Alboroto y motín"
(letter to Admiral Pez, 1692),
    160–64, 169–201, 208; alliance
    with Conde de Galve, viceroy,
    160, 161, 172, 203; "Anotaciones
    críticas," 105–9; as antiquarian,
    19, 23, 53, 98–99, 130, 147–57,
    251, 259; archive of, 19, 22–25, 28,
    104, 147–50, 154–57, 163, 167–69,
    179–81, 195, 253–58; *Armada de
    Barlovento,* 204; as astronomer, 23,
    315n21; on astrology, 18; as author,
    20–22, 271n68; Baroque style of,
    19–20, 24, 261; biography of, 18;
    cartography of, 19, 167, 243–49; as
    chaplain, 18, 205; "Ciclografía,"
    149, 154–55; death of, 250–51,
    254; dispute with Eusebio Kino,
    203, 242, 246, 309n13; "Fenix
    del occidente," 23, 77; *Glorias de
    Querétaro,* 94–101, 109, 144–45,
    210; as historian, 20, 153–54,
    157, 163–64; *Infortunios de
    Alonso Ramírez,* 203–41, 245; as
    Inquisitorial censor, 18; intellectual
    circle of, 23; Ixtlilxochitl family
    and, 23, 130, 154–57; and Jesuits,
    18, 24, 255–57, 270n61; *Libra
    astronómica,* 19, 21 fig. 2, 242;
    Mapa de Sigüenza and, 147–50; as
    mathematician, 18, 167–69, 174–
    76, 243, 247; *Mercurio volante,*
    204, 210–12, 245; "Noticia
    cronológica," 153–54, 152 fig. 16,
    247; *Oriental planeta evangélico,*
    257; *Parayso Occidental,* 20, 57,
    157, 252–53, 287n39; patriotism
    of, 18, 20–22, 23–24, 251, 256,
    269n50; and patronage, 18–19, 113;
    Pegasus, personal device of, 21 fig.
    2, 21–22; and Pensacola Bay, 19,
    160, 203, 209, 226, 242–43, 242
    fig. 21, 312n69, 313n108; *Piedad
    Heroyca,* 105; as polymath, 19;
    Primavera indiana, 19, 93–94;
    propaganda of, 208–9; publication,
    lack of, 19, 26–27, 251; on *pulque,*
    183–84; racism of, 160, 161–62,
    163–64, 181, 189, 233–34; Riot of
    1692, participation in, 193–97; as
    Royal Cosmographer, 19; *Theatro
    de virtudes,* 22, 113–47, 134–35
    figs. 10–11; Torquemada, Juan de,
    and, 23, 129–30, 133, 167; *Triunfo
    parthénico,* 57–65, 68, 81, 91–92,
    104; *Trofeo de la justicia,* 204,
    240–41; Vetancurt, Agustín and,
    23, 257; on Virgin of Guadalupe,

Index

19, 93–101, 104–9; women, attitude toward, 20, 160, 186–90
Silva Prada, Natalia, 160, 185, 305n100
slavery, 235, 238–39; African, 212–15, 217, 231, 233, 238–39, 240; indigenous, as natural slaves, 35; as metaphor, 233; and race, 235, 238–39
Solís, Antonio de, 54, 304n81
Solórzano Pereyra, Juan de, 29–32, 36–39, 40–41, 55, 71, 107; on apostasy, 80–81; on Creoles, 29, 40–41; on mulattoes and mestizos, 29–30, 31; on neophytes, 30–31
sovereignty, 51, 220–21, 229; colonial, theory of, 42; divine, 65. *See also under* Creoles
sovereignty, Spanish imperial, 10, 14, 25–26, 33, 36–37, 42–43, 52; attacked by other states, 36, 223, 229; as debt, 99–100, 117, 145; Christian universalism and, 36, 141, 203, 228; festivals and, 111–15; and law, 10–11, 37–38, 220, 229–30, 279–80n84; and papal bull of 1493, 32, 34; paternalism of, 38, 45, 80, 164–65, 236–37, 277n55, 279n79; Roman empire, compared to, 37, 101, 111, 115, 137–41; and Tordesillas, treaty of, 32; tribute in, 65, 100, 276n36; Valladolid debate and, 35; voluntarism and, 32, 34, 139, 163, 179, 191, 306n129. *See also* Spanish empire
Spanish empire, 117–19, 202–3; Audiencias, 33; Casa de Contratación, 33; competition with European states, 202–3, 207–8, 223; Consejo de Indias, 33, 119, 159; Creoles and, 6, 119, 225, 240–41, 249; geopolitics of, 17, 27, 36, 172, 202–3, 206–9, 215, 222–23, 228–30, 245; as monarchy, 118; and seventeenth-century crisis, 6, 18, 27, 36, 201; viceregal policy, 17, 33–34, 181–82. *See also* sovereignty, Spanish imperial; viceroyalties; viceroys

Taussig, Michael, 177, 179, 192
Taylor, Diana, 48–49
Taylor, William, 53, 91, 185
Tenochtitlan: conquest of, 1, 177; in Mexica migration, 125, 130–32, 133, 147, 147 fig. 13, 149 fig. 14; representation of, 1–4, 65, 67

Teotihuacan, 56, 156. *See also* Ixtlilxochitl family
Tepeyac, 81, 83, 105–6, 107; chapel at, 87, 90; landscape of, 81, 93
Thomas the Apostle, Saint, 15, 23, 69–80, 74 fig. 4, 81, 89, 142; and Mesoamerican calendar, 89, 107
Thomism, 32, 34, 43, 229, 236
Thompson, E. P., 185
Torquemada, Juan de, 7, 53, 102; influence on Sigüenza y Góngora, 23, 129–30, 133, 167
Trabulse, Elías, 260
tradition, 12–13, 14–15, 45, 48–49; authority of, 53, 75, 254; decline of, 45, 55, 161, 183–84; invention of, 12–13, 15–16, 268n34; orality and, 12, 72, 75; Virgin of Guadalupe and, 86, 87, 92
triumphal arches, 111–12, 123, 137–40; in Spanish America, 111, 123. *See also under* emblems
Tuck, Richard, 229

University of Mexico, Royal, 17, 57, 58–62, 87, 92; compared to European, 59–60; Constitutions of, 60, 286n15; as a republic, 62, 286n22

Valeriano, Antonio, 94, 105
Valeriano, Piero, 112, 121
Vasconcelos, Simão de, 75, 77
Veracruz, 219; San Juan de Ulúa fort, 172, 203, 242–43
Vetancurt, Agustín, 54, 181; on *pulque*, 181, 186; and Sigüenza y Góngora, 23, 257; *Teatro mexicano*, 23, 68–69, 257
Viceroyalties: American, as anomalous, 33, 119, 275n27; Audiencias and, 33, 40; established, 33; Habsburg decline and, 18, 38; peninsular bureaucrats and, 39, 119, 159, 162; regionalism and, 16–17, 269n52. *See also cabildos,* New Spain; Peru; viceroys
viceroys, 33, 52, 116–17, 118–19, 133–36, 199, 205; 1624 uprising against, 158; Conde de Galve, 5, 159, 160, 161, 164, 172, 196; entrances of, 111–13; Marqués de la Laguna, 113, 144; restrictions on, 119; tensions with the Archbishop Palafox, 158
Villalpando, Cristobal de, 201 fig. 18

violence: allegory and, 139; commercial, 226, 228; racial, 224–25, 230; in Riot of 1692, 176–81; Spanish Conquest and, 4–5, 96, 138–39, 177; of time, 61, 101, 109
Virgil, 21 fig. 2, 22, 126, 136
Virgin of Guadalupe, 8, 17, 81–90, 213 fig. 19, 236; apocalypse and, 84, 91; Becerra Tanco, Luis, on, 87–89, 85 fig. 7, 94, 102–3, 290n110; Creoles and, 81, 91–92, 103; Cruz, Mateo de la and, 87; cult of, 90–91; Florencia, Francisco on, 90, 94, 101–5, 107–8; historicity of, 81, 86, 87, 90, 101–2; image of, 84, 90–91; Immaculate Conception and, 91–92; indigenous worship of, 87–88, 102–3, 104, 105; inquiry of 1666, 87; landscape and, 81, 93, 105–6; Lasso de la Vega, Luis and, 86, 90; miracle attributed to, 100–101; narrative of, 81–84, 290n92; and paradise, theme of, 85, 92, 105; Querétaro chapel for, 97, 100–101; Querétaro festival for, 93–101, 144; race of, 104; Sánchez, Miguel, on, 17, 81–87, 82 fig. 6, 88, 90, 91, 92, 93; Sigüenza y Góngora on, 19, 93–101, 104–9. *See also* Juan Diego; Tepeyac
Virgin of Remedios, 86, 175, 196, 268n37
Vitoria, Francisco de, 34, 276n37, 279n81; appropriated by Spain's enemies, 36, 276n43

Wallerstein, Immanuel, 217
Weber, Max, 44–45, 300n12
women, 136, 190–91; *pulque*, associated with, 185–86; in Riot of 1692, 160, 186–91, 305n106, 307n149; Sigüenza y Góngora, on, 160, 186–90

Zumárraga, Juan de, Archbishop, 82–84, 92, 290n108, 293n178

ACKNOWLEDGMENTS

This book is itself an archive of influences. Its greatest debt is to Anthony Cascardi and José Rabasa, who lent to the project their dual visions of early modern Spanish imperialism, their intellectual rigor, and, above all, their constant support. I would also like to thank Emilie Bergmann, Margaret Chowning, Francine Masiello, and William Taylor for expanding my understanding of Latin America and Spain. Although my encounter with him was brief, I learned much from the late Antonio Cornejo Polar about the relationship between colonial and modern Latin America. A special thanks goes to Julio Ramos, a friend and mentor who has contributed his incessant and creative insight, his humor, and his deep knowledge of Latin American culture. My colleagues in the Department of Spanish and Portuguese at the University of California, Los Angeles, have supported this book in many forms. I would especially like to acknowledge Adriana Bergero, Michelle Clayton, Verónica Cortínez, John Dagenais, Randal Johnson, Jorge Marturano, and Maite Zubiaurre. José Luiz Passos's move from Berkeley to Los Angeles allowed us to continue our conversations on new ground. Barbara Fuchs's recent arrival has stimulated many new projects on early modern empires and I gratefully acknowledge her presence and support. Finally, I would like to thank Teo Ruiz, whose brief stint as department chair came at a crucial moment in this project. He and other colleagues from the Department of History, Kevin Terraciano and Robin Derby, as well as Charlene Villaseñor Black from Art History, have provided a rich interdisciplinary dialogue so necessary for a project such as this one.

In the many years it has taken me to write this book, I have had opportunities to give parts of the argument as papers in various venues. I would especially like to thank Alicia Mayer, who invited me to participate in an international conference on Sigüenza y Góngora at UNAM. In Berkeley and Mexico, Margo Glantz generously offered her advice and knowledge on colonial Mexican society. I would also like to thank Lisa Voigt, Stephanie Kirk, Galen Brokaw, and Gustavo Verdesio for conversations and conference panels that have enriched my ideas. After having just met me at the MLA, Rolena Adorno invited me to coffee and told me enlightening and endearing stories about her personal friendship with Irving Leonard, a pioneer in studies of Sigüenza y Góngora. Without even knowing me, she enthusiastically encouraged this project and for that I thank her. From early on, Kathleen Ross also generously supported a new project on Sigüenza y Góngora. To Alcir Pécora I owe thanks for an invitation to speak at Universidade de Campinas. He and João Adolfo Hansen have been valued friends and interlocutors on possible comparisons between colonial Brazil and Mexico. Yolanda Martínez San-Miguel invited me early on to deliver a paper at the University of Pennsylvania and has been supportive of this and other projects in a myriad of ways. Finally, Orlando Bentancor and Ivonne del Valle have shaped my ideas in more ways than it is possible to acknowledge. I thank them for combining humor, intellect and ethics in an enduring dialogue.

This book would not have been possible without the financial support from many institutions. An early fellowship at the John Carter Brown Library allowed me to delve into its impressive collection of printed works from seventeenth-century New Spain. Like any fellow under his tenure, I received warm and constant support from the then director, Norman Fiering. While a fellow, I also benefited from dialogues with Candida Barros, Bruno Feitler, Douglas Cope, and Stephanie Merrim and from the generous hospitality of my aunt and uncle, Rebecca and Tim More. The Spanish Ministry for Cultural Cooperation generously supported research at the Archivo General de Indias in Seville. A year-long fellowship for research in the humanities from the University of California Office of the President permitted me the extensive time I needed to revise the manuscript. The University of California, Los Angeles, contributed complementary leaves necessary for both the research and writing phases of the project. Without the help of several research assistants, the project never could have taken the shape it eventually did. I would like to thank Allison Ramay, Yasmine Rivera-Beale, Nora Zepeda, Peter Villella, and Rafael Ramírez for their diligence and hard work in uncovering specifics of Sigüenza's life and times. A very special word of gratitude goes to Bryan Green, who aided the project in innumerable ways over several years. In Mexico City, my dear friend Karla Jasso was able to secure a reproduction of the "Mapa Sigüenza," without which the book would not have been complete. This project benefited immeasurably from the wise advice and generous support of Jerry Singerman of the University of Pennsylvania Press. I thank him and Caroline Winschel for their saintly patience and good humor. I am also indebted to the anonymous reader for the Press whose suggestions greatly improved the final manuscript. A special thanks goes to Tim Roberts and Robert Milks of the Modern Language Initiative for assiduous and efficient copyediting of the final version of the book.

Finally, I would like to thank friends and family who provided the emotional support and intellectual dialogue necessary to complete this project. I thank especially Soledad Falabella, Jody Blanco, Marisa Belausteguigoitea, Kristin Huffine, Paula De Vos, Lisa Surwillo, and Erin Graff Zivin. In Mexico, Pablo Miranda, Jorge Bustamante, Azucena Hernández, and Marilene Marques de Oliveira welcomed me into their lives and introduced me to the subtleties of life in "el df." To Artemio Rodríguez I owe the ambiguous reminder that "cuando leas, pasan cosas." In Brazil, Cristhian Teófilo da Silva and Mireya Suárez of the Universidade Nacional de Brasilia provided me with a rich interdisciplinary dialogue. I also thank Daniela Broitman, Alexandre Rudáh, Márcia Guedes, Mario Volpi, and my extended Brazilian family, especially Odenir, Lázara, Luzia, and Carlos, for their support and friendship. In both Los Angeles and Brasília, Fernanda Melazo and Warner Bento Filho provided companionship, warmth, and the last minute child care necessary to finish writing. Another thank-you goes to my dear friends Rebecca Hellerstein and Mica Pollock, who have also offered the constant support and encouragement it takes to finish a long project.

My colleague and friend Gil Hochberg, her partner Keri Kanetsky, and their children Ella and Omri have been my family in Los Angeles. To them I give special thanks. My late grandparents Billy and Bo Hickenlooper also supported my work on a project far from their own experiences. My "third" grandmother, Harriet Hughes, contributed her deep sense of dignity, humor, and critical spirit. My brother Paul's comment that my project was a Hobsbawmian "invention of tradition" allowed me to adapt that idea to early modern New Spain. Thanks to him, Marta, and Luka for hosting me innumerable times in San Francisco. To my parents, John and Livy More, I surely owe my intellectual curiosity for things past, my love of reading and writing. My mother's keen proofreading caught many a preposition contaminated by Spanish and Portuguese; my father read the entire manuscript and assiduously checked all the Latin translations. Most of all, I thank the loving support of my partner and companion, Benedito Dos Santos, whose own political activism has kept me from having to leave academia to save the world. Our daughter Clarice has given me the energy to endure over the course of this project even while she has had to put up with many writing weekends. Our newest addition, Olivia, made finishing the last revisions a joyful affair and will surely help me transition to the next. To Bene, Clarice, and Olivia, I dedicate this book.

A very preliminary version of Chapter 3 was published as "La patria criolla como jeroglífico secularizado en el *Teatro de virtudes*," in *Carlos de Sigüenza y Góngora: Homenaje, 1700–2000*, edited by Alicia Mayer, 2: 47–77, 2 vols. (Mexico: UNAM, 2002).